Language Intervention Series
Volume II

LANGUAGE INTERVENTION STRATEGIES

LANGUAGE INTERVENTION STRATEGIES, edited by Richard L. Schiefelbusch, Ph.D., is the second volume in the **Language Intervention Series**—Richard L. Schiefelbusch, series editor. Other volumes in this series include:

Published:

Volume I **BASES OF LANGUAGE INTERVENTION** edited by *Richard L. Schiefelbusch, Ph.D.*

In preparation:

LANGUAGE INTERVENTION FROM APE TO CHILD   edited by *Richard L. Schiefelbusch, Ph.D., and John H. Hollis, Ph.D.*

NONSPEECH LANGUAGE AND COMMUNICATION   **Analysis and Intervention**   edited by *Richard L. Schiefelbusch, Ph.D.*

EMERGING LANGUAGE IN AUTISTIC CHILDREN   edited by *Warren H. Fay, Ph.D., and Adriana Luce Schuler, M.A.*

DEVELOPMENTAL LANGUAGE INTERVENTION   **Psycholinguistic Applications**   edited by *Kenneth F. Ruder, Ph.D., and Michael D. Smith, Ph.D.*

EARLY LANGUAGE INTERVENTION   edited by *Richard L. Schiefelbusch, Ph.D.*

Language Intervention Series
Volume II

LANGUAGE INTERVENTION STRATEGIES

Edited by

Richard L. Schiefelbusch

University Professor
and
Director, Bureau of Child Research
University of Kansas

Technical Editors
Marilyn Barket
Robert Hoyt
Bureau of Child Research
University of Kansas

University Park Press
Baltimore

UNIVERSITY PARK PRESS
International Publishers in Science and Medicine
233 East Redwood Street
Baltimore, Maryland 21202

Typeset by American Graphic Arts Corporation.
Manufactured in the United States of America by The Maple Press Company.

Jacket design by Myron Sahlberg.

Library of Congress Cataloging in Publication Data
Main entry under title:

Language intervention strategies.

(Language intervention series; v. 2)
Includes index.
1. Speech disorders in children.   2. Children—
Language.   I. Schiefelbusch, Richard L.   II. Series.
[DNLM: 1. Language disorders—Therapy.   2 Education,
Special.   3. Language disorders—In infancy and child-
hood.   WM475.3 L287]
RJ496.S7L348   618.9′28′5506   78-5715
ISBN 0-8391-1238-6

contents

contributors

Donald M. Baer, Ph.D.
Department of Human Development
and Family Life
University of Kansas
130 Haworth
Lawrence, Kansas 66045

Joseph K. Carrier, Jr., Ph.D.
Bureau of Child Research
University of Kansas
223 Haworth
Lawrence, Kansas 66045

Doug Guess, Ph.D.
Department of Special Education
University of Kansas
377 Haworth
Lawrence, Kansas 66045

Betty Hart, Ph.D.
Bureau of Child Research
University of Kansas
223 Haworth
Lawrence, Kansas 66045

John H. Hollis, Ph.D.
Bureau of Child Research, and
Kansas Neurological Institute
3107 West 21st Street
Topeka, Kansas 66604

Mabel Rice, Ph.D.
Bureau of Child Research
University of Kansas
223 Haworth
Lawrence, Kansas 66045

Ann Rogers-Warren, Ph.D.
Bureau of Child Research
University of Kansas
223 Haworth
Lawrence, Kansas 66045

Wayne Sailor, Ph.D.
Department of Special Education
San Francisco State University
1600 Holloway Avenue
San Francisco, California 94132

Richard L. Schiefelbusch, Ph.D.
University Professor, and Director,
Bureau of Child Research
University of Kansas
223 Haworth
Lawrence, Kansas 66045

Jean Bragg Schumaker, Ph.D.
Department of Human Development
and Family Life
University of Kansas
130 Haworth
Lawrence, Kansas 66045

James A. Sherman, Ph.D.
Department of Human Development
and Family Life
University of Kansas
130 Haworth
Lawrence, Kansas 66045

Gerald M. Siegel, Ph.D.
Department of Communication
Disorders and Center for Research
in Human Learning
University of Minnesota
110 Shevlin Hall
Minneapolis, Minnesota 55455

Joseph E. Spradlin, Ph.D.
Bureau of Child Research
University of Kansas
223 Haworth
Lawrence, Kansas 66045

Kathleen Stremel-Campbell, M.A.
Parsons Research Center
Parsons State Hospital and Training
   Center
Parsons, Kansas 67357

Sebastian Striefel, Ph.D.
Exceptional Child Center, and
   Psychology Department
Utah State University
Logan, Utah 84322

Carol Lynn Waryas, Ph.D.
Department of Communicative
   Disorders
University of Mississippi
University, Mississippi 38677

Bruce Wetherby, Ph.D.
Box 512
MRL—Rm. 416C
John F. Kennedy Center for Research
   on Education and Human
   Development, and
Psychology Faculty
George Peabody College for Teachers
Nashville, Tennessee 37203

Language Intervention Strategies is the second volume in the University Park Press series on language intervention. It calls for examples of programmatic applications for a range of language-delayed and language-impaired individuals. The assumption is that a number of strategies can facilitate the design of individual interventions.

In the first volume the editor described language intervention as a design science. Many clinicians who adopt programs for special children may not regard themselves as scientists. However, they acknowledge that they design individualized programs and that they do indeed employ strategies.

The term *strategy* is an imprecise concept. It covers many different components and many possible functions. That is why the first chapter in this book delineates a number of strategies that clinicians and researchers may use. This establishes a dimensional analysis that is amplified in the intervention programs that follow.

The strategy delineation is followed by a chapter on *identification*. Clinicians who work with severely handicapped, i.e., retarded, cerebral palsied, autistic, or deaf, children may have no difficulty identifying children who need language-training activities. However, there are many other children with less obvious problems and less obvious language delays. Identifying children among this group may be more difficult.

Rice, Chapter 1, provides an update on program selection. Much of her discussion is based on research. Nevertheless, as she explains, the challenge of decision making must eventually be left to the clinician and to parents and teachers who make language intervention efforts feasible, and who must also participate in the referrals and in the planning for optimal intervention.

The rationale for choosing the intervention prototypes in this volume becomes apparent in the Introduction, especially in the section that describes "program strategies." The programs are: 1) nonspeech language intervention, 2) a syntax-teaching program, 3) a functional program for nonverbal adolescents, 4) a milieu program for preschool children, 5) a parent-administered program for young children, and 6) a matrix-training system for language intervention. The last is an experimental strategy that currently lacks extensive application designing but nevertheless provides a rationale for specialized intervention efforts.

The intent is to present a range of different strategies, but not a comprehensive set of intervention designs, that would fit all possible language-learning contexts. Nevertheless, the language programs are prototypes that clinicians can adapt and from which individualized approaches can be derived. The programs explain "how to" and "what for" but not always "when to." The prototypes sometimes leave much of the decision making for individualizing the "how to" up to the clinician. The clinician, however, has the advantage of knowing that the programs work for the experimental formulators and usually for their students, colleagues, field testers, and friends. The operations and task functions have been selected carefully for intervention plans managed or monitored by clinicians. They are not "armchair" designs.

The final chapter by Siegel and Spradlin provides a perspective on the content of the entire book. The strengths and weaknesses of the current state of our knowledge are considered. From this discussion the reader can derive a picture of the field as it currently exists and the directions we may be headed in our further efforts to instruct children with language impairments.

As explained in Volume I, *Bases of Language Intervention,* if language is to be taught (or learned), the adult and the child must share the intervention experience. The contingencies for learning must be reciprocal, and the successes and failures must be shared. The changes noted in intervention contexts are the products of a transaction in which communication events of a complex and largely unfathomed nature have taken place. Our task is to understand this process as well as we can so that the effects of our participation are as instrumental as possible. Needless to say, our exploration of this task is far from complete. Perhaps our efforts to design strategies have just begun.

The editor wishes to acknowledge the contributions of a large number of language researchers who have given background or foreground information to strategies of language intervention. The contributors include many from Parsons State Hospital and Training Center, where research on language intervention has been maintained continuously for 20 years. It was at Parsons that several of the strategies for special language intervention were designed. It was also at Parsons that the importance of strategic designs was first perceived by the editor of this volume. Among the numerous contributors, past and present, whose designs and ideas are alluded to in this book, are Bill Bricker, Joseph Carrier, Robert Fulton, John Hollis, Lyle Lloyd, James McLean, Seymour Rosenberg, Gerald Siegel, Joseph Spradlin, Kathleen Stremel-Campbell, Sebastian Striefel, Carol Waryas, and Bruce Wetherby.

Other Kansas colleagues whose work and counsel are reflected in this volume include Donald Baer, Melissa Bowerman, Earl Butterfield, Doug Guess, Betty Hart, Ann Rogers-Warren, Todd Risley, Mabel Rice, Ken Ruder, Wayne Sailor, Jean Schumaker, and James Sherman.

The list of relevant contributors from the national and international audience is even longer. The editor wishes to express special gratitude to Jon Miller, David Premack, Norma Rees, Robin Chapman, Audry Holland, Dave Yoder, and Diane Bricker for stimulating suggestions and timely contributions.

The base of information for this volume is broad. The editor is grateful to all contributors who provided the information on which effective strategies can be built.

Finally, I wish to acknowledge my own special office colleagues Robert Hoyt, Marilyn Barket, Thelma Dillon, and Mary Beth Johnston. Their efforts prevented the collapse of this project at every step along the way.

R. L. S.

Language Intervention Series
Volume II

LANGUAGE
INTERVENTION
STRATEGIES

Introduction

Richard L. Schiefelbusch

University Professor
and
Director, Bureau of Child Research
University of Kansas
Lawrence, Kansas

contents

The current trend in our society is to place handicapped individuals in less restrictive environments and to provide an appropriate education for *all* children. These changes are improving communication training for handicapped persons as increasing numbers of teachers, clinicians, and other specialists undertake language teaching. Fortunately this trend is based on an expanding knowledge of the structures and functions of language, a growing interest in how language is acquired and a confidence that language behaviors can be taught. The trend also reflects an understanding of language as a critical part of larger educational plans for special children. A child's success in the educational environment—in both social and academic domains—depends largely upon how he[1] uses language.

A child's ability to express language (speech) and to use language interpersonally (communication) is enhanced by many of the activities built into all teaching programs. However, for many children language acquisition is a special problem. These children need special language programs that involve a technology based on psycholinguistics, instructional programming, and functional analysis of behavior. The procedures and the maintenance features of this technology are not simple but they are attainable. In the opinion of the author/editor, this technology is likely to assume a place in education alongside the technology for teaching reading or arithmetic. However, there are important and perhaps unique differences between language teaching and other teaching programs.

First, the language to be taught is a *first* language. The child may not have a language through which a teacher can provide the instructions needed to explain the "assignments." Instead, the lessons may require a special "clinical" arrangement or a functional environment so that meanings can be understood by the child.

Second, many operations performed in classrooms require the communication of messages. The language-deficient child can hardly become a fully effective part of the classroom process until he can express and receive information. Therefore, language training is antecedent to other programs.

Finally, language is a basic part of the child's cognitive and communicative behavior. Language is evaluated by the schools when assigning the child to an ongoing program. Until the child's language is evaluated and, indeed, until the range of progress in language training is estimated, the status of the child as a learner cannot be determined. Plans for an individualized curriculum and for individualized instruction for the child must include such language-training information.

---

[1] Masculine pronouns are used throughout the book for the sake of grammatical uniformity and simplicity. They are not meant to be preferential or discriminatory.

3

In using the technology demonstrated in this volume, the teacher/clinician will be able to extrapolate from prototypical programs so that the teaching of any child may be enhanced. A generalized program suitable to every child is not yet available, but the information presented here will help any enterprising teacher/clinician who wishes to teach language to special children.

Information is also included for specialists who wish to go beyond current frontiers to do research in other features of language acquisition and intervention. The field of language is a challenging domain for professional workers of many persuasions. The teacher/clinician is perhaps the most important link in implementing new developments. The language of special children will certainly continue to be an important part of the programs of such workers.

CHILDREN IN NEED OF LANGUAGE TRAINING

Several different levels of language deficit require us to try to teach new language forms and functions. One form is a severe language deficit that prevents a child from communicating with adults and peers in either social or training environments. The most severe type of language deficit is found in the child who is nonverbal. The child may have a few gestures and primitive vocal signals but no conventional language system. More prevalent language deficits are seen in children who have limited and often incomprehensible modes of expressive speech. Even though a child may have (or may seem to have) considerable comprehension of language, his limited ability to express language somehow limits the range of communication with adults and peers. Such limitations frequently necessitate nonspeech language systems such as manual signs or communication boards. Still more common forms of severe language deficits involve poor conceptual development. The child may have echolalic speech but not comprehend or use language for communication. This problem may be regarded as *delayed language* in a semantic sense.

Another level of language malfunctioning is poor language use. A child may have considerable understanding of language and an adequate ability to express language under optimal circumstances but may still be an ineffective communicator. For instance, the child may not listen to the teacher or comprehend instructions in a normal, noisy, cluttered group setting. Or the child may seldom ask questions, give instructions, volunteer information, or talk with peers. In other words, his language functions are not adapted to normal social and learning requirements. The child has a *communication problem* even though his language comprehension does not seem to be delayed seriously. Such children may have marked deficits in the pragmatic functions of language.

A third level of language deficit is apparent when certain specific *speech behaviors* are objectionable to listeners. These behaviors are often subtle and call for fine tuning to overcome articulation defects, voice disorders, or stuttering. Although the defects in question may comprise only a small feature or segment of the total language of the speaker, if they interfere with communication, they require attention. The dramatic feature of a speech disorder is that the child may receive disturbing feedback that alters confidence in interpersonal contexts, so that what seems to be a "simple" speech disorder may in reality also be a communication disorder as well.

Rice (Chapter 1) examines the issues pertaining to identification of children with language disorders. She is concerned with what behaviors to look for in identifying children for language intervention programs. She concludes that the present state of scientific knowledge is not complete enough to specify conclusively what is "disordered language." Supplemental information in the form of teacher or parental referrals and clinical intuition and judgment based in part upon experience are essential for identifying many children with language problems.

Rice (this volume) and Haring and Schiefelbusch (1976) point out that a language disorder is usually predicted by the existence of mental retardation, deafness, or an extensive developmental disorder. The extensive communication problems of children with severe developmental delays have drawn increasing attention from language intervention specialists. Much of the programmatic work discussed in this volume was developed with severely delayed children.

This brief overview of language problems suggests that we must allow for a wide range of differences in the levels of language children have already acquired. Some children have language with near normal syntax and phonology, whereas others are virtually lacking in all linguistic structures. Some are relatively adequate in receptive language but are extremely limited in expressive features. Because language instruction programs must allow for a range of differences among their clients, it is necessary for a technology for language intervention to take into account these wide divergencies and still represent a procedure that is appropriate for individual instruction. Siegel and Spradlin discuss the use of language programs in Chapter 8.

A language program must be extremely functional if it is to span this wide range of language delays and dysfunctions. In this book the range is bridged by several programs, each representing different strategies. The programs and the strategies are presented in considerable detail.

THE ISSUE OF STRATEGIES

Analysis of first language instruction is perhaps best begun by discussing strategies. *Strategy* is the art of devising or employing plans or stratagems to reach a goal. Our goal is to promote the *acquisition and continued use of functional language and communication.* This rather complex goal includes a number of dimensions and requires a process of decision making based upon informal options. However, for now we want to simply posit that strategies are *plans* or *stratagems* to reach goals.

Strategies can be grouped into four classes: *general strategies, design strategies, instructional strategies,* and *program strategies* (Schiefelbusch, 1977). These classes of strategies are further divided into subclasses and issues in the following pages. They are related to the language programs developed in Chapters 2, 3, 4, 5, and 6 of this volume. Although the classes and subclasses overlap somewhat, each provides a special feature or rationale for planning or analyzing a plan of language intervention.

General Strategies

General strategies denote an informal rationale for initial adaptation of language procedures to impaired or limited children. They suggest an adaptive quality of intervention services that acknowledges the nature of the children. For instance, nonverbal children usually cannot deal with complexity or with unstable learning contexts, and they often fail to understand why something should be learned. Each of these issues should be considered functionally.

Complexity   The opposite of complexity is simplicity. The question is whether or not a given child with limited processing abilities has an environment for language acquisition that is functional, as contrasted to one that overtaxes his perceptual abilities. The point is that poor language learning suggests that the child's environment is not functional. Hollis and Carrier (Chapter 2) suggest that conditions (complex or simple) can be analyzed with the functional operant—a behavioral equation in which the stimuli, the responses, the contingencies, and the consequences arranged by the clinician can be examined. It is one thing to opt for simplicity and another to provide functional arrangements for simplicity. In any event, language events should be arranged for handicapped children in the simplest, most functional way possible in a context in which language is spoken or otherwise presented.

Stability   Children who learn to talk and who develop a large linguistic repertoire are children who are able to cope with a great deal of referential diversity. They also adjust to an array of inconsistent stimuli, variable contingencies with adults, a range of contexts, and variable rates and rhythms of life. They are expected to adapt and to conform to the wishes of virtual strangers (clinicians, aides, teachers) in contexts of unknown and even disturbing uncertainties. Faced with those instabilities, some children have learned to not initiate communication and they often seem less competent than they are even under favorable conditions. An optimal design for language intervention must include a setting with stable and familiar features. Hollis and Carrier (Chapter 2) also acknowledge this issue in their discussion of *environmental interaction.*

Utility   It is possible to design a language-learning program in which referential terms, action, and imaginary people (and animals) are taught to the child in great profusion without ever using language features that are *functional* for the child. "Functional" in this sense means responded to by the child or initiated by the child. It also refers to the child's probable need to use the language feature in other contexts. Otherwise, the child is not likely to use the language in any of the many interactions of his daily life. The child will merely go through an exercise that will not generalize the language use beyond the context in which it is taught. A child will develop more communication if a few words and functions are taught for which the language is needed and for which the child will use language frequently. This issue is discussed in considerable detail by Waryas and Stremel-Campbell under "Structure in the Pragmatic Approach" in Chapter 4, by Guess, Sailor, and Baer under "Dimensions [of Functional Language Training]" in Chapter 3, and by Hollis and Carrier under "An Intervention Strategy for Language Deficiencies" in Chapter 2.

The general strategies are considered to be especially important for lower functioning children in the earlier stages of training. However, to train for generalization the general features may be made more complex in later phases of training in order to approximate conditions in the natural environment.

Design Strategies

Design strategies are required to adapt intervention procedures to programmatic objectives and to the individual characteristics of children. Design strategies can be of many types. Only five are described here: 1) development, 2) mode, 3) form, 4) function, and 5) transaction.

Development   The training program developed by Waryas and Stremel-Campbell (Chapter 4) utilizes a developmental strategy. Their approach considers delayed functions in both semantic and pragmatic use by the children to whom they teach grammatical forms.

Hart and Rogers-Warren (Chapter 5) also plan from a developmental design as they establish a milieu training model. The milieu is established in a preschool and is designed to enhance the child's evolving social role.

Schumaker and Sherman (Chapter 6) utilize a developmental design in working with parents. The developmental strategy was also used by

Miller (1978) in designing evaluation procedures and by Ruder (1978) in developing programmatic procedures for language intervention.

Mode A number of recent studies have emphasized that language can be analyzed apart from phonology and independent of auditory process. Such research recognizes that human language systems are overwhelmingly audible and are strategically phonemic in nature. Nevertheless, the evidence points to a need for nonspeech approaches for many individuals. Lexical displays or manual signs are used increasingly in designs that do not require speech. Various other response modes are taught and situationally used (see Lloyd, 1976).

Hollis has analyzed these strategic systems (see Hollis, Carrier, and Spradlin, 1976; Hollis and Carrier, Chapter 2, this volume; Hollis and Schiefelbusch, in press).

Form Premack's (1970) basic analysis of the functions of language involves four issues: 1) discrimination of symbols, 2) discrimination *among* symbols, 3) discrimination among environmental objects and events, and 4) discrimination among sequential arrangements of the symbols. In this delineation three of the functions involve a discrimination of symbol forms, arrangements, and sequences. This places a heavy emphasis upon the structure or form of language.

If this emphasis is carried into the design for teaching a first language, strategies must be included for teaching the forms so that the child can acquire (learn and remember) them, so that the child can use them appropriately to express the intended meaning, and so that the child can map the forms as a grammar for meaning in both concrete and abstract contexts. Waryas and Stremel-Campbell (Chapter 4) have designed a strategic procedure for teaching grammatical structure. They hold that "new theoretical formulations of the semantic and pragmatic factors in language serve to refocus the role of structure in language by placing it in the framework of the *how* of language which expresses the *what* (semantic functions) and the *why* (pragmatic functions)" (p. 187). Language training is conceptualized as a process of teaching the child to behave as if he knew the rules, producing congruence between his speech and that of his language community so that communication functions can be carried out.

Function Function training as a strategy has been used by Hart and Risley (1975) and Hart and Rogers-Warren (Chapter 5) in teaching ghetto children, by Bricker and Bricker (1974) in teaching handicapped infants and young children, and by Guess, Sailor, and Baer (Chapter 3) in teaching older, severely retarded children. These are only four of many projects that have attempted to design language repertoires to match the actual language performed by children in the contexts in which they normally use language. This language-training strategy is not arranged just as a simulation for communication events but includes the actual contexts (as nearly as possible) so that children gain generalization functions in actual practice. The training also includes the concepts and the functional events that the language denotes. Thus, the language forms map the semantic features of the environment to make language a more definitive feature of the child's social and academic behavior.

Transaction This strategy reflects recent emphases upon pragmatics, i.e., the context and the intent of the speaker (which reflects in both expressive and receptive skills in language transaction). The primary point here is that the child must learn to convey his communicative intent and must learn to discern the intent of other speakers (Rees, 1978). The purpose of language is to achieve the needs and purposes of the language user. The *why* of language use thus becomes central to language training—the reasons why a child communicates and the reasons for continuing communication as a function of probable feedback from others as well as his skilled behaviors in evoking responses from others (Hart and Rogers-Warren, Chapter 5). Other researchers who have developed designs for transaction training are McDonald and Blott (1974), Bruner (1975), Holland (1975), McLean and Snyder (1976), and Prutting (1977). Each of these provides environmental and transactional variables for explaining or planning training interventions.

Instructional Strategies

The statements in this section closely reflect the information presented in Chapters 6, 7, and 8 in *Bases of Language Intervention*, Volume I of the Language Intervention Series. Five instructional strategies are identified: 1) initial evaluation, 2) program development, 3) program maintenance, 4) program evaluation, and 5) program extension.

Initial Evaluation and Planning The *initial evaluation* discusses ways to determine the child's current level of language functioning and suggests a point of departure for language training. In a behavioral sense the initial evaluation should provide a baseline for planning, for making comparisons with subsequent stages of development, and for making decisions about the design of the language program, the maintenance strategies, and the subsequent evaluations. In a functional sense the initial evaluation should map out the child's concepts to form a basis for word acquisitions and linguistic relationships (see Miller, 1978).

The initial evaluation should provide the instructor with information to be used directly in planning for the language-training program. For instance, Guess, Sailor, and Baer (Chapter 3) use a plan for initial evaluation of skills prerequisite to the program, and Waryas and Stremel-Campbell (Chapter 4) have a plan for assessing the developmental forms and functions of language as a first feature of their language program.

Program Development   Program development refers to the language curriculum that the instructor will attempt to teach. It includes a sequential series of phases that will be used to reach the projected goal for this child. The curriculum includes both the structures and the functions of language that the instructor determines to be necessary for the child to reach the projected level of language functioning (see Ruder, 1978).

A language program is built upon information derived from the initial language evaluation. Several assumptions are necessary in designing a program. The first is that language is acquired or learned in a series of phases or stages. Thus, the instructor can set down a sequential design of language units. The design is a practical curriculum that includes a goal in addition to the sequential series of phases. The goal is a specified level of language use. The child who fits into this hypothetical program may be a child in any age range or at any level of language functioning. The language curriculum could be the sequential progress that we think happens to a small child in a natural environment with the informal assistance of parents, other children, and friends.

In this volume, both Guess, Sailor, and Baer (Chapter 3) and Waryas and Stremel-Campbell (Chapter 4) provide language curricula, each designed from a different strategy. Carrier (1974) also has a comprehensive curriculum for teaching a nonspeech language initiation program (Non-SLIP).

Program Maintenance   The *program maintenance* part includes the scheduling, the selecting, and the arranging of stimulus materials and the training environment, the criteria levels used for each sequential phase, the incentives to be used for each child, and the management to be used as part of the long-term program. The chief purpose of the maintenance program is to ensure that the effectiveness of the program is continued throughout its full range (see Ruder, 1978).

The term "maintenance strategies" suggests that there are instructional procedures that help the teacher/clinician conduct the program effectively from start to finish. This literally is the design of the maintenance program. The program has two subparts. One part relates to behavior management and the other to language training. Two principal features of behavior management are 1) the application and alteration of contingencies and 2) language maintenance. Maintenance includes scheduling, materials selection, and criteria. A number of the maintenance strategy issues are presented in Chapters 4 and 5 but are presented in more complete form elsewhere by Carrier and Peak (1975) and by Guess, Sailor, and Baer (1976).

Program Evaluation   *Program evaluation* includes probe evaluations and periodic short- and long-term evaluations. Both are formative evaluations, but each is intended to provide different information. The probe evaluations provide frequent checks upon the effectiveness of the instructional sequences and strategies. The periodic evaluations help the instructor evaluate the general progress of the child and guide the redesigning of the program if the data indicate that the planning and the maintenance strategies are inappropriate (see Ruder, 1978). Program evaluation issues are also presented carefully in Carrier and Peak (1975) and Guess, Sailor, and Baer (1976).

Training Extensions and Integration   A training extension may be any effective carry-over or transfer (in time or location) beyond the context of the training session. It is assumed that the child must learn to initiate language, must actively seek new referents and new skills, and must eventually secure favorable feedback from his communication attempts.

Guess, Sailor, and Baer (Chapter 3) have developed an interesting procedure for effecting self-extended control. They reason that, as the child with limited language learns to control his immediate environment with the word units at his command, he finds great need for other units he does not know. He does not know the necessary labels for the things, actions, and actions-with-things he wishes to use. Thus, it is important to extend the child's referents, mainly by teaching him to request further instruction in specific contexts.

Wetherby and Striefel (Chapter 7) extend the instruction of broad classes of behavior to include both receptive and expressive language functions. Their treatment of receptive language is especially meaningful to the generalization concept because Guess, Sailor, and Baer deal exclusively with expressive language.

The term *integration* implies that language is or becomes an integral part of the child's behavior. Stated simply, language that is learned is used. New forms become active forms. Information gained through questions is stored and used. A new speech form that is correctly articulated in the clinic also is used correctly in the home or in the play activities at school.

Instructional procedures should contribute to integrations. Indeed, strategies for integration are among the most important in language teaching. Terms such as *carry-over, generalizations,* and *transfer of training* are frequently used to identify techniques developed by different clinicians. The techniques frequently serve to generalize the usage from one context to another within the formal teaching environment (see Guess, Keogh, and Sailor, 1978).

Control, extension, and integration strategies should be developed to be used in a range of natural environments. These and similar procedures could greatly reduce the time required by teachers and clinicians in teaching language to special children. A good example of the application of these procedures is found in Guess, Sailor, and Baer (Chapter 3).

Program Strategies

In addition to general strategies, design strategies, and instructional strategies, there are also *program strategies*. Program strategies incorporate most of the strategies just described. Nevertheless, there is a valuable purpose served in illustrating five of the more effective program strategies that have emerged in language intervention research: *early intervention, nonspeech intervention, functional language intervention, structured language intervention,* and *milieu intervention.* Each of these program strategies offers special advantages and should be available to teachers and clinicians who teach language to children.

Perhaps the most natural question is, "What program strategy will most likely help the child attain specified objectives?" For instance, what programmatic strategy will help a child acquire initial language forms or concepts or a larger reference vocabulary, or social functions, or generalized use?

Early Intervention   The rationale for early language intervention is compelling. As described by Bricker and Bricker (1974) and Ruder and Smith (1974), early intervention provides the child with concept training (functional use of objects and the meaning of actions) and with other antecedents to formal language. Individualized relationships are established with the child so that levels of functioning can be matched with the early performance stages of normal children.

As developed by Bricker and Bricker (1974), the program involves: 1) assessment of the infants' repertoire in specific areas (to determine a program plan and to serve as a basis for determining progress), 2) to determine and train prerequisite behaviors, 3) to select and design training stimuli, 4) to arrange a context for generalized relations of agents, actions, and objects, and 5) to arrange small social groups that involve individualized stimulation. Their program moves through a sequence of steps that involves verbal imitation, comprehension, and production training. They advocate a mix of normal and handicapped children, beginning as early as six months.

Schumaker and Sherman, in "Parent as Intervention Agent: From Birth Onward" (Chapter 6), emphasize infant stimulation. In part their plan is designed to enhance the concept of early intervention. Hart and Rogers-Warren (Chapter 5) also seek to use the strategy of early intervention by designing a training milieu for preschool children.

Nonspeech Intervention All infants receive many nonspeech impressions that influence their learning language and communication skills. Nevertheless, it is correctly assumed that the auditory-vocal channels are the critical modes of language acquisition. Speech provides the dominant design for delivering language in human communication. Nevertheless, some children are unable to acquire language via the auditory-vocal modes. For them there should be alternatives for language intervention. The rationale should be to determine the factors of "risk" and to introduce the alternative designs as soon as possible. In this manner, the interventionist may actualize the same positive early intervention tactics that are described in the previous section. This issue is given comprehensive treatment in *Nonspeech Language and Communication: Analysis and Intervention*, a subsequent volume in the Language Intervention Series.

McDonald (in press) has described a procedure for early detection of children with severe respiratory-motor problems who are at risk for speech communication deficits. It seems logical that other parameters of development should come under the same kind of functional scrutiny. For instance, infant detection of cognitive and auditory processing might alert parents and interventionists that intensive visual and tactual experiences are indicated to provide for an adequate conceptual base for language. Unfortunately, we do not yet have fully designed programs for sensory-perceptual training of infants. Nevertheless, progress has been made (see Butterfield and Cairns, 1974, 1976).

For children of preschool and school age, however, a number of manual, lexical, or plastic form systems of language instruction are available. Extensive discussions of these nonspeech systems are presented in Lloyd (1976) and Schiefelbusch (1978).

Functional Language Intervention The issue of functional language is discussed in increasing detail in the pragmatic literature (Rees, 1978), in the communication literature (Prutting, 1977), and by developmental psycholinguistics (Bowerman, 1978). However, Guess, Sailor, and Baer (Chapter 3) may be the first to design a strategy to teach functional language to children with limited (or no) language. In a previous publication (Guess, Sailor, and Baer, 1976), the program was laid out in 61 steps in a prototypal design that starts with labeling and ends with extended sentences. However, the more distinctive feature of their program is functional language training. The dimensions include *reference, control, self-extended control, integration,* and *reception*. Each dimension represents a function concept that is implemented with the child. Throughout the program the language acquired by the child is functional for his communication needs in contexts beyond the training sessions.

Structured Language Intervention   The role of grammatical training in language intervention designs has been analyzed in considerable detail by Waryas and Stremel-Campbell (Chapter 4). On the way to a presentation of their strategy of intervention, the authors acknowledge the importance of semantic and pragmatic features of functional language. They assume a complex interaction between language structure and its function. They also assume that "rather than obviating the importance of structural training, new theoretical formulations of the semantic and pragmatic factors in language serve to refocus the role of structure in language by placing it in the framework of the *how* of language, which expresses the *what* (semantic functions) and the *why* (pragmatic functions)" (p. 187). The skill in language intervention work, in their view, is in making the language concepts real (and functional) in the language setting.

The program that Waryas and Stremel-Campbell present, then, is a reanalysis of the role of grammatical training. They present grammatical training not as an end in itself but as a means for demonstrating how language concepts can be made real in the training setting.

Milieu Intervention   The milieu intervention strategy, described by Hart and Rogers-Warren (Chapter 5), builds upon an incidental teaching model (Hart and Risley, 1975). It also has a number of characteristics in common with an environmental strategy developed by McDonald and Blott (1974).

The milieu design involves preparation in three areas: 1) arranging the environment in order to prompt the use of language, 2) assessing a child's current skill level in order to select for functional language, and 3) training adults to ensure that the child works with language and that the child's language works for him. These functions always interact in the design of a milieu, whether in the home, the classroom, the cottage, or the playroom.

In brief, the environment must be arranged to provide impetus and support for language. There must be a variety of attractive materials and activities immediately accessible to the child. Actual child engagement should be the measure of environmental richness (Cataldo and Risley, 1974). At the same time, certain other materials and activities must be available to the child only on request. The adult mediates materials and activities, uses materials to reinforce verbalizations, and demonstrates how language works to obtain objects and events from the environment.

The strategy has been designed to integrate aspects of both the training (structured) and the talking (natural) environments. "It focuses on building high rates of spontaneous language in natural settings (with a variety of persons), about objects and events, and it elaborates the topography of language through imitation and differential reinforcement procedures" (Hart and Rogers-Warren, Chapter 5, p. 219).

SUMMARY

This chapter uses the strategy of writing about strategies. The categories of strategies in reference have been *general, design, instructional,* and *program.* These categories have been strategically arbitrary. Each language clinician should be able to supplement or to substitute additional strategies.

In Chapter 8, Siegel and Spradlin provide a somewhat different discussion of decision making in their section on "The Use of Language Programs." Their practical discussion places the emphasis upon individualization and should lead the clinician to make rational and perhaps selective utilization of the content of this book. The introductory chapter should also be used in that selective manner.

Six strategic issues appear in various parts of the book:

1. An essential outcome of language intervention training should be functional communication.
2. Low functioning children learn language best in a context in which *simple, stable,* and *useful* features are taught.
3. A combined system of language (both nonspeech and speech) may facilitate acquisition for many multiply handicapped children.
4. *Early* language intervention is preferred to all other time-related strategies.
5. For most children a natural environment provides the greatest range of functional language stimulation.
6. Home-based programs monitored and taught by parents often show the greatest gains and the most lasting effects.

REFERENCES

Bowerman, M. 1978. Semantic and syntactic development: A review of what, when, and how in language acquisition. *In* R. L. Schiefelbusch (ed.), Bases of Language Intervention, pp. 97–189. University Park Press, Baltimore.

Bricker, W., and Bricker, D. 1974. An early language training strategy. *In* R. L. Schiefelbusch and L. L. Lloyd (eds.), Language Perspectives—Acquisition, Retardation, and Intervention, pp. 431–468. University Park Press, Baltimore.

Bruner, J. S. 1975. From communication to language: A psychological perspective. Cognition 3:255–287.

Butterfield, E. C., and Cairns, G. F. 1974. Infant reception research. *In* R. L. Schiefelbusch and L. L. Lloyd (eds.), Language Perspectives—Acquisition, Retardation, and Intervention, pp. 75–102. University Park Press, Baltimore.

Butterfield, E. C., and Cairns, G. F. 1976. The infants' auditory environment. *In* T. D. Tjossem (ed.), Intervention Strategies for High Risk Infants and Young Children, pp. 143–160. University Park Press, Baltimore.

Carrier, J. K. 1974. Application of functional analysis and a nonspeech response mode to teaching language. *In* L. V. McReynolds (ed.), Developing Systematic Procedures for Training Children's Language. ASHA Monograph No. 18. American Speech and Hearing Association, Washington, D.C.

Carrier, J. K., and Peak, T. 1975. Nonspeech Language Initiation Program (Non-SLIP). H & H Enterprises, Lawrence, Kan.

Cataldo, M. F., and Risley, T. 1974. The Resident Activity Manifest: Handbooks for Observers. Center for Applied Behavior Analysis, Lawrence, Kan.

Guess, D., Sailor, W., and Baer, D. 1976. Functional Speech and Language Training for the Severely Handicapped, Parts 1 and 2. H & H Enterprises, Lawrence, Kan.

Guess, D., Keogh, W., and Sailor, W. 1978. Generalization of speech and language behavior: Measurement and training tactics. *In* R. L. Schiefelbusch (ed.), Bases of Language Intervention, pp. 373–395. University Park Press, Baltimore.

Haring, N., and Schiefelbusch, R. L. 1976. Teaching Special Children. McGraw-Hill Book Co., New York.

Hart, B., and Risley, T. 1975. Incidental teaching of language in the preschool. J. Appl. Behav. Anal. 8:411–420.

Holland, A. 1975. Language therapy for children: Some thoughts on context and content. J. Speech Hear. Disord. 40:514–523.

Hollis, J., Carrier, J., and Spradlin, J. 1976. An approach to remediation of communication and learning deficiencies. *In* L. L. Lloyd (ed.), Communication Assessment and Intervention Strategies, pp. 265–294. University Park Press, Baltimore.

Hollis, J., and Schiefelbusch, R. L. A system of analyzing language and communication. *In* R. L. Schiefelbusch (ed.), Nonspeech Language and Communication: Analysis and Intervention. University Park Press, Baltimore. In press.

Lloyd, L. L. (ed.). 1976. Communication Assessment and Intervention Strategies. University Park Press, Baltimore.

McDonald, E. T. Early identification and treatment of children at risk for development of intelligible speech. *In* R. L. Schiefelbusch (ed.), Nonspeech Language and Communication: Analysis and Intervention. University Park Press, Baltimore. In press.

McDonald, J. D., and Blott, J. P. 1974. Environmental language intervention: The rationale for a diagnostic and training strategy through rules, context and generalization. J. Speech Hear. Disord. 39:244–256.

McLean, J. E., and Snyder, L. K. 1976. A transactional approach to early language training: Derivation of a model system. Final report, Contract No. OEC-0-74-9185. U.S. Office of Education, Bureau of Education for the Handicapped, Washington, D.C.

Miller, J. F. 1978. Assessing children's language behavior: A developmental process approach. *In* R. L. Schiefelbusch (ed.), Bases of Language Intervention, pp. 269–318. University Park Press, Baltimore.

Premack, D. 1970. A functional analysis of language. J. Exp. Anal. Behav. 14:107–125.

Prutting, C. A. 1977. Pragmatics and the assessment and remediation of communicative behaviors. *In* Proceedings of the Second Annual Language Symposium Functions of Language Intervention Programs. San Jose State University, School of Education, San Jose.

Rees, N. S. 1978. Pragmatics of language: Application to normal and disordered language development. *In* R. L. Schiefelbusch (ed.), Bases of Language Intervention, pp. 191–268. University Park Press, Baltimore.

Ruder, K. F. 1978. Planning and programming for language intervention. *In* R. L. Schiefelbusch (ed.), Bases of Language Intervention, pp. 319–371. University Park Press, Baltimore.

Ruder, K. F., and Smith, M. D. 1974. Issues in language training. *In* R. L. Schiefelbusch and L. L. Lloyd (eds.), Language Perspectives—Acquisition, Retardation, and Intervention, pp. 565–605. University Park Press, Baltimore.

Schiefelbusch, R. L. 1977. Strategies for language intervention. *In* Proceedings of the Second Annual Language Symposium Functions of Language Intervention Programs. San Jose State University, School of Education, San Jose.

Schiefelbusch, R. L. (ed.). 1978. Bases of Language Intervention. University Park Press, Baltimore.

chapter 1

Identification of
Children with
Language Disorders

Mabel Rice

Bureau of Child Research
University of Kansas
Lawrence, Kansas

contents

The question of how to identify children with language disorders has received a great deal of attention recently as a result of rapidly expanding services for handicapped children. Recent federal legislation and legislation in many states require services for children with developmental disabilities, with "children" defined as inclusive of the age range birth to 21 years. (See Bensberg and Sigelman, 1976, pp. 36–37, for a discussion of recent federal legislation.)

There are several immediate consequences of these new laws. The first is that professionals providing services are responsible for locating children in need of services. Whereas in the past the clinician could wait for someone else to identify a child as having a language problem and then respond to the referral, the clinician is now initiating the identification process.

Another consequence is a strong interest in determining the prevalence of communication disorders and other handicapping conditions. Bensberg and Sigelman (1976) call for a "large-scale, interdisciplinary prevalence study to determine the number and characteristics of our handicapped population" (p. 66). To conduct such a survey, criteria for identifying children with communication disorders must be determined. Bensberg and Sigelman note that "accurate identification of the scope of the problem is the bedrock upon which sound programming must be based" (p. 66). However, programming, in the form of service to children with communication disorders, has not been postponed until a means of identification has been agreed upon. Instead, professionals responsible for the programming for such children have already operationalized procedures for identifying language disorders.

The recent emphasis on accountability and objectivity requires many professionals to define a communication disorder with such terms as "at least one year delayed" or "at least three or four deviant language forms." While this would be a difficult enough task within a "normative" school-age population, i.e., normally developing, white, middle class, English-speaking children, it becomes next to impossible with very young children, or in nonnormative school-age populations such as those of certain cultural or socioeconomic environments, second-language or dialect-speaking, or children with other handicaps.

GENERAL PROBLEMS

Several dilemmas arise when one has the task of identifying children with communication disorders. The first is the lack of a firm reference point for "normal verbal communication." Unfortunately, communication does not have the objectivity inherent in identifying normal vision or dentition. The reference commonly used in formal assessment techniques is that of standard adult English, usually the formal written language system. However, this is not generally the system used in casual, spontaneous, verbal communication. If the ability to communicate effectively in a casual manner is the goal of programming, perhaps it is not appropriate to judge "normal" in comparison to formal written language systems. Hall (1960) defines "good" language as "language which gets the desired effect with the least friction and difficulty for its user. That means, of course, that 'good' language is going to vary with the situation it is used in" (p. 27). It is this contextual variability, in combination with social and dialectal variations, that makes it exceedingly difficult, if not impossible, to agree upon a universal reference point for "normal verbal communication" for all children, of all ages, of all socioeconomic and dialectal circumstances, in all geographic locations. This means that different clinicians facing these conditions must determine standards that are consistent with the standards of the local community and with the expectations of the parents and children involved.

A second dilemma associated with identification pertains to the selection of appropriate procedures. Various assessment procedures are available. They are not discussed in detail here because they are treated at length elsewhere in this series (see Miller, 1978). However, it is appropriate to consider some general limitations of various assessment procedures for the purposes of identification.

As presented by Miller, assessment procedures can be categorized as tests, scales, or behavioral observations. Formally administered tests generally reflect a theoretical bias. They often sample language behaviors of interest to the theory, which may or may not differentiate normal from atypical language users. Another problem with formal tests is that the children are often too young or too unfamiliar with testing situations to perform adequately on the various tests. In addition, even if representative behaviors are elicited, the norms are often inappropriate for the child's environmental circumstances, such as rural or impoverished home environments, the presence of a dialect or second language, or the presence of additional handicaps such as visual problems.

The use of behavioral observations also has limitations. In order to decide what to observe and how to interpret the observations, one has to be familiar with the developmental psycholinguistic literature, which is a challenging and time-consuming task in itself. Many data analysis methods reported in the literature are so time consuming that they are impractical to use with large numbers of children. Furthermore, there is scant information available that directly addresses the identification question. The little that has been reported is regarded as preliminary or exploratory in nature.

Legal mandates to provide services for all handicapped children emphasize the need for identification of children with communication disorders, ages birth to 21 years. Clinicians are under considerable pressure to be accountable and objective. There are several problems associated with the task that are not readily solvable. These take the form of the following questions:

1. Which communication behaviors should be assessed, in terms of which behaviors differentiate normal from disordered language?
2. How should these behaviors be sampled to determine under which set of circumstances the deviancy is apparent?
3. To what standard should the performance be referenced, in terms of chronological age, mental age, or linguistic level, e.g., mean length of utterance?

This chapter addresses these questions in detail. First, a brief look at the dominant theories in the child language literature is presented to account for why the question of identification has received little direct attention in the theoretical literature. Following the development of a theoretical perspective, each of the three questions posed above is discussed in terms of the relevant research. Identification of children with language disorders within a clinical perspective follows the review of the research, with suggestions for integrating behavioral observations into a basis for clinical judgment.

THEORETICAL PERSPECTIVES

The study of child language during the past 15 years has been characterized by two dominant but opposing theoretical positions. The behaviorist position (sometimes referred to as the associationist position), with Skinner (1957) as the foremost spokesman, relies upon concepts such as "stimulus," "imitation," "reinforcement," and "practice" to account for how language is acquired. The nativist position (sometimes referred to as a content approach), put forth in the writings of Chomsky (1957, 1959), McNeill (1966), and Lenneberg (1967), is based upon the premise that the ability to acquire language is determined biologically and that children are innately endowed with information-processing abilities specific to language or with knowledge of certain linguistic structures. Another approach, described as a cognitivist or process theory, has emerged as a reaction to the learning/biology dichotomy of the behaviorist/nativist positions. This third position combines aspects of the learning versus biology dichotomy by shifting the emphasis to the child's underlying cognitive abilities, i.e., innate generalized process mechanisms, instead of a specific innate language ability. Such writers as Bloom (1970, 1973), Brown (1973), Slobin (1973), Bowerman (1976), and Cromer (1974) emphasize that language maps a cognitive base. Children do learn language, but this language learning interacts with underlying cognitive processing.

Two of these theoretical positions are reflected in the content and sequence of various language programs. The nativist position has had little direct impact upon language programming because of the minimal significance it attributes to the environment. Hence the debate concerns the relative merits of the behaviorist versus cognitivist positions in terms of program effectiveness. The position of the behaviorists is reflected in the Parsons Language Sample (Spradlin, 1963), the functional analysis approach to language programming (Girardeau and Spradlin, 1970; McReynolds, 1974), and recent language programs developed by Gray and Ryan (1973) and Guess, Sailor, and Baer (1974). The recent influence of the cognitivist position is apparent in newly developed language programs that relate underlying cognitive skills and the normal sequence of language development to the training of language behaviors. Programs developed by Bricker and Bricker (1974), Miller and Yoder (1974), Stremel and Waryas (1974), and MacDonald (1975) exemplify this position.

Because the influence of these differing theoretical positions has been considerable for both language assessment and programming, it is important to gain a clear delineation of the defining characteristics of each. For those readers interested in a detailed discussion of the three theories, Reber (1973) offers a lucid and integrative analysis. At this point, however, a more concise statement of the differences between the behaviorist and cognitivist positions is sufficient. Staats (1974) provides a clear description of the differences:

> It is suggested, thus, that there are general positions involved here that are antagonistic. The radical behavioristic approach is concerned with the manner in which the environment affects behavior. The position is deterministic; the search is for causal, elementary laws that apply across the phylogenetic scale. The position rejects concepts of inferred mental processes that are not observed, that allegedly determine the individual's behavior (for example, the concept of rules). Biological variables are deemphasized, in effect at any rate, since the study is not directed toward such variables.
>
> Cognitive theory, on the other hand, has as a main goal a description of the characteristics of the mind that determine human behavior. These are usually thought to be in large part special to man, and biologically based. Cognitive theory resists the concept that man is merely the product of his experience (learning) and insists that man is original, spontaneous, and creative (p. 627).

Staats (1974) reviewed presentations by noted researchers in the area of child language representing both the cognitivist and behaviorist approaches and concluded that the two are beginning to interact, with each acknowledging the merits of some of the other's points, in preliminary indications of a rapprochement. However, he cautions that there are real, deep, and valid differences remaining.

Perhaps one reason that there seems to be a "rapprochement" in language development theories is attributable not so much to a "regression toward the mean" in terms of the sharing of theoretical components as it is to an apparent mutual agreement as to how to divide the territory, the domain of language development/language programming. Roughly speaking, this amounts to the psycholinguists representing the cognitive approach studying normal acquisition patterns and constructing theoretical explanations of language acquisition, while the behaviorists develop the technology of behavior change and experimental confirmation of the psycholinguistic findings. This "division of duties" is outlined explicitly by Guess, Sailor, and Baer (1974, pp. 542–543). They outline the contribution of an operant orientation to the development of language-training programs as consisting of: 1) offering effective teaching and procedures, 2) providing an experimental approach, and 3) generating comprehensive language-training programs.

They see the role of the developmental psycholinguist as providing normative data and "reminding the language trainer of the importance of attaching meaning to the child's utterances and of the necessity for training speech and language within a context that has direct applicability and function for the child" (p. 543). Baer, as quoted by Bateman (1974, p. 610), stated that program developers needed (presumably to be supplied by the psycholinguists): "1) accurate and usable descriptions of language behavior and 2) data on what constitutes prerequisites for these behaviors." He further specified that this information would be most useful if stated in behavioral terms.

By and large the respective theoretical camps have recognized the implicit division of the territory. Behaviorists have occasionally wandered over to strike a blow at a psycholinguistic explanation of a particular language skill, such as the challenge to the "rule-governed" explanation of morphological development (the series of studies are summarized in Guess and Baer, 1973), but the psycholinguists have generally stayed in their territory and left the intricacies of programming entirely to the behaviorists. However, Bowerman (1976) recently ran a quick sortie into the behavioral territory by questioning the role of corrective feedback in developing certain language skills.

Although this division of interest is generally satisfactory for those involved, there are several gaps left for the clinician/trainer to fill. The most critical gap is one of identification, i.e., how to know when a child is "deficient" in language skills, in terms of knowing which behaviors to assess, how to sample them, and how to interpret the findings.

The first decision to be made in language programming for a child with language disorders is made before the initiation of the formal training sequence. This decision is one of determining if, indeed, the child's language behaviors indicate a language disorder, and, if so, which language behaviors or skills are involved. Unfortunately, virtually all language programs begin after this decision has been made. While the behaviorists have emphasized the importance of specifying and assessing specific behaviors in order to arrive at a baseline for training, they have not addressed the question of judgment of "normal" versus "deviant" behaviors. This judgment is presumed to be in the territory assigned to psycholinguists, i.e., the determination and description of normal language development. However, it is not that simple. The description of what is "normal" does not lead automatically to a description of "deviant" or "disordered," as if one were the inverse of the other.

Neither the behaviorists nor the psycholinguists (neither the cognitivist nor the nativist position), or a combination of the two approaches, provide an answer to the question of how to identify children with language disorders. Instead, the clinician/trainer is left with the formidable task of seeking the information he[1] needs from the available literature, keeping in mind the theoretical bias of the authors and bearing the frustration of finding few studies or writings that directly address the issue. Such a search of the available literature is summarized in the following section, presented in terms of the questions of what behaviors to look for, how to sample them, and how to interpret the findings.

REVIEW OF RESEARCH

What Behaviors to Look For?

What language behaviors or skills differentiate the child with disordered language from the normal language user? There are several components of language from which to choose, such as phonology, morphology, syntax, semantics, and pragmatics, in addition to the related speech production variables of fluency and voice (pitch, quality). Phonology, morphology, and syntax have received considerable study. Semantics and pragmatics are such recent theoretical developments that there has been little formal study done on either an experimental or a naturalistic basis.

Although language has been divided arbitrarily into these components for the purposes of linguistic description and analysis, the relationships among the components are not known, in regard to independence or interrelatedness. In normal children the acquisition of the

---

[1] Masculine pronouns are used throughout for the sake of grammatical uniformity and simplicity. They are not meant to be preferential or discriminatory.

various parameters is usually so rapid that it seems to be simultaneous. For example, at the earliest stages of language development new sounds (phonology) are acquired within the same time period as new meaningful units of form (morphemes), as new ways of ordering elements within an utterance (syntax), as new vocabulary items and meaningful relationships between words (semantics), and as new social uses of the verbal communication (pragmatics). While observations of normal children yield an immediate impression of a great deal of interdependence among the various components of language, there is evidence also of independence of components in the performance of some individuals with communication disorders, e.g., the very specific kinds of language deficits often observed in aphasic patients, both adult and children.

The question of whether or not the components of language are distinct bears directly on the question of "What behaviors to look for?" It would be very convenient (if it were possible) to differentiate deviant language behaviors on the basis of one or more distinct components, such as syntax. But Dale (1976) cautions against such a simplistic approach: "It is probably unrealistic to seek a single measure, a 'linguistic age' that can represent language development. But just how many distinct components exist is far from clear" (p. 301). He speculates that articulation and syntax are independent of each other, with vocabulary development distinct from syntactic development, and social uses of communication distinct from vocabulary and syntax (p. 301). Although these proposed independent components, i.e., articulation, syntax, vocabulary, and social uses, seem to be intuitively reasonable, it is obvious that their independence is relative, e.g., a child with an articulation disorder or very limited vocabulary is not likely to have sophisticated social uses of verbal communication, and it is possible that a severe articulation disorder could limit maximal vocabulary development insofar as it reduces the opportunities for the child to use vocabulary items in a unique productive fashion in his own verbal communication.

Given the unknown degree of interrelatedness among the components of language, and that the search for a distinct component to differentiate normal from disordered language is probably unrealistic, the discussion here nevertheless is organized in terms of the various identified components of language. This means of presentation is expedient because it reflects the focus of most of the relevant research and the organization of most formal assessment procedures. It also reflects the clinician's responsibility to be descriptively objective and specific, as expressed by Leonard (1972):

> The clinician's major responsibility rests in determining which specific aspects of the child's language behavior make his language different from that of his peers (p. 431).

Phonology   Speech pathologists have devoted a large proportion of their professional interest to the area of phonology, with a relatively well-defined standard for "deviant" behaviors, based on age norms of standardized tests. Thus phonology offers a variable that has a reference for "normal" versus "deviant," which generally has been accepted. But will it help in identifying language-disordered children? Dale (1976) says perhaps not.

> . . . Informally it seems that articulation and syntactic development are largely independent of each other. Some children articulate clearly relatively primitive language, whereas others produce highly developed, complex sentences in an almost unintelligible manner. It is suggestive that among children with language disabilities, disturbed syntax is almost always accompanied by disturbed articulation, but that articulation difficulties are often not accompanied by disturbed syntax (p. 301).

Although the presence of an articulation disorder, in itself, is generally not regarded as indicative of a more general language disorder, it still might be necessary to sort out the interrelationship between articulation and other language components, such as morphology. For example, the omission of a final /s/ sound may be phonemic in nature in the case of an articulation disorder, or morphological in nature in the case of a missing plural or possessive marker on nouns, or a missing third-person singular marker on a present-tense verb, or a missing copula marker in a contracted verb form. It would be necessary to look closely at the distribution of omissions to determine if the problem was phonemic or morphological.

Morphology and Syntax   Chomsky's (1957) theory of transformational grammar inspired a series of studies of syntax and morphology as variables differentiating normal from disordered language users, with a rather confusing course of outcomes.

Menyuk (1964) used Chomsky's (1957) system of analysis of phrase-structure transformations and morphology to compare the language of a group of 10 normals, ages three to five years, 10 months, with that of a matched group of 10 deviant language users. She reported qualitative differences between the two groups in terms of fewer transformations and more restricted or ungrammatical forms for the deviant group than for the normal, as measured by the number of children using each structure. However, the two groups indicated a statistically significant (0.05 level of confidence) difference on only one of 33 structures.

Leonard (1972) followed Menyuk's study by comparing the language of a group of nine normals with that of a matched group of nine deviant language users, with a mean chronological age of five years, three months for both groups. The same three aspects of language, i.e., phrase structure, transformations, and morphology, were analyzed.

Leonard's findings did not support those of Menyuk's in that he reported that no qualitative differences were apparent between the two groups (p. 434). He concluded,

> Deviants tend to differ from their normal peers on the basis of the frequency with which they use certain deviant forms and transformations—not on the number of different deviant forms and transformations used and not on the developmental level of the structure used (p. 443).

However, he did suggest that certain structures meet adequate criteria for clinical attention, with one of the criteria being that of different usage by deviant and normal language users (in terms of frequency data). The structures suggested were verb-phrase omissions and noun-phrase omissions (p. 438). He also suggested that the less frequent use of certain forms, such as indefinite pronouns, personal pronouns, and main verbs, in combination with a normal mean developmental score on the Developmental Sentence Scoring (Lee and Canter, 1971), could be indicative of a "deviant" language user as compared to "delayed" (p. 441).

Morehead and Ingram (1973) continued the search for grammatical differences, using a different criterion for matching subjects than the chronological age match used by Menyuk (1964) and Leonard (1972) and more comprehensive linguistic analyses. They matched 15 young normal children to 15 linguistically deviant children on the basis of mean number of morphemes per utterance, selected to represent five linguistic levels at the beginnings of language acquisition. Grammars were written for the language sample of each child. Five aspects of syntactic development were analyzed: phrase-structure rules, transformations, construction (or sentence) types, inflectional morphology, and minor lexical categories. They reported few significant differences for the more general aspects of syntax, such as phrase-structure rules, frequently occurring transformations, inflectional morphology, and the development of minor lexical categories. However, significant differences were found for the less general aspects of syntax, such as infrequently occurring transformations and the number of major syntactic categories per construction type. They also noted that the deviant group showed a marked delay in the onset and acquisition time for learning base syntax. Morehead and Ingram summarized their findings as follows:

> . . . linguistically deviant children do not develop bizarre linguistic systems that are qualitatively different from normal children. Rather, they develop quite similar linguistic systems with a marked delay in the onset and acquisition time. Moreover, once the linguistic systems are developed, deviant children do not use them as creatively as normal children for producing highly varied utterances (p. 344).

Their findings suggest a relationship between delayed language acquisition and a specific cognitive deficit. The implications are that the search differentiating normal and deviant syntactic and morphological usage is more complex than the identification of a particular linguistic structure or process that is used differently by normal and deviant users. Instead, such differences (according to Morehead and Ingram) are more superordinate in nature, reflecting cognitive functioning.

At this point it is appropriate to look at the methodologies of the studies just cited. The research paradigm used a normal group of children and a disordered group of children, collecting samples of their language behaviors, analyzing the samples according to syntactic and morphological relationships, and then looking for possible differences.

A critical question should be asked: How were the language-deviant children so identified in the first place? The studies do not report criteria for labeling the language-deviant group as such—just that the children had been so labeled by a speech clinician or were enrolled in a special class for children with language problems.

Leonard's (1972) nine defective language users attended a public school kindergarten and had an average age of five years, three months, whereas Morehead and Ingram's (1973) deviant group of 15 children was selected from a special school setting for children designated as aphasic, and the age range was three years, six months to nine years, six months. The nature and extent of the differences found in the studies may be a function of the particular sample of children using "disordered language."

It is possible that the criteria employed for identifying a child as having disordered language within the context of a public school kindergarten were quite different from the criteria used within the context of a special school setting for children as young as three years, six months who were designated aphasic. It is conceivable that these two disordered language groups demonstrated different patterns of language behaviors.

The inability to specify criteria for identifying children with language disorders leads to a circular kind of logic. To learn more about how disordered language is different from normal language, one needs to sample children labeled as "disordered" in terms of some criteria. It is difficult to evaluate the comparisons of normal versus disordered across studies without more information about what is being compared with what. Greater specificity is needed in the definition of "language disordered," in terms of a behavioral description of the particular criteria used.

One such means of defining the deviant language group is level of intellectual functioning. The preceding studies limited their subjects to those indicating normal intelligence. Several studies have addressed the question of whether or not there are grammatical differences between normal speakers and mentally retarded speakers.

Lackner (1976) did a very thorough analysis of the language behaviors of five retarded children, mental ages two to nine years, and compared their language to that of five normal children. He first collected 1,000 utterances from each retarded child, from which he wrote a preliminary grammar. From this grammar he constructed imitation and comprehension tasks that were used to modify the original grammar for a broader representation of each subject's linguistic competence and then used to match the retarded to the normal subjects on the basis of comprehension and imitation tasks and mean length of sentence. Lackner's findings were consistent with those reported by Leonard (1972) and Morehead and Ingram (1973) in that he found that the linguistic systems of retarded children follow developmental trends similar to those of normal children. Specifically, he summarizes the comparison as follows:

> . . . an ordering is maintained between the complexity of the grammars and the mental ages of the retarded children, and the chronological ages of the normal children. . . . [T]hese findings suggest that the language behaviors of normal and retarded children are not qualitatively different, that both groups follow similar developmental trends, but that the most severely retarded children become arrested in their development and remain at a lower level of normal language acquisition (p. 195).

The studies cited thus far that compared the grammar of deviant language users to that of normals have all used Chomsky's (1957) systems of analysis. Although the writing of transformational grammars has provided much useful descriptive information as well as considerable impetus for theoretical formations, it does have its limitations. Leonard (1972) presents examples of the theoretical limitations, such as some of the theoretically more complex structures were used by as many deviant language users as normals, or at an earlier age by normals than supposedly simpler forms (p. 444). Lackner (1976) notes that children's, especially normal children's, grammar changes so rapidly that it is impossible to write grammars to reflect current grammatical status. He also acknowledges that transformational grammar has inherent limitations when applied to children's grammar. It is possible to write more than one grammar to account for a child's utterances, with no way of choosing one over another (p. 195). Another very immediate and practical limitation is the time required in sampling, transcribing, and analyzing utterances. The amount of time involved greatly limits the feasibility of using transformational grammars to identify children with language disorders. Furthermore, and most important, as the foregoing studies have indicated, transformational grammar does not necessarily identify particular qualitative differences between normal and disordered language patterns.

Naremore and Dever (1975) used a performance grammar to compare the spontaneous speech of 30 educable mentally retarded children and 30 normal children at mental age levels six through 10 years. They analyzed both syntactic and functional performance variables. Significant differences in syntax were found for two variables, that of subject and predicate elaboration and that of relative and subordinate clauses. However, this difference was age related, with significance reached only at mental age 10; for mental ages six through nine, there were no significant differences. The authors suggest that, although there may be few qualitative differences at the younger levels, such differences may become apparent when the normals develop more sophisticated language structures, such as relative and subordinate clauses. Because the available research is focused upon earlier stages of development, further study of more complex syntactic forms is needed. The functional performance variables also indicated significant differences for filled pauses, repeats, and false starts.

A recent study by Johnston and Schery (1976) specifically concerned grammatical morphemes, comparing the use of grammatical morphemes by 287 linguistically deficient children, ages three years to 16 years, two months, with that reported for normal children. The subjects attended public school classes for children with language disorders, and they were identified in terms of performance on standardized IQ measures (all were normal) and auditory verbal language scales (two standard deviations or more below expected mental age performance levels). A 90%-usage-in-obligatory-contexts criterion was used, for morphological acquistion, to provide data analysis comparable to that reported in the normative literature. The findings indicated that atypical children acquired the same grammatical morphemes in much the same order as normal children (and with the same general relationship to overall language development level) but at later language levels, as defined by mean length of utterance, and also reflected in older age levels. The authors reported some indications of differences in addition to a later age of acquisition for the deviant users in terms of evidence for a longer course of acquisition, i.e., the deviant language users first used many morphemes at the earliest levels but took longer than normals to reach the 90% criterion.

Another means of comparing normal and deviant language users that has received considerable attention is the system of Developmental Sentence Scoring, developed by Lee and Canter (1971). It provides a system for analyzing spontaneous speech according to eight syntactic categories, with a scoring system that weighs the various structures according to developmental level, i.e., later developing forms receive a greater number of points. Data were collected on 200 children ages two to six years to establish norms for the various structures (Lee, 1974). In earlier publications, Lee (1966) suggested that such procedures could differentiate normal and deviant speakers in terms of specific structures. Leonard (1972) also advocated the use of the Developmental Sentence Scoring to differentiate "different" versus "delayed" language (pp. 439–441). However, in more recent writings, Lee (1974) deemphasizes the use of Developmental Sentence Analysis as a means of identifying specific deviant syntactic structures and instead advocates it as a descriptive map from which to generally compare the child's performance to the norms and then select behaviors and a sequence for training, based upon the normal developmental sequence (pp. 176–201). She acknowledges the practical limitations involved in using Developmental Sentence Analysis for the purpose of identification, indicating that it is "far too complicated to be a satisfactory initial diagnostic tool" (p. 170). Instead, she suggests it is better used as a means of documenting a change in behaviors and determining when to dismiss from therapy (p. 170).

Before concluding this discussion of the research on differences in grammatical forms between normal and disordered language, another issue remains to be addressed. If differences were apparent on some specific structure within a particular system of analysis, such as relative and subordinate clauses within the Naremore and Dever (1975) system of analysis, would those differences be among those picked up by a clinician or other listener/observer as indicating a language disorder? In other words, do those differences have validity for identifying children using disordered language? In the studies cited here, only Leonard (1972) has addressed the question of validity. He asked two speech pathologists to rank the protocols of the deviant and normal language users according to syntactic and morphological performance. These rankings were then compared with the frequency of use of the structures by the deviant and normal groups. He found that the rankings and frequency data did not always coincide, i.e., some structures used frequently by the deviant group and less frequently by normals (or vice versa) did not correlate highly with judgments of grammatical performance. As Leonard notes (p. 438), to obtain clinical significance a given structure should be used differently by normal and deviant language users, but it also should be related directly to judgments about the child's relative grammatical performance.

This question of validity of differences applies not only to grammatical differences between normal and deviant language users, which have been discussed so far, but also to possible semantic and pragmatic differences, discussed in following sections. It is easy to lose sight of the validity issue while following the elegant theoretical formulations presented in the literature to account for observations of possible differences. Such theorizing is thought provoking and leads to new research questions. Yet, for the purpose of identification, an observed language difference is irrelevant, no matter how interesting it is to a given theorist or how elegantly accounted for, if it does not serve as a means of sorting normal from deviant speakers in the listener's judgments. Almost all present research investigating possible differences needs to have additional corroboration in the form of validity data before it can be used with confidence for identification. This issue also extends to assessment techniques and procedures. There are virtually no studies identifying which items on standardized tests differentiate normal from deviant.

An additional observation is that the studies cited have used spontaneous utterances as a data base for comparing grammars, with the exception of the Lackner (1976) study, which included imitation and comprehension performance in the determination of the mentally retarded children's grammars. In none of the studies is there a comparison of the grammatical comprehension abilities of normal versus deviant language users.

Semantics   The recent shift of emphasis in developmental psycholinguistics from syntax to semantics (Bloom, 1970; Bowerman, 1973; Brown, 1973) provides the theoretical impetus to explore another parameter of language that may differentiate normal from deviant language users. Several recent studies use methods of data analysis based upon the systems of classification developed by Fillmore (1968) and Schlesinger (1971). The bases for comparison of normal and language-disordered speakers are the semantic relations involved between words in multiword utterances. Such semantic relations as agent-action, action-object, agent-object, possessor-possession, and entity-attribute are included in the analysis systems.

Leonard, Bolders, and Miller (1976) compared groups of three- and five-year-old normals and language-deviant children, with a total of 40 subjects. The language-deviant children were so designated by a speech pathologist on the basis of performance on various test instruments. None of the language-deviant children was mentally retarded, neurologically impaired, or emotionally disturbed. Comparisons of normal and disordered children were made under both matched utterance length and matched age conditions. The results indicated that when normal and disordered subjects were matched for utterance length there was no difference in the semantic relation utterance types reflected in their language, although the disordered subjects were chronologically older. This finding was interpreted as supporting the proposal that the disordered subjects possessed a semantic relation system suggestive of that of a younger, normal child (p. 383).

Similar findings were reported by Freedman and Carpenter (1976) in a study of the semantic relations encoded in the utterances of language-disordered and normal subjects at the earliest two-word stage of language development. The language-impaired group ranged in age from three years, five months to four years, 10 months and were regarded as language-impaired if they indicated normal hearing and intellectual abilities and "significant delays in both receptive and expressive language acquisition as determined by a speech pathologist" (p. 786). The children were matched to normals on the basis of their mean length of utterance, with all subjects within Brown's (1973) Stage I. Using a type-token ratio as a dependent variable (as compared to Leonard et al. frequency data) the authors reported that at the Stage I level of linguistic development the language-impaired children demonstrated a system of semantic relations no different from that of normal children.

The previous two studies investigated the semantic relations evident in children's verbal productions. Another recent study by Duchan and Erickson (1976) provides a much needed look at the comprehension of semantic relations by normal versus language-disordered children. Their subjects were 12 normal and 12 mentally retarded children who were enrolled in a special education class for children with intelligence quotients between 50 and 80. All subjects had mean lengths of utterance between 1 and 2.5. The experimental procedures consisted of a 60-item comprehension test including the four semantic relations of agent-action, action-object, possessive and locative in three verbal contexts: *expanded, telegraphic,* and *nonsense* forms. The authors reported no significant differences in the performance of the normal and language-disordered children of the same mean length of utterance.

The studies cited so far have investigated the semantic relations between words in multiword utterances. At this point some general comments are in order about semantic relations as a means of analysis of children's utterances. It is a system of analysis used by the developmental psycholinguists for the purposes of describing and accounting for normal language acquisition at the earliest stages of development. There are some very real limitations. Perhaps most important is the lack of evidence indicating how to define the categories of semantic relations so that they represent the child's semantic intentions. Just as the three studies cited here used different systems of categorization, there are a number of different systems reported in the psycholinguistic literature. As Brown (1973) observed, the relations or roles are abstract taxonomies applied to child utterances. That it is not known how finely the abstractions should be sliced and that no proof exists that the semantic levels hit on by any theorist, whether Bloom, Schlesinger, Fillmore, or whomever, are psychologically functional (p. 146).

He comments later that "description in terms of a set of prevalent semantic relations may be little more than a technique of data reduction, a way of describing the meanings of early sentences short of listing them all" (p. 173). Although the problem may seem to be only a theoretical debate in the psycholinguistic literature, it has practical consequences in determining how many categories to use and how to define the utterances within categories.

Another related problem in analyzing a corpus of spoken utterances is that of determining a criterion for productivity. Put another way, how does one decide that a child "has" a given semantic relation, such as agent-object, as compared to "having" a random strategy of word combinations or having memorized a few combinations? Leonard, Bolders, and Miller (1976) used an arbitrary frequency criterion (a given semantic relation utterance type must have occurred twice within a sample (p. 378)),whereas Freedman and Carpenter (1976) did not report such a frequency criterion for establishing a semantic relation category. Related to this difference in productivity criterion were differences in sample size, with 50 utterances as sample size in the Leonard et al. (1976) study and 300 utterances in the Freedman and Carpenter (1976) study. There is a lack of consensus in the psycholinguistic literature about establishing a criterion for productivity. In his recent monograph, Braine (1976) discusses the development of a rationale for determining a criterion for productivity.

Interestingly, the criterion at which Braine (1976) arrived for determining semantic relations is quite different from that used by Bloom, Lightbown, and Hood (1975) for similar purposes. While these methodological issues can be complex, they are also too important to overlook. Different criteria for productivity and different sample size lead to quite different findings from one study to the next. As long as the same analysis system is used within a study for describing both normal and disordered language, the semantic relations categories are directly comparable. However, it is not possible to compare specific categories across studies without a careful analysis of the methods used.

A more sophisticated limitation of semantic-relations categories appears in regard to statistical analysis. Frequency data from a corpus of spontaneous speech, such as that used by Leonard, Bolders, and Miller (1976), are ipsative in nature, that is, "each score for an individual is dependent on his scores on other variables, but is independent of, and not comparable with, the scores of other individuals" (Hicks, 1970, p. 167). In this case, the frequency data are "ipsative" in that the number of times a child produces one category, such as agent-action, reduces his opportunities for another category, such as locative-object. Because the data violate the assumption of independence of scores, such parametric means of analysis as analysis of variance are not appropriate. The statistical analysis of ipsative data presents a dilemma, with no known procedures to determine the extent of artefactual findings (see Hicks, 1970, for a detailed discussion). One means of avoiding the problems of ipsative data is to use a type-token ratio instead of frequency data, as was done by Freedman and Carpenter (1976), which can then be analyzed by a nonparametric statistical procedure.

The aspect of semantics discussed so far is that of semantic relations, i.e., the semantic intentions expressed in combinations of words. Another area of semantic investigation receiving considerable interest in recent psycholinguistic writings is word meanings, particularly at the earliest stages of development (Clark, 1973; Nelson, 1974; Bowerman, 1976, 1978).

Although there are no published studies that have applied the recent psycholinguistic theories of word meanings to the utterances of deviant children, some preliminary work has been completed. Lee (1975) has explored the efficacy of case grammar and generative semantics for revealing differences in the use of particular lexical items by language-disordered and normal children. She selected five semantically related verbs for comparison: *give, get, put, take,* and *have.* Groups of grammatically delayed children, mentally retarded children, and normally developing children were matched for level of grammatical development, according to Developmental Sentence Scoring (Lee, 1974). The children were compared in their frequency of use, variety of meanings, and types of semantic problems with the five verbs. Lee found that "different types of children, matched for level of grammatical development, showed differences in lexical usage, suggesting that grammatical structure and lexical structure are separate and distinct parameters of language learning" (p. 2). While such findings are exciting in terms of implications for differentiating normal from deviant speakers in terms of lexical use, Lee cautions that the methods of analysis have some limitations, such as a great deal of complexity and variability in the classification systems and a very small data base for some levels of analysis (such as only 31 sentences out of 2,000 verbal utterances remaining for one level of analysis).

The study of normal children's word meanings has led to some recent and yet untested implications for the identification of deviant speakers. Bowerman's (1978) systematic observations of the use of causative verbs by her two daughters have revealed evidence of "progressive regression," i.e., errors in the use of particular words that indicate a more sophisticated understanding of relationships among words than is evident at an earlier stage of errorless but more restricted use of the same words. These indications of "progressive regression" in the utterances of normal speakers add another dimension to the search for linguistic behaviors differentiating normal language from disordered language. It is not enough to identify "errors" in a child's language. It is necessary to look closely at the nature of the errors to determine if the errors are the probable result of limited understanding of a linguistic structure or the result of a generalization to an inappropriate use, which is based on a more sophisticated understanding of linguistic relationships. A possible example of such "progressive regression" is reported as an unexplained finding in the Leonard, Bolders, and Miller (1976) study cited earlier, in the observation that "one of the structures that theoretically represents a deviant form (inversion of verb number) is used more by normals" (p. 444). Further analysis of such errors as *There's the bears!* (Leonard, Bolders, and Miller, 1976, p. 433) may indicate that such errors are indicative of sophisticated, rather than limited, linguistic strategies.

Pragmatics   The recent focus on the function of language use in a social context, the pragmatics of language, offers an area rich with potential for differentiating deviant from normal speakers. Bates (1976) describes pragmatics as "the rules governing the use of language in context" (p. 420). Pragmatic structures are traditionally identified as performatives, presuppositions, and conversational postulates (Bates, p. 426), with *performatives* describing the speaker's intentions (p. 427), *presuppositions* referring to information assumed to be shared by speaker and listener, in the sense of a psychological presupposition (p. 439), and *conversational postulates* referring to assumptions about the nature of human discourse (p. 446).

As Dale (1976) notes (p. 258), very little is known about the development of pragmatic knowledge in children, but much important work is being done. Numerous recent studies apply systems of pragmatic analysis to the earliest utterances of normal children, often with the goal of relating early communicative intents and functions to underlying cognitive development.

The first attempt to specifically investigate possible differences in pragmatic use between normal and language-disordered children has been completed recently. Snyder (1975) compared the pragmatic performance of a group of 15 normal and 15 language-disabled children at the one-word stage of linguistic development. The subjects were matched for mean length of utterance and socioeconomic status and were screened for normal mental development. The mean age of the normal group was 14.9 months and of the language-disabled group was 24.2 months. Language-disabled children were defined as follows:

> Subsequent evaluation by a speech pathologist confirmed the presence of a language disability and the absence of complicating oral apraxias. The presenting initial symptom of all members of the language-disabled group was a significant delay in the onset of language comprehension and/or use and a slow rate of language acquisition (pp. 83–84).

The two groups were compared on their performance on pragmatic tasks designed for the experiment and on their cognitive skills, as measured by a standardized Piagetian measure of sensorimotor intelligence. The pragmatic tasks sampled three areas:

1. The children's presuppositional abilities, in terms of ability to encode the most informative element in a context
2. Declarative performatives
3. Imperative performatives

The declarative and imperative performatives then were related statistically to measures of underlying cognitive abilities.

Snyder reported finding significant differences in the pragmatic performances of the two groups of children. The language-disabled subjects had difficulty encoding the most informative element in the context with a linguistic symbol (although there was no difference between the groups in sensorimotor presuppositional encoding). The language-disabled subjects achieved significantly lower scores than the normal subjects on the declarative and imperative performative tasks. The language-disabled subjects exhibited pragmatic behaviors consistent with a stage of cognitive development earlier than that indicated by the normals. These results were interpreted as indicating "support for a specific representational deficit in the language disabled child which affects the dynamic aspects of symbolication" (p. 167).

Snyder's (1975) findings of pragmatic differences between normal and language-disabled children at the earliest stages of language development are certain to inspire further studies along this line. Although such limited evidence is preliminary in nature, the area of pragmatics offers considerable promise as a valid means of defining "language disorder," with "valid" used in the sense described earlier, i.e., corresponding to the social definition of the listeners' judgments of what constitutes a "language problem."

For example, at linguistic levels more advanced than the earliest stages, clinicians frequently observe that language-deviant children lack the subtle language differentiations involved in appropriate social functioning, such as when to ask directly for something as opposed to a more subtle form of hinting, or how to offer a comment that sounds polite versus one that seems rude, or how to appear respectful in a request to an authority figure instead of sounding insolent. Such pragmatics of language seem to come close to the heart of defining "language deviation" from a social and functional perspective. A pragmatics analysis may help delineate the kind of problem referred to by Schiefelbusch, Ruder, and Bricker (1976) as a "communication problem," i.e., the child with apparently adequate linguistic skills (in terms of phonology, morphology, and syntax) but with language functions not adapted to normal social and learning-task requirements.

To summarize this discussion of the components of language that may differentiate language-disordered children from those progressing in a normal fashion, several points can be made:

1. Reflecting prevalent psycholinguistic trends, syntax has received the most attention as a linguistic component differentiating normal and deviant language users. The search for differentiating specific structures or forms has been unsuccessful within present systems of analysis. There is some evidence to indicate that there may be differences in syntactic forms at more complex levels of acquisition that warrant further study. It seems safest to conclude that deviant language users are characterized by a delay in acquisition of morphology and syntax and a generally restricted pattern of use.

2. Recent advances in psycholinguistic descriptive analysis systems have inspired recent studies of semantic relations among words at the early stages of linguistic acquisition. The few studies completed have reported no difference in semantic relations when normal and disordered language users are matched on the basis of mean length of utterance. Another area of semantics featured in recent psycholinguistic writings is that of word meanings, again at the earliest stages. One exploratory study indicated that patterns of lexical use were different in normal, language-delayed, and mentally retarded children, when matched for level of grammatical development.

3. The study of word meanings in normal children's language development has led to the observation of "progressive regression," i.e., errors in word use that reflect a more advanced rather than a limited understanding of linguistic relationships. There have been no investigations of the word usage patterns of language-disordered children designed to explore the possibility of a qualitative rather than a quantitative difference in their errors.

4. Very recent psycholinguistic writings in the area of pragmatics offer the possibility of differentiating normal from language-disordered children on the basis of their social uses of verbal communication. The one study completed indicated differences in pragmatic use

between normal and language-disordered children at the earliest stages of language acquisition, when matched for mean length of utterance.

5. There is some evidence from syntactic and pragmatic analyses of differences indicating a specific cognitive deficit differentiating language-disabled children from normals. The possible cognitive deficit has not been identified or described specifically.

6. Although the psycholinguistic literature has identified linguistic components for analysis, has drawn attention to a complete analysis of verbal communication, including semantics and pragmatics, and has developed descriptive systems of analysis, there are limitations to the psycholinguistic methods when applied directly to group comparative studies or to identification of large numbers of children. The limitations include theoretical issues, problems with specification of analysis systems, methods of comparative data analysis, and time constraints. At the present time, the practicing clinician would be hard pressed to apply most of the research procedures directly to the immediate dilemmas of identification.

How to Sample the Behaviors?

To compare a child's language performance to that of normal children, in order to determine whether or not his language is indeed different, the clinician must first consider how to sample the behaviors. There are two aspects of how to sample for identification purposes. The first and more general question is how to sample in order to arrive at a representative sample of all areas of a child's linguistic performance, which can then be compared to what is known about the performance of normal children (as is advocated and outlined in detail by Miller, 1978). The second question is how to sample in ways to specifically elicit different performances from normal and deviant language users, i.e., a task with performance requirements that differentiate normal from atypical language.

There are a number of ways of sampling or eliciting language behaviors for the purpose of obtaining a representative sample of all areas of linguistic performance: 1) observing and recording spontaneous speech in the natural setting, 2) using some means of eliciting language (imitation or questions to visual stimuli and/or objects are the techniques most frequently used), 3) assessing language comprehension versus language production, and 4) manipulating the social environment. Each sampling procedure has advantages and disadvantages in obtaining a "true picture" of the child's language skills and performances.

Many differences evident in reported levels of language competence at various ages reflect differences in sampling methods. These are particularly evident when comparing language observed in the natural setting and language elicited in experimental settings. Brown (1973) points out the problem in regard to observed differences in dates of acquisition for morphemes:

> . . . assessments of particular kinds of linguistic competence based on experimental findings "date" the competencies in question later than do assessments based on naturalistic data. The performance on which the estimates are based are always different especially with regard to the need to direct and hold attention. I think the naturalistic data can yield a truer estimate in the sense of an estimate that is less dependent on performance skills not routinely developed in the child. But the experimental data, needless to say, can often be complete, where the naturalistic data are seriously fragmentary (p. 293).

In addition to the general problem of differences in performance under spontaneous versus elicited circumstances, which generally refer to the child's verbal productions, there is also the problem of different levels of competence for a given linguistic form in comprehension versus production. Recent studies of normal children show different linguistic strategies operating in comprehension versus production tasks (Bowerman, 1978) and possible developmental influences upon the relationship between comprehension and production (Bloom, 1974).

Recent attention to the pragmatics of language introduces another parameter for sampling a child's total linguistic functioning. If rules of social use may differentiate normal from deviant language users, then it will be necessary either to devise a series of communication tasks within a social context or to observe the child's communication performance within a social situation in his natural environment, or both.

There is little information available about the second aspect of how to sample, that of a sampling procedure that may elicit differential performances. As mentioned earlier, there are virtually no studies investigating which items of standardized tests elicit differential performances. The only means of comparison is by overall performance, in the form of subtest scores or total scores, and then comparing those total scores representing performance on all items to the scores obtained by a sample of normals.

There is some evidence that a sentence-repetition task elicits different syntactic performance from normal compared to language-disordered subjects. Menyuk and Looney (1976) compared a group of 13 language-disordered children (mean age of six years, two months) and a group of 13 normal-speaking children (mean age four years, six months), who were matched according to their scores on a standardized comprehension vocabulary test, on their performances on sentence-repetition tasks of varying length and complexity. The results indicated "striking differences in the sentence repetition abilities of the normal-speaking and the deviant-speaking children" (p. 266). The differences were evident in both number of errors and pattern of errors, with the deviant-speaking children having more "difficulty in repeating the negative, question, and negative subject and the passive sentence than the active-declarative and imperative sentences" (p. 267).

However, Lackner (1976) reported that, when comparing the performance of normal children with five mentally retarded children on imitation and comprehension tasks, there were no qualitative differences (p. 193).

Part of the reason for the discrepancy in findings between the Menyuk and Looney (1976) and Lackner (1976) studies may be found in the methodologies used. Lackner's (1976) retarded subjects were matched to normals on the basis of specific linguistic criteria, which included comprehension and imitation tasks in addition to mean length of utterance. The matching included several indices of linguistic competence. In contrast, Menyuk and Looney's (1976) subjects were matched only on the basis of their scores on a standardized comprehension of vocabulary test, representing a relatively narrow measure of linguistic competence. While the Lackner (1976) procedures allowed a comparison of imitation, comprehension, and production performances, Menyuk and Looney (1976) looked only at imitation.

The sentence-repetition, or imitation, tasks have come under careful scrutiny recently about whether or not they elicit a representative sample of a child's general linguistic competence. Prutting and Connolly (1976) recently reviewed the relevant literature and concluded that elicited imitations alone may underestimate, overestimate, or accurately describe the child's language performance. They suggest that elicited language samples be used in conjunction with a spontaneous language sample (p. 420), as was done by Lackner (1976). What was missing in the Menyuk and Looney (1976) study was some evidence that the elicited utterances corresponded to the linguistic structures evident in the children's spontaneous speech.

While it would be very helpful to discover a linguistic task that elicits differential responses from normal and language-disordered children, it must be a task that elicits behaviors representative of general language competence.

Which Reference to Use for a Judgment of Deviancy?

When the language behaviors of a particular child are being evaluated as possibly deviant, to whom or to what should the behaviors be compared? Several references are possible, namely, chronological age, mental age, and linguistic level, such as mean length of utterance. As Leonard,

Bolders, and Miller (1976) note, the different comparisons yield different types of normal-disordered differences and may account for some of the discrepancies in experimental findings. For example, Menyuk (1964) referenced the differences to chronological age, whereas Morehead and Ingram (1973) compared normal and language-disordered children matched for mean length of utterance. Most of the studies cited here, including those looking at syntax, semantic relations, and pragmatics, compared normal and language-disordered children when matched for mean length of utterance or other linguistic measures of performance.

As a general rule, the usual reference point for clinical comparisons is chronological age. That is the criterion for comparison in standardized language tests. Comparisons in the area of syntax offer enough evidence that language-disordered children are slower in acquiring syntactic structures when compared to their chronological peers. There certainly is not enough evidence to draw conclusions about semantic relations, word usage, or pragmatic development as compared to chronological peers.

There may be circumstances when reference to mental age may be more appropriate than chronological age, as in the case of the mentally retarded child. Naremore and Dever (1975) used mental age to match mentally retarded and normal children. However, it is possible that the retarded children's linguistic abilities do not correspond to their mental ages. In the Lackner (1976) study, mental age was the criterion for initial selection of mentally retarded subjects, who were further matched to normals on the basis of linguistic performance. This was also the procedure followed by Lee (1975), who specifically used as subjects mentally retarded children whose grammatical performances were not consistent with their mental ages. Hence, mental age was the immediate reference for "language disordered" in her sample of mentally retarded children.

Comparisons to indices of linguistic performance, such as mean length of utterance or measures of grammatical complexity, are pertinent to the issue of "deviant" versus "delayed," in the sense of differentiating language behaviors atypical in need of treatment from language behaviors indicative of earlier normal patterns in a "slower" development that would not require treatment. For example, if a child's linguistic performance is consistent with that of children at equivalent linguistic levels, although younger in age, he could be considered "delayed" in language acquisition, in that he appears to be following a normal pattern but at a slower acquisition rate. On the other hand, a child whose linguistic performance indicates different language structures or behaviors than those used by children at equivalent linguistic levels could be considered "deviant" in language acquisition, in that his pattern of acquisition is unlike that of normals and he therefore presumably could be in need of therapy or some form of intervention programming. Leonard (1972) has argued for the possibility of such differentiation.

CLINICAL IDENTIFICATION

The preceding sections have provided frustrating examples of how little is known about how to identify children with "disordered" language—frustrating in the sense of being inadequate for the practicing clinician's needs. The methods of behavioral science are laborious and time consuming. Research studies, which carefully control the many variables that can confound language performance, are gradually but slowly adding bits of knowledge for a clearer understanding of what constitutes "disordered" language. The theorists have been working much faster than the researchers, sometimes providing alternate and conflicting explanations of the difference between normal and disordered language faster than the researchers can substantiate them or the practicing clinician can assimilate them into a working perspective. But, in the meantime, the clinician is faced with the immediate task of identifying children with disordered language. With mandated services comes the responsibility for screening large numbers of children to identify those with language problems, often children who are very young, or very unfamiliar with verbal sampling situations, or are of a cultural setting with dialectal differences—all of which are variables that complicate the identification of children with language disorders. Added to the responsibility of identification is often the charge to do so in a manner that is "accountable," that is, in terms of specific, identifiable behaviors and predetermined criterion levels. Because the limited knowledge available from research studies does not provide adequate information, the clinician is compelled by his responsibilities to look for information elsewhere.

One of the most often overlooked sources of information is the clinician himself. Siegel (1975) reminds us that a clinician needs to develop his own resources, in addition to closely monitoring new knowledge coming out of research laboratories. Instead of depending only on the knowledge painstakingly arrived at through carefully controlled studies, each clinician has to call upon his own experience, intuitions, and good judgment. Siegel's comments indicate that this applies in particular to identification:

> The question of whether or not a youngster ought to be provided speech services is, ultimately, based on the considered judgment of a professionally educated and experienced clinician, and not by the application of some set of norms (1975, p. 214).

If the clinician has to develop and rely upon his "intuition" and "good judgment," then it would be helpful to define some general characteristics of children with disordered communication patterns, some observations of behaviors and relationships to serve as a basis for this "good judgment." Such general characteristics can often provide valid clinical information, even before they have specific confirmation within a research framework.

One such characteristic that has received wide verification is the greater probability of a language disorder in the presence of other handicapping conditions. When other handicaps have been confirmed, or neurological trauma (such as that caused by falls or illnesses) is a possibility, the child is a high risk for problems with verbal communication. Such handicaps as mental retardation and hearing loss typically have an effect upon language development commensurate with the extent of the retardation or hearing loss. In such cases, prior confirmation of the retardation or hearing loss often serves as ipso facto identification of a communication problem. However, there is also cause for caution before one accepts the obvious assumptions, particularly in the case of the child identified as mentally retarded. This judgment is often based upon tests that require verbal abilities. Hence, a child may be erroneously identified as retarded, for reasons that have to do with his inability to function on a verbal test, such as having a language disorder without accompanying mental retardation, having a hearing loss with or without an accompanying language disorder, or speaking a foreign language without comprehending English. In such cases further information is needed from nonverbal assessments to sort out the relationships among retardation, hearing ability, and language performance.

When the child indicates normal abilities in other performance areas, the identification of a language disorder as the sole handicapping condition becomes much more difficult. The characteristics of such children are much more vague and difficult to differentiate from the wide range of normal communicative behaviors. However, there is one group of children without other handicaps that can be characterized immediately as "high risk," i.e., those who are referred for an evaluation. The assigning of high-risk status to referrals reflects the general observation that children with language disorders draw attention to themselves as a result of their atypical performances. For some reason some adult has singled that child out as being different. Even if the referring adult cannot specify the communication differences, the general impression is significant enough to warrant a clinician's careful assessment of the child's linguistic behaviors. Referrals also merit high-risk status in view of sampling limitations. Language behaviors are so complex and so context bound that it becomes virtually impossible for the clinician to sample all of a child's verbal communication behaviors. Hence, any information or judgment of deviance by others merits careful investigation.

The assessment of a child who has been referred will be more helpful if it addresses all aspects of verbal communication. As noted in the previous review of the research, until recently the only areas of verbal communication to receive emphasis were phonology and syntax. The available normative assessment tests and scales generally reflect this emphasis, providing information only about phonology and syntax. With this set of circumstances, the clinician, who relied upon such standardized tests and research findings, could evaluate a child who had been referred and could conclude "no problem," on the basis of adequate syntax and phonology. This would be possible when the referral was initiated on the basis of problems with word usage (semantics) or social context (pragmatics). At such times, both the referring adult and the speech clinician may regard the other's judgment as being inaccurate, when they were actually not addressing the same communication behaviors or did not have a common notion of "language problem." It is a reflection of recent theoretical developments that the informed clinician can now extend his good judgment to include such parameters as word usage and social context. All the parameters of language need to be assessed in an effort to identify which behaviors were responsible for his being singled out to begin with. As noted earlier, the child with language problems can be expected to draw attention to himself. The problem is to determine if it was, indeed, his verbal communication that was the basis for the referral, and in what ways it is different.

In the absence of a referral or evidence of related handicaps, more subtle characteristics can indicate children with communication problems. These characteristics are often revealed in relationships between the comprehension and production of language within a social context, in relation to the apparent cognitive level at which the child is functioning. Such complex interactions are usually manifested in unstructured situations, such as in spontaneous free-play situations or social interchanges. There are undoubtedly many clues for which experienced clinicians learn to watch in such situations. Sometimes the clues form an identifiable pattern or characteristic that serves as an indication of a child having trouble with verbal communication. Such identifiable patterns are based on the assumption that a child's language disorder will affect his behavior in social situations in ways that differentiate him from other children.

Characteristic Behaviors

Among such possible identifier-characteristics are the following:

1. The child who does not interact verbally with his peers in social contexts, the one who seems to be overly shy or embarrassed about talking. A typical example would be the child who observes the play activities of other children from the fringe areas, with little or no involvement except when directly approached. Such a child may only

be shy, but there is the possibility that his embarrassment is justified. Certainly his ability to use verbal communication with facility in a social situation (his pragmatic abilities) would be suspect.

2. The child who does not follow through on verbal commands or information presented verbally, particularly if he seems to be visually alert. A typical example would be the child who does not react until the other children do when the teacher presents new information verbally. There is the possibility that his comprehension of language is limited, with the use of visual alertness developed as a compensatory mechanism. Such a child often has very limited expressive language.

3. The child who does not talk much and yet has elaborate compensatory communication, such as very expressive hand gestures, facial expressions, or vocal inflections. An example would be the child who can give very clear, often detailed, directions or descriptions, but when he has finished his listener is surprised to realize how few actual words he used. An obvious suspicion is that his expressive language is not adequate for what he has to say, whether it be a problem with phonology, syntax, or semantics, or all of the expressive components.

4. Closely related to the previous pattern of behavior is the child who seems to have very well developed comprehension or socially very appropriate things to say but whose verbal productions are limited in either quantity or quality. Such a child may not use the elaborate compensatory communication as in the preceding example but instead may typically offer minimal verbal responses and let it go at that. A typical interchange would be when an adult asks, "What's your favorite TV show?" and the response is something like, "Oh, cartoons, that's all." The verbal responses are typically errorless but minimal in length or structure, as if the child realizes his own limitations. The child's cognitive and social performances are age appropriate. Such children are often bilingual or bidialectal. Again, such patterns lead to a suspicion that the child's verbal communication may not be adequate for his needs.

As a recapitulation, the present state of scientific knowledge is not complete enough to specify conclusively what is "disordered language." Supplemental information in the form of the clinician's "intuition" and "good judgment" is required in order to identify children with language disorders. Such clinical intuition and good judgment are acquired through experience and observing patterns of behavior that are characteristic of children having problems with verbal communication. Among such children and characteristic behavioral patterns are the following:

1. Children with related handicaps, such as hearing loss or mental retardation

2. Children referred for evaluation
3. Children demonstrating subtle patterns of communication failure, such as:
    a. The child who does not talk with his peers
    b. The child who does not follow through on verbal commands
    c. The child with limited verbalization and sophisticated compensatory communication
    d. The child who deliberately monitors his verbal communication for minimal length and complexity constraints

The identification of children with language disorders in a clinical setting is neither completely objective nor procedurally invariant from one child to the next. The identification process usually involves the collection of some normative data, the observation of some particular language performances in both structured and nonstructured circumstances, and the gathering of additional related information, in terms of the aforementioned characteristic behavioral patterns, which are deemed pertinent for that particular child.

An example is provided of a child who was identified as having a "language problem" primarily on the basis of the clinical characteristics just described. It was necessary to rely heavily on "clinical judgment" because this particular child just happened to represent several of the present gaps and weak areas in the available scientific knowledge, in that she was young, at the early stages of language acquisition, of a minority group, and unfamiliar with verbal sampling expectations. However, the available related information corresponded to several of the clinical identifier-characteristics of a child whose verbal communication was inadequate for her needs.

Case History Example

Patricia, age 3 years, 0 months, was referred for evaluation by her day-care teachers, who reported that Patricia was not toilet trained and seemed unable to follow verbal directions when they attempted toilet-training procedures. Patricia was an Indian child, an only child who lived with her mother (who is attending an Indian Junior College and works in a library). English was the only language spoken at home and at the day-care center. It was reported by her teachers that Patricia's mother was overly protective, with very limited expectations for Patricia's self-help behaviors.

An observation of Patricia in her day-care group indicated that her verbal participation was minimal. She offered very few spontaneous comments, usually one word in length, and seemed to passively ignore verbal directions from adults. Her teachers confirmed that this lack of verbal participation was typical for Patricia.

When Patricia was seen in an individual session with an examiner she was very shy and reluctant to respond verbally to direct questions. The Peabody Picture Vocabulary Test (Dunn, 1965), Form B, was administered, with Patricia obtaining a raw score of 10, which is more than two standard deviations below the mean for her chronological age group. The Denver Developmental Screening Test (Frankenburg and Dodds, 1969) indicated performance within chronological age expectations for personal-social, fine motor, and gross motor areas of development, but performance below the norms in the language area. An auditory assessment indicated hearing within normal limits for speech. Her articulatory movements were within normal expectations on simple sound- and word-imitation tasks.

Given Patricia's apparent unfamiliarity with the expectations of a test situation and her "unstandard" background, extensive formal standardized testing was regarded as inappropriate. Instead, Patricia's spontaneous language behaviors, both comprehension and production, were evaluated in a free-play situation. Her spontaneous utterances consisted almost entirely of single words, almost all of which were the names of toy objects.

A total corpus of 55 unimitated utterances was recorded, with a mean length of utterance (MLU) of 1.6. Compared to Brown's (1973, p. 55) two children, Adam and Sarah, Patricia's MLU would be less than expected. However, the comparison is limited because of Patricia's initial shyness and unfamiliarity with the situation, and the very limited sample obtained.

Within the corpus were several multiword combinations, such as "Sit doll a chair," "fix da there," "see a door," "I make a house," "I did a house," "that a chair?" When asked to imitate a three-word agent-action-object sentence, Patricia omitted one of the elements, either the subject or the verb, or reversed the word order to agent-object-action. Similar agent-action-object series were presented as comprehension tasks, with Patricia being asked to act them out with the appropriate toys. She was unable to consistently perform successfully with a change of objects or agents (with the verb kept constant), or when she was asked to perform with herself as actor (such as *kick chair, drop cat, push car,* etc.). When presented with simple pictured objects she could match like objects and those with categorical similarities, such as different kinds of dogs or birds.

Given this information, which took approximately two hours over three different sessions to obtain, how is Patricia's language performance to be judged: normal or deviant? What about the various components of language? Patricia's phonology is within the established norms (Winitz, 1969, p. 59). What about her syntax, semantics, or pragmatics? Unfortunately, there are no established norms for any of these three aspects of language when observed in the spontaneous speech of a three-year-old. Although observation studies of some normal children have been reported in the psycholinguistic literature, Bowerman (1978) cautions that there is little or no information available about normal variability. Hence, even if Patricia's language productions are different from those described in the normal psycholinguistic literature, that does not indicate "deviant" without some estimate of normal variability. While there is some available normative literature describing language productions, there is very little describing comprehension abilities and certainly not enough to constitute a reference for "normal." It is important to keep these vague reference points in mind for evaluating the language performance of a three-year-old when reading studies that present the identification of two- and three-year-olds as "language disordered" as part of the routine responsibilities of a speech clinician.

Patricia's communication behaviors certainly could not be described as advanced or probably not even "average" in the sense of "most typical" for her age, as evidenced by her being singled out from among her peers by her teachers. But does being less verbal, or less responsive to verbal commands, constitute a "language problem"? After all, Einstein did not begin to talk until he was nearly three years of age (Farb, 1975, p. 277).

Although decisive, firm, and objective evidence was not present for a judgment of Patricia's language as being "disordered" or "deviant," several clinical identifier-characteristics were evident. These included being referred for evaluation, very limited verbal participation in a social context with her peers, and limited or nonexistent response to verbal commands. While the objective evidence for "language disorder" was equivocal, the subjective, clinical evidence strongly indicated some problems with verbal communication, in that her performance was not adequate to meet her needs within the day-care setting. Given this distribution of evidence, the final clinical judgment was that of "language disorder," with appropriate intervention programming provided.

CONCLUSIONS

The identification of children with language disorders is a professional responsibility that is typically overlooked in the programming literature. At this stage of our professional development, the available knowledge in regard to what constitutes "disordered language" is very limited. Each clinician must supplement the available professional knowledge with his own clinical judgment, derived from his experience and repeated observations of children's communication behaviors. Given this present state of affairs, several conclusions are warranted:

1. While there is considerable pressure to be objective and specific in establishing criteria for identification, it is possible to be more "accountable" than is consistent with what is known. For example, the specification of particular language structures as "deviant" would be consistent with efforts to be accountable but inconsistent with the available research findings. The one "sure" criterion emerging from research findings is that children with language problems acquire competence with grammatical forms at a later age than their normal peers. Efforts to be more precise or specific must be recognized as the assumptions and hypothetical propositions that they may be.

2. The available information is particularly limited for young children under school age and children from "non-normative" circumstances, i.e., non-white, non-middle-class, non-standard-English speaking. The designation of "language-disordered" for these children requires confirmation of several of the clinical identifier-characteristics in addition to comparisons with what few normative observations and standardized scores are available.

3. There is growing evidence from the normative literature, as more children are observed, of considerable variability, particularly among younger children, in both their linguistic strategies and their patterns of production. The implication is for some caution in designating children as having "language disorders," especially if there is a possibility of negative consequences, such as removal from the peer group. This would be particularly true when the clinician is screening large groups of children, without benefit of prior information in the form of a referral.

REFERENCES

Bateman, B. 1974. Discussion summary—language intervention for the mentally retarded. In R. L. Schiefelbusch and L. L. Lloyd (eds.), Language Perspectives—Acquisition, Retardation, and Intervention, pp. 607–611. University Park Press, Baltimore.

Bates, E. 1976. Pragmatics and sociolinguistics in child language. In D. Morehead and A. Morehead (eds.), Normal and Deficient Child Language, pp. 411–463. University Park Press, Baltimore.

Bensberg, G., and Sigelman, C. 1976. Definitions and prevalence. In L. L. Lloyd (ed.), Communication Assessment and Intervention Strategies, pp. 33–72. University Park Press, Baltimore.

Bloom, L. 1970. Language Development: Form and Function in Emerging Grammars. MIT Press, Cambridge, Mass.

Bloom, L. 1973. One Word at a Time: The Use of Single Word Utterances Before Syntax. Mouton, The Hague.

Bloom, L. 1974. Talking, understanding and thinking. In R. L. Schiefelbusch and L. L. Lloyd (eds.), Language Perspectives—Acquisition, Retardation, and Intervention, pp. 285–311. University Park Press, Baltimore.

Bloom, L., Lightbown, P., and Hood, L. 1975. Structure and variation in child language. Monogr. Soc. Res. Child Dev. 40(2), Serial No. 160.

Bowerman, M. 1973. Early Syntactic Development: A Cross-Linguistic Study with Special Reference to Finnish. Cambridge University Press, Cambridge, Mass.

Bowerman, M. 1976. Semantic factors in the acquisition of rules for word use and sentence construction. In D. Morehead and A. Morehead (eds.), Directions in Normal and Deficient Child Language. University Park Press, Baltimore.

Bowerman, M. 1978. Words and Sentences: Uniformity, individual variation, and shifts over time in patterns of acquisition. In F. D. Minifie and L. L. Lloyd (eds.), Communicative and Cognitive Abilities—Early Behavioral Assessment, pp. 351–398. University Park Press, Baltimore.

Braine, M. 1976. Children's first word combinations. Monogr. Soc. Res. Child Dev. 41(1), Serial No. 164.

Bricker, W., and Bricker, D. 1974. An early language training strategy. In R. L. Schiefelbusch and L. L. Lloyd (eds.), Language Perspectives—Acquisition, Retardation, and Intervention, pp. 431–468. University Park Press, Baltimore.

Brown, R. 1973. A First Language. Harvard University Press, Cambridge, Mass.

Chomsky, N. 1957. Syntactic Structures. Mouton, The Hague.

Chomsky, N. 1959. Review of Verbal Behavior by B. F. Skinner. Language 35:26–58.

Clark, E. 1973. What's in a word? On the child's acquisition of semantics in his first language. In T. M. Moore (ed.), Cognitive Development and the Acquisition of Language. Academic Press, New York.

Cromer, R. 1974. The development of language and cognition: The cognition hypothesis. In B. Foss (ed.), New Perspectives in Child Development. Penguin Books, Baltimore.

Dale, P. 1976. Language Development. Holt, Rinehart and Winston, New York.

Duchan, J., and Erickson, J. 1976. Normal and retarded children's understanding of semantic relations in different verbal contexts. J. Speech Hear. Res. 19:767–776.

Dunn, L. M. 1965. Peabody Picture Vocabulary Test. American Guidance Service, Circle Pines, Minn.

Farb, P. 1975. Word Play: What Happens When People Talk. Bantam Books, New York.

Fillmore, C. 1968. The case for case. In E. Bach and R. Harms (eds.), Universals in Linguistic Theory. Holt, Rinehart and Winston, New York.

Frankenburg, W. K., and Dodds, J. B. 1969. Denver Developmental Screening Test. University of Colorado School of Medicine, Denver.

Freedman, P., and Carpenter, R. 1976. Semantic relations used by normal and language-impaired children at Stage I. J. Speech Hear. Res. 19:784–795.

Girardeau, F., and Spradlin, J. (eds.). 1970. A functional analysis approach to speech and language. ASHA Monogr. No. 14.

Gray, B., and Ryan, B. 1973. A Language Program for the Non-Language Child. Research Press, Champaign, Ill.

Guess, D., and Baer, D. M. 1973. Some experimental analyses of linguistic development in institutionalized retarded children. *In* B. B. Lahey (ed.), The Modification of Language Behavior. Charles C Thomas, Springfield, Ill.

Guess, D., Sailor, W., and Baer, D. 1974. To teach language to retarded children. *In* R. L. Schiefelbusch and L. L. Lloyd (eds.), Language Perspectives: Acquisition, Retardation, and Intervention, pp. 529–563. University Park Press, Baltimore.

Hall, R. A. 1960. Linguistics and Your Language. Anchor Books, Garden City, N.Y.

Hicks, L. 1970. Some properties of ipsative, normative, and forced-choice normative measures. Psychol. Bull. 74:167–184.

Johnston, J., and Schery, T. 1976. The use of grammatical morphemes by children with communication disorders. *In* D. Morehead and A. Morehead (eds.), Normal and Deficient Child Language, pp. 239–258. University Park Press, Baltimore.

Lackner, J. 1976. A developmental study of language behavior in retarded children. *In* D. Morehead and A. Morehead (eds.), Normal and Deficient Child Language, pp. 181–208. University Park Press, Baltimore.

Lee, L. 1966. Developmental sentence types: A method for comparing normal and deviant syntactic development. J. Speech Hear. Disord. 31:311–330.

Lee, L. 1969. Northwestern Syntax Screening Test. Northwestern University Press, Evanston, Ill.

Lee, L. 1974. Developmental Sentence Analysis. Northwestern University Press, Evanston, Ill.

Lee, L. 1975. A study of normal and atypical semantic development. Unpublished manuscript, Northwestern University, Chicago.

Lee, L., and Canter, S. 1971. Developmental sentence scoring: A clinical procedure for estimating syntactic development in children's spontaneous speech. J. Speech Hear. Disord. 36:315–338.

Lenneberg, E. H. 1967. The Biological Foundations of Language. John Wiley & Sons, New York.

Leonard, L. 1972. What is deviant language? J. Speech Hear. Disord. 37:427–446.

Leonard, L., Bolders, J., and Miller, J. 1976. An examination of the semantic relations reflected in the language usage of normal and language-disordered children. J. Speech Hear. Res. 19:371–392.

MacDonald, J. D. 1975. Environmental language intervention: Programs for establishing initial communication in handicapped children. *In* F. Withrow and C. Nygren (eds.), Language and the Handicapped Learner: Curricula, Programs and Media. Charles E. Merrill Books, Columbus, Ohio.

McNeill, D. 1966. Developmental psycholinguistics, *In* F. Smith and G. A. Miller (eds.), The Genesis of Language. MIT Press, Cambridge, Mass.

McReynolds, L. (ed.). 1974. Developing systematic procedures for training children's language. ASHA Monogr. No. 18.

Menyuk, P. 1964. Comparison of grammar of children with functionally deviant and normal speech. J. Speech Hear. Res. 7:109–121.

Menyuk, P., and Looney, P. 1976. A problem of language disorder: Length vs. structure. *In* D. Morehead and A. Morehead (eds.), Normal and Deficient Child Language, pp. 259–279. University Park Press, Baltimore.

Miller, J. 1978. Assessing children's language behavior: A developmental process approach. *In* R. L. Schiefelbusch, Bases of Language Intervention, pp. 269–318. University Park Press, Baltimore.

Miller, J., and Yoder, D. 1974. An ontogenetic teaching strategy for retarded children, *In* R. L. Schiefelbusch and L. L. Lloyd (eds.), Language Perspectives—Acquisition, Retardation, and Intervention. University Park Press, Baltimore.

Morehead, D., and Ingram, D. 1973. The development of base syntax in normal and linguistically deviant children. J. Speech Hear. Res. 16:330–352.

Naremore, R., and Dever, R. 1975. Language performance of educable mentally retarded and normal children at five age levels. J. Speech Hear. Res. 18:89–95.

Nelson, K. 1974. Concept, word and sentence: Interrelations in acquisition and development. Psychol. Rev. 81:267–285.

Prutting, C., and Connolly, J. 1976. Imitation: A closer look. J. Speech Hear. Disord. 41:412–422.

Reber, A. S. 1973. On psycholinguistic paradigms. J. Psycholing. Res. 2:289–319.

Schiefelbusch, R., Ruder, K., and Bricker, W. 1976. Training strategies for language-deficient children: An overview. *In* N. Haring and R. L. Schiefelbusch (eds.), Teaching Special Children. McGraw-Hill Book Co., New York.

Schlesinger, I. 1971. Production of utterances and language acquisition. *In* D. Slobin (ed.), The Ontogenesis of Grammar. Academic Press, New York.

Siegel, G. M. 1975. The use of language tests. Lang. Speech Hear. Schools 6:211–217.

Skinner, B. F. 1957. Verbal Behavior. Appleton-Century-Crofts, New York.

Slobin, D. I. 1973. Cognitive prerequisites for the development of grammar. *In* C. S. Ferguson and D. I. Slobin (eds.), Studies of Child Language Development. Holt, Rinehart and Winston, New York.

Snyder, L. 1975. Pragmatics in language disabled children: Their prelinguistic and early verbal performatives and presuppositions. Unpublished doctoral dissertation, University of Colorado, Denver.

Spradlin, J. E. 1963. Assessment of speech and language of retarded children: The Parsons Language Sample. *In* R. L. Schiefelbusch (ed.), Language Studies of Mentally Retarded Children. J. Speech Hear. Disord., Monogr. 10.

Staats, A. 1974. Behaviorism and cognitive theory in the study of language: A neopsycholinguistics. *In* R. L. Schiefelbusch and L. L. Lloyd (eds.), Language Perspectives—Acquisition, Retardation, and Intervention. University Park Press, Baltimore.

Stremel, K., and Waryas, C. 1974. A behavioral-psycholinguistic approach to language training. *In* L. McReynolds (ed.), Developing Systematic Procedures for Training Children's Language. ASHA Monogr. 18.

Winitz, H. 1969. Articulatory Acquisition and Behavior. Appleton-Century-Crofts, New York.

chapter 2

Intervention Strategies for Nonspeech Children

John H. Hollis

Bureau of Child Research
and
Kansas Neurological Institute
Topeka, Kansas

Joseph K. Carrier, Jr.

Bureau of Child Research
University of Kansas
Lawrence, Kansas

contents

COMMUNICATION AND NONSPEECH CHILDREN

Communication

This chapter's title implies that nonspeech children do, in fact, have the capacity to communicate and to learn language. This assumption is supported by the work of Hollis (1966), who developed food sharing, cooperation, and communication within dyads of severely retarded children. The basic question, "Are these children capable of developing language?" can be answered on scientific grounds, for example, by the behavioral evidence in the work of Carrier (1974).

In an attempt to provide a basis for developing intervention strategies, a brief definition of communication and its processes is presented here. In the broad sense, communication is a social affair in which one individual attempts to transmit an idea or thought to another individual (Cherry, 1961). In the analysis of communication, the mode of idea or information transmission becomes *symbols* and the rules for establishing meaning and the sequencing of symbols become *linguistics*. This dual structure model of language provides a unique foundation for the development of intervention strategies and is discussed in detail in a subsequent section of this chapter.

A simple analysis of the communication process suggests that there are at least four components (Glucksberg and Danks, 1975):

1. *Mapping.* The sender and receiver have mapped the environment, i.e., they have general or specific knowledge about events, persons, places, things, or ideas that are to be communicated (Premack and Premack, 1974; Bowerman, 1976).
2. *Symbols.* The message can be reduced to a symbolic form that represents the information to be transmitted and received (Cleator, 1961; Pollio, 1974; Clark and Woodcock, 1976).
3. *Transmission.* The sender has developed the rules (language) necessary for the organization of an idea or information that is to be transmitted (Bloom, 1970; Bowerman, 1973, 1978).
4. *Interpretation.* The receiver comprehends or knows the meaning of the symbols transmitted, i.e., possesses the same or a similar set of rules as the sender (Cherry, 1961; Langacker, 1973).

Communication is generally a reciprocal system, although the sender and receiver may transmit symbols that are not necessarily identical. In any event, they both abide by the same set of rules. Each of the communication components involves complex cognitive abilities and assumes some degree of reciprocity between the sender and the receiver.

Preparation of this chapter was supported by Grants HD 00870 and HD 07339 from the National Institute of Child and Human Development.

In view of the foregoing, how can the handicapped child best be provided with a thought (cognitive map) that can be translated into a sequence of symbols? And when these symbols are received by someone else, how do they elicit a second thought that approximates the original one? Although answering these questions is difficult, an attempt is made in this chapter to specify some observable and manipulatable elements critical to the development of communication and language.

When A wishes to convey an idea or information to B, the symbols that A produces to do so form a sequence of pictures, hierographs, idiographs, signs, sounds, and so forth. B cannot observe A's idea directly; he[1] can only observe and interpret the symbols A produces or emits. From them B must somehow deduce what A's thought might be. In such a communicative system language is neither the symbols nor the sound passing through the air nor the idea or the thought they represent. *Language is a set of semantic and syntactic rules that allows* A *and* B *to correlate their environmental maps or distinctions and symbols.* We are talking about a set of principles that make it possible for A to reduce the cognitive *map* to *symbols* and *transmit* specific aspects of the map by means of an overt response to B for *interpretation* (Langacker, 1973, p. 23).

Nonspeech Communication

Animals interact with their environment through communicative behavior. The communication is accomplished through *signs* such as scent marking, vocalization, postures, and other methods. The signs are context dependent. It is likely that man's symbolic communicative behavior evolved from signs. Thus, as early man's social world expanded, symbol systems evolved that were not context dependent. To communicate within a temporal framework or to preserve ideas, visible signs or symbols, used conventionally, were necessary. Some early attempts at graphic communication, dating back more than 20,000 years, have been found in caves, e.g., those discovered in northern Spain. The cave drawings provide information on early life. However, it is impossible to ascertain whether they were merely attempts at aesthetic expression or were a means of preserving ideas and communicating a message. These pictures certainly served a purpose independent of spoken language.

Nonspeech Children

The normal child learns to talk before he learns to read and write (Carroll, 1964). While the young child is learning basic language, he is also

---

[1] Masculine pronouns are used throughout for the sake of grammatical uniformity and simplicity. They are not meant to be preferential or discriminatory.

learning to conceptualize his environment. The way in which a child maps or conceptualizes his environment may be affected by the interactions of his language development and the language usage of persons within the environment. Thus, the child will most likely learn to conceptualize the environment in a manner conceptually similar to that of his parents, peers, teachers, and others. Carrier (1974) suggests that "The interaction between language and nonlanguage learning is so strong that it is doubtful that a child can make much progress in learning one without acquiring skills in the other" (p. 47).

Many handicapped children, especially those diagnosed as deaf or retarded, demonstrate significant deficiencies in communication and language development. Although some of these children may communicate by gestures, facial expressions, tantrums, and role playing (nonspeech behavior that functions in a communicative fashion), they often fail to learn language and speech even when given special training. Only with extensive training does the severely hearing-impaired child learn to understand language and to speak. The training programs frequently result in failure (Moores, 1974). The same conclusions can be drawn from studies with retarded children. Thus, spoken language, as used in communication, may not be feasible with children lacking certain cognitive and physiological abilities (Hollis and Carrier, 1975; Rozin, 1976). One reason for lack of success in teaching language to these children is that therapists attempt to teach language and speech simultaneously. In addition, little attention has been given to the analysis of language prerequisites and the development of systematic training programs. Failure to understand the problems of language prerequisites and to develop systematic training programs has resulted in the proliferation of so-called "total communication programs" that emphasize alternative response modes but provide little help for teachers or clinicians in determining prerequisite behavior. In this chapter, some basic prerequisites for language development are outlined, some systematic training steps are suggested, and an overview of nonspeech response modes is presented.

A BASIC COMMUNICATION SYSTEM

What does a child need to know to develop a functional communication *system* and language *models*? This is a complex and most difficult question to answer. However, it is imperative that we attempt to answer if we hope to succeed in developing functional communication and language programs for nonspeech children. First, a *strategy* would provide the teacher or clinician with a method for the direct application of *model(s)*, so as to afford maximal support to language-training programs. Second, the models would provide a functional design for the description of a *system.* Third, at the highest level a system would provide a method for grouping related language models that together perform vital functions in communications.

The delineation of basic communication requirements pinpoints those characteristics or behavioral attributes an individual must possess in order to engage in functional communication. These characteristics or attributes must either be inherent within the individual (Lenneberg, 1967; Rozin, 1976) or amenable to development with training. On at least an a priori basis there seem to be three basic communication requirements, which are defined as follows (Premack, 1976, personal communication):

1. *Representation.*   The development of a cognitive map; for example, the attributes, location, and/or function of persons, places, and things.
2. *Selective attention.*   The categorization and classification, for example, of persons, places, and things within the cognitive map.
3. *Displacement.*   The ability to emit overt responses to specific aspects of the cognitive map; for example, overt responses to persons or things not present within the individual's surrounding or immediate sensory environment.

These three basic communication requirements are compatible with the simple analysis of communication processes presented in the opening section of the chapter. The discussion of a basic communication strategy is extended in this section to cover environmental interaction models and a dual structure language model.

Environmental Interaction Model

An important aspect of a child's development involves his interaction with the environment. Some of these interactions may result in positive consequences and thus be maintained. Other interactions may result in aversive consequences and subsequently be eliminated from the child's repertoire. The degree to which a child effectively interacts or copes with the environment is frequently referred to as his level of adaptive behavior (Heber, 1959). There are variables specific to the child or the environment that control the probability of adaptive and nonadaptive behavior (Hollis, 1965). These variables may involve the senses (e.g., visual or auditory), motor abilities, and level of cognitive functioning. Environmental characteristics, such as physical objects, spatial layout, and social attributes (people), may play an important role in determining the intensity and duration of interaction. Some children may have to be given specific training in order to establish functional environmental interactions.

In the development of a basic language strategy, it is imperative that the characteristics of the child and the environment be considered. In other words, what does the child know about the salient aspects of his physical, spatial, and social environment? If he is to learn to communicate, the child must have something to communicate about and a system for expressing it. For example, we might pose several questions about water: *What does it look like? What sounds does it make? What does it feel like? How does it taste? Where do we find it?* It is interesting to note that one of the first words learned by Helen Keller (deaf and blind) was water (Keller, 1972). There are an infinite number of exemplars that could be given to illustrate the cognitive elements that relate to environmental interactions.

A Communicative Channel Model

As a prerequisite for teaching the nonlanguage severely handicapped, the clinician or teacher must of necessity locate or establish a *functional* communication channel before the acquisition of new or the modification of existing behavior can take place (Osgood, 1957; Hollis, Carrier, and Spradlin, 1976). At a fundamental level, the communication channel involves *sensory-input, integrative processes,* and *response-output.*

Communication Channel Model

Stimulus (S)	Organism (O)	Response (R)
Input Sensory Mode	Integrative and Mediation Functions	Output Response Mode

Although it is not possible to intervene directly with neurophysiological processes (see Sanders, 1976), it is possible to institute training procedures that will modify the relationships between input and output. When selecting a stimulus input mode two factors must be considered: 1) type and degree of sensory impairment, and 2) the degree of stimulus permanency (i.e., What does the individual have to remember about the stimulus and for how long?). The development and use of a communication channel model have been discussed in detail by Hollis, Carrier, and Spradlin (1976).

The sensory input mode selected for the development of a communication channel depends on the individual's type and severity of impairment. Four common sensory input modes are: 1) visual, 2) auditory, 3) tactile, and 4) olfactory.

A second step in the development of the communication channel model is the delineation of integrative processes. These are cognitive functions that are traditionally attributed to neurophysiological processes (see Rosenberger, 1978). The four integrative processes selected with respect to the development of communication channels form a hierarchy of processes that can be defined and programmed. The four integrative functions are: 1) *imitative*, identity matching or match-to-sample, 2) *nonimitative*, use of symbols to represent objects, events, etc., 3) *constructive*, the sequencing of words or symbols, and 4) *transformative*, change in the order sequence of words or symbols.

The output or response mode forms the third step in developing the communication channel model. This step is necessary because many handicapped children are unable to reproduce the complicated motor movements required for the production of speech. In fact, some even have neurological impairments that preclude them from making the motor movements required for the production of manual signs. The response output modes selected for the terminal slot of the communication channel model are: 1) gross motor movements, 2) signing, 3) writing, and 4) speech.

In summary, it is the clinician's or the teacher's task to assess the child's handicapping condition(s) and select the communication channel that has the highest probability of being functional for that child. For example, if the child is retarded and has an auditory impairment, it might be possible to establish a functional communication channel as follows: 1) *input*-visual, 2) *mediation/function level*-imitation, and 3) *output*-gross motor. The selection of input, process, and response levels will depend on the type and degree of handicapping condition(s) exhibited by the child.

The Child's Archetypal Model

What distinctive features does a child incorporate into his model of the environment? His archetype (original pattern or model, i.e., nonlinguistic cognitive map) must depend upon the salient stimulus characteristics of the environment. For example, the normal child has receptive and integrative capabilities for the processing of visual, auditory, tactile, olfactory, and other stimulus information. For these types of information, over the course of development, it is assumed that the child builds a cognitive map or schema of his environment (Tolman, 1932; Piaget, 1957). In the normal child, as language ability evolves, the archetype also changes and expands. However, in the case of the severely handicapped nonlanguage child the child's archetype has not been subjected to the influence of language and therefore the child's cognitive map is very limited. In short, the child's archetype is the foundation upon which language is laid (Schlesinger, 1974; Bowerman, 1976). What does a child's archetype look like? Unfortunately we cannot get inside him and take a look. However, it is possible to make some gross inferences based on types and levels of impairments.

Figure 1 presents a schema for a mapping archetype. The archetype schema is developed from four conceptual elements, A, B, C, and D. The elements may be taken to represent various sensory inputs and related information. The conceptual elements could stand for the information about the environment obtained through the sensory input channels of the visual, auditory, tactile, and olfactory receptors.

What elements of an archetype do two individuals share? As an extreme example consider two nonspeech children, one blind and one deaf, communicating about a horse. For simplicity, the horse can be mapped with four conceptual elements as follows: 1) visual, 2) auditory, 3) tactile, and 4) olfactory. The visual dimensions, for example, show that the horse has four legs, a head, tail, is brown in color, and so forth. The auditory dimension shows that a horse makes characteristic sounds— whinny, hoof clacking, etc. Tactilely a horse feels hairy, warm, wet, and so forth. The olfactory dimension indicates that a horse has characteristic odors. These conceptual elements together form the bases for the concept of horse. It is from sensory inputs that the child is able to construct a map or archetype for the horse. If a sensory modality is severely

A MAPPING ARCHETYPE

(CONCEPTUAL ELEMENTS: A, B, C, & D)

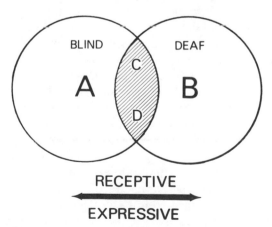

RECEPTIVE

EXPRESSIVE

Figure 1.   A mapping archetype. The schema presented shows the conceptual or sensory environmental events shared in common by blind and deaf individuals. The basic sensory elements are noted as follows: A = auditory; B = visual; C = tactile; D = olfactory. See text for discussion.

impaired or totally nonfunctional, this conceptual element will not be a functional component of the child's archetype. For example, the blind, nonspeech child will not have mapped the visual characteristics of a horse, and the deaf child will not have mapped the auditory characteristics of a horse. With language ability, however, these characteristics of a horse could be synthesized.

Consider an extreme example (Figure 1), a blind and a deaf child communicating expressively and receptively about a horse. What conceptual elements of their respective archetypes do they have in common? In Figure 1 it can be seen that their archetypes of a horse have only two conceptual elements in common. These are the tactile and olfactory elements. In this extreme case, the children can only communicate about a horse with respect to the way it feels and smells. It is understood that as their facility for language use increases they will be able to substitute symbols and words for the missing conceptual elements.

The point to be made here is that the sensory-impaired nonlanguage child is unable to develop environmental archetypes that are the same as those for the normal child. Therefore, in the development of nonspeech language intervention strategies the child's mapping archetype, however limited, provides the only foundation that we have upon which to map language. Premack and Premack (1974) state, "Language can be viewed as the mapping of existing distinctions" (p. 354). In this case the existing distinctions become the child's archetype or environmental model.

A Dual Structure Language Model

Premack (1970), in developing a *functional analysis* of language, demonstrated that communication and language can be separated into two distinct parameters. Figure 2 provides a graphic illustration of the dual structure language model. The first parameter is delineated by the rules for developing symbols (e.g., speech, writing, signs, etc.) or, in other words, the symbol system or response mode. Linguistic rules make up the second parameter of the language model. It in turn consists of two sets of rules and principles, those for semantics and those for syntax. The dual structure model provides the clinician or teacher with a schema for separating linguistic rules from symbol systems. This permits the two parameters to be taught and/or programmed independently.

Symbol Modes   The first parameter of the dual structure language model (Figure 2) is concerned with the development and use of symbol modes. In functional language the symbol mode becomes the individual's response form, which may be taught or programmed independent of linguistic rules. The symbol mode or response forms are classified as follows: 1) speech, 2) writing, 3) manual signing, and 4) gross motor movements, e.g., manipulating plastic chips as in Non-SLIP (Nonspeech

LANGUAGE
A DUAL STRUCTURE MODEL

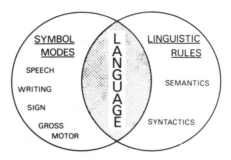

Figure 2.   A dual structure language model. The model divides the communication process into two distinct components, symbols (response modes) and linguistic rules.

Language Initiation Program) or operations of communication boards. For a detailed discussion of this subject see "Symbol Systems: Response Modes," pp. 80–95.

Linguistic Rules   The linguistic-rules parameter of the dual structure language model (Figure 2) consists of two sets of rules, semantic and syntactic. These rules are independent of symbol systems and generalizable across many symbol systems.

1. *Semantics.*   This set of rules consists of those used for the establishment of symbols to represent different meanings (Bowerman, 1973; Clark, 1973; Carrier, 1974). For example, a specific symbol may be used to represent *boy* (nonimitative match), a young male human, and another symbol might be used to represent the action of running (i.e., the name of running). In addition to labeling objects and naming actions, symbols can be used to name locations, relationships, attributes, and so forth.

2. *Syntax.*   This set of rules or principles determines the sequential arrangement of symbols (construction) in a standard grammatical response (English: phrase-structure grammar). For example, in an active declarative sentence, the subject noun precedes the verb. These rules also cover the permissible rearrangements of symbols and/or symbol sequences (transformations).

AN INTERVENTION STRATEGY FOR LANGUAGE DEFICIENCIES

A salient characteristic of many severely and/or multiply handicapped children is a deficiency in communication and language; that is, the

clinician or teacher may be confronted by a child with minimal communication skills, e.g., a total absence of language or even vocalizations
(Miller and Yoder, 1974). Although there is much research to be done, it
is possible at this time to delineate some behavior that is necessary for
the development of language. The objective of this section is to outline a
strategy for the prosthesis of language deficiencies. Prosthesis is defined
as the addition of functional components or substitutions for deficient
components in a nonfunctional system. Thus, if a child's communication
or language system is deficient, additions to or substitutions in the child's
learning system, archetype, or language model would be made. It should
be emphasized that this is not a developmental model and that entry into
the lattice or exit from the lattice may be any one of a number of points.

Figure 3 presents a language prosthesis lattice. In short, this is a
strategic map for the assessment of language deficiencies and a series of
models for specific types of intervention training. The abscissa of Figure
3 denotes a series of independent behavioral models that are assumed to
be related to the communicative processes and language development
(see Sidman and Cresson, 1973; Premack and Premack, 1974; Premack,
1975b). The ordinate of Figure 3 delineates the critical steps within each
model and labels the terminal state or behavior resulting from their
attainment. Thus, taken as a whole, the lattice provides a systematic
method for the prosthesis of language deficiencies; that is, it presents
steps for developing a child's archetype and the mapping of environmental distinctions with language.

For an overview of current approaches to language training the
reader is referred to the work of Kent (1972), Stremel (1972), Bricker
and Bricker (1974), and Guess, Sailor, and Baer (1974).

Environmental Interaction Model

One characteristic of many severely or multiply handicapped children is
their limited interaction with the environment. If language is construed
as a map of existing distinctions (Premack and Premack, 1974), then it is
assumed that the child has formed these distinctions before language
learning or training. This being the case, then language is used to
construct a symbolic map of a child's archetype or environmental model.
The shallower the depth or smaller the size of the model, the less the
child has that can be mapped symbolically. The first step in the development of environmental interactions is the establishment of a functional
operant (Lindsley, 1964; Hollis, Carrier, and Spradlin, 1976).

Functional Operant (see A, Figure 3)   For a child to acquire new
interactions or maintain previously learned ones, it is necessary that we
have a functional operant (see Hollis, Carrier, and Spradlin, 1976). Basic
to the functional operant is the *behavioral equation* $(S \rightarrow R \rightarrow K \rightarrow C)$,

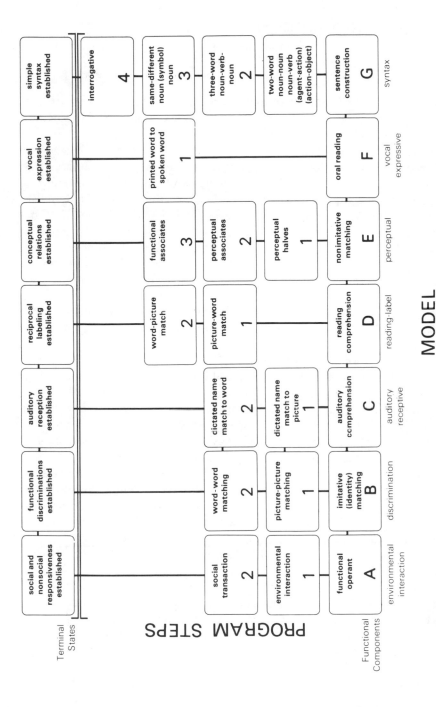

Figure 3.   Language prosthesis lattice. A language intervention model for the training of basic cognitive and prerequisite language skills.

which provides a method for the solution of learning problems across all categories of handicapping conditions.

Behavioral Equation

$$S \xrightarrow{\hspace{2.5cm}} R \xrightarrow{\hspace{2cm}} K \xrightarrow{\hspace{2cm}} C$$

Stimulus   Response   Contingency   Consequences

Thus, if a child is not acquiring new behavior or fails to maintain performance on previously learned behavior, there are four specific places to look in the behavioral equation. These are: 1) the stimulus presentation mode (S); 2) the child's response mode (R); 3) the contingency or schedule of reinforcement (K); 4) the consequence or reinforcer (C). Frequently, in the case of severely handicapped children, one or more of the equation components are nonfunctional. As the first step in establishing a base for language intervention it is imperative that a functional operant be established. The four-component behavioral equation $(S \rightarrow R \rightarrow K \rightarrow C)$ can be solved for only one unknown at a time; therefore, it is necessary to have established three of the components as functional before attempting a solution. Lindsley (1964) and Hollis, Carrier, and Spradlin (1976) discuss and outline procedures for component building. In the final analysis, before attempting language intervention, demonstration of learning or operant behavior is a necessary prerequisite.

Environmental Interaction (see A1, Figure 3)   If in fact a functional operant has been established for a child, then this child (no matter how limited) is interacting with the environment. Hollis (1965) has demonstrated that even profoundly retarded children interact with certain aspects of their environment. Although these interactions are frequently of short duration and may involve simple physical contact with objects, they may be made into lasting and more meaningful relationships by using operant principles. In short, before communication and language can be considered for a handicapped child, it is imperative that a functional interaction (operant) be established with the environment. The variables that can be manipulated to achieve this end were specified above by the behavioral equation $(S \rightarrow R \rightarrow K \rightarrow C)$.

Social Transaction (see A2, Figure 3)   As Premack and Premack (1974) have pointed out, it would be a difficult task to teach, for example, the predicate *give* to an individual who does not engage in the act of giving. The social transaction may be considered a prerequisite to communication, and a reasonable task to map subsequently with language. When the environmental interaction requires only one participant, the social interaction requires two or more individuals. Thus, in a social transaction, the child must learn to "give" some stimulus object (token or symbol) to a second individual (e.g., teacher or parent), and this individual in turn delivers a reinforcer to the child (e.g., some form of food, physical contact, or verbal statement). The ultimate goal for this form of social transaction would be to map it with language. For example, a symbol or word could be substituted for the stimulus object in the transaction. By doing this, for example, it would be possible to have one symbol or word for "milk" and a second for "cookie." In this case the class of the reinforcer would be correlated with the symbol used in the transaction. When the child gives the teacher the symbol of milk he receives milk as a reinforcer and when he gives the symbol of cookie he receives a cookie.

Discrimination Model

To learn rules for selecting symbols and to arrange them in correct sequence, a child must be able to discriminate. At a very simple level, the child in language training must be able to discriminate between familiar objects and simple symbols. If the child has not already learned these simple discriminations, it is possible to teach them. This can be accomplished, provided a functional operant has been established (Hollis, Carrier, and Spradlin, 1976).

Premack's (1970) language analysis suggests that communication be viewed in terms of discriminative responding, that is, the child (communicator) must have learned: 1) to discriminate among various sets of symbols (words), 2) to discriminate among various classes of environmental events or stimuli that call for different and specific symbolic responses, 3) to discriminate among various sequential arrangements of stimuli (e.g., sentence construction or transformation), and 4) to associate sequential arrangements with meanings.

Although these types of discriminative behavior will not necessarily guarantee that an individual can learn to communicate, it is highly unlikely that functional human communication can be established if the child cannot make any of these discriminations.

For a detailed description of training procedures for the development of discriminative responding, the reader is referred to Carrier (1974) and Carrier and Peak (1975). House, Brown, and Scott (1974) have conducted an extensive review and discussion of discrimination research with children.

Imitative (Identity) Matching (see B, Figure 3) This type of discrimination problem requires the child to learn matching-to-sample; that is, when provided with a sample (model stimulus), the child is able to select from a pool of two or more stimuli the one that is identical to or matches the stimulus sample. Procedures for teaching imitative matching to nonspeech children have been presented and discussed in detail by Carrier (1974). Initial imitative matching can involve three-dimensional objects, such as a toy car, dolls, or a spoon. Familiar environmental objects may prove useful in the early stages of imitative matching. Subsequently more abstract stimuli may be introduced, such as pictures, drawings, and various types of symbols (Rosenberger, Stoddard, and Sidman, 1972).

Picture-Picture Matching (see B1, Figure 3)   Because many language and prereading programs employ visual stimuli to elicit a response from the child, it is important that the child be able to discriminate between pictorial stimuli. For example, the ability to perform imitative matches with pictures proves to be a basic prerequisite in Carrier's (1974) nonspeech language program and in Sidman and Cresson's (1973) reading research.

Word-Word Matching (see B2, Figure 3)   For the purpose of this discussion, the term "word" is used to refer to words printed or written in traditional English orthography, and any type of symbol that functions as a word unit, e.g., Non-SLIP (Nonspeech Language Initiation Program) plastic chips, and Exact English manual signs. The procedures for teaching imitative matches for words are the same as those used in developing picture-picture matching and have been explicitly detailed by Carrier (1974) and Rosenberger, Stoddard, and Sidman (1972).

Auditory-Receptive Model

Many handicapped children have developed some auditory-receptive language or possess the ability to develop it. Within this group of handicapped children fall some of those labeled retarded, cerebral palsied, and nonspeech preschoolers. For those children with normal hearing the auditory input mode is of special importance because it provides a significant base for developing speech. Second, the auditory input mode in its own right provides an important channel for the input of information and directions to the nonspeech handicapped child and therefore should be utilized to its fullest extent (see Hollis, Carrier, and Spradlin, 1976).

Auditory Comprehension (see C, Figure 3)   Demonstration of auditory comprehension frequently involves two types of stimulus equivalence, one intramodal and the other intermodal (Hollis, Carrier, and Spradlin, 1976). The intramodal equivalence occurs when a word dictated by the teacher is matched by a word spoken by the child. The second type of equivalence, intermodal, involves responding across sensory modalities, e.g., auditory input and the child's response to a visual stimulus (e.g., picture).

Cross-modal transfer, e.g., transfer across sensory modalities, has important implications with respect to the cognitive development of children. In the development of reading and language, Peters' (1935) Mediate Association paradigm provides a model for auditorily relating events, objects, words, etc. If, for example, the child is provided with an auditory label "C" for object "A" and picture "B" then he has been provided sufficient information to form the conceptual association between object "A" and picture "B." This paradigm forms the bases for a functional analysis of reading (Sidman and Cresson, 1973; Hollis, Carrier, and Spradlin, 1976). This same technique is applicable to words and other associations.

Dictated Word Matched to Picture (see C1, Figure 3)   This is a problem of intermodal equivalence (Hollis, Carrier, and Spradlin, 1976), that is, stimulus equivalence across sensory modalities. In this case the transfer is from the auditory input mode to the visual response-output mode. Specifically this aspect of reading skill involves learning equivalences between auditory (input) stimuli and visual (response-output) stimuli. Basically the task requires that the child learn to match pictures to words dictated by the teacher or clinician. For example, the teacher says "spoon," and the child's task is to select the spoon picture from a group of two or more pictures (Sidman and Cresson, 1973).

Dictated Name Matched to Word (see C2, Figure 3)   This task is essentially the same as the one involving the intermodal equivalence of auditory input and visual response-output, except that the response output requires the selection of a word (symbol) instead of a picture. For example, the teacher says "spoon," and the child's task is to select the word (symbol) from a group of two or more words (see Sidman and Cresson, 1973).

Reading-Label Model

One of the most important programs in the prosthesis of language deficiencies is the teaching of labeling. The child must learn to use symbols to label objects, pictures of objects, and so forth (Carrier, 1974). Labeling is a form of nonimitative matching and requires that the child be able to make abstract associations. Thus, the child is presented with symbols, plastic symbols (Carrier, 1974), or printed words (Sidman and Cresson, 1973) and must learn to associate them with objects or with pictures of objects (i.e., labeling). This type of training involves the use of symbols in context. At this simple level, labeling with symbols could be expanded to include actions, attributes, spatial relationships between objects, locations, and so forth. The Non-SLIP (Nonspeech Language Initiation Program, Carrier and Peak, 1975) provides a step-by-step model for teaching labeling to nonspeech children.

Reading Comprehension (see D, Figure 3)   Simple reading comprehension involves learning intramodal equivalences, i.e., stimulus equivalence within a specific sensory modality (see Hollis, Carrier, and Spradlin, 1976). In the case of the reading-label model (Figure 3) only the visual sensory modality is involved. Development of simple reading comprehension involves two steps, the ability to perform two types of matching: imitative and nonimitative. The *nonimitative match* requires the ability to match, for example: 1) the matching of a printed word or symbol to a picture, and 2) the matching of a picture to a printed word or symbol (see Sidman and Cresson, 1973). In simple terms this task requires that the child learn that "X" is the name of "Y."

Picture-Word Match (see D1, Figure 3)   This nonimitative matching problem is designed to teach the child that the picture of a spoon is equivalent to the printed word "spoon" or some other symbol (see Sidman and Cresson, 1973). For example, the child is presented a picture of a spoon, and the child's task is to select the word "spoon" from a group of two or more printed words or symbols.

Word-Picture Match (see D2, Figure 3)   This nonimitative matching problem is the reverse of the picture-word match. For example, the child is presented a printed word or symbol for "spoon," and the child's task is to select the picture of a spoon from a group of two or more pictures (Sidman and Cresson, 1973).

Perceptual Model

Nonimitative Matching (see E, Figure 3)   It is generally assumed that by the time a child reaches school age he has developed a variety of perceptual categories, e.g., things that perceptually go together, things that are associated, things that function together. The developmentally deficient child may not, for a variety of reasons, have developed these perceptual distinctions (an archetype) necessary to form a basis for language. The normal child as a preschooler has learned to match identical objects (imitative matching) or to select the odd object that does not match (nonimitative matching) in a specified situation. In an imitative match the child is presented with a sample stimulus, a matching stimulus, and an odd (nonmatching) stimulus. In this situation the matching (identical) stimulus is the correct response. In the case of the oddity test (nonimitative match) the odd stimulus is the correct response. Perceptually, many objects are composed of parts or elements. Thus, one could conceive of a number of elements that go together perceptually to make up the whole object or unit. A complex example would be a puzzle. However, from the standpoint of initial language intervention programs, other, perhaps simpler, perceptual categories would be appropriate. Premack (1975a) has suggested three perceptual categories that on a priori grounds are functional with respect to the degree of association or dependence between parts or elements.

Perceptual Halves (see E1, Figure 3)   This class is defined by the use of dismembered objects. In this class, because the original object was bisected asymmetrically, there is an extremely high degree of association between the stimulus and response objects. Examples of perceptual halves could include the following objects: doll's body and doll's head, cup and handle, blossom and stem. In a typical test situation the child could be presented with a doll's head or doll's body and some unrelated object(s). Nonimitative matching would be indicated by the child responding with a choice of the doll's head. If, for example, the child had selected the doll's body, the response would have been imitative. As we shall see, the ability to select symbols or words as labels for objects also involves nonimitative matches, but at a higher level.

Perceptual Associates (see E2, Figure 3) A second class of nonimitative matching is labeled perceptual associates. This class is defined by two parts of an object that are separable but normally are observed to go together. Common examples of perceptual associates include such items as: a jar and lid, a lamp and light bulb, a shoe and a shoelace. These are typical associations learned by the normal child. Their distinctions are mapped readily by the child's language. However, in the case of the severely handicapped child they may not even be a part of this archetype; therefore, it may be necessary to invoke specific training programs so that the child may learn them.

Functional Associates (see E3, Figure 3) The final class of nonimitative matching to be discussed is labeled functional associates. This class consists of two or more separate objects that are used together normally or frequently. The association between the objects may be relatively weak in some cases, and in others very strong. However, without prior observation or experience with their function, many of these objects do not provide intrinsic cues that would indicate that they function together. Some possible examples of functional associates include such objects as: cup and saucer, mirror and hairbrush, hammer and nail. Again, these are typical associations learned by the normal child. The normal child readily maps these distinctions by his language. However, in the case of the severely handicapped child, they may not even form a part of his archetype; they therefore must be taught explicitly.

Vocal-Expressive Model

Hopefully most children training in nonspeech communication will eventually achieve spoken communication. As pointed out previously, speech is a response mode and not language per se. Therefore, if language is learned using nonspeech response modes, the problem is one of transferring the rules (semantic and syntactic) from the nonspeech response mode to that of speech symbols (see Figure 2).

Operant techniques, in particular, have been used to develop sound production and speech and to correct inappropriate speech patterns

(Sailor, Guess, and Baer, 1973). These applications include establishing sound production (Hollis and Sherman, 1968), establishing functional speech (Risley and Wolf, 1967), developing imitative speech (Lovaas et al., 1966), and establishing vocalizations (Salzinger et al., 1962; Buddenhagen, 1971).

Oral Reading (see F, Figure 3)   Gibson and Levin (1975, Figure 4-1) suggest that there is a significant relationship between hearing-speaking and reading-writing. The importance of this relationship is substantiated by the research of Sidman and Cresson (1973) on reading and cross-modal transfer. Although reading and reading comprehension can be established in the nonspeech child, oral reading represents an advance with respect to an alternative response mode (see Figure 2, and Hollis, Carrier, and Spradlin, 1976).

Oral reading involves the establishment of an intermodal equivalence between printed words or symbols and the speech response mode. This requires that the child has or can develop the ability to produce and distinguish between utterances and phonemes. In turn he must be able to sequence the 39 segmental phonemes of English to produce in speech the morpheme or smallest unit of the language (Gibson and Levin, 1975). Kuntz (1974) has demonstrated some degree of success in transfer from nonspeech language in retarded children to the speech response mode (Hollis, Carrier, and Spradlin, 1976). For the child who has learned nonspeech language, oral reading involves only a transfer to the speech response mode because the prerequisite discriminations, rules, and so forth have been learned already (Carrier, 1974; Kuntz, 1974).

Printed Word to Spoken Word (see F1, Figure 3)   From the foregoing discussion it should be apparent that the learning of language and the learning of speech are independent aspects of communication (see Figure 2) and thus can be trained independently. However, if the handicapped child can learn to use the speech response mode, then the oral reading level of equivalence involves the use of speech as a response mode to printed words or symbolic stimuli. For example, the child is presented the printed word "spoon" and responds with the spoken word *spoon* (Sidman and Cresson, 1973).

Syntax Model

The dual structure language model (Figure 2) provides a systematic method for the separation of symbols (response mode) from language (rules of semantics and syntax). In essence, the function of syntactic rules is to link conceptual structures (the child's archetype, Figure 1, or cognitive map) with surface structures (symbols). At this point little is known about archetypes or cognitive maps. However, the organization of surface structures is relatively easy to analyze (Langacker, 1973) and provides the basis for a description of syntactic systems.

In conventional school grammar the description of written or spoken sentences is referred to as syntax. Thus, syntax delineates the rules by which words are combined into phrases, and the phrases combined into sentences. In contemporary tests, linguistic description of grammar is referred to under several rubrics, for example, *generative* and *transformational* grammar (Glucksberg and Danks, 1975). It is important to note that these related grammars differ from conventional classroom and structural grammar in that they do not depend on the analysis of a specific sentence nor do they involve the description of speech production (MacLeish, 1971). As such, they are compatible with the dual structure language model (Figure 2) and with nonspeech language intervention strategies. From this vantage point, syntax is the base of grammar and consists of three sets of rules (MacLeish, 1971): "(1) Phrase structure rules, which generate basic sentences . . .; (2) Lexical rules of selection, which substitute words for the complex symbols in the phrase structure string . . .; (3) Transformational rules, which add to, rearrange, and subtract from the phrase structure string . . ." (p. 121). (Also see Figure 4.)

Sentence Construction (see G, Figure 3)   A sentence is a collection of words (symbols) arranged by syntactic rules so as to constitute a grammatically complete sense unit. For the purpose of this discussion a sentence is a sequence of words or symbols forming a unit, which consists of a noun-phrase subject and a verb-phrase predicate. Figure 4 provides an examplar sentence for phrase-structure grammar. The sentence was selected arbitrarily to illustrate various symbol systems (response modes) discussed in the final section of this chapter.

Two-Word Sentences (see G1, Figure 3)   Although Carrier (1974) has demonstrated that severely retarded children can learn to sequence and comprehend seven-word sentences, it is likely that sentences with simpler syntax (Miller and Yoder, 1974) may prove more economical with some handicapped children. Table 1 provides a number of simple two-word sentences appropriate for initial communication and the development of a handicapped child's language (see Dale, 1972). Miller and Yoder (1974) suggest that "The need for syntax arises on the part of the child in order to make his expression of semantic concepts understood by others in the community" (p. 516). Simple syntax-teaching programs have been developed by Carrier (1974) and Miller and Yoder (1972).

Three-or-More-Word Sentences (see G2, Figure 3)   Once a child has learned to map existing distinctions (i.e., perceived objects and so

SENTENCE STRUCTURE

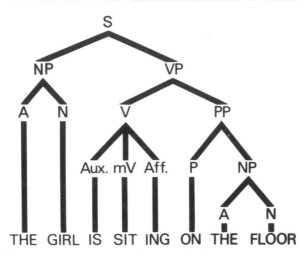

Figure 4.   Phrase-structure grammar. An example of the constituent structure of the English sentence, *The girl is sit (ing) on the floor*. Each constituent in the sentence has a characteristic name, as indicated by the symbols: noun phrase (NP); verb phrase (VP); article (A); noun (N); verb (V); prepositional phrase (PP); auxiliary verb (Aux.); main verb (mV); verb affix (Aff.); preposition (P) (see Dale, 1972).

forth), his lexicon increases in size, permitting the expression of new relationships in new situations. Miller and Yoder (1974) state:

> Children must be able to comprehend S-V-O construction with contrasting word order to be credited knowledge of basic grammatical relations. . . . That is, word order is basically a syntactic phenomenon and if the child has syntactic knowledge he should be able to use word order to determine subject and object in contrasting sentences on a comprehension task (p. 512).

Table 1.   Simple sentences in child language

Structural Meaning[a]	Form	Examples
1. Recurrence	More + N	more juice
2. Possessive	N + N	Mommy drink
3. Locative	N + N	dish sink
4. Agent-action	N + V	Mary go
5. Agent-object	N + N	Daddy car
6. Action-object	V + N	push ball

Adapted from Dale (1972, p. 47).
[a] May be context dependent.
N = Noun; V = Verb.

In Carrier's (1974) nonspeech language-training program, a rote sequencing program is presented, which is designed to teach the operations necessary for learning to sequence seven-word sentences (see Figure 4) by severely handicapped nonlanguage children.

Same-Different Concept *(see G3, Figure 3)* Although imitative matching (match-to-sample) can be demonstrated by a child, it may not be an appropriate assessment for demonstrating the concept of "same-different" (Premack and Premack, 1974). The two tasks differ both on the arrangement of stimuli and the judgmental requirements for a solution. In imitative matching problems three objects or stimuli are present, whereas only two are present in same-different. In imitative matching the child's response is the selection of an object or stimulus that matches the sample. However, in same-different language training the child is required to select a word or symbol and place it between two objects or stimuli (Premack and Premack, 1974). In addition, the same-different problem requires both a positive and negative judgment, whereas imitative matching requires only a positive judgment. These differences may seem trivial to the normal adult, but they most likely are important distinctions with respect to prelanguage training. For a detailed discussion of this concept the reader is referred to Premack and Premack (1974).

Interrogative *(see G4, Figure 3)* An interrogative sentence is one that can be answered either by *yes* or *no* or by providing information relating to *What? Why? When? Where? Who? How?* and the like (MacLeish, 1971). Premack and Premack (1974) have developed a procedure for teaching simple interrogatives at the prelanguage level. The basic prerequisites are imitative matching (match-to-sample) and development of the same-different concept. The simple interrogative is taught using hybrid sentences. The format of the sentences looks like this (Premack and Premack, 1974):

Spoon	?	Spoon
Spoon	?	Glass

Or, what is the relationship between a spoon and a spoon, between a spoon and a glass? Having learned the same-different concept, the child must learn to remove the ? and replace it with the correct word or *symbol: same* or *different*. In a different format, for example,

?	"same"	Spoon
?	"different"	Glass

the child is provided with real objects or symbols and required to replace the interrogative *marker* with the correct object or symbol. For a detailed discussion of the simple interrogative the reader is referred to Premack and Premack (1974).

SYMBOL SYSTEMS: RESPONSE MODES

Language intervention tactics are only necessary when we are confronted with children who demonstrate significant *individual differences* with respect to behavior and/or sensory impairment, that is, children who differ significantly with respect to the norms on sensory input and motor output (see Hollis, Carrier, and Spradlin, 1976). When teaching language to these children, intervention tactics must be developed to provide alternative sensory input and response modes. This section presents and discusses some of the more common symbol systems and their applicability to children with various types of handicapping conditions.

It is of fundamental importance to understand that symbol systems are not language nor do they map existing distinctions. Symbols only provide a response or output mode for language that has mapped existing distinctions. As pointed out previously in this chapter (Figure 2), language is made up of semantic and syntactic rules. Symbols take the form of a response mode. The distinction between language and response mode is a critical one when considering the development of nonspeech language intervention strategies. Many programs currently in use (Signing Exact English, Bliss, and others) confound language with symbol systems. In short, if we were dealing with individuals who differed little from the norm, this probably would not be a serious problem. However, in the case of significant deviation from the norm, this may be a most serious problem.

An overview of communication and language systems for the handicapped reveals a number of symbol systems currently in use. These systems have evolved, in part, to overcome receptive or transmission problems with handicapped children who are cerebral palsied, deaf, blind, or mentally retarded. Table 2 provides a classification schema for three types of symbol systems: orthographic, word-unit, and mixed or concept-based symbols. The table indicates which of three symbol classes applies to each symbol system. The symbol classes are defined as follows:

1. A *representational symbol system* is one in which the specific symbol manifests one or more of the critical attributes of the signified nonlinguistic referent (Brown, 1958). This class of symbols is frequently referred to as *pictograms* and is entirely independent of speech. For example, sketches of the sun and moon are unmistakable in respect to their referent but lack the luminosity and heat dimensions. The icon even at its best is only an abstraction of environmental referents. Even a high-grade color photograph provides only a two-dimensional representation, reduced in size and so forth. As one progresses from photographs, to detailed line drawings, to outlines, the degree of abstraction increases markedly. Stick drawings of man are another example that preserves

Table 2.   Symbol system classification

Symbol System	Symbol		
	Representational	Semantic	Phonetic
1. Orthographic			
a. Alphabet			X
b. Braille			X
c. Fingerspelling			X
2. Word Unit			
a. Words		X	
b. Signing Exact English		X	
c. Non-SLIP		X	
d. Speech			X
3. Compound			
a. Rebus	X	X	X
b. Bliss	?	X	
c. American Sign Language (ASL)		X	

some of the critical elements of skeletal relations. Illustration by picture or other visual representation is known as *iconography*. Thus, an icon is a pictorial representation of an object or event.

A study of the history of pictographic writing suggests that, over time, pictorial representations (icons) were transformed from representational drawings to highly abstract figures and symbols. Premack (1975a) states, "The distance between iconic and noniconic use is less great than many discussions suggest, and a transition from one to the other is not hard to imagine" (p. 236). That is, with succeeding transformations the referent's icon changes to such an extent that it could be considered an arbitrary abstract figure. Premack (1975a) notes, "It is contextual dependence that makes symbols iconic, not physical appearance, and therefore symbols that originate as icons need not remain so" (p. 236). The use of a symbol has little to do with the physical resemblance of the symbol and referent; whether a symbol is used iconically or noniconically is not of significant importance.

2. *Semantic symbols* are arbitrary signs that stand directly for an idea and that in some cases may have been derived from icons, e.g., using a heart-shaped sign to represent emotion, or using the number three to stand for a set of objects, events, etc. In the case of the heart sign for emotion, the drawing is used to represent an idea and not the thing pictured. This class of writing or drawing is called ideograms. In symbol systems that use words, numbers, manual signs (e.g., Signing Exact

English), or plastic chips (Non-SLIP) the notation or configuration of the sign is purely arbitrary and does not embody any of the critical elements or attributes of the referent.

3.   In a writing system using *phonetic signs*, each sign represents an individual sound (alphabetic writing) or individual syllables (syllabic writing). This type of system contrasts markedly with ideographic writing in which the graphic character, symbol, or figure merely represents the idea and provides no information with respect to the spoken sound(s). The common communication systems incorporating traditional orthography (TO) are the alphabet, Braille, and fingerspelling. Irrespective of the notation or transmission method, all the orthographic systems provide for the representation of a phoneme within a discrete unit. (It should be noted, however, that there are exceptions.) Examples include the letters of the alphabet, the hand and finger configurations in fingerspelling, and the configurations of raised dots in Braille.

Table 3 summarizes the transmission characteristics of the various symbol systems (see Vicker, 1974). It provides a subjective analysis of each type of symbol system with respect to permanency, complexity, transmission time, and types of automation. *Permanency* of transmission refers to the degree to which the communicative stimuli continue or endure without fundamental or marked changes. The *complexity* of message transmission refers to the physical difficulty encountered by the sender and in some cases the receiver with respect to the symbol system. For example, printing letters or fingerspelling requires fine and specific finger movements, whereas the Non-SLIP system (Carrier, 1974) requires only gross motor movements. The *transmission* or *production time* for a message may be related to the physical disabilities of the sender or may be an inherent part of the nonspeech system. Thus, transmission time will be the result of the interaction among difficulty of stimulus production or response mode, the degree of the child's handicap, and the problems encountered in decoding the symbols. *Automation* refers to the degree to which the initial levels of transmission can be aided by mechanical, electromechanical, and electronic types of prosthetic devices.

Language Structure   Descriptive linguistics provides an important source of input for determining training goals for the development of a communication program. Premack (1970) demonstrated how language learning could be accomplished independently from its traditional response mode, i.e., speech. However, programs intended to teach communication should address the problem of structure. Structure plays a significant role in human communication. Therefore, the descriptive linguistic literature should be consulted to determine what structural rules are basic to English communicative responses (Langacker, 1973; Lyons,

Table 3.   Transmission characteristics of symbol systems

Symbol system	Response mode	Receptive mode	Transmission			
			Permanency	Complexity	Time	Automation
1. Orthographic						
a. Alphabet	Writing	Visual	Lasting	Very high	Moderate	Electric Typewriter Autocom[c] Optacon[d]
b. Braille	Typewriter	Tactile	Lasting	Very high	Slow	Automatic Typewriter
c. Fingerspelling	Fine finger	Visual	Fleeting[a]	Very high	Slow	N/A
2.						
a. Words (printed)	Word-blocks	Visual	Semi-permanent	Low	Variable	Autocom Optacon
b. Signing Exact	Arm-Hand-Finger Movements	Visual	Fleeting	High	Variable	N/A
c. Non-SLIP	Plastic Symbols	Visual	Semi-permanent	Low	Slow	N/A
d. Speech	Complex motor Movements	Auditory	Fleeting[a]	High	Rapid	N/A
3. Compound						
a. Rebus	Printed symbols	Visual	Variable[b]	Moderate	Variable	Autocom
b. Bliss	Printed symbols	Visual	Variable[b]	Moderate	Variable	Autocom
c. American Sign Language (ASL)	Arm-Hand-Finger movements	Visual	Fleeting	High	Moderate	N/A

[a] Requires the ability to remember the sequence of letters or sounds transmitted.
[b] Depends on transmission method, e.g., flip board versus autocom.
[c] Developed by Vanderheiden et al., 1975.
[d] Tactile receptive mode.

1968). Figure 4 provides a sample sentence, "The girl is sitting on the floor," for delineating some structural rules. This model sentence is used here in subsequent illustrations of various symbol systems currently in use. The rules defining structure may be sorted into various categories. The categories include the rules for producing noun phrases, rules for producing verb phrases, and rules for selecting and indicating verb tense, among others.

Orthographic Symbol Systems

Underlying communication systems and language is a representational or symbol system for transmission. For purposes of discussion, this chapter deals only with English orthography (spelling). In English, each spoken phoneme is usually represented by the characteristic (Roman) letter (Dale, 1972). However, for individuals with significant auditory and visual impairments, the printed letter spoken phoneme may be nonfunctional for general communication purposes. The deaf individual may be able to learn to read words made up of printed letters but he is unable to produce the phonemes required for speech without special training. On the other hand, the blind individual may be unable to learn to read printed words but he is able to learn to use words in spoken communication. It becomes readily apparent that these problems involve communication channels, that is, sensory input and response output modes (see Hollis, Carrier, and Spradlin, 1976). When teaching language to very young or retarded children the use of orthographic systems is in doubt because the child must be able to learn to spell and remember his last response.

Three symbol systems that fit traditional English orthography have been selected for discussion. They were selected because they are the ones most commonly used for providing handicapped individuals with either a receptive or an expressive response mode. The three orthographic systems discussed are: printed letters (alphabet), Braille, and fingerspelling.

Printed Letters (Alphabet)   There are 26 written characters in the English language. In their conventional order, each letter represents isolated or individual sounds or phonemes. Letters are normally put together to form morphemes, the smallest independent meaningful unit.

Although handwritten communication is a viable alternative to oral speech, in many cases it is not feasible with severely handicapped individuals. First, it requires that the individual have the ability to or has learned the traditional orthography (spelling); that is, the individual must have some knowledge of the phoneme-grapheme relationships in the English language. Second, using handwritten letters requires that the individual have the ability to produce legible handwriting. Many handicapped children and other individuals do not have the ability to properly grasp a pen or pencil and make the necessary fine motor movements required to produce letters. This is because of various types of neuromuscular involvement. Such systems as Non-SLIP (Carrier and Peak, 1975), discussed subsequently, circumvent this problem.

The use of printed words in receptive and expressive communication is discussed in another section on word-unit systems. Research to date suggests that severely developmentally deficient individuals are able to learn to label and read using word units, providing they do not have to produce the words by handwritten method (Sidman and Cresson, 1973; Carrier, 1974).

Braille   The early systems of writing for the blind, before the development of Braille, used various systems of raised letters. These systems provided tangible alphabets, that is, they used letters engraved in wood, cast in lead, or cut in cardboard. In many ways these methods of presenting letters to the blind were similar to some of the methods developed by Montessori (1965) for teaching other handicapped individuals. For at least two centuries the tactile input mode has been the universally accepted method for use with the blind and visually impaired. (It should be noted that many legally blind individuals read print; see Jones, 1961.)

Today the universally accepted system of writing for the blind is Braille.[2] Braille was developed by Louis Braille in 1824 when he was 15 years old. The basic unit of Braille is a six-dot cell (see Figure 5) in which the dots are raised or embossed on paper. The Braille system consists of 63 characters, which include the alphabet, arranged within the six-dot cell. The characters are read (tactually) by passing the fingers lightly over the embossed dots.

An example of the Braille cell is provided in Figure 5, and the sentence *The girl is sit* (*ing*) *on the floor* is illustrated graphically, using black dots to represent the Braille embossed dots.

The Braille system of writing is phonetic. By incorporating the alphabet it permits the use of traditional orthography (spelling). It should be noted that a partial shorthand has developed, that is, some very commonly used words (e.g., articles, prepositions, affixes) are denoted by a single cell's configuration. The restrictions and limitations for Braille usage with the handicapped are essentially the same as those described for printed letters.

Fingerspelling   This is a manual communication system primarily used by the deaf. Fingerspelling uses the manual alphabet, which consists

---

[2] Division for the Blind and Physically Handicapped. *Braille Alphabet and Numerals.* The Library of Congress, Washington, D.C. 20542.

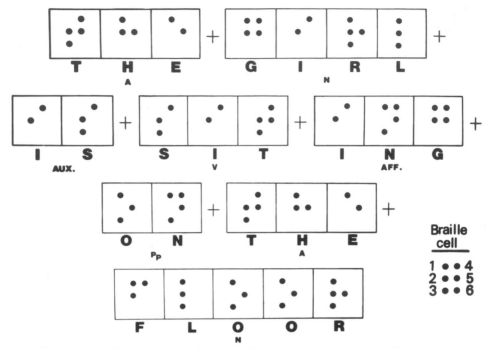

Figure 5.   Braille. An example of using Braille to construct the sentence *The girl is sit* (*ing*) *on the floor*. (Note: Normally, the dots of the Braille cell are embossed on Braille paper.)

of 26 letters. Words are spelled letter by letter, thus putting heavy demands upon one's spelling ability; that is, there is a one-to-one correspondence with traditional orthography (TO) or conventional spelling. Although fingerspelling normally is considered a visual-receptive system, it has been adapted for use with the blind/deaf as a tactual system (Keller, 1972).

Figure 6 illustrates a sentence formed using the manual alphabet. In manual spelling, the hand is held in front of the chest and the letters are produced by variations in hand and finger configurations. Moores (1974) reports that the rate of presentation for an accomplished fingerspeller is equivalent to a slow rate of speech and somewhat faster than that of an accomplished typist. The symbol system may have limited use because most auditorily intact individuals, those not in the deaf community, have not learned the manual alphabet and therefore are unable to comprehend the communication.

A major advantage of fingerspelling over some other systems (e.g., American Sign Language) is that the manual alphabet response mode is independent of morphological, syntactic, and semantic systems. Moores

(1974) provides examples of variations in the manual alphabet used in various parts of the Soviet Union, where fingerspelling is taught to preschool children in primary programs for the deaf.

The use of fingerspelling with severely handicapped individuals, such as retarded, cerebral palsied, and multiply handicapped, would be very limited. Children who fall into these categories typically have some form of neuromuscular involvement that precludes them from making the fine hand and finger movements necessary to produce the manual alphabet. Second, at least at the preschool level, most children are not able to use the traditional methods in the English orthographic system.

Word-Unit Systems

In the normal course of development, the young normal child arrives at school with language. The child is able to speak and has learned the basic rules of semantics and syntax. However, he is frequently unable to read; that is, he has not learned the alphabet, the phones each letter represents, the relationship of letters to words, or the sequencing of the words to form a written sentence. Educators argue about the proper units for teaching reading (Gibson and Levin, 1975). Should the units be letters, syllables, or words? From this argument a controversy has grown over

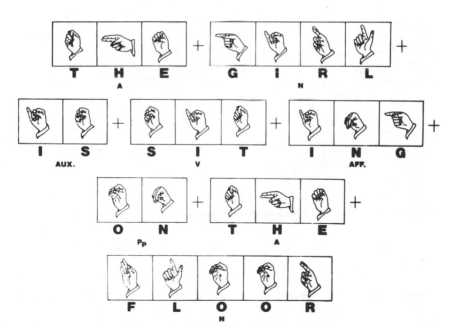

Figure 6.   Fingerspelling. An example of using fingerspelling to construct the sentence *The girl is sit (ing) on the floor* (as viewed from in front of the speller). (Reference: Talkington and Hall, n.d.)

whether reading should be taught using the phonetic or the word-unit approach. As a result, basic reading programs have been developed that are either totally phonetic or a strict word-unit approach. A normal child will have to learn both eventually.

If we are to succeed in teaching language to nonspeech children, the ideal system would be one that avoided the problems associated with the phonemic approach and provided the child with a visual or tactile set of symbols. Children who would benefit most from a word-unit symbol system are nonspeech preschoolers, deaf, blind, and retarded children. The system selected would depend to a large degree on the type of handicap involved. For the purposes of this presentation, three word-unit systems have been selected for discussion. The systems are compatible with English phrase-structure grammar (Figure 4) and should provide generalization within the English language. The word-unit systems are printed words, Signing Exact English, and Non-SLIP (plastic symbols).

Printed Words   The whole-word-versus-phonetic unit controversy has continued in educational circles for many decades. It is based on the assumption that one unit, either the letter or the word, must be chosen for emphasis (Gibson and Levin, 1975). However, when developing language intervention strategies for nonspeech children the word-unit method has several advantages. The word-unit method preserves traditional orthography while circumventing the problem of learning phonetic rules. Word units can be adopted as functional symbols for children who, for whatever reason, will never be able to develop speech. When teaching language (semantics and syntax), the word-unit method corresponds in a one-to-one relationship with English and thus is highly generalized to other response modes (writing and speech).

By printing words on blocks of wood in large letters or using other devices, word units can be used and manipulated by various handicapped children. For example, the word-unit method could be programmed like Carrier's (1974) Non-SLIP program. Sidman and Cresson (1973) have used the word-unit technique for teaching labeling (use of nouns) to severely mentally retarded individuals. This approach has also been used successfully by Hollis (unpublished data) with nonspeech preschool children as well as visually and auditorily impaired children. In the case of visually impaired children, very large print was used (48–96-point type).

In summary, the word-unit method for teaching language retains traditional orthography and English grammar while avoiding the pitfalls of phonemic production (speech). Second, the word-unit system poses no problems with respect to generalization, that is, the rules and symbols are universal within the English-speaking population.

Signing Exact English   This manual symbol system is an attempt to make signing compatible with English by providing a more direct translation of English into visual symbols than either Signed English or Manual English (Gustason, Pfetzing, and Zawolkow, 1972; Wilbur, 1976). Thus, Signing Exact English, which is word-based, may be contrasted with American Sign Language, which is idea, or concept, based. The rationale for Exact English is that the child will see and use actual English (semantics and syntax), and thus his language abilities should be more comparable to those of his hearing peers. In general, Signing Exact English is compatible with transformational phrase-structure grammar (see Figure 4).

A visual representation of a sentence is presented in Figure 7. With respect to the use of Signing Exact English, Gustason, Pfetzing, and Zawolkow (1972) have made the following statement:

> This concept of signing by word or morpheme leads to some pitfalls. In an effort to avoid as many of these as possible, some rules were set up. Words are considered as either compound, complex, or basic. A basic word is a root word with no additions or inflections, as girl, talk, sit. A complex word is a basic word plus an inflection or affix, as girls, talked, sat, sitting. A compound word is a word composed of two or more basic words, as chalkboard, undercook (p. 4).

Signing with manual symbols or word units has obvious advantages over the use of fingerspelling. It avoids the problems of traditional orthography, while attempting to maintain English morphology, semantics, and syntax. Although Signing Exact English was developed for education of the deaf, it has been incorporated into some communication programs for the retarded and the aphasic. It should be easier for the retarded to learn than fingerspelling. Irrespective of the handicapping condition, the greatest error made by teachers is attempting to teach language (semantics and syntax) simultaneously with teaching the motor movements required for signing. In addition, any children with neuromuscular involvement of the arms, hands, and fingers would have great difficulty producing the manual signs. For example, many retarded children have trouble with tasks requiring fine motor movements. This certainly would hold true for cerebral palsied children.

Non-SLIP (Plastic Words)   The Non-SLIP system is an attempt to reduce the complexity of language training for severely retarded, nonverbal children. In this system developed by Carrier and Peak (1975) plastic chips are used to represent English words. Figure 8 illustrates a sentence written with the plastic word symbols.

Plastic word symbols are only part of Carrier's extensive language-training program commonly referred to as Non-SLIP (Nonspeech Lan-

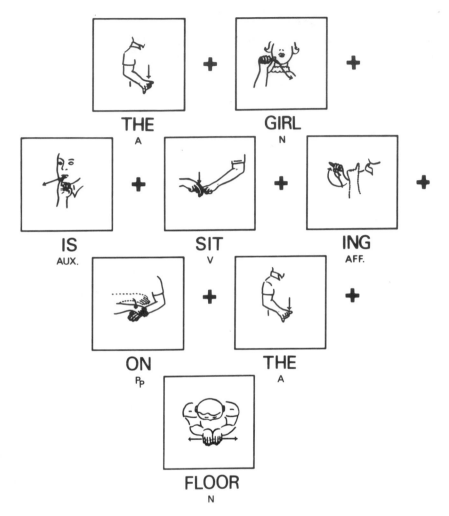

Figure 7.   Signing Exact English. An example of using Signing Exact English to construct the sentence *The girl is sit (ing) on the floor* (as viewed from in front of the signer). (Reference: Gustason, Pfetzing, and Zawolkow, 1972.)

guage Initiation Program). The Non-SLIP program and plastic word symbols are based on the research of Premack (1970) in which he attempted to teach communication skills to chimpanzees. Premack's work with chimpanzees is particularly pertinent because of its implications for language training with many children who have not learned language. The plastic word symbols permit the handicapped child to use symbols correctly without producing them, i.e., they are prefabricated. This is in marked contrast to systems using spoken words or manual signs. Thus, the plastic word symbols provide a tangible method for the production of language without using the auditory or vocal communication channels (see Hollis, Carrier, and Spradlin, 1976).

The word symbols illustrated in Figure 8 are cut from 3-mm milk-white plastic and measure approximately 7 × 7 cm. Each symbol in the Non-SLIP kit (Carrier and Peak, 1975) is unique in shape (abstract or arbitrary configuration), color coded, and keyed to indicate in which sequence in the program it is to be used. The word represented by each

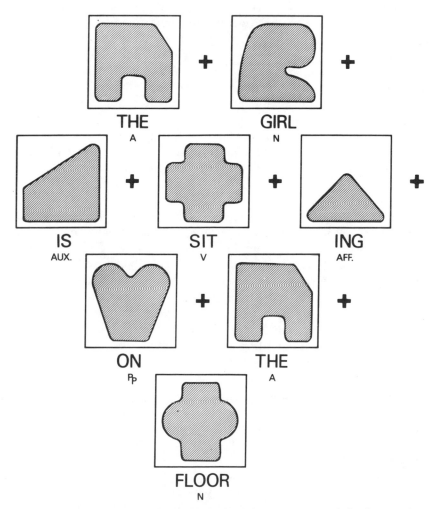

Figure 8.   Non-SLIP (Nonspeech Language Initiation Program) symbols. An example of using Non-SLIP (plastic words) to construct the sentence *The girl is sit* (*ing*) *on the floor.* (Reference: Carrier and Peak, 1975.)

plastic symbol is written on the symbol. Manipulation or placement of the symbols requires only gross motor movements of the hands and fingers; however, in the case of cerebral palsied children it may be necessary to mount the symbols on small blocks of wood to enable children to either grasp them easily or knock them over in order to indicate word choices.

Compound Systems

This section concerns three types of symbol systems in which the basic symbols may be classified as representational or semantic. The basic symbol may either represent (picture) or stand for an idea or thought (abstract symbol). However, these symbol systems may use letters to indicate affixes (e.g., ing, s). The three symbol systems (in some cases) correspond in a one-to-one relationship with English phrase-structure grammar (Figure 4). For children with receptive language, but having handicapping conditions with respect to response mode, these systems may prove valuable for developing educational programs. The Rebus system is useful in remediating reading problems (Woodcock, Clark, and Davies, 1968). The Bliss system has provided a viable response mode for the cerebral palsied youngster (Vanderheiden, 1976). American Sign Language has been incorporated into many educational programs for the deaf (Moores, 1974).

Rebus   Simple rebuses represent a word or part of a word by a picture (pictograph) or a picture of a thing with a similar name. Several rebuses may be combined to produce a phrase or sentence. Some literary rebuses combine letters, numbers, musical notes, pictures, or specially placed words to form a type of sentence puzzle. Complex rebuses typically combine pictures and letters to make sentences. They have sometimes been used to instruct or inform illiterate persons directly or to assist children in learning to read. Figure 9 provides an illustration of complex rebuses used in writing a sample sentence. In the sentence *The girl is sit (ing) on the floor*, some of the symbols are highly abstract in nature. This is true even for the drawing representing floor.

Of a less abstract nature are the rebuses used internationally for airport signs, road signs, and equipment or automobile controls. In these cases the logograph may represent an idea or more than one word. Although anyone can design rebus symbols, there is a published set of rebuses entitled the *Standard Rebus Glossary* (Clark, Davies, and Woodcock, 1974). In brief, the glossary contains 818 different rebuses and several hundred combinations of rebuses or rebuses with letters.

Woodcock (1965) developed an experimental reading program, *The Rebus Reading Series*, in which the children learned to read using a vocabulary of rebuses and then transferred to traditional orthography

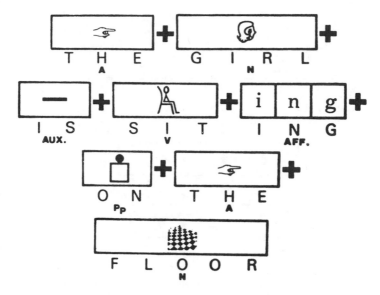

Figure 9.   Peabody Rebus symbols. An example of using Rebus symbols to construct the sentence *The girl is sit (ing) on the floor.* (Reference: Clark, Davies, and Woodcock, 1974.)

(TO). This research resulted in the development of the *Peabody Rebus Reading Program* (Woodcock, Clark, and Davies, 1968). In providing communication techniques (in early language development programs) for children with neuromuscular involvement (e.g., cerebral palsy), rebuses have been used as symbols on communication boards (Vanderheiden, 1976). It simplified the learning task by: 1) avoiding traditional orthography (TO), e.g., selecting the rebus(es) that conveyed the idea or thought, and 2) requiring only a pointing, looking, or touching response, or a simple sequence of responses.

Bliss Symbols   The Bliss symbol system is ideographic in that the symbols represent an idea or concept, that is, the symbols suggest the idea of an object without expressing its name. They may also represent an abstract idea or quality. Although some of the symbols retain some representational characteristics of objects (e.g., a heart for emotion), for the most part they are abstract. The use of symbols to produce a sentence is illustrated in Figure 10.

While Charles Bliss was serving as an engineer in China during 1942 he attempted to design an international symbol system patterned after written Chinese. The system was formerly called "semantography" because it was believed to be based on symbolic logic, semantics, and ethics (Bliss, 1965). In Bliss' system, symbol combinations frequently

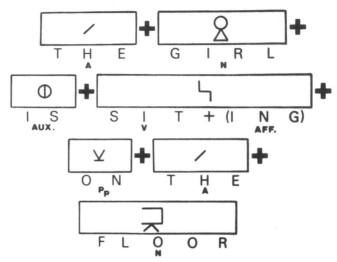

Figure 10.   An example of using symbols similar to those of Bliss to construct the sentence *The girl is sit (ing) on the floor*. It should be noted that the symbols and syntax are *not a facsimile* of Blissymbolics.

represented concepts or ideas and thus were similar to Chinese characters in function (see Rozin, Ooritzky, and Sotsky, 1971).

The initial Bliss system of visual symbols contained 340 symbols. However, the basic set of symbols used with children contain 100. Although the Bliss symbol system is not widely known, its use was initiated by McNaughton and Kates (1974) in Canada for education of cerebral palsied individuals and has since been incorporated into Communication Boards by Vanderheiden (1976) in Wisconsin. The number of symbol combinations has been extended to over 400 and modified so that sentences can be formed that fit within the framework of phrase-structure grammar (see Figure 4).

When using this symbol system for communication, the printed word in traditional orthography is always paired with the Bliss symbol. This enables the uninitiated to read the message sent by the handicapped individual without having to translate the Bliss symbols.

There has been little research on teaching language using Bliss symbols. However, they were used as a prosthetic device for expressive communication with cerebral palsied children by McNaughton and Kates (1974) and Vanderheiden et al. (1975). In these educational projects the children have developed at least minimal auditory-receptive language before the language of Bliss symbols. The symbols only provided them with a unique response mode. For example, they have been used as symbols on communication boards and incorporated into the computerized communication boards (e.g., Autocom) developed by Vanderheiden. To date there is no intergrated language program for Bliss symbols. This most likely is because the educators working with Bliss symbols are not trained in language. It would be difficult to arrive at any valid conclusions concerning the use of Bliss symbols with severely handicapped children.

American Sign Language (ASL)   In general, ASL is not merely a symbol system; it is a language in its own right. That is, when compared to English, ASL differs in vocabulary, syntax, and morphology. Thus, articles, prepositions, copulas, participles, and inflectional endings do not occur in ASL (Bergman, 1972). This problem, in part, has been circumvented as noted in the discussion of Signing Exact English.

In discussing the roots of ASL, Moores (1974) states:

> The roots of the American Sign Language do not lie in the English language but can be traced back to a variant of the French Sign Language developed by de l'Epee to reflect French syntax. The French Sign Language was brought to the United States by Laurent Clere who became the first teacher at the American School for the Deaf in 1817. Although a competent user of English can sign and spell in grammatical English patterns, many of the basic signs remain cognates with the original French ones (p. 380).

Although this manual system and its derivations have a high degree of intelligibility throughout the deaf populations of the United States and Canada, its disadvantages most likely outweigh its advantages when attempting to provide handicapped children with a communication system. First, manual signing presents a formidable problem for those individuals who have neurological involvement of the upper extremities. Second, the most important with respect to language learning and development, there is not a one-to-one relationship with English.

SUMMARY

Many children who have not learned to speak and understand speech are capable of learning language and learning to communicate. Their failure to develop normal speech in spite of intense attempts to teach them to communicate in the speech mode probably is caused by a variety of factors. First, there are some children who simply do not process auditory stimuli. This group includes, of course, the deaf, but it may also include some children who hear. Second, there are some children who have severe neuromotor problems that preclude the highly elaborate and complex motor movements required to produce spoken words. Third, there may be some children who have specific neural associative problems that preclude or interfere with the use of an auditory verbal system.

Fourth, it may be that the typical procedure of teaching the production of speech simultaneously with the language structure may interfere with learning.

The present authors maintain that speech is not necessary for the development of language and communication. Furthermore, when other symbol systems are used, nonspeaking children sometimes develop language and communication skills rather rapidly.

Communication is an interaction process that involves a sender and a receiver. A certain knowledge of the environment (or cognitive map) is assumed for both the sender and the receiver. This cognitive map involves classification of events, objects, actions, and persons. There is a set of symbols that has a similar relationship to aspects of the cognitive map for both the sender and the receiver. The sender must be able to select and organize the symbols that relate to his cognitive map, and the receiver must be able to translate the symbols to his cognitive map.

There are four sensory channels and four output modes that determine in part the structure of the cognitive map and what channels may be used for developing a functional communication system. The input channels are the visual, auditory, tactile, and olfactory. The output modes are gross motor output, signing, writing, and speech. Both the input mode and output mode are subject to basic disorders that may severely impede or prevent the use of a given input or output mode. For example, blind and deaf children are severely impaired in their respective abilities to respond to visual and auditory stimuli, and cerebral palsied children and dysarthric children may be severely handicapped in their respective use of writing and speech. The critical point in teaching is to pick input and output modes for children that result in functional communication channels.

Sensory modality deficits will have an effect on the kind of cognitive maps developed by a child and the type of communication symbol systems that are practical.

Numerous symbol systems have been used in attempts to teach handicapped children to develop a functional communication system. These include sign language, Braille, Rebus symbols, Bliss symbols, printed words, spoken words, and plastic forms. These symbol systems are evaluated in terms of iconicity versus arbitrariness, the input and output modes used, permanence versus transitivity, complexity versus simplicity, time required for transmission, and degree to which presentation can be automated.

Finally, examples are given concerning how the American signs, Non-SLIP symbols, Rebus symbols, and Bliss symbols may be used to form a simple English sentence.

ACKNOWLEDGMENT

The author is indebted to Carlyn Ogden for the figure preparation and artwork.

REFERENCES

Bergman, E. 1972. Autonomous and unique features of American sign language. Am. Ann. Deaf 117:20–24.

Bliss, C. K. 1965. Semantography-Blissymbolics. Semantography Publications, Sydney, Australia.

Bloom, L. M. 1970. Language Development: Form and Function in Emerging Grammars. MIT Press, Cambridge, Mass.

Bowerman, M. 1973. Structural relationships in children's utterances: Syntactic or semantic? *In* T. E. Moore (ed.), Cognitive Development and the Acquisition of Language, pp. 197–213. Academic Press, New York.

Bowerman, M. 1976. Semantic factors in the acquisition of rules for word use and sentence construction. *In* D. Morehead and A. Morehead (eds.), Normal and Deficient Child Language, pp. 99–179. University Park Press, Baltimore.

Bowerman, M. 1978. Words and sentences: Uniformity, individual variation, and shifts over time in patterns of acquisition. *In* F. D. Minifie and L. L. Lloyd (eds.), Communicative and Cognitive Abilities—Early Behavioral Assessment, pp. 351–398. University Park Press, Baltimore.

Bricker, W. A., and Bricker, D. D. 1974. An early language training strategy. *In* R. L. Schiefelbusch and L. L. Lloyd (eds.), Language Perspectives—Acquisition, Retardation, and Intervention, pp. 431–468. University Park Press, Baltimore.

Brown, R. 1958. Words and Things. The Free Press, New York.

Buddenhagen, R. G. 1971. Establishing Vocal Verbalizations in Mute Mongoloid Children. Research Press, Champaign, Ill.

Carrier, J. K. 1974. Application of functional analysis and a nonspeech response mode to teaching language. ASHA Monogr. Nov. 18.

Carrier, J. K., and Peak, T. 1975. Nonspeech Language Initiation Program. H & H Enterprises, Lawrence, Kan.

Carroll, J. B. 1964. Language and Thought. Prentice-Hall, Englewood Cliffs, N.J.

Cherry, C. 1961. On Human Communication. John Wiley & Sons, New York.

Clark, C. R., Davies, C. O., and Woodcock, R. W. 1974. Standard Rebus Glossary. American Guidance Service, Circle Pines, Minn.

Clark, C. R., and Woodcock, R. W. 1976. Graphic systems of communication. *In* L. L. Lloyd (ed.), Communication Assessment and Intervention Strategies, pp. 549–605. University Park Press, Baltimore.

Clark, H. H. 1973. Space, time, semantics and the child. *In* T. E. Moore (ed.), Cognitive Development and the Acquisition of Language, pp. 27–64. Academic Press, New York.

Cleator, P. E. 1961. Lost Languages. The John Day Company, New York.

Dale, P. S. 1972. Language Development: Structure and Function. Dryden Press, Hinsdale, Ill.

Gibson, E. J., and Levin, H. 1975. The Psychology of Reading. MIT Press, Cambridge, Mass.

Glucksberg, S., and Danks, J. H. 1975. Experimental Psycholinguistics: An Introduction. John Wiley & Sons, New York.

Guess, D., Sailor, W., and Baer, D. M. 1974. To teach language to retarded children. In R. L. Schiefelbusch and L. L. Lloyd (eds.), Language Perspectives—Acquisition, Retardation, and Intervention, pp. 529–563. University Park Press, Baltimore.

Gustason, G., Pfetzing, D., and Zawolkow, E. 1972. Signing Exact English. Modern Signs Press, Roosmoor, Cal.

Heber, R. 1959. A manual on terminology and classification in mental retardation. Am. J. Ment. Defic. 64(Monogr. Suppl.).

Hollis, J. H. 1965. The effects of social and nonsocial stimuli on the behavior of profoundly retarded children: Part I. Am. J. Ment. Defic. 69:755–771.

Hollis, J. H. 1966. Communication within dyads of severely retarded children. Am. J. Ment. Defic. 70:729–744.

Hollis, J. H., and Carrier, J. K. 1975. Research implications for communication deficiencies. Except. Child. 41:405–412.

Hollis, J. H., Carrier, J. K., and Spradlin, J. E. 1976. An approach to remediation of communication and learning deficiencies. In L. L. Lloyd (ed.), Communication Assessment and Intervention Strategies, pp. 265–294. University Park Press, Baltimore.

Hollis, J. H., and Sherman, J. A. 1968. Operant control of vocalizations in profoundly retarded children with normal hearing and moderate bilateral loss. J. Kan. Speech Hear. Assoc. 9:30–37.

House, B. J., Brown, A. L., and Scott, M. S. 1974. Children's discrimination learning based on identity or difference. In H. W. Resse (ed.), Advances in Child Development and Behavior, Vol. 9, pp. 1–45. Academic Press, New York.

Jones, J. W. 1961. Blind Children: Mode of Reading. M. S. Office of Education, Bulletin No. 24, Chapter III, pp. 12–19.

Keller, H. 1972. The Story of My Life. Dell Publishing Co., New York.

Kent, L. R. 1972. A language acquisition program for the retarded. In J. E. McLean, P. E. Yoder, and R. L. Schiefelbusch (eds.), Language Intervention with the Retarded, pp. 151–190. University Park Press, Baltimore.

Kuntz, J. B. 1974. A nonvocal communication development program for severely retarded children. Unpublished doctoral dissertation, Kansas State University.

Langacker, R. W. 1973. Language and Its Structure. Harcourt Brace Jovanovich, New York.

Lenneberg, E. H. 1967. Biological Foundations of Language. John Wiley & Sons, New York.

Lindsley, O. R. 1964. Direct measurement of prosthesis of retarded behavior. J. Educ. 147:62–81.

Lovaas, O. I., Berberich, J. P., Perloff, B. F., and Schaeffer, B. 1966. Acquisition of imitative speech by schizophrenic children. Science 151:705–707.

Lyons, J. 1968. Introduction to Theoretical Linguistics. Cambridge University Press, London.

MacLeish, A. 1971. A Glossary of Grammar and Linguistics. Grosset & Dunlap, New York.

McNaughton, S., and Kates, B. 1974. Visual symbols: Communication system for the prereading physically handicapped child. Paper presented at the AAMD Conference, June 5, 1974, Toronto, Ontario, Canada.

Miller, J. F., and Yoder, D. E. 1972. A syntax teaching program. *In* J. E. McLean, D. E. Yoder, and R. L. Schiefelbusch (eds.), Language Intervention with the Retarded: Developing Strategies, pp. 191–211. University Park Press, Baltimore.

Miller, J. F., and Yoder, D. E. 1974. An ontogenetic language teaching strategy for retarded children. *In* R. L. Schiefelbusch and L. L. Lloyd (eds.), Language Perspectives—Acquisition, Retardation, and Intervention, pp. 505–528. University Park Press, Baltimore.

Montessori, M. 1965. Dr. Montessori's Own Handbook. Schocken Books, New York.

Moores, D. F. 1974. Nonvocal systems of verbal behavior. *In* R. L. Schiefelbusch and L. L. Lloyd (eds.), Language Perspectives—Acquisition, Retardation, and Intervention, pp. 377–417. University Park Press, Baltimore.

Osgood, C. E. 1957. A behavioristic analysis of perception and language as cognitive phenomena. *In* J. S. Bruner et al. (eds.), Contemporary Approaches to Cognition. Harvard University Press, Cambridge, Mass.

Peters, H. N. 1935. Mediate association. J. Exp. Psychol. 18:20–48.

Piaget, J. 1957. Logic Psychology. Basic Books, New York.

Pollio, H. R. 1974. The Psychology of Symbolic Activity. Addison-Wesley Publishing Co., Reading, Mass.

Premack, D. 1970. A functional analysis of language. J. Exp. Anal. Behav. 14:107–125.

Premack, D. 1975a. Putting a face together. Science 188:228–236.

Premack, D. 1975b. On the origins of language. *In* M. S. Gazzaniga and C. Blakemore (eds.), Handbook of Psychobiology. Academic Press, New York.

Premack, D., and Premack, A. J. 1974. Teaching visual language to apes and language deficient persons. *In* R. L. Schiefelbusch and L. L. Lloyd (eds.), Language Perspectives—Acquisition, Retardation, and Intervention, pp. 347–376. University Park Press, Baltimore.

Risley, T. R., and Wolf, M. M. 1967. Establishing functional speech in echolalic children. Behav. Res. Ther. 5:73–88.

Rosenberger, P. B., Stoddard, L. T., and Sidman, M. 1972. Sample matching techniques in the study of children's language. *In* R. L. Schiefelbusch (ed.), Language of the Mentally Retarded, pp. 211–229. University Park Press, Baltimore.

Rosenberger, P. B. 1978. Neurological processes. *In* R. L. Schiefelbusch (ed.), Bases of Language Intervention, pp. 13–41. University Park Press, Baltimore.

Rozin, P. 1976. The evolution of intelligence and access to the cognitive unconscious. *In* J. M. Sprague and A. N. Epstein (eds.), Progress in Psychobiology and Physiological Psychology, Vol. 6, pp. 245–280. Academic Press, New York.

Rozin, P., Ooritzky, S., and Sotsky, R. 1971. American children with reading problems can easily learn to read English represented by Chinese characters. Science 171:1264–1267.

Sailor, W., Guess, D., and Baer, D. M. 1973. Functional language for verbally deficient children: An experimental program. Ment. Retard. June:27–35.

Salzinger, S. K., Salzinger, K., Portnoy, S., Eckman, J., Bacon, P. N., Dentsch, M., and Zubin, J. 1962. Operant conditioning of continuous speech in children. Child Dev. 33:683–695.

Sanders, D. A. 1976. A model for communication. *In* L. L. Lloyd (ed.), Communication Assessment and Intervention Strategies, pp. 1–32. University Park Press, Baltimore.

Schlesinger, I. M. 1974. Relational concepts underlying language. *In* R. L. Schiefelbusch and L. L. Lloyd (eds.), Language Perspectives—Acquisition, Retardation, and Intervention, pp. 129–151. University Park Press, Baltimore.

Sidman, M., and Cresson, O. 1973. Reading and crossmodal transfer of stimulus equivalences in severe retardation. Am. J. Ment. Defic. 77:515–523.

Stremel, K. 1972. Language training: A program for retarded children. Ment. Retard. 10:47–49.

Talkington, L. W., and Hall, S. M. n.d. A Manual Communication System for Deaf Retarded. Austin State School, P.O. Box 1269, Austin, Texas 78767.

Tolman, E. C. 1932. Purposive Behavior in Animals and Men. Century, New York.

Vanderheiden, D. H., Brown, W. P., MacKenzie, P., Reinen, S., and Scheible, C. 1975. Symbol communication for the mentally handicapped. Ment. Retard. 13:34–37.

Vanderheiden, G. C. 1976. Non-Vocal Communication Techniques and Aids for the Severely Physically Handicapped. University Park Press, Baltimore.

Vicker, B. (ed.). 1974. Nonoral Communication System Project 1964–1973. Campus Stores Publishers, Iowa City, Iowa.

Wilbur, R. B. 1976. Manual language and manual systems. *In* L. L. Lloyd (ed.), Communication Assessment and Intervention Strategies, pp. 423–500. University Park Press, Baltimore.

Woodcock, R. W. (ed.). 1965. The Rebus Reading Series. Institute on Mental Retardation and Intellectual Development, George Peabody College for Teachers, Nashville, Tenn.

Woodcock, R. W., Clark, C. R., and Davies, C. O. 1968. Peabody Rebus Reading Program. American Guidance Service, Circle Pines, Minn.

chapter

3

Children with
Limited Language

Doug Guess

Department of Special Education
University of Kansas
Lawrence, Kansas

Wayne Sailor

Department of Special Education
San Francisco State University
San Francisco, California

Donald M. Baer

Department of Human Development
and Family Life
University of Kansas
Lawrence, Kansas

contents

In 1957, B. F. Skinner asserted systematically and in detail that language might be a system of behavior, similar to other systems of behavior in its function although different in topography. Function being more basic than topography, this argument immediately implied that language should be susceptible to instruction, remediation, and elaboration at any time in a human's life and at any stage in any person's development. That statement of theory was not necessary for the pursuit of attempts to develop language in its absence or to repair it when it was wrong (cf. Itard (1962) and the entire tradition of speech pathology and speech teaching). However, Skinner's statement was the stimulus for the flood of systematic, technological research that followed. A review of that research by Sailor, Guess, and Baer (1973) includes examples of the recovery of speech in mute persons who previously had adequate language; the repair or elaboration of specific speech patterns in those showing deviant, distorted, or deficient language; and the development of selected instances of speech in children who had never displayed recognizable language skills.

Much of the research, especially in recent years, was aimed at developing teaching methods to produce not only a specified element of language skill but also a generalization of that element to untaught exemplars of it—essentially, the teaching of pieces of the surface *grammar* of language. (Some of this research has been reviewed by Guess and Baer, 1973.)

The research, coupled with the preexisting practices and traditions of speech training and speech pathology, logically implied three questions of considerable theoretical and practical import:

1. Given the reported success in establishing and/or correcting those targeted examples of language behavior, would it prove true that any aspect of language would be teachable or correctable in any deficient human with adequate vocal physiology?
2. If any elements of language could indeed be established in anyone needful of them, would those elements summate to the pattern of interpersonal behavior that is recognized as useful language communication?
3. If useful language communication is indeed the end result of a sequence of instruction in the elements of language, then by what curriculum could such instruction best proceed? In other words, which elements should be taught in what order, for maximal results from minimal teaching?

Preparation of this chapter was funded in part from USOE/BEH Grant OEG-0-74-2766 to Doug Guess, Wayne Sailor, and Leonard Lavis at Kansas Neurological Institute; and in part from USOE/BEH Contract OEC-0-74-9184 to Doug Guess and Wayne Sailor at Kansas Neurological Institute.

These three questions are neither trivial nor answerable as yet. However, the assertion that "no" is the answer to the second question was produced at exactly the same time as Skinner's analysis that prompted the second question (cf. Chomsky, 1959). In effect, it can be argued that language is a system of behavior that inevitably will be acquired by humans, in virtually any environment wherein language is already used, because the genetic inheritance of (most) humans powerfully predisposes them to learn and to use language in certain forms. Those forms, which by hypothesis are more basic than the surface grammar forms taught to school children, are by hypothesis the true underlying structure of language. Then it may be that those deficient, retarded children, who have never displayed language, despite environmental modeling of it in their childhood, may be lacking in the genetic predisposition at the most basic levels of its structure, and perhaps should be considered to be permanently barred from its acquisition. Whether or not this harsh implication is logical, the assertion of such "deep structures" strongly implied that both Skinner's theoretical analysis, and the resultant behavioral programs for establishing language in deficient children, could neither explain nor produce a language performance that would deserve the label.

Despite such strong, if exceptionally complex, arguments against the probability that supposedly simplistic language-training programs could succeed in accomplishing the acquisition of language by severely or profoundly retarded children, simple language-training programs have been designed, and continue to be designed. A survey of programs has been sketched by Guess, Sailor, and Baer (1976a, 1976b). There are several dozen in existence. Most of them are intended to accomplish some major part of what may be imagined to be the total problem of language acquisition and usage by retarded children. A few are suggested to be (at least by hypothesis) nearly complete programs. All are far more thorough and systematic than the research reported so far, which successfully established and generalized usage of specific elements of language in such children. A few of these programs exist in published form. Most exist as mimeographed manuals or as progress reports to sponsoring research/development agencies (usually agencies of the federal government, most often through the U.S. Department of Health, Education, and Welfare). There exist even more in such form that have escaped this survey, and no doubt still more are being produced around the world. The problem is too real and the stimulation too optimistic for this possibility to be left unattempted.

Most of these programs share a common teaching technique. Almost without exception, they use the methods of operant conditioning:

reinforcement of correct behavior; extinction and brief timeout from the opportunity to gain more of that positive reinforcement, contingent on incorrect, inappropriate, disruptive, or inattentive behaviors; careful, detailed programming of small new increments to be learned; and repetitive modeling of those new responses, usually coupled with the fading and shaping techniques well known in operant technology. (Modeling, or imitation, is considered here to be an operant technique, following the analysis exemplified in Baer, Peterson, and Sherman, 1967.)

Thus, there is no perceived need to add a fourth question to the preceding three—no one is asking, "How can language responses be taught?" or even, "Do some language responses require fundamentally different teaching techniques?" Nevertheless, it should be noted that the answer to this possible fourth question is no more settled (except by common practice) than are the answers to the other three. Perhaps speech teachers and programmers find their efforts sufficiently reinforced by these methods to preempt their trying alternatives. However, satisfaction is not equivalent to proof.

It is in the answer to the third question that the most systematic and persistent disagreement occurs: "What is the best curriculum for language training?" At least two logics may be discerned, one which may be called *developmental*, and another which may be termed *remedial*.

Developmental logic supposes that the best way, or perhaps the only effective way to teach language to a deficient child, is in the same sequence in which normal children learn language. If language has a complex structure, such that parts of it depend for their function on other parts of it already being mastered, then the normal developmental sequence must represent at least one effective sequence of learning those interdependencies. Conceivably, there is no alternate sequence in which language can be learned, at least by children learning it at the usual stages of their development. This possibility is bolstered by the reported uniformity with which children acquire language. If there were several possible sequences, or many, then would not at least some children manifest different sequences?

Remedial logic, by contrast, supposes that children being taught language relatively late in their lives, because they have failed to acquire it adequately in their earlier experiences, no longer possess the same collection of abilities and deficits that normal children have when they begin to acquire language. Instead, the usual recipient of systematic, experimental language training will be a retarded child, well past the second-year level of motor development, possessed of a certain deviant means of interacting with peers and adults and securing some service from them, and with some acquaintance with the physical ecology of the world and its mechanics—all deficient, all oddly sorted and conditioned by years of institutional life or the sheltering a home-based retardate receives, but none of it any longer representative of the concantenation of knowledge and ignorance, ability and inability of the 18-month-old normal child.

Remedial logic, then, will not ask in what order the retarded child needs to learn language but rather in what order the language taught most quickly will accomplish some improvement in the child's communication. The success of past studies that taught such children quite arbitrary elements of language, with virtually no regard for their "readiness" to learn that particular element, no doubt reinforces this tendency. Remedial logic also presupposes that if every element of language that the child is ever to use must be taught directly, through a well-designed program of operant techniques, then the problem is insoluble, because such teaching will require too much effort to find either willing teachers or students whose life expectancy is sufficient to endure the necessary programs. Language must indeed have the characteristic called "generative" by the linguists (cf. Chomsky, 1959) if it is to be taught after its natural acquisition has failed. That is, language must be self-generating; some new elements of it must be produced by the child, not by the teacher; and all new elements must follow the rules of language that the rest of us follow, otherwise they will not be understood by us (and thus will not be language). A remedial approach cannot assume that self-generating language is inherent in the child's genetic endowment. Indeed, these children have already failed to acquire language in an environment that modeled it for them, sometimes as well as do the environments in which normal children learn their language. If that failure results from the children's genetic predisposition to learn language, then it has already shown that the predisposition is faulty. Then an alternative will be required. Behavioral approaches will usually invoke generalization of surface grammar rules as one alternative, and the development of systematic listening-imitation skills as another, at least.

Furthermore, a remedial logic will be most concerned with motivating the child not only to learn language from the teaching program but also to learn it from ongoing interactions outside the teaching program. If that is to happen, the child must find that language—even the small amount that has been learned so far in the program—is useful in accomplishing better reinforcement of the child's behaviors than was possible without that language. Thus, a program based on remedial logic will try to establish first the most useful elements of language that the child might need. What they are will depend on the child's environment. Surely those first elements need to be labels, but more importantly they should be labels of reinforcers *for the child*, and they should be labels the child can use as requests that will be granted by those attending the child. Supplying a child with the name for an object that is reinforcing, but that is almost never present in the child's everyday environment, will not provide everyday experiences showing that possession and use of that name are reinforcing. Similarly, giving the child the name of a reinforcer that the child's parents or parent surrogates believe is improper for the child to have, again will not provide much reinforcement for using that name as a request. Thus, remedial programs will supply a child with language responses that maximally enhance control of the environment *that* child encounters. The curriculum for the next child may well be different, if the next child lives in an environment different enough to require different names and requests to control it. But, in each case, the key concept is control of the environment by language. The remedial assumption is that, if a child encounters systematic control not only of the language teacher but also of much of the rest of the environment, through the language responses taught by the language teacher, then a motivation is established that could prompt the child to learn how to listen to a language-using environment, to learn by observation, to learn the skills of *asking* for language training from language users (e.g., *What's that?* is a request for training in a new label), and to learn the skills of remembering what is gained by these tactics for later productive use in gaining even more control of the environment. Just as a program aimed at teaching the child that language controls the environment establishes motivation to learn such skills, a thorough program then will capitalize on that motivation by directly teaching those skills. The program described subsequently in this chapter includes such teaching. However, unlike the logic of normal development, remedial logic suggests that there may be many alternate sequences of instruction, any of which could well embody the experience of control by language, the motivation to control by language, and the skills of acquiring more language to extend and elaborate that control. Some of these alternate programs may do better at those lessons than others, but that becomes an empirical issue rather than a theoretical one, and it may be resolved by appropriate comparative research (discussed later).

To emphasize to the child that language controls the environment, it is important that productive language predominate. Receptive language, although undoubtedly of immense value to a child (relative to no language capability at all), nevertheless is the medium whereby the child is controlled by others, rather than a means by which the child achieves some personal control of others. Presumably skill in receptive language will enhance a child's life and gain reinforcement otherwise lacking (by receiving invitations to encounter positive reinforcers and warnings against negative reinforcers), but it seems almost inevitable that the motivation to acquire more language through the child's own efforts cannot be as powerful in an exclusively receptive language domain as it would be in an effectively constituted productive domain.

This conclusion occasionally produces sharp criticism from students of normal developmental logic. In normal development it seems clear that receptive skill precedes the corresponding productive abilities. Thus, it is often advised that children being taught language in a systematic training program first should undergo extensive receptive training, followed by productive training. The remedial program described here nonetheless emphasizes productive skills over receptive, and typically teaches the productive version of each target skill before establishing its receptive discriminations. This is true for at least three reasons: 1) it is possible to do so without undue teaching effort, 2) productive skills are taught first so that control, rather than being controlled, will be experienced first, and 3) in the final analysis, the children engaged in this program indeed have extensive early receptive training—they have all been taught (or polished in) the skills of generalized vocal imitation before learning their first productive label-requests. Verbal imitation, especially when brought to the level of wide generalization, is intrinsically a skill requiring very precise receptive discrimination; that is, to imitate a sound, one must first discriminate it receptively—discriminate it from all other sounds that one can also imitate. Thus, any accomplished vocal imitator is by the same token a highly sophisticated receptive-speech connoisseur. Consequently, emphasis on productive language does not in fact contradict the linguists' well-founded insistence on the primacy of receptive skill; in that productive speech is dependent on imitative ability, it is founded on receptive skill, even in this program.

This last argument may well be characteristic of many that arise in the consideration of developmental and remedial logics, that is, the differences between the two approaches may be fewer than their similarities. After all, the two logics are not contradictory to each other, but only different. Thus, their areas of overlap may well be extensive. The extent to which this is true cannot be evaluated at present, however, for two reasons: 1) there are many possible remedial programs, some of which may resemble developmental logic more, and others less, and 2) developmental logic is not itself well established at the level of detail necessary to yield a teaching curriculum for this problem. (Indeed, as that detail is worked out in future years, it may prove true that developmental logic is not monolithic, that not all normal children develop language skills in so uniform a sequence as is presently supposed. Current descriptive linguistic data are, after all, fairly limited in number, scope, and reliability of measurement. Thus, new findings may conceivably hold some surprises for everyone.)

Consequently, it may well be the case that, at present, the best research tactic and the best educational tactic are identical: to develop some thorough language-training programs that are effective and to evaluate their effectiveness with careful measurement procedures and extensive observation of their generalization to nonteaching environments. Language skills that exist only in the ear of their teacher, or only in that teacher's proximity, are not language skills in any useful sense of the word. But those that can be understood and answered by nonteachers, and are used by the children to enlist nonteachers in their aid, education, and general human interactions, represent solutions to the problem posed by language-deficient children. The value of language to any child, and to that child's society, is too obvious to require specification here. Thus, any research or development effort that produces a language-training program that works in a generalized manner, is thereby an important project.

The next issue will be to see if remedial language-training programs are sometimes effective, if developmental language-training programs are sometimes effective, and if the two types of programs are in fact different from each other in their curricula. If the answer to those questions is "yes," then (and only then) will the stage be set for some exceptionally difficult and expensive comparative research. Such research would compare a representative sample of remedial programs, in all relevant aspects of effectiveness and cost, to a representative sample of developmental programs, looking for consistent, systematic differences that might establish both the theoretical and the practical superiority of one approach over the other. The answers to that comparative research, as far as can be said now, could be anything. One might prove more effective and easier to use than the other; one could prove more effective but more difficult to use; one might be better for certain classes of children but not for others; or there might be no consistent, systematic differences between the approaches, compared to the differences that arise from local details such as the level of training of the teachers, the times and hours per day available for the training, the settings available for training and generalization, the cooperation of nonteaching personnel, etc. However, before any such answers can be hypothesized, it is necessary first to have some effective programs.

What follows is one proposal for a program, based on remedial logic for the most part, that may prove useful in this context.

SKILLS PREREQUISITE TO THE PROGRAM

Sensory and Motor Abilities

The program is designed to teach productive and receptive language. Accordingly children should be able to hear at a normal conversational level with or without the use of a prosthetic hearing device. The ability to identify objects and actions visually is required also, although normal vision is unnecessary if there are special adaptations and prosthetic devices to compensate for sensory impairment.

Children entering the program should have intact the physiological speech mechanisms that enable speech sounds, although perfect articulation is by no means required. (Pilot work is currently underway to adapt the training sequence to communication boards for use with children who have extensive motor impairment in their speech mechanisms. The program is also being adapted to an oral signing system for retarded children with severe hearing losses.)

Etiology and Medical Diagnosis

The program is being field tested with severely handicapped children variously labeled profoundly retarded, autistic, brain damaged, etc. Many have seizures, some are cerebral palsied, and some come from impoverished home environments. So far, neither etiology nor diagnosis has been seen to predict progress, apart from citation of complicating motor and sensory impairments.

Level of Functioning and Chronological Age

The vast majority of children field tested are severely or profoundly retarded. To date, their IQ scores do not predict their success; however, their overall level of adaptive behavior may. For example, at present, nonverbal children scoring higher on the TARC Assessment Scale (Sailor and Mix, 1975) progress more rapidly in the program than nonverbal children with lower TARC scores.

The field test now involves 400 individuals ranging from about three to 50 years of age, with a mean of 10 years. So far, their chronological age (apart from level of functioning) has not been significantly related to progress. However, a recent use of the curriculum with preschool children might change this conclusion. Initial reports suggest that these younger severely handicapped children progress more rapidly, compared to the initial, somewhat older, subject population.

Verbal Imitation

Most theorists believe that if children can hear, discriminate sounds, and reproduce the sounds they hear, one fundamental skill for later language learning has been mastered. This important skill is verbal imitation. Earlier descriptions of the curriculum (Sailor, Guess, and Baer, 1973; Guess, Sailor, and Baer, 1974) described imitation-training procedures to prepare children. Of all entry level skills, verbal imitation is consistently the most significantly predictive of success in training. Its absence is also prognostic for failure in the program. To date, of children entering the program with no vocal-verbal imitation skills, only about 60% have shown successful progress in the steps of the speech and language sequence. Furthermore, the majority of this successful 60% took nearly two years to acquire generalized verbal imitation (under the training procedures included in the program).

Operant conditioning techniques have long been used to establish generalized imitative repertoires in previously nonimitative children. Typically, the training strategy has been to present a model of the sound to be imitated (e.g., *John, say "ma ma"*), wait briefly for the child to approximate an imitation, and reinforce the approximation. This training continues until the child begins to imitate new models the first time they are presented. At that point, the child has learned a *generalized* imitative repertoire and is ready to learn that sounds can be used to label and ask for things.

Successful as these procedures have been, more sophisticated methods must be developed to teach nonverbal children to imitate. The present procedures are arduous and time consuming, sometimes requiring the presentation of the same sound thousands of times before the child begins to imitate it. Then, a second sound must be trained and brought under imitative control; then a third, and so on. In some cases, this method of instruction can continue for years before the child becomes a skillful, generalized imitator.

Another major concern is the total-failure rate of current imitation-training procedures. Many children do learn to imitate when these procedures are used systematically, but some (40% in our sample) do not. That failure rate is sufficiently high to require a closer look at the imitation procedures presently being used.

The literature provides some clues as to how to begin. For example, Baer, Peterson, and Sherman (1967) trained nonimitative retarded children to imitate motor responses before training on vocal ones. They reasoned that vocal imitation training might be enhanced if the subjects first mastered the topographically less difficult motor imitations. Furthermore, motor-imitation training before verbal-imitation training allows the teacher to assist the child physically much more easily than in the vocal mode. Sloane, Johnston, and Harris (1968), using much the same rationale as Baer et al., required their subjects to master motor imitations before training in the vocal mode, but they also chose motor imitations that involved movements of the mouth and tongue (e.g., open mouth). Once the children were imitating the motor movements, training began to include a vocal component as well (e.g., open his[1] mouth and say "ah"). Another strategy was to bypass motor imitation training altogether. For example, Lovaas et al. (1966) taught autistic children to imitate words by selecting training sounds that possessed salient visual and auditory cues (i.e., "ma" instead of "ka"), reasoning that some children discriminate sounds with visual (e.g., lip closure) and auditory cues more easily than those with only auditory components.

Perhaps these imitation-training procedures have not provided sufficient rationale for the *type* of response that should be trained. In most cases, the program teaches specific imitations that are *not* already in the child's behavioral repertoire. Thus, the children are to emit new and often quite difficult responses. These may seem quite simple (e.g., "ah," "oh," "ee"), but they require complex coordination among the various voicing structures. Severely handicapped children often have tremendous problems in producing such complex responses. Admittedly, the operant techniques of shaping, prompting, putting-through, and fading are invaluable tools for teaching responses that lead to at least a close approximation of the target speech sound. However, for many nonimitative children, the practitioner may be premature in attempting to teach some new sound productions.

A possible solution is first to identify responses already established in the child's repertoire, and to select out some of these responses for imitative training. In this case, we already know the child can produce the responses. Our task is to bring these responses under stimulus control so they are produced in the presence of a model. By first teaching a set to imitate, we can then embark on the more difficult task of teaching the child *new* (and more useful) responses, or to shape the newly taught responses into more functional ones.

This concept is not novel in imitation training. Following a Piagetian model, Bricker, Dennison, and Bricker (1975) described a similar procedure in their imitation-training program for preschool handicapped children. These authors, however, used a procedure in which positive consequences (reinforcers) are made contingent on spontaneously occurring responses emitted by children during the course of their natural interaction with the environment. One difficulty, however, is finding sufficient opportunity to reinforce these responses, because they may be emitted very infrequently by some children.

A second major concern in current imitation-training procedures is the issue of *response functionality*. Most imitation-training programs

---

[1] Masculine pronouns are used throughout for the sake of grammatical uniformity and simplicity. They are not meant to be preferential or discriminatory.

have included motor responses such as *touch the table, clap hands, stand up,* etc. These and similar responses have limited or no utility for the child in most situations. The child would hardly engage in them in isolation from some larger response chain. These responses per se provide little in the way of "inherent" reinforcers. For example, in the course of their daily interaction with the environment, children would have little reason to merely touch a table. They would likely stand up only as part of a motor chain to go somewhere else; and they would clap their hands, if at all, only when expressing delight or approval. The point is that these responses are not intrinsically useful or reinforcing to the child; thus, their teaching requires the use of arbitrary reinforcers (e.g., food) both to establish and maintain them. Furthermore, these responses are not likely to occur frequently in the child's daily life, other than as part of a larger chain of motor responses (e.g., standing up to go somewhere else).

Functional responses, on the other hand, are those that have their own immediate (usually natural) consequences. Examples include turning a radio knob (response) to hear music (consequence), pressing a lamp switch (response) to produce light (consequence), or peering into a kaleidoscope (response) to see a colorful design (consequence). It is apparent that many functional responses include the use of objects appropriate to the response. Indeed, a recent unpublished study by Carpenter (1975) found that imitations using objects are acquired more rapidly than corresponding imitations of similar topography that did not use objects. Similarly, a study by Saunders, Sailor, and Taylor (1976) indicated that specific reinforcers given for specific responses would accelerate acquisition of a receptive discrimination task. In this study, three retarded children were taught a receptive discrimination among pairs of toys to which nonsense labels had been assigned. All three could "point to" upon instruction. The subjects were pretested for baselines of time spent playing with various toys and toy preference in a choice situation. The baseline level of pointing to any nonsense-labeled toy, preferred or otherwise, was chance. The subsequent experimental conditions then established the nonsense labels as functional, controlling for toy preference; that is, in one condition, subjects were taught that for certain labels spoken to them, if they made a correct point, they received a consistent one of the preferred toys, i.e., they got what they pointed to, for 15 seconds of play. In a contrasting condition, a correct point resulted in a random access to sometimes one, sometimes another of two preferred toys. Rate of acquisition of correct pointing was higher in the first condition (in which a label, when responded to, meant a specific result) than in the second condition (in which a label, when responded to correctly, meant a nonspecific result—an unpredictable one of two possible results). A third condition controlled for the effects of two reinforcers per se as a stimulus and motivational difference between the first two methods, by using two nonspecific but less preferred toys as the consequence. The results showed that specific consequences were superior to nonspecific consequences, regardless of toy number or preference.

Thus, at our present level of analysis, *functional* responses may be defined as those that 1) produce an immediate consequence for the child, 2) the consequence is potentially reinforcing, 3) the consequence is specific to the response, and 4) the response is natural to the child's interaction with the environment.

To summarize briefly, the curriculum presented here is designed to begin functional speech and language training with a speech-deficient child. The child must have certain minimal auditory and visual entry skills (pending further developments in the nonspeech mode applications) and must be capable of generalized vocal imitation. The curriculum does not contain an instructional sequence for the production of imitation. Ongoing research in our own laboratory, as well as others, is leading to the refinement of a general technology of imitation training. The development of a curriculum for general instruction that attends to the issues of response selectivity and response functionality remains a working objective for the present. The instructional technology for proceeding *past* imitation language development is, in these authors' opinion, in a rather advanced state of design. The instructional sequence presented here (adapted from Guess, Sailor, and Baer, 1976a, 1976b) is only one example of that technology.

FUNCTIONAL LANGUAGE
TRAINING FOR THE SEVERELY HANDICAPPED

Dimensions

The complete instructional curriculum includes 60 individual training steps subsumed under five dimensions. The dimensions represent a basic structure and framework in accordance with the particular training emphasis and theoretical underpinnings of the program. These dimensions, described below, include *reference, control, self-extended control, integration,* and *reception.*

Reference   This dimension is used to represent a fundamental function of language—learning that certain sounds (words) represent (or symbolize) objects and events in our environment, or attributes of these objects or events. For example, the word "ball" represents a specific object of finite size, color, and texture. The word "eat" represents an activity describing the process of delivering food to one's mouth. "Red" is used to symbolize a color which can vary in hue, and which can be an attribute of an infinite number of objects. "Big" is used to describe the relative size among objects and events, etc. *Reference* is used in numerous contexts in the program, including the rather basic labeling of objects, the description of actions, the identification of ownership (my, your), the attribution of color, and the description of relational properties between objects (size, position, location).

Control   This dimension introduces to children the power of language by teaching them various forms of requesting behavior, such as *I want (object or action)*, *I want (action-with-object)*, and *I want you to (action-with-object)*. The specific purpose of including the request forms is to emphasize to children the importance of language to them in managing their environments and to give them the skills necessary to initiate speech in relation to their specific needs. Further explicitness about the controlling function of language is then added through the inclusion of possessive, descriptive, or relational and locational properties that further identify the object or event appropriate to the request forms.

Self-Extended Control   *Reference* and *control* dimensions are useful for children to manage their environment within the limitation of the referents known to them. However, speech-deficient children often have only a meager number of referents at their disposal (i.e., they simply do not know the necessary labels for all the objects, actions, and action-with-objects that they wish). Thus, a *self-extended control* dimension is included in the program, designed to teach children to request more complete, specific information based upon their own determination of what they do not know from what they already know. *Self-extended control* is developed by teaching children to ask such questions as *What is that?* in response to unknown objects, *What are you doing?* in response to unknown actions, *Whose (object)?* when identifying ownership of objects, *What size?* to inquire about the largeness or smallness of objects, *What color?* when confronted with novel color stimuli, and *Where (object or location)?* to establish or identify the relationship between objects or the locations of either objects or persons.

Integration   Language skills taught in *reference, control,* and *self-extended control* are put together in such a manner that previously taught skills are integrated with currently taught skills to maximize appropriate interaction with the environment. *Integration* presents training steps that teach children to discriminate when to seek appropriate information via question asking, and when to respond with appropriate referents when the information already exists in their language repertoire. A second function of *integration* is "dialogue," which, conceptually, provides a teaching format requiring the children to chain together all or some of the previously learned skills, such that they can carry on a simple but appropriate conversation centered around a functional activity or theme.

Reception   Corresponding to specific attainments in productive speech, concepts are also taught at the receptive level, to make complete the children's ability to speak and understand. In this curriculum, however, a productive skill is taught before the corresponding skill is taught at the receptive level. For example, children are trained to label objects before they are taught to identify these same objects receptively. The training of productive skills in the program, followed by receptive training (if necessary) of the same skill, is intended not to minimize the importance of receptive training but to emphasize the productive nature of the program, which, by design, has the purpose of bringing the children rapidly into the speaking community (as contrasted to the mute instruction-following community).

Content of the Curriculum Sequence

The 60-step training sequence is divided into six content areas: Persons and Things, Actions with Persons and Things, Possession, Color, Size, and Relation/Location. The number of steps in each of these content areas is presented in Figure 1. The content areas are grouped into four separate parts, which represent the training order of the program.

Persons and Things[2]   The initial nine steps in this content area teach the student to label common objects, to identify the same objects receptively, to request objects using a two-word utterance (*want* [*object*]) in Step 3, and later, *I want* (*object*) in Step 8. In this part of the training sequence, the student also is taught to ask *What's that?* when confronted with unknown objects, to discriminate when to ask *What's that?* and when to label objects, and to remember the labels of novel items given in response to the question. In addition, the student is trained to use *yes* and *no* as receptive indicators for understanding object labels (Step 7) and to chain two previously learned responses together (in Step 9).

Action with Persons and Things   This content area includes 19 individual teaching steps that center around the expressive and receptive use of verb actions. In the sequence the student is taught both to express and identify a large number of common verb actions. The verb actions first are trained separately (e.g., *I play*) and then in combination with the objects of the action (e.g., *I play ball*).

Interwoven in the training sequence is the teaching of the second person pronoun *you* and the appropriate discrimination between the first and second person pronouns (I/you). At a later point in the sequence, children are taught to expand their own repertoires by asking questions to identify actions which are novel to them (e.g., *What are you doing?*).

---

[2] All four parts of the training program are available in published form from H & H Enterprises, Box 3342, Lawrence, Kansas 66044.

CONTENT CATEGORIES

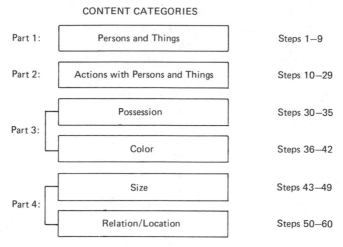

Figure 1.   Schematic of the training sequence.

Also, there is further expansion of concepts and skills taught in the Persons and Things sequence, including increases in object labels, extension of the yes/no concept to identify actions, and more varied use of requests. Actions with Persons and Things systematically increases the length of response utterances required, and integrates these utterances into new and different response chains as part of trained conversational units.

Possession   Steps 30–35 are concerned with teaching the concept of possession appropriate to the pronouns *my* and *your*. In this six-step sequence, the students are taught to identify the ownership of objects using the productive pronouns *my* and *your*, to identify ownership receptively using *yes/no* as indicators of their understanding, to request objects using the correct possessive pronoun (e.g., *I want my/your (object)*), to ask the question *Whose (object?)* when ownership is unknown, and to use the possessive pronouns appropriately in the context of a simple conversation that involves requests and the descriptions of actions. In this latter instance *my* and *your* are integrated with previously taught responses, thus expanding the length of the student's utterances and systematically adding possessive pronoun usage to previously learned concepts.

Color   In Steps 36–42 the students are trained to use color descriptors. They are taught initially to label common colors, and then to label objects using the correct color descriptors. The students are next taught to identify objects of various colors receptively via a pointing response. The other steps in the sequence teach the students to make requests to open boxes of various colors, to then identify the same action at the receptive level using *yes/no* as indicators for correct responses, to ask *What color?* when presented with unknown color labels, and to integrate color in conversation that centers around the activity of coloring. This final step combines a number of previously learned responses and concepts to accentuate the use of color descriptors.

Size   Steps 43–49 teach the students to use the size descriptors *big* and *little*. In this sequence, students are taught *big/little* as referent labels, to identify big and little objects with the appropriate size descriptors, to state the location of objects placed in big or little boxes, to identify receptively the location of items placed in big or little boxes using *yes/no* responses, to ask *What size?* when given a request for objects, to identify receptively the size of objects given to them using the *yes/no* response, and to engage in a brief conversation that integrates both color and size descriptors.

Relation/Location   The last sequence in the program (Steps 50–59) pertains to the functional use of position descriptors (*on/under*) and location descriptors (*inside/outside*). Students are taught to use *on/under* and *inside/outside* as reference labels, to identify receptively the position and location of objects and persons using the *yes/no* response, to request objects placed in the *on/under* position, to request a person to go *inside/ outside* various locations (e.g., *I want you to go outside the room*), and to ask questions (e.g., *Where is my (object)?* and *Where are you going?*). The position/location concepts are integrated in a brief conversation in Step 59.

One final step (60) concludes the program. Step 60 provides an integration and review of the skills and concepts trained in all the concept areas. This step integrates the concepts of verb actions, possession, color, size, position, and location in a rather lengthy interaction between the students and their language trainer.

Integration of Steps in the Program

The entire 60-step program is divided into six content areas, each containing its own sequence of instruction. Nevertheless, it is important to realize that the design of the program sequence emphasizes the gradual introduction of new skills prefaced by more fundamental concepts. Thus, the 60-step sequence is interlocking, so that new skills are introduced as soon as possible in the context of previously learned skills and such that the students are not exposed abruptly to concepts for which adequate prior training has not taken place. In addition, the length of the response utterances required is increased gradually across the training sequence. For example, the mean response length of utterances required in the productive training steps in the initial Persons and Things category is 1.9 words; the longest verbal response type in that same category is three words. By the time the students reach the final content area of the program (Relation/Location) the mean response length has been expanded to 4.4 words, and the longest sentence type is seven words. Similarly, the trainer's response length in presenting instructions and questions also increases and becomes more rapid across the 60-step sequence.

Structure of the Training Steps

Each individual training step in the program follows a similar outline, which includes the Training Goal, Training Item, Procedures, Training Instructions, Scoring Form, Summary Form, and Programming for Generalization.

Training Goal   This section describes the specific skill or concept to be trained in the step, a brief statement as to how the step is integrated with previous steps, and the identification of the step with whichever of the five dimensions (reference, control, self-extended control, integration, reception) it embodies.

Training Items   This section describes the specific type of materials or objects needed for the step. The stimulus items and props required for each step are frequently left to the discretion of the trainers, whose selections can be made through their knowledge of the students and their living environment. For the most part, however, the training stimuli include common, readily available, and functional items. The use of objects rather than pictures is preferred, to increase the authenticity of the training environment.

Procedures   For each trial in a session the trainer provides the student with a stimulus, which can be a question, command, or the presentation of an object or the modeling of an action. The student, in turn, can emit a correct response, a partially correct response, a wrong response, or no response at all. The trainer must respond accordingly. When correct responses are given, the student is usually reinforced and praised. Trainers select the types and amounts of reinforcers dispensed for correct responses. However, considerable effort has been made to construct many steps so that a correct response is *intrinsically* reinforcing for the student, especially in the later steps.

Obviously students will not respond correctly on every trial. Indeed, some students may require lengthy periods of training before correct responses, or even partially correct responses, are emitted. Thus, the trainer must be prepared to deal with partially correct responses, incorrect responses, or no responses. The various steps in the program use one of two basic procedures when correct responses are not given on the first presentation of a trial. These are the Training and Correction Procedure and the Two-Trainer Training and Correction Procedure.

The Training and Correction Procedure describes how language trainers should use prompts, put-throughs, and shaping techniques to correct errors made by the student. The Training and Correction Procedure allows for flexibility in reacting to individual, idiosyncratic responses made by the student, yet provides a systematic framework that allows the trainer to be consistent when correcting errors.

There are certain skills and concepts for which a second trainer can best serve as a model for the correct response, following an error or no response by the student. These situations occur when the concept to be taught involves a reversed or conditional discrimination that depends on the person who originated the response. The concept of *I/you* serves as a case in point. The first person singular pronoun *I* is used by a speaker, whereas the second person singular pronoun *you* generally refers to the person or persons spoken to. In teaching the *I/you* discrimination, a second trainer is helpful because that person (whether it be another adult or another child who has already mastered the concept) can provide the correctly modeled answer by assuming the same speaker-listener role as the student. Accordingly, a Two-Trainer Training and Correction Procedure is used in those steps in the program when a reversed or conditional discrimination is taught.

Training Instructions   Each step includes instructions to the trainer, describing the order in which items and trials are to be presented, what the trainer says to the student, and the expected response from the student. The trainer's instructions to the student are always printed in capital letters (e.g., WHAT IS THAT?) The expected response from the student is printed in small letters with quotation marks (e.g., "ball"). When appropriate, the instructions also explain how training items are to be arranged for the session, and the position or location of the student in the room. For some steps, the instructions also describe a skill test that allows the student to either skip altogether a particular step or to exit from the step without having to undergo further training.

Scoring Form and Summary Form   Each step includes a scoring form (data sheet) specifically designed for the skill being trained in that step. This form also provides descriptive information for the trainer to assist in correctly following the instructions. The scoring form includes space for the student's name, the name of the trainer, the date, and session number. Each form also includes a summary table for tabulating percentages of correct responses for every session. Percentage conversion tables are provided for the trainer to assist in the rapid and accurate tabulation of correct responses.

A summary sheet is also provided for each step to record program progress across sessions. Additional space on the summary sheet is used to indicate the date when training was started for that step, the date when criterion performance was reached, and the total number of sessions required to achieve that criterion performance. The program also includes instructions for graphing data from the summary sheets for those trainers wishing to have a visual display of progress for their students.

Programming for Generalization   Many of the steps in the program have an additional section that describes extending a newly learned skill to the student's natural environment. Ordinarily the generalization-training procedures are to be administered by the student's parents, parent surrogates, teacher, or other significant person who has daily contact with him. The purpose of the generalization procedure is to increase the use of a newly taught skill with persons other than the trainer and in environments different from the student's training setting. Additionally, the generalization training procedures assist in keeping other persons aware of the student's progress across time. Thus, the student's parents or parent surrogates become familiar with the skills available to the student as he advances through the program so that such skills can be attended to (and reinforced) when they occur spontaneously.

An Illustration   The following reproduction of a training step serves to demonstrate how each step is organized in accordance with the structure described in the preceding section. Step 3 from the Persons and Things category of the program is presented. This particular step is designed to teach the student to request things using a two-word response, *Want* (object).

Step 3
(Requesting Items)

Training Goal.   To train the student to request items using a two-word response, "Want (item)." This step initiates training in the *control* dimension of language, i.e., saying things that require another person to do something.

Training Items.   Ten items (food, liquids, toys, etc.) that are reinforcing to the student. The most important thing in making your selection of items for the step is that the student *wants* them. It is also important that the student be able to label the items. Thus, items for Step 1 should be used if they are important to the student. If new items are used, you should make sure that the student can label them.

Procedures.   Use the *Training and Correction Procedure* (from the Part I Training Manual: Guess, Sailor, and Baer, 1976), realizing that considerable shaping may be required.

Step 3 Training Instructions

1. Hold up each item, one at a time, and ask, WHAT WANT? A correct response must include the word "want" plus the correct label for the item (e.g., "want car"). The student is given the item for correct responses. For example, if you hold up a cookie and ask WHAT WANT? and the student responds, "want cookie" then you give the student the cookie (or a portion of it). If the item is nonconsumable, let the student play with it before asking that it be given back for use in further trials. When you ask for the item back, extend your hand and say, I WANT (ITEM). Partial responses by the student are of particular importance in the Step. If partial responses are given (e.g., labeling the item without first saying "want"), you should emphasize the missing component when modeling the correct response (e.g., WANT (ITEM)). Some examples of typical trials, using the Training and Correction Procedure, are

Table 1.   Example trials for Step 3 training

Trainer	Student
Trial 1	
(Holds up cookie)	
WHAT WANT?	"Cookie"
THAT'S CLOSE, DICK. LET'S TRY AGAIN. SAY, WANT COOKIE.	"Wa cookie"
THAT IS MUCH BETTER, WANT COOKIE. (Gives portion of cookie to student for coming close and scores ($-$) on Scoring Form for the first response "cookie." Here the trainer chose to reinforce the student for a good attempt "wa cookie" following the correction procedure. This would not be done in later trials if the word "want" is being correctly articulated.)	
Trial 2	
(Holds up cup of Coke)	
WHAT WANT?	"Wa Coke"
GOOD! YOU WANT COKE. (Gives cup with small portion of Coke to student and scores (S) on Scoring Form for shaped response.)	
Trial 3	
(Holds up piece of candy)	
WHAT WANT?	"Want candy"
VERY GOOD TALKING, DICK! (Gives piece of candy to student and scores ($+$) on Scoring Form.)	

Table 1.   Example trials for Step 3 training (*continued*)

Trainer	Student
Trial 4	
(Holds up toy car)	
WHAT WANT?	"Car"
NO DICK, YOU WANT CAR. (Scores (−) on Scoring Form.)	
WHAT WANT?	"Want car"
THAT'S RIGHT. WANT CAR.	
Trial 5	
(Holds up milk)	
WHAT WANT?	(No response)
(Scores (NR) on Scoring Form)	
DICK, SAY WANT MILK, WHAT WANT? (Note the trainer provided the correct model (WANT MILK) and quickly asked the question, WHAT WANT?).	"Milk"
(Says nothing and goes to next trial; trainer should consider whether student really wants the milk.)	
Trial 6	
(Holds up ball)	
WHAT WANT?	"Want ball"
THAT IS REALLY GOOD! (Gives ball to student, scores (+) on Scoring Form.)	
(Lets student play with ball for a short while, then holds hand out.)	
I WANT BALL.	(Gives ball to trainer)
THANK YOU.	

presented in Table 1. These examples are keyed to the first six trials shown in the sample Scoring Form for Step 3, Figure 2.

2. Present the 10 items three times each in a session (for a total of 30 trials), as indicated on the Scoring Form for Step 3.
3. Count the number of correct (+), incorrect (−), shaped (S), and no response (NR). Refer to 30 Trial Session in Appendix A (from the Part I Training Manual) for converting these numbers to percentages, and enter percentages on the bottom of the Scoring Form.
4. Record percentage of correct responses for each session on Summary Form for Step 3. (See sample summary form for Step 3, Figure 3.) Continue training until criterion performance is reached (80% correct in one session or 12-in-a-row correct in one session).
5. Advance the student to Step 4 when criterion performance is reached and initiate generalization training for Step 3.

Student _Dick_   Date _4-3-75_   Session No. _1_

Trainer _Bill_

List items used:

(1) _Cookie_   (2) _Coke_   (3) _Candy_   (4) _Car_   (5) _Milk_

(6) _Ball_   (7) _Apple_   (8) _Drum_   (9) _Book_   (10) _Gun_

Present this item: Ask, WHAT WANT?	Expected response: "Want (item)" (Score)	Present this item: Ask, WHAT WANT?	Expected response: "Want (item)" (Score)	Present this item: Ask, WHAT WANT?	Expected response: "Want (item)" (Score)
(1)	—	(1)	—	(1)	—
(2)	S	(2)	S	(2)	—
(3)	+	(3)	+	(3)	+
(4)	—	(4)	NR	(4)	—
(5)	NR	(5)	—	(5)	+
(6)	+	(6)	S	(6)	+
(7)	+	(7)	+	(7)	+
(8)	S	(8)	+	(8)	—
(9)	S	(9)	S	(9)	+
(10)	—	(10)	S	(10)	+

Score trials as correct (+); incorrect (−); shape (S); or no response (NR)

"want + (label)" Percent Summary for Session

	+	−	S	NR
Score	12	9	7	2
Percent	40	30	23	7

Figure 2. Scoring Form for Step 3.

Note: Use only items that the student really wants for this Step, and make sure to give the item to the student for correct responses. Training on this Step will be difficult and nonfunctional if these two considerations are not met.

Programming for Generalization

When the student has reached criterion performance on the Step, parents and parent surrogates should periodically present the trained items to the student and ask, WHAT WANT? The item and verbal praise are given for correct responses. Additional, nontrained items should be included if the

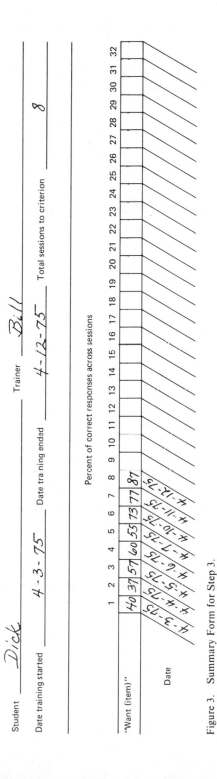

Figure 3. Summary Form for Step 3.

student maintains a high level of performance. Parents and parent surrogates should be particularly sensitive to spontaneous requests by the student that include the newly trained response. Such spontaneous (or self-initiated) requests should be heavily reinforced.

COMMON PROBLEMS AND SPECIAL STRATEGIES

The procedures and instructions for the training steps in the program have been written and developed for the severely handicapped child, regardless of etiology or medical diagnosis. Results and observations to date indicate several common problems. Additionally, some children present idiosyncratic training problems that require special strategies not discussed in the written procedures and instructions.

Common Problems

One of the major concerns of language trainers is poor articulation by the children, especially in the early steps of the sequence. Many trainers fail to recognize that well-articulated speech is not normal in any child's early acquisition of language. Certainly, many severely handicapped children have various degrees of motor impairment of their speech mechanisms, or other physical anomalies that mitigate against speech clarity. Thus, we do not expect (and rarely observe) near perfect articulation among children in the program. Trainers who persist in requiring perfect speech from the children will likely become discouraged, as will their children. However, we do expect that the utterances produced can be understood by persons familiar with the child and, eventually, by most other persons. In aid of this goal, several early steps use programmed imitation procedures to train some of the more difficult utterances required: for example, the question *What is that?* in Step 4 of the program.

Articulation does seem to improve as the child moves through the program, even without additional articulation therapy. Children labeled as autistic usually progress faster to well-articulated speech than children diagnosed as profoundly retarded, and much faster than children diagnosed as cerebral palsied.

A second common problem concerns the use of speech in nontraining environments and with persons unfamiliar to the child. At this point, nothing other than anecdotal reports relevant to this area is available. These reports indicate that, indeed, some children use their newly taught language skills appropriately in nontraining environments but that other children show little if any generalization. Interestingly enough, the question *What's that?* is one of the trained skills that is said to be used appropriately in other environments. In fact, one child made a very nice nuisance of herself by the repeated use of this question to other persons.

Optimal generalization occurred with one boy who, after separate trainings to say *I want (object)* and *I eat (object)*, combined the two in spontaneous requests of the form, *I want eat (object)*. In general, and predictably, requests—*I want (object)*, *I want you (action-with-object)*—are the instances of considerable appropriate generalization. These anecdotes reinforce the control-of-environment logic underlying the design of this training program.

Unfortunately, some children show little use of their new speech in other settings. Currently, we are in the process of assessing some socioecological conditions that support or inhibit generalized language use and of developing practical procedures for achieving generalized speech when it does not occur. Results from these investigations may improve the Programming for Generalization procedures currently included in most steps in the program.

It should be apparent that specific speech and language training for severely handicapped children will require a combination of individual training sessions and generalization programming in other environments. The individual training sessions provide particular language skills and concepts, systematically taught in a structured sequence. For many children, it is not likely that these skills can be trained efficiently in a group setting, nor can the skills be expected to develop alone in even the most stimulating environments. On the other hand, the trained speech skills must be maintained and expanded in environments that set the occasion for, and demand the use of, these skills. This is especially important for children who exhibit little spontaneity in their speech.

Special Strategies

Occasionally, specific procedural changes in the program are required to expedite learning. Typically, these changes are based on idiosyncratic response patterns, and thus do not occur frequently enough to be included as procedural deviations in the training instructions. One specific example was observed with a nine-year-old boy being trained to say *Want (object)* in Step 3. This step requires that 10 items be presented in each training session—items that are highly salient for the child. This boy perseverated with one label: he said "Want pants" for the majority of trials regardless of what item was being presented (and even when the pants were not present). Pants were removed entirely from the list of training items. "Want pants" continued, however, at a high rate. Consequently, a deviation from the instructions was implemented. Only two items (both foods) were presented, instead of the usual 10 items. The child then stopped requesting pants and asked correctly for the two food items presented. A third item was added, then a fourth item, etc., until the desired object-discriminated requesting behavior was firmly established for 10 different items (including pants). This example shows how an ad hoc change in training was successful in eliminating an inappropriate response.

In other cases, only slight procedural changes have been used to bring about acquisition of a particular skill when no progress was being made. In one example, a 10-year-old, profoundly retarded boy was having difficulty in one of the phases of the *yes/no* training in Step 7 of the program. The addition of inflectional voice cues by the trainer to help the boy discriminate when to answer with a *yes* or *no* produced dramatic results in the desired direction. These inflectional cues were subsequently faded out, such that the object stimuli were sufficient for the child to make a correct discrimination with the appropriate *yes/no* response. Other similar inflectional and nonverbal cues have been used successfully to assist a child in making the appropriate discriminated response when acquisition was not occurring. In other cases, changing the training items or even slightly changing the verbal instructions to the child produced similar results.

The use of special strategies that deviate from the written procedures and instructions is usually applied by experienced trainers who know the program well and who have a good grasp of basic behavioral techniques and procedures. Unfortunately, these are the types of behaviors that come with experience and are difficult to include in even the most carefully prepared set of instructions.

RESULTS FROM FIELD TEST EFFORTS

The comprehensive speech and language curriculum has been undergoing extensive field test research with approximately 400 severely handicapped children and adults in classrooms, day-care centers, and institutions in Kansas, Nebraska, and Arkansas. These data, accumulating since 1972, are used to make decisions regarding program refinement. The program has undergone four major revisions since field testing began, the revisions taking two forms: First, modular steps within the 60-step sequence were reordered in sequence, when data confirmed that they provided more success in different positions in the sequence than those in which they were originally placed. Second, a task analysis was conducted on each step that was found to be difficult, relative to other steps in the sequence. These task analyses in turn generated new or revised procedures to meet the objective of the step, and a new module was placed into field test.

For example, some preliminary results of the field test effort were reported in Guess et al. (1976), concerning the sequence of the Persons and Things category (Steps 1–9) as it existed in 1974. These data demonstrated that a substantial savings in trials to criterion accrued across the nine steps. However, the data also revealed that Step 4 was different relative to the other five steps in the block, requiring twice as many training trials to attain criterion as the average of the other eight steps. On the basis of this finding, Step 4 was substantially revised and a new sequence was entered into field testing.

Figure 4 presents the results of the new (1974–1975) sequence, in terms of mean number of sessions required to train the objective of each of the nine steps in the Persons and Things category. Data from 30 students are included in the figure. (Subsequent computer analysis of a larger sample became available too late for this chapter, but did not significantly alter the averages reflected in the figure.) The results again suggest a substantial reduction in training trials across successive steps in the sequence. Step 4 continues to require more trials than the others in the block, but significantly fewer, following revision, than were required to train the step as it was constituted in the 1974 sequence.

These data may be interpreted by the reader as *roughly* predictive of the amount of time required to move a student through the first block of the published curriculum (Guess, Sailor, and Baer, 1976). The ideal training situation, recommended in the teacher's manual, calls for two 15–20-minute sessions per day, one to be administered in the morning and one in the afternoon. Based on the averages from the field test shown in Figure 4, nine weeks can be expected for the nine steps of this block. This average, however, must be considered in terms of the possible variability.

Table 2 presents averages and variabilities for the sample displayed in Figure 4.

An analysis of Table 2 indicates a relative homogeneity of progress in Steps 1–4, but Steps 5, 6, and 9 were subject to extreme variability. The time projection from these data would suggest an expected interval for the nine-step block ranging from five days to completion at the highest extreme, to 222 days at the lowest rate of progress. Because the mean of nine weeks is much closer to the rapid end of this range than the slow end, it may be assumed that progress for the usual student will be less than 15 to 20 weeks.

Figure 5 presents the mean sessions-to-criterion results from the field test on Steps 10–35. These data are preliminary, pending final revision and resequencing of the second and third blocks of training modules.

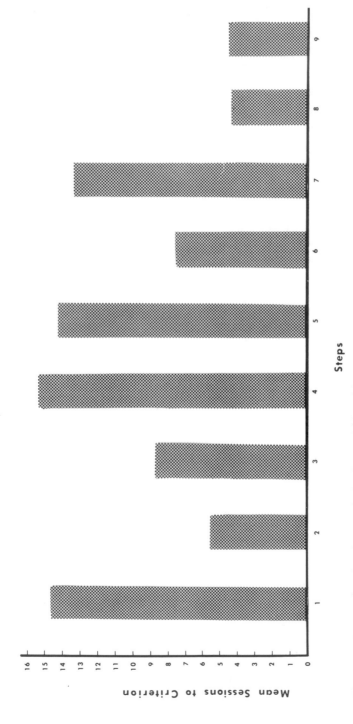

Figure 4.   Mean number of sessions to criterion for acquisition of Steps 1–9.

Table 2.   Array statistics for Steps 1–9 (Persons and Things)

	Steps								
	1	2	3	4	5	6	7	8	9
Mean sessions to criterion	14.52	5.64	8.78	15.39	14.30	7.53	13.28	4.15	4.52
Standard deviation	15.80	5.46	8.86	14.93	24.67	14.36	16.52	3.49	9.44
Range	1–48	1–16	1–33	1–45	1–146	1–79	1–52	1–13	1–13
N	42	37	38	38	33	30	21	20	21

The data again suggest a relative economy in training time accruing across successive steps in the sequence—until Step 31. The last five steps shown in this figure are currently undergoing revision on the basis of these data and additional field testing. The average number of days required to train each step after Step 9 drops from about nine to about five, up to Step 31. Variability around the means of each step is somewhat lower than that of the first nine steps (except for Step 28, which showed a range across 15 students from one session to 102 sessions, respectively).

To summarize, the initial field test indicated a relatively stable performance across the steps comprising the Persons and Things category, with an indication of increased relative difficulty in acquiring Step 4 (self-extended control, *What's that?*) and Step 7 (*yes/no*). The steps that introduce verb usage, Action with Persons and Things (Steps 10–29), progress very smoothly and more rapidly than the introductory sequence, with the exception of increased variability in performance on Step 28 (a combination of *self-extended control* and *integration*).

Figure 5 also indicates that when students come to the sequence on Possession (Steps 30–35), they experience considerable difficulty relative to the section on verb usage. Step 33 in particular is characterized by extreme variability (3–133 sessions) as well as a high mean number of sessions needed to reach criterion (34.28). The Possession sequence is currently undergoing task analysis and revision, the result of which will probably be the addition of some intermediate phases within these steps.

The remaining steps, Color (Steps 36–42), Size (Steps 43–49), and Relation/Location (Steps 50–60), have an insufficient field-test base as of now to merit presentation of summary results in this chapter. The data available suggest that these steps progress similarly to those of Action with Persons and Things, that is, relatively few training sessions are required for each step in the sequence. Apparently, Possession, or the teaching of correct *my/your* usage, is one of the most difficult concepts for the authors to program.

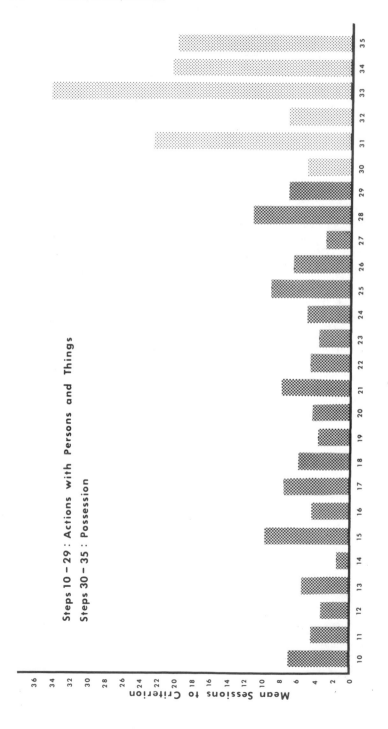

Figure 5.   Mean number of sessions to criterion for Steps 10–35.

Three Case Examples

Three children from the field-test population were selected for the purpose of presenting their progress in some detail. The three examples were not selected at random but rather were chosen because they exemplify quite different cases of severely handicapping conditions. All three were relatively young, institutionalized, severely or profoundly retarded children.

The first child, David, whose progress in language training has been documented extensively in Firling (1976), entered the program at the age of seven with a diagnosis of early childhood autism. He had no speech and demonstrated extremely poor social relations. David did show some receptive language skill at the onset of training, especially in the areas of object recognition and the ability to follow simple commands. He began with a verbal-imitation training sequence. After three months of that training, David was able to articulate words of few syllables (e.g., *apple*) in response to a model by the language trainer. At this point, he was started in the earliest version of the language curriculum.

In Step 1 of the curriculum, David was taught to label common objects, a component of the *reference* dimension of the Persons and Things category. The objects used in his case were *apple, cookie, Coke, milk, car,* and *ball.* (In this step, the child, having learned to verbalize a word in response to the word modeled by the language trainer, now learns to transfer the expression from a verbal stimulus to a visual one: the object that the word represents.) Figure 6 shows David's progress through training on Step 1. After labeling training in Step 1, David was able to identify the same items receptively (Step 2) without training.

David was next taught to exert *control* over his environment by using the newly learned referent labels. He was taught a number of new labels and then trained to respond to the question *What (do you) want?* with *I want (label).* Figure 7 illustrates David's acquisition of the verbal request for one of the trained items, cookie.

As also indicated in Figure 7, a second trainer was used to model correct responses, following a schedule that thinned out in ratio schedules of 2:1, 4:1, and 8:1, that is, the second trainer initially modeled the correct response every time. Once David reached a criterion of 80% correct, the second trainer modeled only every other time, and so forth. It should also be noted that the second trainer initially modeled only *Want (object).* When criterion was reached with this response form, David was then trained to respond with *I want (object).*

Space considerations do not permit a detailed examination of acquisition by David of the subsequent training steps. The reader is referred to Firling (1976) for this material. Figure 8 presents his progress through

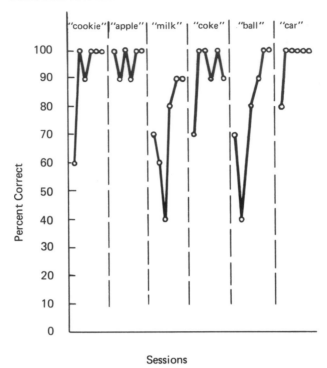

Figure 6.   Progress of David acquiring object labels in the earliest version of the program.

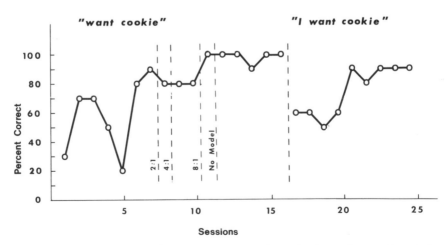

Figure 7.   Progress of David learning to request items in the earliest version of the program.

the 49 steps, expressed as a cumulative curve of the sessions to criterion needed at each step. Figure 8 reveals an effect that was to become an early lesson for the authors in later revisions of the training sequence. David was one of the first children to complete the program as it was initially constructed. At that time, the *yes/no* training procedure was Step 4. David, as the figure shows, required more sessions (and therefore time) to acquire Step 4 than he required for the rest of the training program. Step 4 subsequently was revised, expanded from 4 to 15 phases, and moved to become Step 7 in the current sequence.

At the time of his departure from the institution to a community-based living arrangement, David had completed 49 of the 60 steps in the total curriculum. He also had made remarkable progress in areas other than those taught to him directly through the speech and language curriculum. He now reads orally, as well as talks conversationally. He answers questions with detail and requests things he wants and needs. His

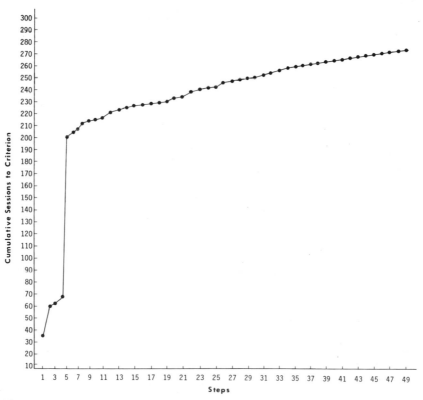

Figure 8.   David's cumulative progress, showing number of sessions to criterion for each of 49 steps.

only real communication deficit is in articulation, and he is undergoing speech therapy to improve this skill, in conjunction with his school activities (he now attends a special class every day).

The second child, Joe, was also an institutionalized profoundly retarded youngster of 11 at the time he began the program. He was diagnosed as a case of mild cerebral palsy. He had some speech at the onset of the program, consisting mainly of single words accompanied by appropriate gestures. Joe was imitative prior to training and thus was placed in the program at Step 1.

Figure 9 presents data illustrating his cumulative acquisition of Steps 1–32, in terms of the number of sessions needed to reach criterion for each step. With the exception of several of the *self-extended control* and *integration* steps within the sequential blocks, Joe progressed smoothly through the first 32 steps and is continuing to progress through the remaining steps at about the same rate. Like David, Joe will require articulation therapy.

The third child was an 11-year-old, Susie, who also resided at a large state institution for the retarded when she began the program. At

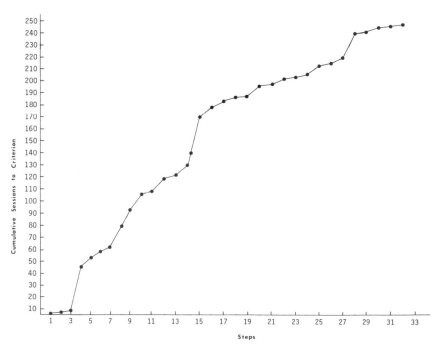

Figure 9.   Joe's cumulative progress, showing number of sessions to criterion for each of 32 steps.

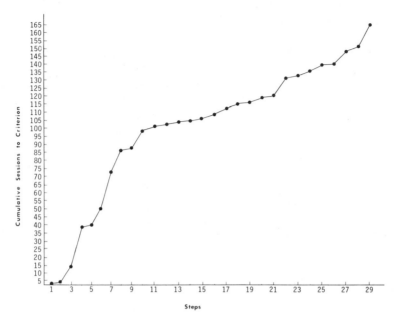

Figure 10.   Susie's cumulative progress, showing number of sessions to criterion for each of 29 steps.

that time, she had a fairly extensive repertoire of receptive communication skills. Susie was in vocal imitation training for about three months before entering Step 1. Imitation training was conducted primarily to improve Susie's very poor articulation.

Figure 10 presents Susie's progress through the first 29 steps of the curriculum, in terms of the number of sessions needed to reach criterion for each step. Again, the figure shows a relatively smooth acquisition curve, with the usual stumbling block at Step 4. As with David and Joe, the Action with Persons and Things category (Steps 10–29) was achieved easily, relative to the initial Persons and Things sequence (Steps 1–9). Under ideal training conditions, Susie would have completed these two blocks in 17 weeks of training at the rate displayed in the figure, but Susie returned to her home at the end of Step 29 and was enrolled in a community-based special education class, partly on the strength of her new language skills. Her improvement in speech and language skills at that time was impressive. At the termination of her program's training, Susie spoke in appropriate phrases and short sentences. Her articulation showed steady improvement, and she engaged in spontaneous and meaningful conversational speech.

Extensions of the Curriculum and Future Developments

For some children, the absence of certain prerequisite skills and other severe physically impairing conditions are such that the development of oral speech is unlikely under any training conditions. The time consumed in training speech skills (i.e., articulatory control and accuracy, respiratory control, voice pitch and quality) for these children is so prohibitive that certain other nonspeech forms of communication must be considered as alternatives.

Still other children have no specific or severe motor impairment in their diagnosis and yet show expressive speech skills that lag far behind their understanding levels. Extensive articulation training may produce only modest results among these children. They continue to be only minimally imitative and display but a few sounds and syllables in their spontaneous vocalizations. A few have highly stereotyped intonation patterns in their speech, indicating that they are using some system of rules in their efforts to communicate. However, the exact rules or system cannot be determined because of unintelligibility.

Obviously methods to develop communication and facilitate speech acquisition are needed for these children. Other chapters in this book discuss nonspeech forms of communication, including the use of symbol systems for teaching basic syntax. Thus, this section is limited to a description of pilot work to modify the program for use with communication boards. Lois Waldo, Speech Pathologist at Kansas Neurological Institute, has been primarily responsible for adapting the program for use with communication boards.

Apparatus and Materials   The communication boards used in training consist of 18″ × 24″ paint canvases placed inside an envelope of clear heavy plastic. For wheelchair-bound students, the boards are placed on their lap trays. For ambulatory students, several boards are placed in critical areas of the living environment.

Noun symbols used for the individual steps in the program consist of black, felt-tipped outline drawings on white cards. The verbs and *yes/no* symbols were selected from the *Peabody Rebus Reading Program* (Woodcock and Clark, 1969). The remaining symbols have been drawn to meet specific needs of the students and to correspond to material in the oral speech version of the curriculum. Regardless of where the students begin in the program, their initial training is conducted with 3″ × 5″ symbol cards. As the student's pointing behavior is refined, the cards are reduced to 1″ × 1″ in size. With the exception of one of the symbol cards, each card represents one word. To communicate with a multiword response, the student must point to more than one symbol card. The exception, discussed later, is the symbol for "no card." The symbols are placed on the board only as needed in training. Once the symbol is used in training, it remains on the board in the same approximate location.

Adaptation of the Oral Speech Program to Communication Boards

Attempts to adapt the first nine steps (Persons and Things) of the program are still in development. Some changes have been made in most of the steps, and procedures for adapting the three steps (4, 5, and 6) that involve question asking have yet to be worked out.

In Step 1 (Labeling), the only change required was that of response definition. The following definitions are used to record responses:

Correct Response.   Student points to the symbol card representing the object label requested.

Incorrect Response.   Student points to more than one card, points to the object, points to an incorrect symbol, touches the board but not on the symbol, or resists a prompt.

No Response.   Student does not point within a 10-second period.

Shaped Response.   Student requires additional cues or prompts to complete an accurate point.

Instructions were added for this step (as well as other steps), describing where the symbol cards were displayed on the communication board.

Step 2 (Object Recognition) required no changes because the communication board (i.e., the expressive mode of communication) is not required in the response, and the student is instructed to point directly to the objects rather than their symbol representations.

Step 3 (Requesting Objects) has required only that the response mode be changed. In responding, the student points first to the symbol for *want,* and then to the picture symbol for the object desired. As is true for the oral speech-training procedures for this step, it is most important that symbols be used to represent objects that the student actually does want, rather than objects selected by convenience.

Step 4 (Asking *What's that?*), Step 5 (Acquiring New Object Labels), and Step 6 (Memory for New Object Labels) have been omitted from the communication board sequence because each of these steps includes a question-asking response. Perhaps the procedural problems associated with this type of response can be worked out, so that this important self-extending communication skill can be taught. In the meantime, it was important to teach the students that they could not respond to every stimulus in their environment with the few symbols available on their boards. Therefore, a training step was included in the program to teach students to reply "no card" when confronted with items that they did not have available as a label symbol. The symbol used to present "no card" is an outlined square with a red slash through it, placed in the upper left-hand border of the communication board. This added training step helps prepare the student for the *yes/no* training in Step 7.

Step 7 (*yes/no*) is done exactly as written in the oral program, except for the response mode. The symbols for *yes* and *no* are again taken from the Peabody Rebus Reading Program.

Procedural changes for Steps 8 and 9 have yet to be developed because, at this early phase, no students have advanced beyond Step 7. The adaptation of the program for Steps 8 and 9 should be easy because only the pronoun *I* is added (in Step 8) to the already established *want* (*object*) skill taught in Step 3; and Step 9 merely combines labeling and requesting in a two-response chain.

Preliminary Evaluation and Observations

Progress of six children currently in the adapted program has been steady and rapid. These children had few functional speech and communication skills before training. The fact that they can now request objects and materials of importance to them is most gratifying. Nonvocal communication is being established at a rate that must be much faster than would be possible with oral speech, considering the history of failure of these children in oral speech training. Even those children who were not pointing well in initial training are improving in response topography. Developing a good pointing response has taken considerably less time than prior attempts to teach vocal imitation or articulation.

There are numerous problems. Methods of making the communication boards more portable for ambulatory children are needed, and there are children with such severe motor impairments that a board display using the number of symbols required in the present method is not realistic. Thus, a system of coding the board for as few separate response areas as possible needs to be developed.

Other Extensions of the Program

At present, a program is also underway to adapt the program for use with a Signing Exact English system. In this extension, signing is used to convey the context of the program taught in the 60-step sequence. This adaptation of the program is being used with students who have a significant hearing loss, and yet who have the physical dexterity to produce signs. Galen Berry, Speech Pathologist/Audiologist at Kansas Neurological Institute, is adapting the program to the Signing Exact English system. Thus, in the future, the program should be available for teaching oral speech to children capable of communicating in these response modes. At some point, the program may also be adapted for children with other severe impairments in both sensory input and expressive output systems. This will likely involve adaptation of the program to include a three-dimensional symbol system, such that the tactual modality can be used for stimulus input, and a simplified motor response can be used for response output. The three-dimensional symbol system discussed by Hollis (Chapter 2) has obvious advantages.

In addition to further adapting the program for use with multiply handicapped children not capable of oral speech, further consideration must be given to assessing children more accurately, so that the most functional communication mode (both input and output) can be identified at an early age. Further research is needed to evaluate whether teaching the program first in the nonspeech mode accelerates later acquisition in the oral speech mode, for children capable of speech.

SUMMARY AND CONCLUSION

This chapter began with a discussion of *remedial* versus *developmental* logic as the basis for structuring a language-development curriculum for severely handicapped children and other speech-deficient persons. Developmental logic, it was pointed out, assumes that language-deficient persons should be taught speech and language in the same sequence, so far as that sequence is ascertainable, as that which characterizes normal infant language development. Remedial logic, on the other hand, seeks to capitalize on deficient persons' immediate environments and their most urgent survival and coping needs as the basis of initial language intervention. That logic stresses the power of language to build itself through instruction in self-generative elements of the linguistic process. It was pointed out that many more similarities exist across the two logical systems than differences, and that eventually psycholinguistics research may present evidence that normal development parallels the functional system that characterizes the remedial logic in acquisition.

A particular language-development curriculum, which uses remedial logic as a basis for language intervention, was presented in some detail (Guess, Sailor, and Baer, 1976). The program was presented as a conceptual framework with examples of several of the actual "steps" or modular, sequential training components. Present changes in instructional tactics since earlier publication of the curriculum framework (e.g., Guess, Sailor, and Baer, 1974; Sailor, Guess, and Baer, 1973) were discussed in detail as were tactics for teaching vocal imitation as a prerequisite skill to entry into the 60-step functional speech and language sequence. Particular stress was put on the issues of response selectivity, response functionality, and response-specific reinforcement tactics as new developments in language intervention. The results of some recent research efforts into these issues were presented briefly.

Special problems in language training were discussed from the framework of the curriculum presented, with special attention given to the teaching of generalization, or the extension of language usage from the training laboratory, or classroom, to the environment at large. Some attention was given to the need for special strategies or procedural changes needed to accommodate to the particular handicapping conditions or deficiencies that characterize some students.

Some early field test results were presented in summary form from the computer data bank of about 400 language-deficient persons currently undergoing the field test research effort. Three case examples were presented in brief form to illustrate progress in acquisition as a function of training time.

Finally, the chapter presented a series of new developments in program extension into the area of nonspeech linguistic development. A particular adaptation of the Guess, Sailor, and Baer (1976) curriculum to communication boards was presented, with a brief discussion of adaptation of the sequence to an English signing system.

It is hoped that the material presented in this chapter will be taken as a stimulus to research and further program development by those researchers committed to the remediation of language deficits in handicapped persons. The authors in no way wish to imply that they have developed the final solution to language training. In fact, the surface of the problem has only been scratched. Although many language-deficient children and adults will succeed in attaining a measure of functional speech and receptive language by careful implementation of the sequence outlined in this chapter, many will fail. This chapter is dedicated to those failures, in the hope that material presented here and elsewhere will help others who will make the breakthroughs needed for the truly successful language-instruction effort of the future.

REFERENCES

Baer, D. M., Peterson, R., and Sherman, J. 1967. The development of imitation by reinforcing behavioral similarity to a model. J. Exp. Anal. Behav. 10:405–416.

Bricker, D., Dennison, L., and Bricker, W. A. 1975. Constructive interaction-adaptation approach to language training. MCCD Monograph Series No. 1. Mailman Center for Child Development, University of Miami, Miami.

Carpenter, J. 1975. An experimental comparison of acquisition rates of motor imitation items with and without manipulable consequences in a group setting. Unpublished paper, Kansas Neurological Institute, Topeka.

Chomsky, N. 1959. Review of Verbal Behavior by B. F. Skinner. Language 35:26–58.

Firling, J. 1976. Functional language for a severely handicapped child: A case study. AAESPH Rev. 1:53–74.

Guess, D., and Baer, D. M. 1973. Some experimental analyses of linguistic development in institutionalized retarded children. In B. Lahey (ed.), The Modification of Language Behavior, pp. 3–60. Charles C Thomas, Springfield, Ill.

Guess, D., Sailor, W., and Baer, D. M. 1974. To teach language to retarded children. In R. L. Schiefelbusch and L. Lloyd (eds.), Language Perspectives— Acquisition, Retardation, and Intervention, pp. 529–563. University Park Press, Baltimore.

Guess, D., Sailor, W., and Baer, D. M. 1976. Functional Speech and Language Training for the Severely Handicapped, Part I: Persons and Things. H & H Enterprises, Lawrence, Kan.

Guess, D., Sailor, W., and Baer, D. M. 1976. Functional Speech and Language Training for the Severely Handicapped, Part II: Actions with Persons and Things. H & H Enterprises, Lawrence, Kan.

Guess, D., Sailor, W., Keogh, W., and Baer, D. M. 1976. Language development programs for severely handicapped children. In N. Haring and L. Brown (eds.), Teaching the Severely Handicapped (Vol. 1). Grune & Stratton, New York.

Itard, J. M. G. 1962. The Wild Boy of Aveyron. Appleton-Century-Crofts, New York.

Lovaas, O. I., Berberich, J. P., Perloff, B. F., and Schaeffer, B. 1966. Acquisition of imitative speech by schizophrenic children. Science 151:705–707.

Sailor, W., Guess, D., and Baer, D. M. 1973. An experimental program for teaching functional language to verbally deficient children. Ment. Retard. 11:27–35.

Sailor, W., and Mix, B. J. 1975. TARC Assessment System. H & H Enterprises, Lawrence, Kans.

Saunders, R. R., Sailor, W. S., and Taylor, C. 1976. An experimental analysis of three strategies of reinforcement on two-choice discrimination learning problems with retarded children. Unpublished paper, Kansas Neurological Institute, Topeka.

Skinner, B. F. 1957. Verbal Behavior. Appleton-Century-Crofts, New York.

Sloane, H. N., Johnston, M. K., and Harris, F. R. 1968. Remedial procedures for teaching verbal behavior to speech deficient or defective young children. In H. N. Sloane and B. MacAuley (eds.), Operant Procedures in Remedial Speech and Language Training, pp. 77–101. Houghton Mifflin Co., Boston.

Woodcock, R., and Clark, C. 1969. Introducing Reading-Book Three, Peabody Rebus Reading Program. American Guidance Service, Circle Pines, Minn.

chapter 4

Grammatical Training for the Language-Delayed Child

A New Perspective

Carol Lynn Waryas

Department of Communicative Disorders
University of Mississippi
University, Mississippi

Kathleen Stremel-Campbell

Parsons Research Center
Parsons State Hospital
and Training Center
Parsons, Kansas

contents

THEORETICAL APPROACHES TO LANGUAGE DEVELOPMENT

The problem faced by the language-delayed child is developing skills necessary to become a full-fledged speaker of his[1] language. As Ervin-Tripp has stated (cited in Slobin, 1967):

> To qualify as a native speaker . . . one must learn . . . rules . . . This is to say, of course, that one must learn to behave *as though one knew the rules* (p. x).

Thus, the problem faced by the language interventionist is one of deciding what form the rules of language should take and what procedures to follow in order to bring the language-delayed child's language behavior into accord with the rules. There have been many diverse and conflicting inputs into the language intervention process, each with its own notions about the nature of the language system, the processes by which it is acquired, the psychological reality of linguistic constructs, and procedures for describing the language system in relationship to the totality of behavior. These competing approaches, their commonalities and differences, have been analyzed by Houston (1971) and Reber (1973). It is important for the applied language practitioner to recognize that all language intervention procedures partake of theoretical biases, either explicitly or implicitly. In other words, when a decision is made to adopt one training procedure, the practitioner is also making a judgment about its theoretical principles. It is important then to reexamine certain factors concerning the nature of the communication process and the language system—its primary transmission medium, the study of the acquisition of language and related analysis procedures, and the inter-relationship of the language-delayed child and the therapy process. This helps provide a framework against which to compare competing theoretical approaches. This does not mean that a language therapist must possess expertise in all areas of language research and theory to be effective. But it does mean familiarity with these areas is necessary for the therapist to make good judgments about the efficacy of different approaches in achieving specific goals, the possibility of integrating different procedures into a unified approach to training, and a rationale for language intervention procedures that will improve the communication ability of the language-delayed child.

Primary focus is placed on the needs of the child who demonstrates some rudimentary communication skills but who lacks appropriate linguistic forms for reception and expression. Programs for children with

---

This work was supported by Grants HD-00870, HD-2528, NS-11601, and OEC-0-74-7991, to the Bureau of Child Research, University of Kansas.

[1] Masculine pronouns are used throughout for the sake of grammatical uniformity and simplicity. They are not meant to be preferential or disciminatory.

no communication skills and for those with fairly elaborate language are presented elsewhere in this volume.

This is an analysis of one approach to ameliorating language deficiency by considering its theoretical bases, as discussed above, by relating it to certain current advances in the theoretical disciplines of language and behavioral analysis, and by suggesting how the language practitioner can utilize this approach in clinical research. The importance of clinical research cannot be overstressed, because the problem of changing language behaviors is not answered by this approach alone, or by any other single approach. In this regard, the language practitioner cannot rely solely upon the theoretical fields for answers, but must choose and integrate innovations into approaches that are then tried, evaluated, and restructured. In this sense, the language therapist is the researcher and the therapy setting is the laboratory.

Grammatical Structure in Perspective

In the past decade many training programs for the language-delayed child have emerged that rely heavily on advances in developmental psycholinguistics for their theoretical rationale. The rapidly changing state of this field has made many practitioners feel as if they were chasing a will-o'-the-wisp. Before a new development in the theoretical field can be incorporated into applied procedures, it has often been rejected, at least in part. This has led many applied investigators to despair of being able to keep pace with advances or to understand where the field is going. This period has been one of rapid reorientation in perspective, witnessing a radical departure from the previously accepted "structural" approach to language and its development, through the "semantic revolution," to the cognitive-pragmatic approach to language. The models should be examined in light of the requirements Ingram (1971) specifies for models:

> The model must be relatively *stable* and it must have a degree of *plausibility*. Further, in interdisciplinary fields it must be seen to be *relevant* and it must be *compatible* with the basic assumptions the user makes about his own field (p. 147).

In light of the theoretical developments discussed above, in particular the move away from a structural approach to the study of language development, it may seem somewhat quixotic for the authors to now stress the importance of the development of grammar as a central focus of language training, yet this is our thesis. We propose that the role of grammatical development in language training needs to be reexamined in light of the foregoing discussion of the semantic and pragmatic components of language, but *reemphasized* as a result of this, rather than relegated to the limbo of outmoded approaches. We are suggesting, in other words, that procedures and objectives in language training—the goal of teaching the child to "behave as if he knew the rules"—should be able to assimilate and accommodate new information without being lost in the process.

As Maratsos (1975) has said:

> Recent work in early grammatical acquisition has tended to emphasize the cognitive and semantic base of language structure. This development has been a healthy one that has rendered more comprehensible the facts of early acquisition. But on the other hand, there has perhaps been an accompanying tendency to dilute or forget the importance of *the acquisition of structural devices per se* (p. 92, italics added).

Bever (1970) has also suggested that we:

> ... expand our horizons beyond the treatment of syntax to more inclusive treatments of language behaviour. However, we must tread carefully lest our enthusiasm to describe all available "facts" about language leads us into the same kind of behaviourist swamp that engulfed the last structuralist period between 1920 and 1950. We can avoid this danger and bring the study of language into line with other areas of behavioral science if we recognize that language behaviour is itself a function of a variety of interacting systems, none of which is logically prior in its influence on language behaviour (p. 169).

It is our contention that the structure of language remains a valid concern particularly for the language therapist and that the structural approach need not be viewed negatively, because its importance is not diluted but only reconceptualized by current advances in the field. As Lyons (1969) emphasized:

> ... structuralism (to use the label which is commonly applied, often pejoratively) ... means that each language is regarded as a *system of relations* (more precisely, a set of interrelated systems), the elements of which—sounds, words, etc.—have no validity independently of the relations of equivalence and contrast which hold between them (p. 50).

It is suggested that the revolutions and counter-revolutions in the field, the apparent incompatibility of new formulations with old, and the formulation, rejection, and subsequent reexamination of old concepts are natural in the development of the study of language as a scientific endeavor (Kuhn, 1962) and should not dismay the applied researcher. It may be that we shall find that, after an analysis of grammatical structure in relationship to theoretical advances in the field, we shall return to where we began but with a new perspective on the original issue.

In this chapter, a reanalysis of the role of grammatical structure in language development is presented in light of current advances in the domains of semantics and pragmatics. In the process, these advances are related to a language-training program previously described by the authors (Stremel and Waryas, 1974) not for the purpose of providing an indepth description of the program itself but rather to provide the practitioner with a vantage point to evaluate these theoretical formulations.

Structure in the Syntactic Approach

The syntactic approach to children's language development, occasioned primarily by Chomsky's (1957, 1965) syntactic theory, is apparent in the work of Braine (1963), Menyuk (1963), Brown and Fraser (1964), Miller and Ervin (1964), and McNeill (1966, 1971). According to most formulations, the child is engaged in active construction of a system of syntactic rules that capture the regularities he perceives in the speech he hears, as represented in a form analogous to that of a transformational grammar.

The problem with this approach, which ultimately led to revisions in it, was that it allied itself too closely with the formulations of the transformational grammar theory of language. While it is true that this theory has made extensive contributions to the study of language, it also possessed two fatal flaws for the study of language development. First and foremost perhaps was Chomsky's (1957) statement that grammar is "autonomous of meaning" (p. 17). Second, because the model of language posits abstract or deep structures that are never evident in surface forms, it was suggested that the child comes somehow "prewired" for these structures. The result of these two factors was to inspire the nativist-empiricist battle over the nature of language development (in addition, increasing the division between behaviorists and psycholinguists) and to rule out, not only the role of experience in language development, but also the role of meaning in language use. The absurdity of this position is seen in its most extreme form, which would analyze a child's utterance such as *I want milk* into a subject-verb-object structure, which just incidentally happened to be lexicalized with the items *want, milk,* and *I.* As Schlesinger (1971) stated,

> . . . it is not very plausible that the child should learn to produce empty structures which he subsequently stuffs with meanings (p. 85).

Moreover, it should be noted that in the strongest formulation of the nativist's position the role of experiential learning, particularly the possibility of language intervention procedures, was ruled out. Morton (1970) has severely criticized the concept of these language-specific innate structures. Moreover, Luria (1974/1975) has discussed the "philosophical dead end" in the development of linguistic theory, which has resulted from this stance.

Brown (1973) has addressed the problem of the relationship between generative grammatical models and models of actual language behavior.

He suggests that, although grammatical models are not adequate models of behavior, the fact that they attempt to formalize the knowledge that a speaker/listener must possess implies that they have a psychological goal. The problem confronted by those who approach grammatical formulations from the position of psychological investigations is: Which of the myriad of competing formulations of the structure of language should be adopted? Brown suggests:

> The way we live with this situation is by noticing that there is a good deal of substance of English grammar that seems to endure through all these disputes, and indeed was partly known before the invention of generative transformational grammars (p. 406, italics added).

Before rejecting the syntactic approach, therefore, it is important to consider some of the important contributions to the study of child language that it occasioned: It is a nontrivial fact that communication in the form of language is lawful. The primary contribution of this theory is that it deals in a precise (if somewhat narrow) way with the regularities of syntax, suggesting that there are relationships that obtain between sentence types, which can be specified by the operation of rules that change word order, combine structures, or add or delete words or structures. These syntactic rules, being relatively unaffected by meaning, permit languages to express an infinite variety of semantic relationships with a limited set of structural operations (Bowerman, cited in Bloom, Lightbown, and Hood, 1975). Thus, it is these rules that permit projection from a finite set of structures into an infinite set of sentences.

As has often been emphasized, the existence of these regularities does not require that the speaker/listener be aware of them for his behavior to correspond to them, any more than one must be aware of the principles of behavioral theory in order to behave in accord with them.

The search for evidence of these rules in children's language led to the discovery that children's syntactic development is also lawful, not merely a random approximation of adult forms or the rote imitation of adult forms with modifications imposed by performance limitations such as memory. Slobin (1965) has suggested three tests for the child's possession of a rule system: production that is regular, extension of regularities (generalizations), and the ability to detect deviations from regularity in both his own speech and the speech of others. The syntactic regularities in children's speech correspond in many respects to the grammatical organization proposed by utterances that can be described by transformational grammar. For example, rules for the formation of syntactic structures appear earlier than those for which it would be necessary to posit transformational rules (Brown and Fraser, 1964; Klima and Bellugi, 1966; Brown 1968). The discovery of these regularities has led to an awareness that certain "errors" in children's speech can be accounted for by the inappropriate operation or overgeneralization of these rules, or "error by analogy" (Ervin, 1964). For example, the development of the rule for forming the regular past tense of verbs may temporarily cause the loss of previously existing correct irregular forms. These regularities have been formalized into a developmental sequence of the emergence of syntactic structures, which have formed the basis for new approaches to the study of the nature of language disorders and language delay. In particular, the notion of hierarchical development of constituents has proved important because it defines how single words can be expanded sequentially into phrases. This developmental sequence provides a series of discrete training goals on the path to full language structure for the language-delayed child and has largely supplanted previously existing patchwork approaches to language training that attempted to teach grammatical classes without regard to syntactic development in the vain hope that they would somehow coalesce into language structures.

The theory of transformational grammar is a method of analysis, and as such is valuable insofar as it produces insights into the nature of the system to which it is applied. In this regard, theories are like grids that may be applied to our primary data, revealing one or another parameter of the data for one or another purpose. Bruner (1974/1975) has discussed the relationship between grammatical theories and the study of children's language development:

> ... to master a language a child must acquire a complex set of broadly transferable or generative skills—perceptual, motor, conceptual, social, and linguistic—which when appropriately coordinated yield linguistic performances that can be described (though only in a limited sense) by the linguist's rules of grammar. Such rules of grammar may bear no closer resemblance to the psychological laws of language production, comprehension, and use than do the principles of optics bear to the laws of visual perception—in neither case can the one violate the other (p. 256).

What Bruner implies is that grammar can only explain specific linguistic aspects of language. It cannot explain the socioaffective, sensorimotor, perceptual, and cognitive skills, which are only partly subsumed by language. Although it appears to fail the test as a theory of language development, the transformational grammar approach is useful as a descriptive device in terms of the structure of language. Moreover, the research on language that has resulted from it, both attempting to prove and disprove it, gives evidence of its utility at least as an impetus to further work. Regardless of whether or not syntactic operations are the force behind language development and use, the fact remains that syntactic operations must be developed if one is to use language appropriately.

Structure in the Semantic Approach

The so-called "semantic revolution" in the study of children's language development, evident in the work of Bloom (1970), Bowerman (1973a, 1973b), Brown (1973), and Schlesinger (1971, 1974), among others, is based on the inadequacy of former approaches to the role of meaning in language. Discussing them, Edwards (1973) said that syntactically based approaches imply that the child in the process of communicating is not attempting to convey messages but rather to structure words to be syntactic. He suggests that one should instead consider how syntax serves the expression of meaning. Thus, syntax should be seen as merely the form and not the function of language.

Bloom (1970, 1974) and Brown (1973) have done extensive analysis of children's development of semantic structures. According to Bloom, children's early language structures result from the interaction of the child's developing cognitive-perceptual organization and his linguistic and nonlinguistic experiences. Children's language should be analyzed not from the point of view of the syntactic structures expressed but rather for the semantic relationships in these early utterances. In this formulation, "Grammar-recognition learning involves recognizing relations between order or function patterns and properties of meaning" (Ervin-Tripp, 1973, p. 275). Schlesinger (1971) stated that ". . . word order is imposed on the utterances as a result of the speaker expressing his intentions, but it is not a part of these intentions" (p. 66). MacNamara (1972) has suggested that meaning serves the function of providing the vehicle for the child's acquisition of syntactic structure. He suggests that ". . . the infant uses meaning as a clue to language, rather than language as a clue to meaning" (p. 1).

Lyons (1966) stated that by the age of 18 months the child already possesses the concepts of "things," "properties," and "situations." These concepts he feels are sufficient to provide the child with language concepts such as "subject-predicate" if he is presented with sufficient "primary linguistic data" (p. 131). These statements reflect the notion that language "maps" the child's conceptualization of his world. It is apparent that this formulation of the child's developing language, emphasizing as it does the central role of semantic intent in the formulation of language structures, seems more logical and compelling than the construction of semantically empty syntactic structures. Brown (1973) has suggested some generalizations concerning the interrelationship of semantic and syntactic development—primarily that the progress of language acquisition will be found to be approximately the same in the development of grammar (syntax) and semantics within a given language, and, more abstractly viewed, across all languages. He suggests that the primary determinants of acquisition are "cumulative semantic and syntactic complexity," that is, the order in which structures are acquired will be related to the complexity of the semantic intent expressed and the syntactic form that it requires for expression. Thus, structures such as relative clauses would be predictably late because they require the conjoining of semantic structures and of syntactic forms. This idea was apparent in an early statement by Guillaume (1973):

> ... one has to take account of the material meaning of the words and of their functions (word order, inflections, particular grammatical devices). Difficulties arise from the inseparable nature of form and content (p. 522).

Brown has suggested that, after semantic concepts are acquired, the course of language development takes the form of learning to more adequately express what is intended (by the acquisition of grammar) so that it can be comprehended by a larger audience. It is obvious that utterances such as Bloom's (1970) example of *Mommy sock* indicate the semantic richness of children's early speech, because it is used to express a variety of meanings. It is potentially the existence of these multiple readings that leads the child to acquire grammatical rules to disambiguate them for his listener and achieve more adequate communication. Brown (1973) also suggests that the child does not possess all possible meanings before he acquires grammar and the fact that the language can express certain meanings leads him to later acquire them.

This view would suggest that abstract syntax, in the sense proposed by the syntactic approach, is not the structure that is acquired directly, but in the process of developing the semantic function of language, syntactic forms used to express them become abstract. This fact was suggested by Paul in 1891 (cited in Derwing, 1973):

> In the process of naturally mastering one's mother-tongue no rule, as such, is given, but only a number of examples. We hear gradually a number of sentences which are connected together in the same way, and which hence associate themselves together into one group. The recollection of the special contents of the single sentences may grow less and less distinct in the process; the common element is always strengthened anew by repetition, and it thus comes about that *the rule is unconsciously abstracted from the examples* (1891, pp. 98–99; italics added by Derwing).

This point was amplified by Bever (1970), who suggested that, as the child extends his mastery of perceptual and productive skills, he is attending to an increasingly wider range of sentences, which causes his organizational (grammatical) schemata to become more abstract in order to deal with them.

Miller and Ojemann McKean (1964) observed that,

> . . . in most general terms, linguistic rules are social conventions of the form "when the same situation occurs again, do the same thing." Such statements would be meaningless, of course, if we could not recognize a new situation as similar to an old one, or if we did not know what it meant to do the same things. Each rule must be supported by a system of recognizable similarities and differences (p. 298).

This new view of linguistic rules obviates the need for positing deep structures and suggests that they directly reflect regularities in behavior. As Derwing (1973) suggested:

> We are talking about a notion of linguistic rules which can be directly "elicited from surface structures" (Schlesinger, 1967, p. 399), hence one which does not put unreasonable demands upon the language learner: all that is required to learn rules of this sort are general capacities which human beings possess: power to discriminate, to generalize and, most important, to extract regularity from the environment (p. 310).

Schlesinger (1971) suggests that semantic intents are formalized as *input markers*, which become outputs through the operation of *realization rules*. Schlesinger (1971) suggests that the child learns relationships such as subject-object separately for the enormous number of sentences that could express this relationship. Rather, the child must acquire certain generalizations to capture the regularities that all such sentences exhibit. This concurs with McCawley's (1968) formulation of a grammar, which consists, according to Olson (1970), of a "formation-rule component" that specifies the semantic representations or intended referents and a "transformational component" that relates these semantic representations to the surface structure (p. 272). The importance of syntactic structure in semantically based approaches has been emphasized by Bloom, Lightbown, and Hood (1975), who demonstrated that form and function may be semiautonomous. They stated:

> . . . [the] ability to say sentences depends upon the child's learning something of an abstract system of semantic-syntactic structure, a grammar, for representing linguistically what he already knows about events in the world (p. 2).

Thus, semantically based approaches to language development must also incorporate the concept of structure, and syntactic approaches must incorporate considerations of meaning. It is as if semantic approaches can no more obviate the role of grammar than transformational grammar could eradicate the role of meaning. Even language intervention programs based on the semantic model (MacDonald and Blott, 1974; Miller and Yoder, 1974) must utilize structural concepts in some fashion. It is apparent that (to paraphrase Halliday, 1975) we must teach a child "how to mean" through the structure forming properties of language.

Structure in the Pragmatic Approach

The most recent innovation in language study has been a rediscovery and reanalysis of the communicative or pragmatic functions of language. According to Halliday (1970), adult language consists of three components: the *ideational*, serving to express the speaker's perception of the world and his own experiences; the *interpersonal*, serving to establish social relationships and to maintain them; and the *textual*, serving to relate language to itself and to the context of use (Halliday, 1975). He suggests that the interpersonal and ideational components are: ". . . mapped onto each other by the structure-forming agency of grammar" (p. 240). He suggests that in learning language, the child uses it for two purposes, for learning and for influencing other behaviors so that needs may be satisfied. Both purposes generate new meanings, which require the addition of new lexical items and new structures. Halliday (1975) conducted an intensive study of one subject, from the age of 9–24 months, which provides us with a description of the developing functions of a child's language. During the initial period (up to the age of 16½ months), four communicative functions were demonstrated by the child, even though words had not yet developed. These were defined as the *instrumental*, serving to satisfy material needs; the *regulatory*, serving to influence others' behavior; the *interactional*, serving to effect the establishment and maintenance of social relations; and the *personal* function, serving as a vehicle of individual expression. In the next month and a half, three more functions emerged in this order: the *heuristic*, serving to obtain information; the *imaginative,* serving to provide make-believe play; and the *informative*, serving to transmit information. During this stage, lexical items were used to express functions, and rudimentary grammatical structures were emerging, the existence of which, according to Halliday, makes it possible to mean more than one thing at a time. Toward the end of this period, the child developed dialogue ability, loosely defined as the adoption and assignment of social roles, as indicated by the ability to respond to Wh-questions, commands, statements, and responses themselves. By the third period, the child had learned "*how* to mean," in Halliday's words, although he had just begun to learn the adult language. He had demonstrated the two general functions of language (which subsume the specific functions listed above): the *ideational*, which arises from the use of language to learn, and the *interpersonal*, which arises from the use of language to act. Schmidt (1974) has extended Halliday's functional model to the speech of a 30-month-old child. He suggests that a much richer functional system exists for the older child as indicated by the verbal control exerted by the child. Moreover, he suggests that there is an important although not complete correlation between functional and structural parameters of language.

Bruner (1975) discusses linguistic concepts as being initially realized in action, specifically, in joint activity and joint attention. He presents a modification of Bowerman's (1973a) analysis of early Stage I semantic relations, demonstrating that the child's initial language is related to action being carried out jointly by himself and another. He suggests:

> It is the infant's success in achieving joint action (or the mother's success, for that matter) that virtually leads him into the language (Bruner, 1975, p. 6).

Viewed in this light, the child's expression of the semantic relations that involve the categories of agent, action, object, and possession is representative of his attempts to establish or to comment on joint action. Attempts to establish joint attention are reflected in the use of demonstrative marking, nonexistence, greeting, location, and feature marking.

Dore (1974) has used the theory of *speech acts* (Searle, 1969), which distinguishes two parts of its utterance—its *proposition* (or information content) and its *illocutionary force* (which specifies how the speaker intends the utterance to be taken by a listener)—in analyzing the early stages of language development. He suggests that the primary motivation for language acquisition is the development of these pragmatic functions of language. He proposed the primitive speech act (single-word utterances) as the unit for studying the pragmatics of early child language. Dore defined a primitive speech act as an utterance, consisting of a single word or a single prosodic pattern, which functions to convey the child's intentions before he acquires sentential structures. He postulated nine primitive speech acts that his subjects displayed at the single-word stage. These were: 1) labeling, 2) repeating, 3) answering, 4) requesting action, 5) requesting answer, 6) calling, 7) greeting, 8) protesting, and 9) practicing. He used the child's utterances, the nonlinguistic behavior, the adult's response, and the relevant, salient aspects of the context of the utterances as four types of behavioral evidence to characterize each of the proposed primitive speech acts. Dore suggests that it is these primitive speech acts becoming "grammaticalized" that gives rise to the syntactic development apparent in children's language.

Bruner (1974/1975) has also placed great emphasis on the pragmatic function of language in the initial stages of language development. He suggests:

> ... neither the syntactic nor the semantic approach to language acquisition takes sufficiently into account what the child is trying to do by

communicating. As linguistic philosophers remind us, utterances are used for different ends and *use is a powerful determinant of rule structures* (p. 283, italics added).

He also reinforces Dore's (1975) notion that the process of attempting to "get different things done with words" directs the child toward the "appropriate devices and conventions" (Dore, 1975, p. 284). In a like fashion, Leontiev (1975) has viewed speech as a process of solving a communication problem. Thus, it could be suggested that the child's cognizance of the "communication problem" leads him to acquire the grammatical "devices and conventions" for solving it.

Brown (1973) has also suggested that the child's need to "get things done" with words explains the driving force behind children's language improvement, which he defines as the increasing convergence of the child's speech with that of the adults around him. He suggests that the child is initially "narrowly adapted" as a speaker, that is, he is effective only with those in his immediate environment who can interpret his ill-formed and incomplete utterances because of familiarity with the child's knowledge and the context. Brown suggests that it is the pressure of having to deal with new people or new experiences that causes the child to learn to express missing obligatory constituents in order to be understood.

Brown's view of the initial "shared-knowledge" support of the environment relates to Mahoney's (1975) suggestion that language develops *after* a system of communication has developed; that is, a child does not learn "language" and then begin communicating; he begins communicating before real evidence of linguistic skills is present. From this viewpoint, training language structures should parallel and be guided by communication. Although a systematic, highly structured approach is often necessary in training language to handicapped children, the function or "use" of language has not been given its share of emphasis in intervention programs. Mahoney (1975) suggests that just as the semantic or syntactic analyses to language acquisition have not taken into account what the child is trying to do by communicating, neither do the behaviorally and linguistically based training programs deal with the necessary communicative functions of language.

The major thrust of Mahoney's ethological approach is to take into account that a critical dimension of language development is its social function, i.e., efficient communication. The linguistic structure is a means for achieving efficient communication within an extended social environment and not an end goal in and of itself. In a like fashion, Brown (1973) suggests:

> . . . language development from the first word to the compound sentence would then be largely a matter of learning how to put more of what is

intended into adequate expressive form. With what useful result? Ultimately with the result of making the utterance more freely "exportable," making it intelligible in a wider community (p. 168).

The form that communication systems take between the parent and the child also influences the course of development. Nelson (1973) has found that children tend in their early language to be either primarily *referential* or *expressive* in their functional use of language, as are mothers in their presentation of language exemplars. The rate of a child's language development as a whole is related to parental acceptance or rejection of their language forms, based on a congruence between maternal and child communication styles. Not only does form follow function, as previously suggested, but the development of language forms may be enhanced or retarded by their functionality in establishing and maintaining social communication.

Structure in Summary

Miller and Yoder (1972) have suggested that in order to use language one must have something to say, a way to say it, and a reason for saying it. This captures the semantic, syntactic, and pragmatic functions of language. What are communicated in language are the semantic content and the pragmatic intent, but the vehicle for their transmission remains the lexicogrammatical structure of the utterance. Regardless of the mode of transmission—spoken language, written forms, manual signs or other symbolic systems—the ordering of elements in accord with structural principles (or syntactic marking imposed by morphophonological operations) is an essential component in order for semantic and pragmatic content of an utterance to be expressed by a speaker and interpreted by a listener.

Despite the dispute concerning the role of structural processes in the development of language, as the process or product or even the byproduct of development, structural factors in language must remain important for the language practitioner for two reasons. First, structure is an observable requisite for language usage, and the language therapist must deal with observable behaviors, whatever we infer their underlying cause to be. Second, bearing in mind the central role of semantic and conceptual factors in the acquisition of language, we must still face the fact that we are providing the child with the means of expression. There is as yet no compelling evidence that we can in fact train these functions in their absence. Schiefelbusch (1974) has stated:

> Language acquisition, either in a normal environment or under the aegis of training, is limited to the extent of the child's conceptual development (p. 659).

The goal of language training should be to provide the child with a means of "cracking the code" (in Bruner's term, 1974/1975) of language, and the framework of the code is structure.

Bloom, Lightbown, and Hood (1975) have discussed three levels of structural considerations: 1) as the combination of elements, which results in the fact that the meaning of the sum is more than that of the separate components, using different components in different situations, 2) as a means of predicting certain parts of a child's linguistic system based on the knowledge of others, and 3) as a specification of the regularities evident in children's language at any point and their sequential development. All three levels of structure are important for the development of language-training programs. In what follows, the concept of structure is used in all three ways—as a statement of the organization of specific sentences expressed by the child or targeted in training, as a statement of the common properties evident across a specific child's language usage, and as a statement of the sequential stages of development and commonalities across all children's language.

Halliday (1975) has posed questions that he feels any current, unified approach to the study of the child's language development must answer:

> . . . how does he master the adult linguistic system, in which grammar is just one part, and structure is just one part of grammar? How does he build up a multiple coding system consisting of content, form, and expression of meaning relations, the representation of these as lexicostructural configurations, and the realization of these, in turn, as phonological patterns? (p. 241).

In a similar fashion Bever (1970) has presented an algebraic equation for the role of syntax in attempting to summarize its position in current theory:

> (Structure of Language Behavior) − (SU + HCS + PM + SS + BUC + CS) = (specifically linguistic structures) . . . (where SU = social urge; HCS = common properties of all human communications systems; PM = psychological mechanisms; SS = semantic structures; BUC = biological universals of communications systems; CS = common properties of all human cognition systems) (p. 168).

The present authors suggest that rather than viewing structure as what is left over after all other components are subtracted as this model does, it should instead be viewed as a *function* of all of these factors in combination.

GRAMMATICAL TRAINING
FOR THE LANGUAGE-DELAYED CHILD

In this chapter the definition of the language-delayed child has been restricted to one who possesses some limited language ability. This suggests that the child being discussed has already begun mapping his conceptualization of his world in the form of language to express certain semantic functions, and to exploit in at least a rudimentary fashion the pragmatic functions of language. The child must make further developments in these areas, but it is probable that there exists a complex interaction between language structure and its function. Slobin (1966) has stated that it is:

> . . . reasonable to suggest that it is language that plays a role in drawing the child's attention to the possibility of dividing nouns on the basis of animation; or verbs on the basis of duration, or determinacy, or validity, or pronouns on the basis of social status, and the like (p. 89).

This is not to suggest that the language system is responsible for the development of the concepts of animation or of duration and the like, because it is obvious that the child possesses these concepts before he learns to speak. As Halliday (1975) and Bruner (1975) have indicated, before the child reaches the two-word stage, he gives evidence of many semantic relations and communicative functions. Rather, the role of the grammatical structure of language would be to serve to indicate which of the possible features of objects or events that he perceives and conceptualizes can be expressed in language and in what fashion. Miller and Yoder (1974) said:

> . . . syntax can be thought of as a general abstract organizational structure which allows the child to use the numerous semantic concepts acquired in comprehension and production in a manner consistent with his linguistic community [to achieve certain illocutionary ends] (p. 513).

Thus, the goal of language training for the child at this level should be directed toward providing him with the means of mapping his existing semantic and communicative intents in a structured form as well as exposing him to new semantic and communicative functions expressed in structured forms that he controls. This fits with both the observation of Werner and Kaplan (1963) that new functions are first expressed by means of old forms and the observation of Slobin (1971) and Brown (1973) that as new forms are acquired by children they are first used to express old functions. As Slobin (1973) has summarized:

> . . . this acquisition process involves the assimilation of information to existing structures, and the accommodation of those structures to new input. . . . Inner linguistic structures change with age as computation and storage space increase, as increasing understanding of linguistic intentions leads the child into realms of new formal complexity, and as internal structures are interrelated and re-organized in accordance with general principles of cognitive organization (p. 208).

It is increasingly elaborated grammatical structures that represent these realms of new formal complexity.

Before departing from the realm of theory to some very real and practical concerns of language training, a moment should be taken to return to Ingram (1971), who has posed the requirements against which theoretical models should be judged. Lest the applied researcher despair of the complexity of theoretical issues, Ingram has written:

> I have at times had the feeling of being up against some monolithic, immovable set of assertions and dogmas, which I could neither fully assent to nor get round. Now, it seems, everything is wide open, and it is possible to question, to re-evaluate, to shift models around so they can be made use of for particular purposes . . . (p. 151).

These issues are considered below for *our* purpose: developing language-training procedures for the language-delayed child.

LANGUAGE INTERVENTION

Just as the theoretical framework supporting language-training programs has been reanalyzed in terms of syntactic, semantic, and pragmatic factors, language-training programs must be reanalyzed, reevaluated, and modified according to continuing developments. The authors have previously described a language-training program designed for the moderately and severely handicapped child (Stremel and Waryas, 1974). The major features of the program are the utilization of a developmental sequence and systematic procedures for training. The pragmatic component of language inherent in the program has been discussed only briefly in the previous publication. In this chapter the importance of a developmental sequence or a structured program is not deemphasized. Rather, more emphasis is placed on the aspect of the communicative function of language as it relates to the linguistic component of language, suggesting that structure follows function rather than the reverse.

In the reanalysis of the training program, the important aspects of the recent pragmatic and semantic developments have been incorporated into our grammatically based program. When we deal with a child at the linguistic level, we are assuming that the child possesses at least the rudiments of pragmatic and semantic development. These components of language are extremely relevant to any language-training program as precursors to and as ontogenetic components of grammatical development. Our main emphasis in training language-delayed children focuses on the relationship of the pragmatic and semantic components to the grammatical components—the lexical, morphological, and syntactic features of language.

Three general areas of the language-training program are discussed. First, the assessment procedures are outlined; second, specific training sequences, procedures, and results are presented; third, strategies to evaluate individual language programs are discussed. The points to be covered are intended not to be prescriptions but simply to be perspectives that a language trainer may consider when designing a language intervention program for any individual child.

Various models of language-training programs for the handicapped child are available to the practitioner. However, these models are often difficult to replicate unless the practitioner can receive direct training. In most cases, the person involved in training language can use a specific model as a basis for training but, in fact, is responsible for designing a program for each individual child. Each child comes into training with specific cognitive, sensorimotor, and socioaffective behaviors. This array of behaviors, which consists of skills and deficits, is not always readily apparent; therefore, the trainer must determine what behaviors occur under specific conditions. The trainer has to also consider the child's environment. Perhaps the child's language development is severely delayed because of past conditioning and an environment *not* conducive to communicating. Often the trainer must rearrange the child's environment before the language training can be effective. Given information concerning the child and his environment, the trainer must outline the initial, medial, and final training objectives. The trainer must also determine what techniques would be the most efficient in training and what type of training materials are available. The type of service model from which the trainer must operate is also a variable in designing a child's program. Trainers do not always have ideal settings for training language, but they are required to function in the setting available to them.

The training program presented here is a series of sequential assessment procedures and training programs for students who display delayed language. The program has been used primarily for the developmentally handicapped student. It is divided into three major sections, with individual programs within each section sequenced according to information from normal language development and data collected in the course of developing the program. The three major sections include:

1. *The Early Language-Training Program.* The student's lexicon is expanded and refined to increase intelligibility. The semantic organization of the lexical items is refined and additional examples of semantic functions are presented. The basic grammatical relations are trained and additional content words are incorporated within the basic structure. A social communication system is introduced early within this section. This system includes a few early forms of dialogue.

2. *The Early Intermediate Language-Training Program.* The length of the student's utterances is extended by expanding the classes of

content words and introducing function words. At this stage the student learns to incorporate internal markers of questions and negation into his utterances. He also learns to use the optional replacive pronouns and to use a variety of different utterances for the same communicative function.

3. *The Late Intermediate Language-Training Program.* The student's language is refined by training more complex structures. He learns to transform existing structures into others and to acquire additional syntactic rules for refining structure. An emphasis is placed on training the student to use his language to gain additional information for learning new skills.

The basic model of the language-training program, the content, and the specific procedures are described by presenting the assessment and training program for one student. To some extent this student is representative of the 200 children who have received this program, and the trainer is somewhat representative of all trainers. However, by focusing on one student, the individual aspects of training can be discussed.

Student

Paul is an 11-year-old, moderately handicapped student who resides at Parsons State Hospital and Training Center. He is ambulatory, but his overall motor functioning is delayed. According to the AAMD classification system (Heber, 1958), Paul functions at a measured intelligence level III and an adaptive behavior level III (low). An audiometric assessment completed by the training center's speech department showed that Paul's hearing is normal.

Environment

Paul lives in a cottage with 28 other moderately handicapped males of the same age group. He is cared for by at least nine different caregivers and shares a room with three other boys. The number of activities and toys within Paul's living environment are limited. Paul is also enrolled in a federally funded educational program that offers full-day training programs in: 1) academics, 2) self-help skills, 3) domestic skills, 4) vocational skills, and 5) communication. Paul is based in a classroom with eight other severely and moderately handicapped students. He goes to the different areas within the school for various training programs. Paul is exposed to more objects, activities, and experiences in the educational setting than in his living environment.

At the beginning of training, Paul's adult interactions consisted mainly of smiling and touching; few verbalizations were noted. Most language directed to Paul consisted of verbal directives that required a motor response. Paul interacted very little with his peers.

The student and environmental information was collected before Paul was seen for a speech and language assessment. This information was general and did not offer data for stating objectives. Specific assessment tests and additional observations were necessary before designing a language program for Paul.

Assessment

Only a few standardized language tests were administered. The results of these tests showed how Paul's scores compared to the scores obtained from normal children and did not indicate specific training objectives. Assessment is important only as it relates to training; therefore, the content and sequence of Paul's training had to be specified by the results of our assessment battery. The assessment was conducted in both nonstructured and structured settings. The spontaneous language samples were collected during five half-hour segments and structured assessment was conducted in five half-hour sessions. The entire assessment occurred over a two-week period.

Paul's assessment included the developmental functions of language, the semantic relations, and the linguistic structures that he displayed. These behaviors were assessed by a battery of three tests: 1) a checklist, 2) general tests, and 3) specific tests. The three assessment tests were directly related but differed in degree, beginning with the gross criterion-based checklist and going to pretest or baseline measures.

The checklist assessed a total of 85 behaviors contained under the categories of prelinguistic communication, receptive language skills, and expressive language skills. Paul's teacher completed the checklist during a one-week observation period and indicated if each behavior was consistently displayed, inconsistently displayed, or not displayed. This measurement provided only a gross estimate of Paul's language behavior. From this information, the trainer selected a number of general tests. The general tests provided more examples of the critical behaviors listed in the checklist and the results could be plotted as percentages.

The general test battery for Paul consisted of 29 tests with each test consisting of 10 to 20 items. A specific set of objects were used across a number of relevant tests to ensure that the tasks themselves and not object familiarity were being assessed. Paul was provided with examples of the behaviors that were being assessed, and he was given positive feedback for correct responses. The general assessment battery was completed when Paul performed below 20% correct responses on five consecutive expression tests and at chance level on five consecutive receptive tests. The percentage score of each test was plotted on a profile, which is presented in Figure 1. The results showed that Paul's expressive language was delayed considerably in comparison to his receptive language. The majority of Paul's single-word utterances were not

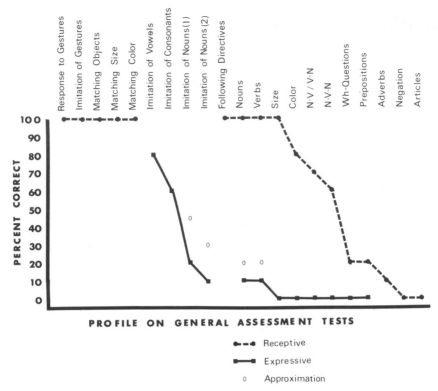

Figure 1.   Profile on general assessment test battery for Paul, an 11-year-old, moderately handicapped student.

intelligible out of context, and correct imitations of nouns were infrequent.

The general test scores were analyzed and a number of specified pretests were selected to obtain additional information on the items to be trained. For instance, a specific noun test measured Paul's comprehension, imitation, and production of 55 nouns under various concept classes. This test determined the additional noun lexicon that had to be trained and specified the basic procedure to be used. Receptive and expressive tests of noun-verb, verb-noun, and other two-word structures, which contained the various semantic relations, were also assessed. Paul scored 100% on the receptive tests and attempted to use two-word structures, but the majority of these utterances were only gross approximations.

Spontaneous speech samples were also used to gain additional information concerning Paul's level of language functioning. The information on both the structured and nonstructured tests was compiled and analyzed to determine the developmental functions of language, the semantic relations, and the linguistic structures that Paul displayed.

Assessment of the Developmental Functions of Language   Halliday's (1975) description of the developing functions of language was used to assess why Paul used language. His utterances were characterized by five factors that occurred in the spontaneous setting: 1) the utterance itself, 2) the nonlinguistic features, such as gestures and facial expressions, 3) the context of the utterance objects, people present, 4) another's response to that utterance, and 5) his response to the listener's response. Paul's utterances were collected primarily in the classroom setting; however, any spontaneous utterances in the structured setting also were recorded. Each utterance was transcribed phonetically, and the likely gloss for the utterance was written. The utterances were categorized under four specific functions:

1. Instrumental—to satisfy own needs
2. Regulatory—to influence others' behavior
3. Interactional—to establish social contacts
4. Personal—to express oneself

Paul mainly expressed these functions by one-word utterances, although some two-word utterances also were noted. The utterances, which were primarily directed to adults, were limited in quality of production and in quantity. The instrumental and regulatory functions served by these utterances occurred with the highest frequency. Paul used utterances to initiate interaction with others but perseverated with the same utterance in order to maintain contact. Many instances of language function were expressed with inappropriate actions, such as knocking objects off the table or noncooperative behavior. These behaviors indicated that Paul needed more appropriate means for expression of these functions.

Assessment of Semantic Relations   Miller and Yoder (1974) provide a description of semantic relations and offer suggestions on how the semantic relations may be trained. Examples of the semantic relations that Paul expressed are listed in Table 1. The phonetic transcription and the gloss are given for each representative example. Because the context of any one environment may not include all of the relations we were trying to assess, specific contextual settings were set up so that there was a high probability of specific responses occurring. A frequency count was necessary to determine if Paul used the relation in other situations or if the utterance was a stereotyped utterance. Again, contextual cues, gestures, and others' responses were used to categorize these utterances.

Paul's mean length of utterance (Brown, 1973) for spontaneous utterances was 1.3 words. The following semantic relations were expressed by two-word utterances in Paul's spontaneous speech: 1) agent-

Table 1. Semantic relations expressed by Paul's one- and two-word utterances

Utterance		Nonlinguistic cues	Context	Response	Semantic relation
Spontaneous (gloss)					
[u/i]	"You eat"	Handed teacher cookie	Snack time	Teacher took cookie	Agent-action
[do/ho]	"Go home"	Pointing to himself	Classroom	"Are you going home?"	Action-object
[wɔ/ka]	"Want car"	Pointing to car	Play time	Teacher gave him car	State-object
[ka]	"Car"	Pointing to car on shelf	After play time	"Mary put car away."	Location
[dʌ]	"Doug"	Pointing to Doug	In hallway	"That's Doug."	Demonstrative
[ha]	"Hi"	Smile	Greeting person	"Hi"	Greeting notice
Structured					
[bɔ]	"Ball"	Took big one	Little and big balls offered	"You want the big ball?"	Feature
[wc/pa]	"Want pop"	Held up empty glass after already drinking	Snacktime	"More pop."	Recurrence
[dæ]	"That"	Gesturing no	Given water, not juice	"You don't want water."	Negation
[tu]	"Shoe"	Pointing to water Pointing to shoe Indicated himself	Ordinary shoe	"That's you shoe."	Possession

action, 2) action-object, and 3) state-object. One-word spontaneous utterances seemed to indicate location, demonstrative, and greeting relations. Paul also demonstrated specific relations in the structured assessment even though these relations were not always expressed with two-word utterances. Many of the one-word utterances were difficult to categorize unless they were accompanied with a gesture or repeated until an appropriate listener response was made. Paul indicated recurrence by using the state-object relation, e.g., "Want pop." He also showed a preference for specific features of objects (big ball, big cookie, little car) even though he did not use the lexicon representing a specific feature. State-object relations occurred more frequently than the other relations.

Assessment of the Grammatical Aspects of Language Paul's receptive vocabulary of object nouns was quite large in comparison to his expressive vocabulary. Again, his articulation skills interfered with obtaining a reliable score on the expressive tests. Paul's reception scores on the functor words (such as prepositions, articles, and third-person pronouns) were low. Paul's utterances were analyzed syntactically and fell into the following categories: 1) noun, 2) verb, 3) verb-noun (V-N), 4) noun-verb (N-V), and 5) noun-noun (N-N). No three-word utterances were obtained in spontaneous speech or in a structured setting. When three-word, noun-verb-noun (N-V-N) structures were presented with an imitative model, Paul imitated only the final noun.

The following spontaneous utterances are shown as examples of how utterances were analyzed across the semantic, grammatical, and pragmatic components.

Speech Utterance	Gloss	Semantic	Grammatical	Function
/i/ /t ʊ ɪ/	"eat cookie"	Action-object	V-N	Regulatory
/wɔ/ /tʲʊ ɪ/	"want cookie"	State-object	V-N	Instrumental

Table 2 shows the initial objectives that were selected from the assessment results as being priority behaviors for training. The objectives within each component were trained not as isolated tasks but rather as interactive tasks. The training of an objective in one component often met the objective criterion in another component. Once the training on an objective was completed at one level, more refined examples of the behavior were introduced.

Training

Once the child variables and environmental variables had been determined and the initial objectives had been outlined, the training setting, training techniques, and materials were selected for Paul. Both structured and nonstructured environments were used for the training settings. The communication area was defined as the structured environ-

Table 2. Initial training objectives within each component

Functions	Grammatical	Semantic	Nonlanguage behavior
1. Require at least one-word utterances before meeting needs.	1. Increase lexical items.	1. Increase types of utterances indicating relations.	1. Decrease drooling.
2. Decrease inappropriate behaviors that exert control.	2. Shape closer word approximations.	2. Train comprehension of unknown linguistic elements.	2. Time out temper tantrums.
3. Increase opportunities for appropriate behaviors that exert control.	3. Increase verb vocabulary.		3. Require shorter response latencies.
4. Decrease perseverated utterances used to maintain contact.	4. Increase number of N-V and V-N structures.		
5. Train utterances to maintain contact.	5. Increase N-V-N comprehension to criterion.		
6. Increase experiences, possessions, and tasks.	6. Train production of N-V-N structures.		
7. Train peer interaction.			

ment. The structured component of training allowed us to arrange conditions that would control the context and that thus would predict the probability of a type of response occurring. The structured training also provided Paul with the opportunity to respond more frequently. The disruptive behaviors that occurred and interfered with Paul's utterances were decreased in the more controlled situation. However, the trainer was interested in communicating with the child and took advantage of and encouraged each spontaneous utterance so that the setting was not artificial and static.

The classroom was defined as the primary nonstructured setting; however, the other training areas also were used as nonstructured settings. Paul had to learn that language was required in a number of settings and was to be directed to a number of listeners. Because language is inherent in a number of skills, we had several potential language trainers operating within the school while they were training the other skills.

A variety of techniques were used within Paul's continued training program. Many of these techniques were general and operated across each training task; others were more specific and were used for only certain tasks. We do not suggest that one set of procedures needs to be incorporated into training for the formulation of an effective, efficient program. Combinations of different procedures have been found to be effective in training both similar and dissimilar behaviors. Certain procedures may be effective but not practical in terms of some training models. For example, the teaching procedure used by Bandura and Harris (1966), involving an experimenter, the child, and a model, is used frequently in research studies. However, most service models cannot provide two trainers for one child, although this might be beneficial in certain instances.

The following general procedures were used for Paul's training program. They are described in detail as Paul's program is outlined.

1. A stimulus-response-reinforcement paradigm
2. A comprehension-referential imitation-production format
3. Concurrent training
4. Prompts
5. Grammatically progressive expansions
6. Specific criterion levels
7. Magnitude of reinforcement

Different materials were used in Paul's training program. Spontaneous and "arranged" events are the most natural stimuli and the most inexpensive. However, waiting for each natural stimulus to occur may take time, and controlling the response may be difficult. A certain

amount of natural stimuli must be used if the student is to use spontaneous language in nontraining settings. Photographs and slides depicting Paul, his peers, and his environment were used for training materials,
and in some individual programs purchased materials and line drawings
were used. Materials and events were interchanged to keep Paul's
interest. Materials often varied somewhat according to specific children
because each child had specific interests and preferences. The most
important "material" can be the trainer. These unwritten rules operated
throughout Paul's training:

1. The student can manipulate the trainer by using appropriate ut-
    terances (within reason).
2. The student has the right to state his preferences and objections,
    which can be affirmed or negated by the trainer (also within reason).
3. The trainer has the right to state personal preferences and objections.
4. The trainer utilizes "change" in that novel objects, persons, and
    events are brought into the training setting.
5. The trainer is an interested communicator.
6. The trainer does not use an unnatural voice quality.
7. The student is allowed to say anything he has heard the trainer say
    (providing it is not direct echolalia).

Paul's actual training program is outlined in phases, with the Early
Language-Training Program containing Phases I, II, and III. Phase IV
was conducted in the Early Intermediate Language-Training Program.
Paul had two different primary trainers at different times, but, because
both trainers operated within the same system, the program format did
not change.

Phase I Training   Paul was seen on an individual basis for half-hour
sessions, four times a week in Phase I training. The objectives trained
within the initial phase of Paul's training were: 1) to arrange events, 2) to
require specific responses, 3) to decrease inappropriate behaviors, 4) to
decrease perseverated utterances, 5) to shape closer word approximations, and 6) to increase lexicon.

Specific events were arranged within the structured setting to
increase the probability of a spontaneous utterance occurring. These
events included giving the child specific possessions, giving the child
some opportunities to control the trainer's behaviors, and requiring
motor actions for certain activities. Table 3 shows the tasks that Paul
was initially required to complete. Later in Phase I training Paul had to
use a single-word utterance before he could initiate a task or activity.

Because Paul often expressed communicative intent by gestures or
stereotyped grunts, an appropriate response was modeled in those situations and Paul was required to imitate that single-word utterance. For

Table 3.   Activities and utterances within the training setting during Phases I and II (with later extensions)

	Utterance extended		
Activity	Phases I & II	Phase III	Phase IV
Getting cup for tokens	"cup"	"I get cup."	"I get my cup."
Getting materials	"picture"	"I get picture."	"I get the picture."
Trading tokens for pennies	"penny"	"I have 5."	
		"I want penny."	"I want a penny."
Taking pictures out of box		"I take out."	"I take the picture out."
Putting pictures in box		"I put away."	"I put the picture in box."
Specifying reinforcer	"juice"	"I want gum."	"Give me some gum, please."
Specifying activities	"blocks"	"I play with blocks."	"I listen to record player."

instance, if Paul wanted the trainer (T) to tie his shoe, he had to approximate the word *shoe.*

Paul's inappropriate behaviors were timed out, even though these behaviors were used for a function. However, other more appropriate behaviors (words) were taught to replace those inappropriate behaviors. Paul learned that he could say "go" when he wanted to leave a situation instead of throwing a temper tantrum. Perseverated utterances were decreased by directing Paul to say something only one time. He was then timed out for repeating an utterance more than once.

Paul exhibited a phonological speech delay; however, he did approximate words within one or two phonemes and for this reason was not placed in a nonoral analogue of the program. Paul's speech had to be considered in conjunction with his language. It is quite easy to fall into two traps when dealing with this issue. The first is training perfect articulation with no language, and the second is having a student using unintelligible four-word structures with only the trainer knowing what they mean. This relates to Brown's (1973) point that too much "shared knowledge" may not be a grammatically progressive influence for the student.

An example of Paul's training goals for closer noun approximations is shown below:

			Training Goals		
Level	Initial Behavior	Referent	1	2	3
	/o/	coat	/to/	/tot/	/kot/
nouns	/o/	home	/om/		/hom/
	/u/	shoe	/tu/	/su/	/ʃu/

At the one-word level, our training goal consisted of getting Paul to produce a consonant sound paired with a vowel sound in reference to an object. Once he had reached this criterion, closer approximations were required. These approximations were not consistent across all students. Phonemic data were collected in relation to both the student's articulation ability and the potential ambiguities caused by faulty articulation. Motokinesthetic techniques paired with imitation were used as a method to initiate the sound and to prompt Paul once he was able to produce the sound in relation to the word. We used the "word-approach" in shaping these sounds because sounds only have meaning when they are paired with a referent. As Paul acquired more nouns and verbs, his word approximations had to become more precise so that we as trainers could discriminate between *put* and *pull, give* and *get,* and *boy* and *ball*, because Paul's lexicon and syntax were providing vehicles for his growing store of meanings, requiring greater clarity of expression for the prevention of ambiguity.

Paul displayed the negation and recurrent relations by gesturing and saying the object or state object relations. He did not display appropriate lexical items for these relations; even though he expressed these relations. Therefore, lexical items, such as "no" and "more," were trained. Paul also used a stereotyped grunt for unknown lexical items. If he did not comprehend the nouns, comprehension and production were trained. Many of these nouns included the names of people involved in his training program. Because Paul displayed a limited verb vocabulary, additional verbs were trained before Phase I training was completed. Closer verb approximations were required as Paul was learning new verbs.

Phase II Training   The objectives in the second phase of training were: 1) to provide opportunities for Paul to explore his environment, 2) to require relations to be expressed in two-word utterances, 3) to increase the number of exemplars expressing relations, 4) to increase his adverb, adjective, and pronoun (first) lexicon, and 5) to increase the N-V, V-N, and other two-word structures. These structures are referred to as N-N structures. However, only possession was trained with a proper noun-noun structure; other two-word structures included feature-noun and demonstrative-noun.

Paul was placed in group training for 45-minute sessions with three other boys. The other students were also based in the same classroom. Another change in the training included the trainer spending an additional 45 minutes a day in that classroom during the teacher's lunch break. Since this was a self-help and free-play period, opportunities for spontaneous speech were frequent. Again, the objectives were trained somewhat concurrently. Once behaviors reached the specified criterion, they were reviewed for maintenance.

It was difficult to determine if Paul did not display exploring behaviors because he was not inquisitive or because of past conditioning. Paul was encouraged to explore new places and unexposed places and situations by following directives. For example, he was told to get the scissors (which were in the desk drawer), and then further directives, which allowed him to open the drawer, were given. He was then required to search for the scissors. Therefore, he was trained to explore his environment for a purpose. If Paul wanted to get a pencil, which he previously spotted in the drawer, he was required to gain approval or denial by using a two-word utterance, "get pencil."

Paul's basic verb and noun vocabulary was expanded during Phase I. He was trained to use those lexical items to express two-word semantic relations in Phase II. Different combinations of the lexical items were also trained so that Paul would increase the number of utterances used within each category. Both structured and nonstructured training was used depending on the specific relation that was being extended.

Paul did not express adverbs, adjectives, or some of the first-person pronouns with words. However, he often used gestures and facial expressions to express concepts such as "smells" and "me." The specific pretests showed which words had to be placed in receptive and expressive training, and which words could be trained without the receptive component of training. The specific adverbs and adjectives that were chosen for training were words that would be functional in Paul's environment. A few of the words (such as color adjectives) were trained in the classroom.

The training criterion for two-word utterances was met when Paul reached criterion on the specific relations that were included within the N-V, V-N, and N-N structures. As each two-word utterance was being trained, a N-V-N expansion was provided for correct two-word utterances. The use of expansions provides discrete (single-word) developmentally sequenced expansions of the student's utterance (Stremel-Campbell and Ruder, 1976). For example, if Paul said, "Tim eat," the expansion, "Tim eat sandwich," was given. Paul was given extra reinforcement for using a three-word utterance, "you drink pop," at the two-word stage of training. However, he was not placed in the next phase of training when he first exhibited a few instances of three-word utterances, but only when he met criterion for Phase II training.

The grammar (vocabulary and structure) trained in Phase II allowed different functions to be combined. As Halliday (1975) states, grammar makes it possible to mean more than one thing at a time. Paul also made advances in dialogue by responding to new commands and responding to Wh-questions. This form of dialogue initially occurred primarily between Paul and the trainer.

Phase III Training   The third and fourth phases of training are described in more detail, emphasizing the procedures that are used to train the specific content. Continued assessment was another aspect of

Paul's program. Ongoing assessment told us if Paul was using trained linguistic elements within other structures or if he had inferred certain relationships from trained structures that were similar. In other words, we were asking if he was "behaving" as though he knew the rules. Many of these assessments took the form of probes. The results of the probes showed if Paul was able to use a trained structure only under specific conditions or if he could generalize its use to other appropriate situations.

The function, semantic, and syntax training continued concurrently as well as sequentially. The specific behaviors within each component were also presented concurrently. The Planning and Evaluation of Resources and Techniques (PERT) schema in the chapter Appendix shows the concurrent training of the grammatical components trained in Phases I, II, and III. Initially, concurrent training included expanding Paul's lexicon while introducing the receptive component of a new linguistic element. In Phase III, training included building, expanding, and refining the simple declarative sentence, negation statements, and questions concurrently.

Phase III objectives included: 1) to increase peer dialogue, 2) to arrange situations for imaginative play, 3) to increase lexicon, 4) to train three-word structures, 5) to train Wh-words in questions, and 6) to initiate internal negation within three-word utterances.

Specific utterances were required before each student could carry out an activity. Many of these activities took place between two of the students. Not only was dialogue required, but the students also learned that they could regulate each other's behavior. A few of the activities and utterances are listed in Table 4. The type of utterances used in Phases I and II was expanded as training continued. Part of the increase in dialogue between the students was not trained directly, but seemed to occur because of previous student-trainer interactions. Situations to increase imaginative play were arranged during the free-play periods within the classroom. These situations included showing the students how to "build a house" with four chairs and a blanket and using a big box for different imaginative purposes.

As Paul learned extended language functions and had more novel experiences, he demonstrated the need for his lexicon to be expanded further. Many of these lexical items did not have to be trained directly, but they were presented to the child in context. Other lexical items were trained within the N-V-N training in order to train more variations of N-V-N combinations.

The syntax training for three-word utterances primarily concentrated on N-V-N training. The semantic relations included within the N-V-N training were agent-action-object, agent-action-location, and

Table 4.   Activities and utterances within the training setting during Phases III and IV

Activity	Utterance extended	
	III	IV
Telling T to write name on data sheet	"Write my name."	"You write my name here."
Asking to be token giver	"I give token."	"I give token to you?"
		"Give me 10 token."
Asking for other child's cup	"I want cup."	"Give me his cup." (T)
		"Give me your cup." (S)
Asking for his cup after completing 10 trials	"I want cup."	"Put token in my cup."
		"Give me my cup."
Ask to take rubber band off cards	"I take off."	"I take band off the card."
Picking up objects that are dropped	"I drop token."	
	"I get token."	"I get token I drop."
Asking to turn pages	"I turn page."	"I turn you page?"
Asking to go outside (other places)	"I go looking."	"I going to the classroom."
Pushing another child in wheelchair	"I push Tim."	"I push Tim to room."
Specifying order of training	"I go first?"	"I be first?"
Regulating peers behavior	"Stop that."	"Tim, don't push me."

person-affected-state-object. However, verb-adjective-noun, verb-noun-noun, noun-verb-demonstrative, and noun-verb-adverb structures were also trained within the third training phase.

Wh-questions were trained concurrently with the N-V-N training. One student would ask the questions, and another student was required to answer. The agents within the questions and N-V-N structures varied according to who was performing the action, who was asking, and who was being asked; therefore, the students did not learn rote questions or statements but had to determine the agent (you, I, proper name) and the use of negation.

Two sets of N-V-N structures were used for structured training. Ten specific structures were included within each set, with the verb and object noun varying in each structure. The training items within Set II paralleled those in Set I with the exception of one element varying.

Stimuli:

	Set I	Set II
1.	"Tim go classroom."	"Tim go home."
2.	"Doug eat cookie."	"Doug eat popcorn."
3.	"Brandon sleep mat."	"Brandon sleep bed."
4.	"Bonnie ride bus."	"I ride bus."
5.	"John drink pop."	"John pour pop."
6.	"I walk cottage."	"I walk school."
7.	"You play car."	"You ride car."
8.	"You write name."	"I write name."
9.	"Curtis sit chair."	"Curtis stand chair."
10.	"I make popcorn."	"Donna make cookie."

The student must learn enough examples so that the rule is expressed by his utterances, that is, regularities are present and nontrained instances are generalized. This sample of trained utterances shows the variation that occurred in order for Paul to realize that certain words may be used in conjunction with many words. For instance, he had to learn that *I want* is not one word, but that each word could occur with an almost infinite set of other words.

The N-V-N training contained four possible training steps. The child could "probe out" of a training step by meeting criterion on a probe test. Since Paul had learned the N-V or V-N structures that were contained within the N-V-N structure, only the agent noun or object noun had to be included within the N-V-N training. A card with three place markers was initially used as a prompt to help Paul realize that he was required to use three words to express those relations formerly expressed by two-word utterances. If Paul made an incorrect response, the error type could be pointed out in terms of "where within the structure did it occur?" Manual signs were also used in training the first personal pronoun (I). Fewer *I-you* confusions were seen when this type of gesture prompt was used. The four training steps included: Step 1, echoic element trained N-V__, __V-N with visual prompt; Step 2, card prompt and pointing prompt; Step 3, self-initiated with card prompt, and Step 4, self-initiated without prompt.

An example of Paul's N-V-N training and Tim's Wh-question follows:

Training: Noun-verb-noun and Wh-questions
Stimulus Conditions: Step 3, Step 2
Stimulus Items: Set I
Criterion: 90% on two blocks

Trainer	Tim	Paul
1. Presents 10 pictures or sets up situations.		
2. Says, "Tim, ask Paul questions."		
3. Points to agent, signs *I*.	"What *I* do?"	
4. Says, "Good," while giving Tim a token.	Puts token in his cup.	"You go classroom."
5a. Says, "Right, Tim go to (gesture) classroom."		
b. Hands Paul a token.		Puts token in his cup.
6. Records responses.		
7. Says, "Tim."		
8. Points to agent.	"What Doug do?"	
9. Says, "Right," while giving Tim a token.	Puts token in his cup.	"Doug cookie."
10. Says, "No, Doug *eat* cookie," while visually prompting and emphasizing verb error.		
11. Records responses.		
12. Presents remaining (3 . . . 10) trials in Block #1.	Completes training block.	Completes training block.

Other three-word utterances were trained to extend Paul's other two-word semantic relations:

Action + possession (+ object)	"Get my ball."
State + recurrent (+ object)	"Want more pop."
Negation + state (+ object)	"No want water."
Action + feature (+ object)	"Get big box."

Spontaneous questions not given with the correct structure were prompted, then answered. Early forms of internal negation were also trained. Paul learned to use simple, functional negation statements, as "Tim not here," and "I not go."

The child was trained the concept of sentence (N-V-N) by the trainer indicating that a more complete utterance was needed. This was done by saying, "Give me a sentence," and/or prompting with the initial word. However, Paul also learned that sentences were not always required. Questions could be answered by phrases, such as, "Who dropped tokens?"—"Bonnie," or "What Tim doing?"—"Play car."

The distance between providing a verbal model and requiring the child to provide utterance without a model was initially too great. Various prompts were often necessary to bridge this gap. The prompts varied accordingly to the specific linguistic element or structure being trained and the specific student. Many of the prompts used in our program consisted of manual signs (Stremel-Campbell, Cantrell, and Halle, 1977). The prompts were a necessary component of the program in that they allowed Paul to succeed without depending on total support (imitation).

Paul was given tokens for correct responses. After collecting 10 tokens, Paul had to initiate the exchange, "I have 10," "I want penny." Natural language contingencies were also available. Responses made by the trainer were set up to function as both reinforcing events and additional stimuli. The goal was not only to increase the use of that specific structure but also to increase communication.

Paul was required to meet the training criterion of 18 correct responses out of 20 possible trials on two consecutive blocks of training before advancing to the next training step. This criterion was consistent across all structured training steps. The criterion level in the nonstructured training was set somewhat lower. Paul had to produce nine correct responses out of 10 trials before the behavior was placed on review.

Phase IV Training   The fourth phase of training consisted of completing the following goals: 1) to train the earlier developing prepositions, 2) to include these prepositions within the appropriate N-V-N utterances, 3) to train the *don't* negation form, 4) to train articles and possessive pronouns, and 5) to train varying structures which specify identical functions.

During the noun-verb-noun training, the trainer's expansions included the /-ing/ form and a limited set of prepositions. The prepositions were those that are seen early in normal language acquisition and those reflected by the majority of our students' utterances. Our students often began using our expansions within their three-word utterances before they completed that program. If the students tended to use the /-ing/ form, it was trained until it was used consistently before the prepositions were trained. Paul imitated the model's "verbing" as a two-word utterance, "eat in." Because this occurred, the /-ing/ training was delayed until Paul could imitate "verbing" as a single utterance.

The prepositions (in, on, to, with, by) were trained with manual signs being used as prompts. Paul used these signs while learning to extend his utterance to four words and dropped these gestures when he no longer needed the support. Thus, Paul, not the trainer, determined when the signs were omitted. Learning a longer structure (four words) and a new concept (prepositions) was a large step. The length had to be decreased until Paul was using the prepositions in phrases, "to school," and in N-Prep-N utterances, "Doug in bathroom," before they were used in N-V-Prep-N utterances. At this stage of training Paul continued to expand his lexicon of nouns, verbs, adjectives, and adverbs. The adverbs were primarily trained in the nonstructured setting. He also demonstrated more questions ("What you doing?") as more changes were introduced and more negation statements ("I (gesture 'no') want that") as more options were available to him. The concurrent features during N-V-Prep-N training were extensions of Paul's current questions and negation statements to more adult-like forms. The progression of these forms was gradual and may be described as:

Affirmative Structure	Question	Negation
N-V/N-V	(Inflection)	(Gesture)
N-V-N	"You doing?" "That"	"No juice"
		"I (gesture no) want milk"
N-V-Prep-N	"What doing?" "What that?"	"No, I want milk"
	"What you doing?"	"I don't want milk"

At this level Paul's questions were still of the Wh-type (who, what, what doing, where), and negation statements included *no, not, don't*. Other forms were to be trained later in the Early Intermediate Language-Training Program.

Paul's nonstructured environment was extended to include more situations that could be expressed by locations, questions, and negation. He heard the more expanded forms of the utterances before they were trained and often demonstrated the understanding of linguistic elements. Again, the ongoing assessment determined if Paul understood specific linguistic elements or if he had combined new structures from trained forms. Particles were also trained within the N-V-Prep-N framework. Even though the particles were initially trained within the N-V-Particle-N structure, expansions included N-V-N-Particle structure. This was one of the first such examples in which Paul learned that different forms expressed identical functions, both equally appropriate.

At this point in training, Paul had a functional communication system; however, he was operating with a limited communication system or with what Bernstein (1967) has defined as a restricted code. More language refinements needed to occur in order for Paul to approximate the adult model. He needed to continue extending his vocabulary, learning new concepts and learning more complex structures. After Paul had completed the preposition and particle training and had learned to use those elements within the basic N-V-N structure, he extended them to other four-word utterances. These structures included additional combinations of the basic semantic relations, such as, "Put on your shoes," "Put car in there," and "I want more milk." Not all of these structures needed to be trained. That is, because the component parts had been trained, new utterances could be generalized. Again, ongoing probes determined if examples of these structures needed to be trained.

While Paul was learning N-V-Prep-N structures and various other four-word combinations, the trainer expanded his utterances to include modifiers. Articles and possessive pronouns were the specific modifiers expanded and thus they appeared next in the basic training sequence. Because Paul was using a large portion of proper names as agents, the articles and possessive pronouns were initially trained to modify the noun within the verb phrase. Paul learned that certain features are expressed by these modifiers, inherent in themselves and in the nouns that they modify. Here again, the relation of the modifier to the noun is often expressed by the structure of the language. The articles may be definite or indefinite and may modify either mass or count nouns, whereas the possessive pronouns may be singular or plural, male or female, human or nonhuman. Communication itself plays a major role in teaching these linguistic concepts. Shared knowledge or previously mentioned information may change an indefinite article to a definite article or determine if a possessive pronoun is used. Paul learned that the use of some possessive pronouns is obligatory, according to the nouns they modify (his arm, her mother); others could be optional (his coat, a coat; her doll, the doll). Examples of various structures needed to be presented within the training tasks in order for Paul's behavior to reflect the rule:

"Bonnie brushing her teeth."	N-V-Poss Pron-N
"Doug putting on his boots."	N-V-Part-Poss Pron-N
"John putting his coat on."	N-V-Poss Pron-N-Part
"I want the big ball."	N-V-Article-Adj-N
"Skipper get his dirty shoe."	N-V-Poss Pron-Adj-N

Paul learned that the modifier occurred in direct conjunction with the noun only if descriptive information was not included within the structure. If additional information was included, the article or possessive pronoun modified the entire noun phrase.

Paul was trained to use different structures to obtain an identical response from the listener. This training insured that sentences did not become rote. For instance, Paul was required to vary structures such as, "I want the ball," "Throw the ball to me," "Throw me the ball," "Give me the ball, please," to obtain the ball.

The development sequence of the program extends the pronoun system to include objective pronouns, and subjective pronouns which will be introduced later. Paul is currently learning to comprehend the objective pronouns. Here again, not only does he need to learn the semantic features and the syntactic case differences, but communication itself is important. Because the pronouns serve a replacive function (replacing the noun phrase), Paul must learn that the proper noun must be mentioned before a pronoun can be used. Once another proper noun is interjected into the conversation or after a certain length of time, the proper noun must be mentioned again.

Results

Paul completed the first four phases of training over a 14-month period. Continuous data were collected during the structured training, and probe data were collected in the nonstructured training. Pretest and posttests were administered for each training behavior. Intermediate probe tests were given to determine if Paul could bypass a training step or if a branching step was required. Generalization tests were conducted to show if 1) trained elements and trained structures would generalize to untrained combinations of the trained structures, 2) trained structures were combined to produce untrained structures, 3) trained structures were generalized to nontraining situations.

Paul's acquisition data for the four training phases are shown in Figure 2. These data represent only the training trials within the structured training setting. Each data point represents a block of 10 trials. The number of errors for each training program are also shown. The graph is divided into training segments, which contain one-word, two-word, three-word, four-word, and five-word utterances. Paul required the most training trials on shaping closer noun approximations. Paul initially used a few two-word utterances during assessment; however, the majority of his utterances were one-word utterances. As Figure 2 shows, Paul required fewer training trials within each segment (word level). An increase of trials is shown across segments, indicating the difficulty Paul displayed when an utterance was increased in length. The data by no means show each behavior that was trained within the 14-month period.

Paul used the expansions provided by the trainer, to some degree. Within the last three training blocks of the two-word (N-V/V-N) stage of training, Paul used 10 three-word utterances. He also used the preposition five times within the last three blocks of N-V-N training. He was using the gesture prompt to indicate the preposition before N-V-Prep-N training was initiated. Thus, a training step within the N-V-Prep-N training could be deleted from Paul's training program. The modifier-noun had been given as an expansion during N-V-Prep-N training. Paul did

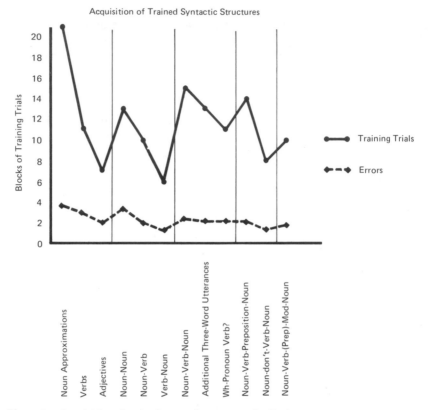

Figure 2.   Acquisition of trained syntactic structures by Paul.

not use the modifier during this training, but scored 80% correct when given an intraverbal pretest after N-V-Prep-N training was completed. This same pretest was given before N-V-Prep-N training, and Paul scored 0% correct. However, Paul did imitate the modifier-noun directly after the trainer gave the N-V-Prep-Mod-N expansion even though no reinforcement was given for imitation at this point.

Generalization of trained structures to untrained combinations occurred at a high rate. Because a number of various combinations were trained, Paul had little trouble using an untrained combination. For example, during N-V-N training, the following examples were trained: "I make popcorn," "Doug eat popcorn," and "Donna make cookie." Paul could use structures, such as "I make juice" and "Doug make cookie," without direct training. Generalization of trained structures to untrained combinations increased as Paul advanced in training. Paul learned

N-V-N structures, as "I want pop," and N-V-Prep-N structures, as "I go to bathroom," and then produced untrained structures, as "I want to play." Paul did not readily use trained structures in nontrained situations that included people and settings not involved in direct training. The use of trained structures occurred with the other language trainers, but these trainers had given Paul prompts and reinforced spontaneous language in nontraining settings. Paul also used the trained and some nontrained structures with his peers that were involved in training. The students often prompted and reinforced one another for good sentences, so, in fact, both the other language trainers and the other students were involved indirectly in language training. At this point in training, Paul will be placed in an articulation program before his language training is advanced. However, trained structures will be reviewed and used within the articulation program.

Language Intervention Program Evaluation

A language intervention program, developed by the trainer or someone else, should be evaluated by asking two basic questions: 1) Is this program appropriate for this student? and 2) Is this program appropriate for the majority of students? In order for either type of evaluation to occur, the trainer must have a measurement system, that is, data must be taken. The more precise and complete the data, the more information the trainer has for the program evaluation.

In deciding if a program is appropriate for a specific student, an ongoing evaluation must be made. The trainer must determine if each program step is appropriate, or if branching steps are needed, or if the student indeed requires each step. To make these decisions, not only must the trainer record data, but that data must also be analyzed. The data analysis and comparative data should provide answers to the following questions:

1. Is the student acquiring the behavior in a consistent manner?
2. What is the rate of acquisition?
3. When is the student failing?

If the data show that the student's behavior is very erratic and that the rate of acquisition is extremely slow in comparison to other students, then branching steps should be included within that student's program. Our program defines failure as 50% incorrect responding on a training block. If a student completes one program, but fails to progress on the next program, several factors may be considered: 1) the criterion on the previous program may be too low, 2) more steps may be needed between the two programs, or 3) the two programs may not be logically sequenced. Once the student completes a specific program, the program must also be evaluated in terms of communication effectiveness. Is the student using the trained behavior in his natural environment? Is he combining trained structures into untrained structures? Is he using untrained examples within trained structures?

If a number of students demonstrate slow acquisition of the behaviors being trained within specific programs, then those programs are not effective and efficient as they stand. The trainer must determine if the problem is a procedure variable or a content variable. Often, only slight procedural changes, branching steps, or a modified program sequence will shape the overall program to be more effective and efficient.

Once a student's progress in terms of the program has been evaluated, the student's progress in terms of trainer effectiveness must also be evaluated. Again, if he is not progressing, the trainer must ask if all of the program components or just a selected few are being used. Perhaps the most important question to be asked is this: Do I enjoy communicating with this person or is training only a job?

The final portion of this chapter has been directed at reanalyzing language intervention in terms of communicative effectiveness. Three specific components were considered in offering suggestions in regard to program development. These components included pragmatics, semantics, and syntax, and their relationship in language intervention. The following outline provides a summary of the important points that have been discussed:

1. Reanalyzing language intervention programs in terms of communicative effectiveness
2. Using a developmental sequence
3. Relating assessment tests directly to training
4. Using a concurrent sequence in training
5. Providing ongoing assessment
6. Using precise and systematic procedures
7. Measuring the student's progress with a continuous data base
8. Using the comprehension-referential imitation-production mode of training
9. Using visual and gestural prompts in training
10. Using progressive grammatical expansions
11. Presenting natural contingencies for language behavior
12. Presenting the pragmatic and semantic components as linguistic precursors

13. Using both structured situations and environmental events in training
14. Using group training to promote communicative effectiveness
15. Considering each individual student
16. Considering service models
17. Considering environmental factors
18. Evaluating each student's progress
19. Evaluating the program's effectiveness

SUMMARY

This chapter is a reanalysis of the role of grammatical training for the language-delayed child from the perspective of recent advances in the study of child language. It has been suggested that rather than obviating the importance of structural training, new theoretical formulations of the semantic and pragmatic factors in language serve to refocus the role of structure in language by placing it in the framework of the *how* of language, which expresses the *what* (semantic functions) and the *why* (pragmatic functions). This chapter suggests that structure must be considered an important goal of language training, not as an end in itself. We must consider it as it serves to improve the child's communication ability, as a means of leading the child to behave as if he "knew the rules," producing congruence between the child's speech and that of his language community, so that communication functions can be carried out. In the process of this reanalysis of structure, specific reference has been made to aspects of a language-training program for the language-delayed child in order to provide a vehicle for demonstrating how some of these concepts can be made real in the therapy setting. A general outline of procedures used within the program, as well as illustrative examples drawn from the development of one child receiving training, is presented.

In summary, two purposes underlie the presentation of this material. The first is to stimulate some language practitioners to assume the role of a "clinical researcher" in the process of training language, and thus to benefit not only the child to whom clinical services are provided but also all others who provide such services. Second, with regard to theory, Lepschy (1975) stated that "Theory is never of any direct interest to the person who trains children or patients" (p. 35). The authors hope that this chapter has helped eradicate this feeling by providing the practitioner with a perspective for understanding and using theoretical formulations of language and its development.

APPENDIX

The Planning and Evaluation of Resources and Techniques (PERT) schema showing the concurrent training of the grammatical components trained in Phases I, II, and III.

PERT

EARLY   LANGUAGE   TRAINING

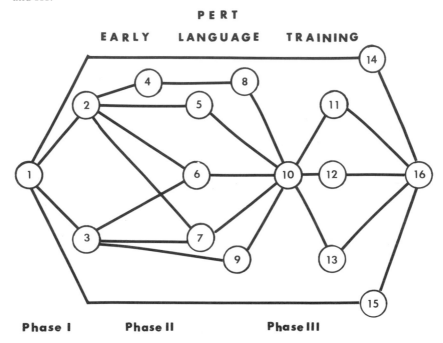

Phase I   Phase II   Phase III

PERT DICTIONARY FOR EARLY LANGUAGE TRAINING

1. Prerequisite behaviors
2. Noun expansion and shaping
3. Verb
4. Adjectives
5. Noun-noun
6. Noun-verb
7. Verb-noun
8. Adjective-noun
9. Pronouns (first personal)
10. Noun-verb-noun
11. Verb-adjective-noun
12. Noun-verb-adverb
13. Verb-modifier (first pronoun)-noun
14. Wh-pronoun-V(-*ing*)
15. Negation
16. Early language training completed

REFERENCES

Bandura, A., and Harris, M. 1966. Modification of syntactic style. J. Exp. Child Psychol. 4:341–352.

Bernstein, B. 1967. Postscript to social structure, language, and learning. *In* J. DeCecco (ed.), The Psychology of Language, Thought, and Instruction. Holt, Rinehart and Winston, New York.

Bever, T. 1970. The integrated study of language behavior. *In* J. Morton (ed.), Biological and Social Factors in Psycholinguistics. University of Illinois Press, Urbana.

Bloom, L. 1970. Language Development: Form and Function in Emerging Grammars. MIT Press, Cambridge, Mass.

Bloom, L. 1974. Talking, understanding, and thinking. In R. L. Schiefelbusch and L. L. Lloyd (eds.), Language Perspectives—Acquisition, Retardation, and Intervention, pp. 285–311. University Park Press, Baltimore.

Bloom, L., Lightbown, P., and Hood, L. 1975. Structure and variation in child language with commentary by Melissa Bowerman and Michael Maratsos; with reply by the authors. Monogr. Soc. Res. Child Dev. 40(2, Serial No. 160).

Bowerman, M. 1973a. Early Syntactic Development: A Cross-Linguistic Study with Special Reference to Finnish. Cambridge University Press, London.

Bowerman, M. 1973b. Structural relations in children's utterances: Syntactic or semantic? In T. Moore (ed.), Cognitive Development and the Acquisition of Language. Academic Press, New York.

Bowerman, M. 1975. Commentary in L. Bloom, P. Lightbown, and L. Hood, Structure and variation in child language. Monogr. Soc. Res. Child Dev. 40(2, Serial No. 160).

Braine, M. 1963. The ontogeny of English phrase structure: The first phrase. Language 39:1–13.

Brown, R. 1968. The development of wh-questions in child speech. J. Verb. Learn. Verb. Behav. 7:279–290.

Brown, R. 1973. A First-Language—The Early Stages. Harvard University Press, Cambridge, Mass.

Brown, R., and Fraser, C. 1964. The acquisition of syntax. Monogr. Soc. Res. Child Dev. 21:1.

Bruner, J. 1974/1975. From communication to language: A psychological perspective. Cognition 3:255–287.

Bruner, J. 1975. The ontogenesis of speech acts. J. Child Lang. 2:1–20.

Chomsky, N. 1957. Syntactic Structures. Mouton, The Hague.

Chomsky, N. 1965. Aspects of the Theory of Syntax. MIT Press, Cambridge, Mass.

Derwing, B. 1973. Transformational Grammar as a Theory of Language Acquisition. Cambridge University Press, Cambridge, England.

Dore, J. 1974. A pragmatic description of early language development. J. Psycholing. Res. 3:343–350.

Dore, J. 1975. Holophrases, speech acts, and language universals. J. Child Lang. 2:21–40.

Edwards, D. 1973. Sensory-motor intelligence and semantic relations in early child grammar. Cognition 2/4:395–434.

Ervin, S. 1964. Imitation and structural change in children's language. In E. Lenneberg (ed.), New Directions in the Study of Language. MIT Press, Cambridge, Mass.

Ervin-Tripp, S. 1973. Some strategies for the first two years. In T. Moore (ed.), Cognitive Development and the Acquisition of Language. Academic Press, New York.

Guillaume, P. 1973. The development of formal elements in the child's speech. In C. Ferguson and D. Slobin (eds.), Studies of Child Language Development. Holt, Rinehart and Winston, New York.

Halliday, M. 1970. Language structure and language function. In J. Lyons (ed.), New Horizons in Linguistics. Penguin Books, Baltimore.

Halliday, M. 1975. Learning how to mean. In E. Lenneberg and E. Lenneberg (eds.), Foundations of Language Development: A Multidisciplinary Approach, Vol. I. Academic Press, New York.

Heber, R. (ed.). 1958. A manual on terminology and classification in mental retardation. Monogr. Suppl. Am. J. Ment. Defic. 64(2).

Houston, S. 1971. The study of language: Trends and positions. *In* J. Eliot (ed.), Human Development and Cognitive Processes. Holt, Rinehart and Winston, New York.

Ingram, D. 1974. The acquisition of the English verbal auxiliary and coupla in normal and linguistically deviant children. *In* L. McReynolds (ed.), Developing Systematic Procedures for Training Children's Language. ASHA Monogr. 18.

Ingram, E. 1971. The requirements of model users. *In* R. Huxley and E. Ingram (eds.), Language Acquisition: Models and Methods. Academic Press, New York.

Klima, E., and Bellugi, U. 1966. Syntactic regularities in the speech of children. *In* J. Lyons and R. Wales (eds.), Psycholinguistic Papers: The Proceedings of the 1966 Edinburgh Conference. Edinburgh University Press, Edinburgh.

Kuhn, T. 1962. The Structure of Scientific Revolutions. University of Chicago Press, Chicago.

Leonard, L. 1975. Developmental considerations in the management of language disabled children. J. Learn. Disabil. 8:232–237.

Leontiev, A. 1975. The Heuristic Principle in the perception, emergence, and assimilation of speech. *In* E. Lenneberg and E. Lenneberg (eds.), Foundations of Language Development: A Multidisciplinary Approach. Vol. I. Academic Press, New York.

Lepschy, G. 1975. Some problems in linguistic theory. *In* E. Lenneberg and E. Lenneberg (eds.), Foundations of Language Development: A Multidisciplinary Approach. Vol. I. Academic Press, New York.

Luria, A. 1974/1975. Scientific perspectives and philosophical dead ends in modern linguistics. Cognition 3:377–385.

Lyons, J. 1966. General discussion to D. McNeill's paper, The creation of language. *In* J. Lyons and R. Wales (eds.), Psycholinguistic Papers. Edinburgh University Press, Edinburgh.

Lyons, J. 1969. Introduction to Theoretical Linguistics. University Press, Cambridge.

McCawley, J. 1968. The role of semantics in grammar. *In* E. Bach and R. Harms (eds.), Universals in Linguistic Theory. Holt, Rinehart and Winston, New York.

MacDonald, J., and Blott, J. 1974. Environmental language intervention: The rationale for a diagnostic and training strategy through rules, context, and generalization. J. Speech Hear. Disord. 39:244–256.

MacNamara, J. 1972. Cognitive basis of language learning in infants. Psychol. Rev. 79:1–13.

McNeill, D. 1966. Developmental psycholinguistics. *In* F. Smith and G. A. Miller (eds.), The Genesis of Language: A Psycholinguistic Approach. MIT Press, Cambridge, Mass.

McNeill, D. 1971. The capacity for the ontogenesis of grammar. *In* D. Slobin (ed.), The Ontogenesis of Grammar. Academic Press, New York.

Mahoney, G. 1975. Ethological approach to delayed language acquisition. Am. J. Ment. Defic. 80:139–148.

Maratsos, M. 1975. Commentary in L. Bloom, P. Lightbown and L. Hood,

Structure and Variation in Child Language. Monogr. Soc. Res. Child Dev. 40:2.

Menyuk, P. 1963. Syntactic structures in the language of children. Child Dev. 34:407–422.

Miller, G., and Ojemann McKean, K. 1964. A chronometric study of some relations between sentences. Q. J. Exp. Psychol. 16:297–308.

Miller, J., and Yoder, D. 1972. A syntax teaching program. In J. McLean, D. Yoder, and R. L. Schiefelbusch (eds.), Language Intervention with the Retarded, pp. 191–211. University Park Press, Baltimore.

Miller, J., and Yoder, D. 1974. An ontogenetic language teaching strategy for retarded children. In R. L. Schiefelbusch and L. L. Lloyd (eds.), Language Perspectives—Acquisition, Retardation, and Intervention, pp. 505–528. University Park Press, Baltimore.

Miller, W., and Ervin, S. 1964. The development of grammar in child language. In U. Bellugi and R. Brown (eds.), The Acquisition of Language. Monogr. Soc. Res. Child Dev. 29:1.

Morton, J. 1970. What could possibly be innate? In J. Morton (ed.), Biological and Social Factors in Psycholinguistics. University of Illinois Press, Urbana.

Nelson, K. 1973. Structure and strategy in learning to talk. Monogr. Soc. Res. Child Dev. 38:1–2.

Olson, D. 1970. Language and thought: Aspects of a cognitive theory of semantics. Psychol. Rev. 77:254–273.

Paul, H. 1891. [Principles of the History of Language.] Trans. by H. A. Strong. Longmans Green, London. (Cited in Derwing, B. 1973. Transformational Grammar as a Theory of Language Acquisition. Cambridge University Press, Cambridge.)

Reber, A. 1973. On psycho-linguistic paradigms. J. Psychol. Res. 2:289–319.

Schiefelbusch, R. L. 1974. Summary. In R. L. Schiefelbusch and L. L. Lloyd (eds.), Language Perspectives—Acquisition, Retardation, and Intervention, pp. 647–660. University Park Press, Baltimore.

Schlesinger, I. 1971. Production of utterances and language acquisition. In D. Slobin (ed.), The Ontogenesis of Grammar. Academic Press, New York.

Schlesinger, I. 1974. Relational concepts underlying language. In R. L. Schiefelbusch and L. L. Lloyd (eds.), Language Perspectives—Acquisition, Retardation, and Intervention, pp. 129–151. University Park Press, Baltimore.

Schmidt, R. 1974. The functional development of language in a child of two-and-a-half years. Lang. Speech 17:358–368.

Searle, J. 1969. Speech Acts: An Essay in the Philosophy of Language. Cambridge University Press, Cambridge.

Slobin, D. 1965. Supplementary statement to grammatical development in Russian speaking children. In K. Riegel (ed.), The Development of Language Functions. Report No. 8, Language Development Program, University of Michigan, Ann Arbor.

Slobin, D. 1966. The acquisition of Russian as a native language. In F. Smith and G. Miller (eds.), The Genesis of Language. MIT Press, Cambridge.

Slobin, D. 1967. A Field Manual for Cross-Cultural Study of the Acquisition of Communicative Competence. University of California ASUC Bookstore, Berkeley.

Slobin, D. 1971. Universals of grammatical development in children. In G. Flores-D'Arcais and W. Leveit (eds.), Advances in Psycholinguistics. American Elsevier, New York.

Slobin, D. 1973. Cognitive prerequisites for the development of grammar. *In* C. Ferguson and D. Slobin (eds.), Studies of Child Language Development. Holt, Rinehart and Winston, New York.

Stremel-Campbell, K., Cantrell, D., and Halle, J. 1976. Manual signing as a language system and as a language facilitator. *In* E. Sontag, J. Smith, and N. Certo (eds.), Educational Programming for the Severely and Profoundly Handicapped. Division on Mental Retardation of the Council for Exceptional Children, Reston, Va.

Stremel-Campbell, K., and Ruder, K. 1976. A Progressive Approach to the Utilization of Grammatical Expansions in Training Language. Parsons Research Center Working Paper No. 328, Parsons, Kan.

Stremel, K., and Waryas, C. 1974. A behavioral-psycholinguistic approach to language training. *In* L. McReynolds (ed.), Developing Systematic Procedures for Training Children's Language. ASHA Monogr. 18.

Werner, H., and Kaplan, B. 1963. Symbol Formation. John Wiley & Sons, New York.

chapter 5

A Milieu Approach to Teaching Language

Betty Hart

Bureau of Child Research
University of Kansas
Lawrence, Kansas

Ann Rogers-Warren

Bureau of Child Research
University of Kansas
Lawrence, Kansas

Most children learn language in their normal day-to-day environments, progressing through predictable developmental stages (see McCarthy, 1954). Some children, though, either fail to acquire language or fail to display progressively more complex language. The causes of the failure may vary (Morehead, 1975), but, since language underlies so many of the skills and abilities that define the "normal" individual, any child who continues to lack language or to deviate in language development is likely to become a candidate for direct language teaching. Such language teaching is directed toward getting the child to produce language that will enable him[1] to function in the normal environment. In current teaching technology this goal is achieved in two overlapping stages. In one stage the emphasis is on form. The child is taught the essential vocabulary and syntax for communication. In the second stage the child is taught the functional use of language in the natural environment. The availability of an explicit and effective first-stage technology for training language production has made direct language teaching a practical reality for all handicapped individuals (Schiefelbusch and Lloyd, 1974). The second-stage technology, the training of functional use in the natural environment, is still in the process of development. This technology is described in this chapter, following a brief delineation of the two environments that form the basis of the technology.

THE TRAINING ENVIRONMENT

The goal in the training environment is to teach the child appropriate language forms, including phonetic, morphological, semantic, and syntactic features. Performance criteria are specified in terms of the precise topography of the language to be produced by the child. Exact repetition is encouraged and closer approximations to an implicit or explicit model are systematically reinforced. The rule of training environments is simply "Practice makes perfect."

The training environment usually involves two persons, the child and the clinician. The training is conducted in an area free from distractions, away from the flow of normal activities and conversation. The environment is arranged carefully. As many task-irrelevant stimuli as possible are removed. The relevant stimuli are both physical and verbal and are chosen and selected carefully to conform to the specifications of the training program. The clinician provides topics for language responses in the form of objects or pictures and accompanying questions for the child. Models for verbalizations are specified clearly, and the child's attention is directed toward them to facilitate imitation. The models provided are only slightly beyond the child's current skills.

The training program provides a sequential order for teaching skills, often (although not always) based on a developmental model. For each

---

[1] Masculine pronouns are used throughout for the sake of grammatical uniformity and simplicity. They are not meant to be preferential or discriminatory.

step of the program the behaviors of both child and clinician are specified in terms of the model to be presented, the response to be consequated, how incorrect responses are to be handled, and the criteria for advancing within the training sequence. Emphasis is on the *form* of language (correct label, appropriate tense marker, complete sentence). Language to the child is largely restricted to stimuli targeted to elicit particular verbal responses. The child's responses are typically limited to prespecified criterion behaviors, and language behavior irrelevant to the training sequence is discouraged. Both the correct language and its consequences are planned carefully. Feedback about the appropriateness of the verbalization is provided for nearly every response.

The effectiveness of this training model has been demonstrated repeatedly with a wide variety of language disorders (see other chapters in this book). The training procedures are particularly effective in teaching discrete verbal responses. Such training is the best, perhaps the only, means of teaching language to children who possess no language skills, children whose initial verbal response must be shaped carefully. The systematically arranged setting facilitates close attention to the topography of language. The child attends to the model and the clinician attends to the response. Thus, fine discriminations are possible. The carefully controlled session also serves to avoid or to limit disruptive behaviors that can interfere with language teaching. The environment is deliberately arranged to optimize the child's use of discrimination and imitation skills requisite to learning the forms of spoken language.

One-to-one training, however, is very expensive. It requires a skilled clinician for each child. Thus, it is likely that only those children with the most severe deficiencies can be treated, and each child can receive training for only a very short period (a half-hour or so) each day. Years of training may be required to build a limited language repertoire, one that is displayed only during training sessions. Transfer to other settings and generalization to other persons and objects must often be programmed as carefully and planned as deliberately as the initial stages of the language training. Too frequently, programming for generalization does not occur. Failure to obtain generalized language use may not be indicative of the failure of the training itself. One-to-one training fulfills its objective: it teaches the *form* of language, not its function. To ensure functional usage of newly trained skills, the training technology must be complemented by and integrated with a technology for teaching talking.

THE TALKING ENVIRONMENT

The goal in the talking environment is simply the functional use of language. In nontraining settings, the language-learning child must learn to use language as a social communication tool. Any language usage, regardless of form, is reinforced as long as it fulfills a communicative function. Topographical features are attended to only if they deviate from the norm enough to make communication impossible. Performance criteria are nonspecific. Any usage that "works" to communicate is likely to be reinforced. Exact repetition is discouraged. The natural environment in which most children learn language is such a talking environment.

The talking environment usually involves a variety of persons and a multiplicity of stimuli. For the child acquiring language the environment is variable and unsystematic, even chaotic. In the home a parent may be seen holding an infant while conversing with a visitor, the infant simultaneously engaged in play with mother's jewelry, in watching, and in babbling. In a preschool it is common to have the teacher speaking to a child, peers speaking to each other, many attractive toys and materials adjacent to the child, and the child nonverbally engaged in an activity, all at the same time. Language to the child in such settings is varied in form and purpose. It includes instructions, questions, and conversational or social comments. It is often unclear whether a language response from the child is even appropriate or desired by the adult. Models for appropriate language occur in the talking environment, but children may or may not attend to their presentation. Because adults are often unaware of a child's precise skill level, many models presented may be overly complex and beyond the child's ability to imitate.

The talking environment provides many opportunities for a child to use language. The child's use of language is cued by adults and is shaped gradually to approximate adult language. In a sense the language of the normally developing child becomes more complex by the adult's rising expectations of the child's communication skills. Adult consequences are usually delivered for language that appropriately communicates the child's needs and wants. During initial language learning, adults are likely to focus on the precise form of the language only when the child's verbalization is not comprehensible to the adult. Function is the central mechanism in the talking environment. A parent does not need to be an expert in language. Natural responsiveness to the social nature of language ensures that improvements in the child's language will receive appropriate feedback from the parent. The parent naturally gives a differential response to language that better communicates the child's needs or more readily engages adult attention. The social nature of language is such that the most appropriate consequence of talking is more talking, particularly talking that tends to elicit elaboration or variation in the language of the other party.

The effectiveness of the talking environment as a setting for acquiring language may lie in this very absence of careful attention to the topography of language. When language usage as a response class is reinforced, without particular attention to topography, it is likely that the child's rate of verbalizing will increase. However, the higher the rate of language use, the greater the likelihood that the topography of this language will come under the control of environmental stimuli. In this way, conditions for generalization and elaboration are naturally arranged. The more the child talks, the more the child encounters environmental feedback about how language works and which language works best. On the basis of this feedback, the child is able to select more appropriate (and possibly more complex) forms for use in future communications.

The talking environment (with its multiplicity of stimuli) is a very inexpensive learning laboratory, but it can be unsystematic. If language acquisition does not go right, the language-deficient child may simply not respond when verbalization opportunities occur, or the child may not attend to feedback directed toward eliciting more complex verbalizations. If the child fails to alter the form of language on the basis of adult feedback, the feedback may cease or become less frequent. There may be no alternative then except to provide a highly structured environment, which includes conditions necessary for learning. This usually means instituting a program of one-to-one language training.

Although a child may learn a great deal of language in a one-to-one training environment, the new language may not be used as a communication tool beyond the training setting. Thus, the child may not communicate much better than before training. Transfer and generalization of newly learned skills may be slow, either because the language repertoire has little relevance to the child's talking environment or because the talking environment has not been arranged to provide the appropriate stimulus events.

The need for a setting intermediary between the training and the talking environments, one which integrates the two and incorporates features of both, is apparent. This integration the present authors have called the milieu teaching model.

THE MILIEU TEACHING MODEL

The first goal of the milieu model is to teach the child to use language in functional ways. As in the natural setting, any language use is reinforced to establish and maintain an increased rate of talking. As soon as a reliable rate is established, the second goal of milieu teaching becomes operative and the child is encouraged to use appropriate forms of language. A specific teaching sequence is employed to teach the child to use specific forms within the context of social communication. These forms are modeled, prompted, and reinforced systematically, much as they might be in one-to-one training.

The milieu teaching model relies on the communications that occur naturally in everyday settings. The language-teaching program is carried out in the environment in which the child spends the majority of his time—in the home, in the preschool classroom, in the ward where the child lives. All the waking hours and normal activities of the child are potentially available as teaching occasions. The child does not leave the normal flow of verbal-social activities to learn new language skills. Rather, persons, events, objects, and contingencies typically present in the setting are incorporated into the teaching program. The setting may be rearranged to accommodate and support language learning, but it is not as stringently structured for that purpose as the one-to-one training environment.

The child's skills in the setting are assessed carefully, as are the language-eliciting and consequating behaviors of the adults in the setting. Based on these assessments, language skills are taught in a teaching sequence determined by the skills of the child and by the skills that child needs most to function in his particular setting. Adults provide topics for language responses in the form of objects, pictures, and activities, with accompanying questions for the child. No matter what the target skill, adults focus on making the child's language functional by consequating it with their attention and with the objects and services requested by the child. Models only slightly beyond the child's current skills are presented when a child's attention is focused and the child is thus optimally motivated to imitate them.

Individual training programs provide a sequential order for teaching language skills. However, skill training takes place only when the rate of spontaneous language persists under differential reinforcement for correct form. The environment is planned to elicit and support a quantity of language, which gradually comes under the control of the natural consequences in the unaltered talking environment. Because emphasis is always on the communicative function of language rather than on form, stimuli and consequences are arranged so the child's current language skills do in fact usually work to affect the environment in the desired way. The setting is also arranged to provide numerous contexts for a wide variety of functional language.

The milieu teaching environment serves as a bridge between the training setting and the natural talking environment. A child learns enough about how language works through milieu teaching to successfully generalize newly trained skills to the completely natural setting. Also, milieu teaching may be a viable alternative to one-to-one training for children who already have considerable language skill. For example, it is ideal for use with children with apparently normal acquisition skills who need to learn the language patterns of another culture or to learn

English as a second language. Milieu teaching is very economical because many children may be taught in a classroom during a limited time. When children have already learned appropriate language, but need to learn to use it in different ways, need to elaborate these forms, or need to use language more frequently, insetting intervention is more appropriate than is one-to-one teaching.

Milieu teaching may be most important, however, as a supplement to the one-to-one language training. Many language-deficient children succeed in learning new skills under the tightly controlled stimulus conditions of the training environment but fail to display these skills in the settings where they spend most of their time. In such cases, an expensive and effective training procedure may result in little apparent benefit to the child. Even when children begin using some of the newly trained language in the natural settings in which they live, the process of transfer is slow. Although the natural talking environment contains the most important occasions for language use, and potentially the strongest reinforcers, it is not sufficiently systematic to aid the child in transferring and extending newly acquired skills. If the child fails to display language skills, important opportunities to learn about the communicative function of those skills may be missed. The deliberate arrangement of the talking environment as a setting for milieu teaching in coordination with the program and goals of the one-to-one training environment ensures that newly learned language is extended to events and contexts outside the training. Milieu teaching ensures the practice of trained items and contact with the communicative function of that language. The milieu teaching model is designed to help the child learn about reinforcement contingencies for the display of language in the day-to-day social communication environment. Because language-delayed children often appear less aware of the communicative demands of normal social interactions than do normal language-learning children, deliberately teaching the child that language has a function is a necessary component of a comprehensive program.

The milieu teaching model integrates the best features of the training and talking environments. It structures the learning of language forms within the context of social communication. In this way, milieu teaching provides opportunities for the child to learn both "what to say" and "how to say it."

The various aspects of one-to-one and natural environments and their integration in the milieu teaching model are summarized in Table 1.

TEACHING LANGUAGE SKILLS VIA THE MILIEU MODEL

Implementing the milieu teaching model involves preparation in three areas: 1) arranging the environment to prompt the use of language, 2) assessing a child's current skill level to select areas for teaching functional language, and 3) training adults to ensure that the child does work with language and that the child's language works for him. Environmental arrangement, assessment, and training always interact in the design of a milieu, whether in the home, the classroom, or the ward. They are separated here only for discussion.

Arranging the Environment

The environment must be deliberately arranged to provide impetus and support for language. There must be a variety of attractive materials and activities immediately accessible to the child. If there is nothing in the environment that children want to have or do, there is little for them to talk about. Regardless of how attractive materials and activities may appear to adults, actual child engagement should be the measure of environmental richness (Cataldo and Risley, 1974). Thus, materials and activities offered to children should be those that they use repeatedly for extended periods. Those not used should be removed. Some materials and activities are, of course, more conducive to social interaction and conversation than others (Quilitch and Risley, 1973). These are preferable, as long as they engage children. (For example, dolls and housekeeping toys provide more opportunities for conversation than do individual puzzles.) In selecting materials, start with materials the child enjoys and with activities in which the child wants to participate.

The materials and activities the child wants must be accessible. The child must be able to see them and should be able to reach them. Their accessibility, like their attractiveness, prompts the child to want to use them. There should be a toy box or a low shelf of toys from which a child can help himself. A moderately high rate of engagement with materials is basic to milieu teaching and may in certain cases have to be established (through training and reinforcement) concurrent with language teaching.

At the same time, certain other materials and activities must be available to the child only on request. In milieu teaching the adult mediates materials and activities, uses materials to reinforce verbalizations and to demonstrate how language works to obtain objects and events from the environment. Removing some materials from the child's reach makes it easy for an adult to use access to them as a language-eliciting and consequating event. This also requires the adult to be continuously and immediately available to ensure that a child's request for a material is consequated appropriately with delivery of the material. If the adult does not hear the child's request, the language response goes unreinforced. If the material is accessible to the child, however, the child could ask, and, if he received no response from the adult, the child might help himself. A rule that certain materials, even though within reach, must be requested is easy to establish: the adult states the rule re-

Table 1. Aspects of one-to-one and natural environments and their integration in the milieu teaching model

Aspect	One-to-one teaching	Natural settings	Milieu teaching settings
Language to the child	Highly specified and structured according to particular training program.	Varied. Content determined by the objects, events, and persons in the setting.	Controlled and balanced to coincide with both the child's skills and the objects, events, and persons present in the setting.
Models of specific language	Presented discretely. The child's attention is directed toward them. Imitations are consequated and matched systematically to the child's skill level.	Occur irregularly. The child's attention may not be directed toward them. They vary in complexity so that many of them may be beyond the child's skill level.	Specific. Delivered in a context that functionally reinforces imitation. Models are provided only when the child is attending. Complexity and frequency of presentation are determined by the child's skills.
Consequences for language usage	Frequent and immediately following child's verbal response.	Vary in frequency but are typically unsystematic. Functional reinforcers are attention from adults and peers, acquisition of needed materials and services, participation in social-verbal interaction.	Frequent and systematic. Same functional reinforcers as found in natural settings.

Demand for language usage	High. The child is required to respond many times during a relatively short period of time.	Low. The child may infrequently be required to verbalize or elaborate his verbalizations.	Selectively high, when it is functional for the child to respond.
Opportunities for language usage	Many opportunities to respond but few opportunities to initiate with descriptions or requests.	Opportunities to ask questions, request needed objects and services, and to engage in social conversation are all present in the setting although the child may not utilize the opportunities.	Same opportunities are present as in the natural setting. The child is prompted to make appropriate responses when these opportunities arise.
Language teaching	Systematic but occurring during a small portion of the child's day.	No systematic teaching.	Systematic and occurring during a moderate portion of the child's day.
Emphasis of teaching	Form, correct structures, etc.	If it occurs, the focus is likely to be communicative function.	Communicative function is primary. Form is secondary.

peatedly, and, when a child takes (or is about to take) a material, the adult enforces the rule. The adult goes to the child and puts a hand over the child's hand on the materials. (The child as well as the adult may continue holding onto the material. Thus, it is clear that the child does "have" the material, and that the issue is not "having" it but "asking" for it.) While they both hold the material, the adult says, "You need to ask for that" (or whatever restatement of the rule has been selected in the particular environment). (What to do if the child does not answer is dealt with below.) Establishing the rule, "Materials must be asked for," is facilitated by the adult being nearby, listening for requests, focusing on the child when he asks for materials and always providing the material when it is verbally requested.

The environment must be arranged so that the adult is readily available to mediate materials and activities. For example, in a classroom, where many materials are available on low, open shelves, the teacher should be either centrally located to supervise an extended play area, or moving around the area, from one play group to another. In a home, where a child's activities are subordinated to the parents' schedule of activities, it may be more effective to place the materials on a small cart or in a large box and bring the materials into the area where the parent is working.

In the milieu model the adult must mediate things that the child wants, the more things the better. For the child progressing normally in the talking environment, the adults mediate attention, approval, affection, assistance, safety, comfort, food, toys, activities, trips, contacts with others—a panoply of reinforcers. Adults present and remove all these reinforcers, not always contingent upon the child's language (what the child wants or what he is saying). The adult in a milieu teaching environment is mediating these same reinforcers systematically. The materials and services provided to the child do not change, but the conditions under which the child obtains these things are arranged to encourage language display. The parent, the preschool teacher, or the ward attendant continues to attend to the child's needs and wants. In addition, the adult actively engages in language teaching. Milieu teaching makes adults very important individuals in a language-deficient child's environment.

In arranging the environment it is necessary to consider: 1) what it is the children do, 2) what they want to do, and 3) what reinforcers the adults mediate for children. Once the environment is arranged so that the things the children really want are located in close proximity to adult consequation, decisions must be made concerning the level of communication expected of the child.

Assessing Functional Language

The communicative skills to be taught in the milieu must be based on an assessment of the child's current language skills. While a child may have numerous skills in other settings, particularly in the one-to-one training environment, if those skills are not exhibited in the milieu teaching setting, it is assumed that the child must be taught to use them there. Although information is collected concerning the child's skills in other settings, a specific assessment of language skill in the milieu setting is necessary. This assessment entails making a detailed transcript of the child's verbalizations and the circumstances in which these verbalizations occur. Such a transcript (although time consuming to record) provides specific information about what the child is saying and what the adult is saying in response to the child. Both types of information are important to the success of milieu teaching. For example, it may not be evident that a child never uses plurals or tense markers unless one specifically looks for such forms. Likewise, it may not be obvious just how much an adult talks without requesting a verbal response from a child, unless the adult's verbalizations are monitored.

In addition to transcriptions of actual language by adults and children, less formal observations of social-communication interactions may be valuable in providing a "feel" for typical social-communication interactions and the opportunities for language teaching that normally occur. Although an observation system employing a code for adult and child behaviors provides the most accurate information in terms of rates of verbalization by both parties, less formalized observations can be used. Even brief samples of rates of verbalization by children and adults may supplement informal, anecdotal observations.

After assessing the general language skill level of the child, an assessment is made of what skills the child needs to function in the setting and what opportunities exist for teaching these skills. For example, children need to know how to indicate when they are hungry or thirsty, when they have had enough to eat, when the food is distasteful, and, eventually, which foods they prefer. Snacks and mealtimes, which occur in nearly every setting, are the occasions when such communications are most likely and most functional. This assessment of the communication demands and the setting benefits the person who will be using the setting as a teaching milieu. It gives them information about language-teaching opportunities that they may not have seen or used before.

Assessment of the communication opportunities in the setting continues throughout operation of the program, and contributes to arranging and rearranging the environment to increase opportunities for communication or to make those opportunities more discriminable to children. New and more complex stimuli are introduced as children progress, and the environment is programmed carefully to elicit increasingly complex language, coinciding with the child's initial acquisition of more complex language forms. The program of language skills to be taught in the milieu setting is designed on the basis of the assessment of the child's communication skills. The program systematically takes the child from the current level to a level of greater complexity or fluency by gradually increasing and extending the functions of language. The primary consideration, however, is that the language be functional. Language for which no function can be arranged in the milieu setting is simply not taught in this setting. For instance, a child is taught the labels *knife* and *fork* at the time that these utensils are used at meals, not while playing on the playground. Children in the milieu teaching setting should know and use the name of every object and activity in their immediate environment and the label for everything they can touch and do, before they learn the name of anything that can only be depicted or illustrated.

One of the most important uses of language is to give and get objects, information, and attention. The language may or may not be vocalized (viz., sign language). The function lies in the communication. Every person, in this respect, communicates, and so has language of some kind. In milieu teaching, the first step is to make language functional, beginning with whatever communicative abilities the child possesses. By making current skills functional, the foundation for the development of more complex language is laid. For example, if a child is just learning to produce sounds in one-to-one training, the milieu teaching procedure would make those sounds functional in obtaining objects and attention. The child might be prompted to make the sound, and, when an approximation is produced, the desired object would be provided with much attention from the adult. Similarly, a child's one-word phrases may initially serve many purposes. Like the "holophrastic" speech of the infant, the child's one word can communicate a complete proclamation, command, or question, when closely bound up with an attitude of response to the immediate surroundings (DeLaguna, 1972). To a child with minimal language skills, the first language taught might be labels. Single words for frequently needed materials and services (*milk, go, me*) can function as requests or comments in varying settings, and as "pivots" to which, in later training, other words may be attached.

Although a child with only a few words may be displaying a very limited language repertoire in the milieu setting, the child is using language within the social communication context. The child's "holophrastic" speech is functional in mediating the things he wants. The adults in the setting ensure that the child's language, no matter how minimal, is consistently functional. This is similar to the circumstances of normal language development. Very young children express needs and wants through single words, but their language is consequated by adults whose expectations in terms of child language are in close accord with the children's actual skill levels (Broen, 1972). Adults using milieu teaching procedures similarly match their expectations for the child's language to the child's skills. At the same time they increase the number of opportunities for the child to use these skills and, thus, to learn about language as a functional communicative tool.

For the slightly more skilled child, milieu teaching begins with functional labels to bring the child into contact with the consequences of language use (adult attention, acquisition of desired materials or services), but the teaching quickly moves on to more elaborate language responses (e.g., label-plus-verb). As the child's skill level increases, the demands for more complex language also increase. If a child is being taught in one-to-one training sessions, milieu teaching gets the child to use newly learned labels or grammatical constructions in the home, classroom, or ward. At the same time, the clinician conducting the one-to-one training may be asked to work with the child on specific words or constructions that are particularly functional in the milieu setting. There must be frequent exchanges of information between the clinician or trainer and the teacher, parent, or ward attendant doing the milieu teaching.

Once a child has skills for minimal functioning in the setting, more elaborate grammatical or semantic forms are selected and made functional in a similar manner. Rather than immediately consequating a child's labeling of food items by providing the desired food, the adult models a slightly more complex response for the child and requests that the child imitate that form. Thus, a progressive teaching program is incorporated into the milieu teaching model. The adult begins with requests for very simple language and systematically moves toward requesting more adult-like verbalizations. This teaching sequence may follow a developmental model but will be determined by the needs of the child in a particular setting. The teaching sequence will move from simple to complex with the child advancing at his own individual rate. At each step the language is functional for the child. For instance, color names are taught only when something of a particular color is present and wanted by the child. Request statements are taught only when there are materials or services the child wants to obtain.

Function may be defined informally by the adult for the child as, "Saying what you want will get it for you." For the child with lesser skills, the definition may be simpler still, "Verbalizing will get it for you." The adult makes the child's language functional by providing the child with attention, materials, or services when the child displays the appropriate language skills. If the adult provides these things to a language-delayed or language-deviant child without placing a demand for language on that child (however gentle or subtle), the adult is teaching the child that language is neither a necessary nor a useful tool for managing the environment.

What the Milieu Teacher Does

As described above, the milieu teacher, parent, ward attendant, or classroom teacher arranges the environment for function and assesses the child's skills level. These two activities are ongoing, with the teacher ever alert to the need to alter aspects of the environment as the child's skills increase. The adult is also an important aspect of the milieu teaching environment. The teacher arranges his behavior to be maximally conducive to child language. Milieu teaching takes place during unstructured, free-activity times. If the teacher is to maintain spontaneity and reciprocity, and retain his own natural language and interaction style, he cannot analyze, count words, or parse sentences, either his own or a child's during conversation. The teacher must focus on how the child is to respond, not on the topography of his own speech. The teacher's goal is to get the child to comprehend and produce more language. When an adult's language is not working toward this goal, the adult should not be afraid to be silent. A good listener may be as effective as a good model and, for the young child, certainly rarer.

The milieu teacher operates on the premise that the language-deficient child must learn three kinds of consequences. First, the child must learn that language *has* consequences. Second, the child needs to learn that language gains things and events. Third, the child must learn how language works to get more language, as in social conversation.

Building Rate

The language-delayed child must first learn that language has a function, that language works. With a child who has no language or only minimal language, it may be necessary to teach the child that a vocal or verbal response will result in attention. This means that the adult must respond to every communicative gesture made by the child, whether verbal, vocal, or physical (whichever has been assessed as the highest level response for the individual child). The response class being reinforced is expansive. It includes all verbal or nonverbal language. The goal is more language use, and thus more communication.

Initially, it does not matter what the adult says when the child uses language. It matters only that the adult does something, anything, so that the child's language has a result. In this way the child is given feedback indicating that language has a consequence that is discriminably different from that accorded silence. In milieu language teaching, the teacher is all ears. The most important occurrence for the teacher is child speech. The teacher lets the child know how valuable this behavior is by the immediacy, consistency, and magnitude of the response to it. This differential responsiveness to verbalization must be maintained even after a child becomes sophisticated in language use. The schedule of reinforcement may be leaned, but deliberate consequation of language use as a response class cannot be neglected. The reinforcement of language, independent of local topography, leads to increase in rate or ensures that rate remains high. A high rate of language use facilitates all operations on topography.

Providing materials and adult attention as reinforcers is critical to milieu teaching. It may be necessary in certain cases for the teacher to establish attention as a reinforcer for the child, and it may be necessary to establish materials as reinforcers. The process of pairing and mediation (see Bijou and Baer, 1965) required to establish materials and attention as reinforcers may take considerable time, but they must come first. It is impossible to increase a child's rate of talking unless teacher attention and access to materials are positive reinforcing events.

Once a teacher has established attention as a reinforcer, the teacher can present it contingent on a child's talking to another child, by coming over and listening, without interrupting. Attention can also be a stimulus for talking when the teacher approaches a child and waits silently for the child to speak in order to get attention. Attention can even enhance the child-perceived value of a material when it is provided contingent on the use of language.

Once the child has learned the importance of language in making things happen, the child is ready to learn specific relations between words and things. The child is ready to learn that certain topographies work better than others to obtain particular results. For example, an infant (or a child with delayed language) learns first how vocalization or how a word such as *Mama* works to communicate a need for food. Later on, the child learns that *cookie* works better when he needs food but does not want milk.

An important aspect of language is that, along with communicating a want or need, it can specify the particular thing that will satisfy a need. In the natural environment, specification normally pays off. It permits the listener to respond more efficiently and effectively. A cry *Get off!* is not responded to in the same way as is a cry *Get off my fingers!* The milieu teaching environment is arranged so the language-delayed child learns better and more elaborate ways to work with language. The goal of milieu teaching is to teach the child how to specify needs and wants. This teaching process, directed toward teaching functional language and based on environmental arrangement, has been termed "incidental teaching" (Hart and Risley, 1975).

Building Requesting

The necessary conditions for incidental teaching are: 1) the child must have rate and repertoire (must emit spontaneous nonechoic speech with sufficient frequency that continuous reinforcement is no longer necessary and must be able to imitate), 2) the environment must contain materials and activities that are reinforcers for the child, and 3) the child must initiate the interaction by specifying a reinforcer, something needed or wanted. If a child does not have the skills that incidental teaching procedures require, those skills must first be taught. In some cases, the child may require one-to-one training in imitation, or must have a program for increasing rate, or a program for establishing materials as reinforcers.

Once the child has the basic language skills (and materials and events have been established as reinforcers) incidental language teaching can occur whenever the child initiates language to express a need or want. The adult can require that the child work with language only when there is something for which to work, something the child wants, and something the adult can, and is willing to, mediate. A child's expressed need to urinate, for instance, can be used for incidental teaching only if there is no risk that the child will wet his pants. An adult can make a meal contingent on verbalization only if the adult really intends to withhold food if there is no verbalization. In practice, there is no need to use access to primary reinforcers as contingencies in incidental teaching. If adult attention and the materials and activities in the environment are not reinforcing for a child, the child is not yet ready for incidental teaching. If these are reinforcers, however, and the incidental teaching interaction is kept brief and positive, and always results in the child getting what is requested, the child will initiate language very frequently. Because the milieu setting is the environment in which the child spends the majority of his time, a child on a ward or in a home may be available for teaching for 12 hours a day or more. In this amount of time there should be (if the environment has been properly arranged) many, many opportunities for casual, incidental teaching.

The more reinforcers an adult supplies in an environment, the more it is likely that the child will initiate language. If reinforcers are plentiful, the adult can afford to wait for the child to use language, rather than having to prompt or nag him to speak. And the adult can afford mistakes. An occasional delivery of attention or a material without requiring more elaborated language from the child is not as serious in a 10-hour session as it is in a half-hour training period. The teacher should relax and focus not on what he says, but on what he wants the child to say. In this way, the teacher continuously varies, adapts, and elaborates language in ways that elicit more and better language from the child. In incidental teaching, the frequency of occasions for teaching is always more critical than the precision of the language interaction.

Table 2 lists classes of teacher behaviors in terms of the desired child response—what the teacher wants the child to do when he uses a particular type of language. Teachers can most effectively elicit language from children by concentrating on their own communicative *intent,* rather than on the content or topography of their language. The child's response provides feedback about how effectively the teacher has expressed his intent. With language-delayed children, the teacher restricts *his* language behavior and adapts to the level of the child to teach the child about communicative intent. Just as a parent does with an infant, the teacher shortens the sentences delivered to a child with a repertoire of one-word utterances and tries to make the distinctions between classes of verbalizations (e.g., questions, greetings, models) clear, so that a child may learn the intent of a particular class. A child's receptive language repertoire is also considered. Whenever a teacher addresses language to a child, he endeavors to make its class or communicative intent as clear as possible. When the teacher presents verbal instructions for the child to comprehend and carry out, those instructions always contain an imperative. When asking the child questions, the purpose is primarily to gain specific information or elaboration and only secondarily to give the child practice in hearing and answering the question. The teacher frequently confirms what the child says ("That's right, you're . . ."). Confirmation increases the likelihood that the child will do more of the behavior the teacher describes, and it provides an opportunity for the child to learn the label for the behavior specified in the confirmation. Confirmations are also models of the language the teacher would like the child to use.

If the teacher knows the exact response he wants from the child, he can tailor verbal behavior to get precisely that response. When initiating language interaction with a child, the teacher usually has time to consider the desired response before beginning to speak. The teacher may not have time to consider his intent as carefully when responding to a child, however. When the teacher wants a child to do something, he selects the simplest, least ambiguous instruction (e.g., *Stop that, Put your toys away, Go to the bathroom*), at least until it is certain the child understands. Then the teacher can introduce the child (when *he* is ready in terms of language progress) to more sophisticated forms of instruc-

Table 2. Teacher behaviors in terms of desired child response

When the teacher presents:	By saying, for example:	He wants the child to:
Attention	"Hi," "Wow!"	Start or continue talking. He wants his attention to tell the child, "I'm available, I'm listening."
Instruction	"Say, 'red'." "Sit down." "Take your sweater off." "You need to tell me." "You need to sit and watch how the other children play without hitting." "Look what John is doing." "If you turn it a little bit, I think it will go in." "If you want to paint, get an apron."	Do what he tells the child to do.
Question	"What color is this?" "Where do worms live?" "What are you doing?" "What do you think?"	Answer with information or elaboration.
Confirmation	"That's right, it's a red truck." "You are really jumping high." "That's exactly the right way to brush your teeth." "It is a big building."	Do more of the behavior described. At some future time, emit a particular language response again or do a particular motor response again, without instruction, simply because it is "right" for drawing adult attention.
Prompt	"Remember?" "Worms live in the . . .?" "It rhymes with 'jar'."	Take the hint and complete the verbalization or do the action without more complete instruction.
Model	"Worms live in the ground." "It's almost time to go home." "This is a car." "It's warm outside, you don't need your coat." "One, two, three." "I don't know."	Say what the teacher said at some later time. The teacher thus informs a child of facts, vocabulary, labels, sentence structure, but he does not want, expect, or require an imitation or even an answering verbalization from the child if the child does not choose to answer.
Display	"That's nice." "I like that." "I don't know why this school buys puzzles for three-year-olds that are too hard even for grown-ups to put together, but then I've never been good at puzzles, maybe that's why I hate them so much."	Do nothing. The teacher is showing the child how much fun it is to talk, that people do this and enjoy it and others enjoy that they do it. Talk like this just makes everybody comfortable. A child needs to be exposed to the fact that language can work in this way.

tion: *It's time to clean up, We don't hit people with blocks.* Only when a child has fairly well-elaborated language should instructions be introduced in the form of rhetorical questions (*How would you like to put up your toys now?* or *Do you have to use the bathroom?*). Similarly, the teacher whose aim is language remediation tries to avoid *yes/ no* questions, because, in adult verbal behavior, these are so often rhetorical in intent.

The adult must also be aware of the purpose of an interaction. The adult should note carefully whether or not a reinforcer is being specified by the speaker. When no reinforcer is specified in a verbalization, no response other than more talking is called for. Conversation (the exchange of talk) generally requires a higher level of language skills. Consequently, in the milieu teaching environment, the emphasis is on language that makes its communicative intent as clear as possible and that specifies a reinforcer. Therefore, the adult largely initiates language to the child with that same purpose for which the adult endeavors to get the child to initiate language—because the adult wants or needs things from the child. Each occasion on which the child initiates and specifies a reinforcer, something needed or wanted, is an opportunity for incidental teaching.

Incidental teaching entails a series of steps that can be best specified in terms of intent. Each step relies on the teacher's ability to adapt to the skill level and response of each child. The process may be used *only* when the child initiates the interaction and specifies a reinforcer. The child's initiation, verbal or nonverbal, is always the starting point for making the child's requesting behavior functional and for requiring more elaborated language from the child.

Incidental teaching begins when a child initiates a request to an adult.

Step 1: Focus Attention on the Child When the Child Initiates   The adult focuses full attention on the child who has initiated the request. This gives immediate response to the child's language. At this point the adult must decide whether or not to ask the child for elaboration. The language here may be verbal or nonverbal. A child may say, "Gimme," or merely point, may vocalize a cry, or just stand there with one arm in a coat waiting for the teacher to put it on. The adult's decision to use the occasion for incidental teaching is based on whether he has the time and whether or not he can request an appropriate elaboration. An appropriate elaboration is one that will be easy for the child in terms of the child's individual language repertoire and one for which there are clearly discriminable environmental cues. For example, consider the child who says to a teacher, "Gimme," and points. The teacher is not likely to use this occasion for incidental teaching if: 1) the child is pointing to something the teacher does not intend to give the child, such as a paring knife, 2) if the child has never or rarely said "Gimme" before, and so the teacher wants the child to learn, first, that this language works immediately and better than just pointing alone, or 3) the teacher is busy with another child. If the teacher decides not to use the child's initiation for incidental teaching, he simply gives the child what the child has asked for or pointed to. When a child points and says "Gimme," the teacher is likely to choose to use the occasion for incidental teaching when the teacher has time. When the child is saying "Gimme" regularly and is pointing to a frequently used toy, such as a car, this is an instance for incidental teaching. The adult, with attention focused on the child, and often holding out the object to the child, goes on to the next step.

Step 2: Model an Appropriate Verbal Response The adult models the language expected from the child. The adult gives the child the answer, and expects the child to respond by repeating the model. If a response occurs, it indicates that the child has discriminated some very subtle cues for imitation; that is, the child has attended to an adult expansion of his own statement. If the child does not imitate immediately, the teacher does not wait for the child to respond to the model but quickly goes on to the next step.

Step 3: Ask a Question The adult asks a question that clearly calls for the response the adult has just modeled. The adult asks, for instance, while holding out the car to the child, "What is this?" The adult may skip the modeling step (Step 2) with a child known to have the response (e.g., a child who has said *car* in the presence of the object on many prior occasions). The teacher may, in the case of a normal child, merely focus on the child and ask a question. If the child answers the question, the teacher proceeds.

Step 4: Confirm the Child's Behavior The adult always confirms the child's verbal behavior. This is done best by doubly informing the child by saying, "That's right, it's a car." The child is told specifically that the answer was correct. The answer is repeated by the adult to let the child know that the adult both heard and understood the answer. It also reminds the child of the correct answer.

If the child does not answer the adult's question in Step 3, the adult has three choices. The adult can prompt the child, instruct the child, or terminate the interaction. The adult should opt to terminate the interaction whenever there is no language immediately available that will elicit the correct answer from the child; that is, if the teacher asks a child a question, gets no response, and cannot think of another way of getting the language from the child, the teacher should just give the child what has been asked for, and repeat the model. E.g., when the teacher asks a child, "What's this?", if the child does not answer and the teacher does not know what more to do, the teacher should say, "It's a car," and give the car to the child. If the incidental teaching episode is kept brief and positive (with the child always obtaining both a desired object and close teacher attention), the child will initiate language again. The teacher can think about how better to get more elaborated language from the child and try again the next time. The teacher never keeps a child waiting while thinking of a way to elaborate language.

The adult should opt to instruct the child whenever the adult is fairly certain that the child knows the answer to the question. If the child does not answer, but the teacher has heard the child label this specific object on a prior occasion, the teacher should instruct the child as to what to say (e.g., *Say, "car"*). If the child answers, the teacher confirms the response. If the child does not answer, the teacher terminates the interaction by labeling the object (*It's a car*) and giving it to the child. If the child cannot imitate or will not answer, other specific training may be needed.

The adult should prompt the child whenever the adult is certain that the child knows the answer but appears to be somewhat unsure in the present circumstances. For instance, if the child does not answer but the adult has heard the child label other cars often in the past, although not this specific object, the adult should prompt or give a hint. The teacher might present part of the word (*It's a c . . .*), or a comparison (*It's not a truck, it's a . . .*), or a relation (*It's what your mother brings you to school in*). The teacher must be able to select a situation-specific and child-appropriate prompt. Success depends on choosing one that works at that moment. The child must have a repertoire of both language and concepts that enable the child to benefit from the teacher's prompts. Skill on the part of both the teacher and the child is likely to come only with repeated practice and experience.

The steps in the incidental teaching process may be summarized as those that are mandatory (attention, question, and confirmation) and those that are optional (the model, prompt, and instruction). Two more examples illustrate how this works.

The first example is the child who just stands with an arm in his coat, waiting, while all the other children go outdoors to play. If outdoor play is reinforcing to this child, so that the child wants the adult's help with his coat in order to contact the reinforcers outside (rather than wanting to hold the adult's attention as a means of avoiding outdoor activity), the occasion may be used for incidental teaching. The adult begins the process by focusing attention on the child. The teacher questions, "What do you need, John?" John says, "Uh." The adult confirms, "That's right, you need help," and puts the coat on the child.

Once John is coming to the adult and showing that he has learned the function of that language response by saying, "uh, uh, uh," as he pulls on the teacher's sleeve, the adult may begin asking for an elaboration of that response. Again, the adult focuses attention, looks into the child's face, models an appropriate word, and then immediately asks a question ("What do you need, John?"). When John says, "Uh," the adult instructs, ("Say, 'help'."). If any aspect of the child's response is closer to the topography of *help*, or even if the response topography differs from *uh* in a discriminable way, the adult confirms ("That's right, you need help."). If John emits an identical "Uh," the adult models, "help, help, help," as the teacher puts his coat on him. Because the adult regularly helps John with his coat, there will be many opportunities to try again.

As a second example, there is a child who has a high rate of saying "Look," or "What's this?" This is a child who knows quite a bit about how language works. The child has learned that certain stimuli will elicit an adult response automatically. The reinforcer specified when this child initiates language is adult attention, usually accompanied by verbalizations. When the child initiates language (saying, "What's this?"), the adult begins incidental teaching by focusing attention on the child and questioning, "What's that?" If the child responds correctly ("Chair"), the adult confirms ("That's right, it's a chair."). When, on a subsequent occasion, this child initiates, "What's that?" in regard to the same chair, the adult focuses attention on the child and models, "That's a chair," following immediately with a question, "What's that?" If the child says, "Chair," the adult instructs, "Say, 'That's a chair'." If the child does not immediately reply as instructed, the adult turns away to do something else. If the child then emits, "That's a chair," or something close to it, the adult returns his attention to the child and confirms the child's statement. If the child does not respond at all this time, the adult waits for the child's next *What's this?* and repeats the above procedure. (In the case of the child who initiates a high rate of *look*, the adult's question *Look at what?* must of course precede the actual looking. The question itself indicates to the child that the teacher is potentially attentive.)

Children's rates of requesting materials and attention are readily increased by requiring that some form of language be used to obtain these things. The forms of requesting language are elaborated through the incidental teaching process. The child who is taught through this process learns that a label and a sentence (*I want a trike, I want to paint*, etc.) work more effectively to obtain a material or access to an activity than pointing. The ability to make requests is the primary focus in remediation because this is both most essential to effective functioning in society and most likely to be maintained by peer responses. At the same time, no opportunity to shape conversational skills should be over-looked, if the goal is for the child to acquire a normal language repertoire.

Building Commenting

In acquiring more sophisticated language, the child learns how to prompt environmental responses without making a demand. The child learns how to initiate and draw attention by giving information that is of interest to others. The child also learns how to respond in ways that will maintain or discourage attention. The exchange of language in a setting of mutual attention is called conversation.

In conversational language, no reinforcer is named. A statement does not specifically request an object or demand attention. Whereas a child is likely to repeat a request or demand for something he wants, a conversational statement is unlikely to be repeated unless an adult specifically asks that it be repeated. For example, a child says, *Hi*, or *My mama's gonna take me to the circus.* If no one responds, the child is unlikely to repeat the statement or the greeting. If an adult responds with *Hi*, or with *That's nice*, the conversation may be effectively ended. Such statements by the adult return the conversation "ball" to the child, who must devise a second statement, an elaboration or addition, that will draw a further response and maintain the attention of the adult. Because the adult's comment has not included cues or support for another child comment, the language-deficient child may be unable to provide a second statement and the conversation ends. Thus, these adult responses tend to suggest to the child that the adult is not very interested in hearing more.

It is often the case that the conversation of children with minimal language is not at all interesting to adults. Adults naturally tend to terminate or avoid uninteresting conversation. To maintain adult attention in conversation, a child may need particular skills. Thus, guidelines for building conversational skills are presented here. As before, it is most helpful if the adult focuses not on topography but on communicative intent. The communicative intent of conversation is social interaction: mutual, attention-maintaining talk. Therefore, the adult focuses on responding to a child's comment with another comment intended to draw or suggest a further comment from the child.

When a child initiates a comment to an adult, the adult proceeds in the following way.

Step 1.   The teacher focuses full attention on the child who initiates with a statement or greeting. The teacher lets the child know that *his* language is important, that it will draw attention immediately, no matter what else the teacher may be doing.

Step 2.   The adult confirms, letting the child know that he has truly been listening and has understood the language. The adult repeats some or all of what the child said. If the adult did not understand, he should take a guess, based on the child's sounds and the immediate context. This gives useful feedback to the child in a context in which the adult is obviously positive, neither correcting nor asking for a repetition. The child gets information about what the verbalization sounded like to the audience.

Step 3.   The adult can ask a question, give an instruction, or model a language response. The adult may leave if he cannot think of anything to say.

For example, a child calls as a teacher passes, "Hey!" the teacher stops and looks at the child (Step 1). If this is a verbally skilled child, the teacher waits for the child to respond to the attention before saying something more. If this is a child with minimal language, the teacher might say, "Hey yourself," repeating what the child said (Step 2). The teacher then immediately asks a question (*How are you?*), models a statement (*That's a big building*), or gives an appropriate instruction (*Try turning it and it will go in*) (Step 3).

In another example, a child says to the teacher, ". . . (incomprehensible) . . . circus . . . ." The adult looks at the child (Step 1), and says (Step 2) "The circus, yes." This gives the child differential feedback about the comprehensibility of his language, and lets the child know what the teacher thinks he is talking about. Then the adult asks (Step 3, question), "Who are you going with?" If, for instance, the child replies, "Mama," the teacher has a conversation, which he undertakes to keep going. The teacher might then try to get the child to talk about other family members also going to the circus, or about all the things to be seen in a circus.

The start of a conversation challenges the adult to use many skills to adapt language immediately and adroitly to the ability level and the topic of the child. Conversation always works best when two persons have a topic of mutual interest to discuss. Second-best conversation occurs when one person has a topic of consuming interest plus a receptive and attentive listener. Language teachers in a classroom must create the conversational context. The child is likely to need to learn the one-sided, second-best conversation, in which the topic of consuming interest is himself, before being expected to discriminate what is a topic of mutual interest. The child may need direct instruction in topics that interest other persons, especially adults, and in how to be a good listener (for example, how to respond as the teacher does, how to imitate the behavior the teacher models). The teacher models the fascinated listener whose every cue communicates, *Tell me more.* This is a skill the teacher develops with practice and with listening.

SUMMARY AND CONCLUSION

The milieu teaching model integrates aspects of both the training and talking environments. It focuses on building high rates of spontaneous language in natural settings (with a variety of persons) about objects and events, and it elaborates the topography of language through imitation and differential reinforcement procedures. Its strategies involve making language functional by arranging situations in which the child works with language and by ensuring that the child's language works to produce attention, things, and events. The environment is designed to include many and varied stimuli that elicit language. Programming starts from the initial, observationally assessed repertoire of the child and relies on carefully arranging contingencies for language use and systematic teacher responses. The model stresses the function of language rather than its form. It is a model based on a communication intent approach to language acquisition rather than on a generative grammar approach (see McNeill, 1970). It is a developmental sequence designed for a child with delayed language and reflects the view that the language of the normal child "is acquired as an instrument for regulating joint activity and joint attention" (Bruner, 1975, p. 2).

CASE STUDY 1

When four-year-old Charles came to the nursery school he was reluctant to talk. However, the teachers soon observed that he used "nonspeaking" as a device to gain desired responses from adults. Often he would withhold speech until the teacher determined his wishes from the cues he arranged in the play context. In effect, he evoked speaking responses from the teacher and in turn avoided talking.

On the basis of their observations of Charles on this first day, as well as during his preliminary visit (when he had played only with puzzles and had spoken only when asked to do so by his mother), teachers suspected that Charles had learned that one way to obtain adult attention was to wait, silent and immobile. In his home, where Charles was the only child, waiting in silence probably worked in a similar way, to draw his mother into interaction. Getting his mother to prompt him into activity had an obvious advantage: she gave her implied approval in advance, and so was unlikely to tell him to stop when he was engaged.

Charles' mother had enrolled him in the preschool because she had been convinced by her mother and her physician that Charles was going to have difficulty in school because of his lack of speech. She contended, however, that Charles talked well, and she demonstrated this to the teachers by having Charles say, on entering, "Good morning," and on leaving, "I had a good time. I'll see you tomorrow." Charles' words, though spoken very softly and without looking at the teachers, were enunciated clearly.

These preliminary judgments led teachers to outline an initial set of objectives for Charles, directed, eventually, toward increasing his rate of using language. The first objective was, of necessity, that Charles use a variety of materials and engage in a variety of activities. His standing and waiting, doing nothing, must be eliminated, because it provided neither practice of present skills nor learning of new skills, and for teachers it provided an inappropriate but compelling context for speech. Teachers commented, for instance, that Charles seemed to have taken over their role: Whenever he wanted to use a preschool material he prompted *them* to use language; he would just stand and wait until a teacher went to him and communicated in some way that he was permitted to take the material.

The first step toward the objective to get Charles to use a variety of materials, then, was to assure him that he was permitted to use all the materials. This involved, at first, rewarding his silence: A teacher who saw him waiting, said simply, "You may take a puzzle." Maintaining communication was an important element in the teacher's acquiring reinforcing properties for children. At the same time, however, the teachers were modeling language as the mode of communication. They turned automatically, immediately, to say at the very least a distracted, "Yes you may," to a child who called, "Can I play with this?"; whereas the teacher who looked up to see Charles standing in silence near a material was never sure how long he may have waited. She hoped, however, that while he was waiting he may have been noticing how relatively more effective, in the preschool environment, was the behavior of the other children (i.e., language) for attracting teacher attention.

At first teachers did not insist that Charles use materials other than the puzzles and books, but they did prompt him repeatedly to use other materials. A teacher said, for instance, as Charles waited by the shelf, "You can use the pegs," as though that was perhaps the material she thought he wanted; after a pause, if Charles did not move she added, "Or you can take a puzzle if you want."

One day when a teacher said, "You can paint if you like," Charles took a step toward the creative area. The teacher immediately told the teacher in the painting area, "Charles would like to try some paint." That teacher said, "Good," and took Charles carefully through the preparatory steps. She said, "First you need an apron so you don't get any paint on your clothes." As Charles stood some distance from the easels and watched the other children painting, the teacher put an apron on him and tied it. Then she said, "This is your place. Here is your paper. Now you need some paint." She turned away to get the paint; when she turned back, Charles had come to stand before his place at the easel. "Now you need brushes," the teacher said as she supplied them, "And you're ready to start painting." The teacher remained beside him, saying, "That's right. That's the way you paint," as Charles tentatively dipped into the paint and put brush to paper. After some time, when Charles paused, the teacher said, "Do you want another piece of paper?" Charles nodded, and the teacher immediately supplied it.

Even as they prompted and encouraged Charles to begin exploring more and more of the materials available, teachers worked at the same time on the second of their objectives for Charles: that their attention and approval become important to him.

To make their approval meaningful, teachers presented it, but only after he was engaged with a material. When Charles was working a puzzle, for instance, a teacher went over to watch and to comment, modeling what she would have liked Charles to say to her. She said, as Charles put a piece in, "That piece goes right there," or, as he worked, "You know how to do that puzzle," or "That's right, you're turning the piece around so it will fit." The teacher never asked Charles a question as she watched, and her attention was usually brief. She could count on being attracted away by some talk from another child. With Charles she tried to make this circumstance clear, by staying and watching him, until another child called her or a conversation broke out between two children. Then she moved away from Charles toward the talking children. From the outset the teacher let Charles know that while she was interested in his skill with puzzles, she was more interested, consistently, in language.

One day in Charles' second week of school the teacher had responded to a child's call to come look at her string of beads and was standing between the girl and Charles when she heard from behind her, "Look teacher." Charles had just completed his favorite puzzle, and the teacher suddenly realized she had forgotten to contact him while he had been working on it. She turned immediately and knelt beside Charles, saying, "Wow, I'm glad you called me. You did that so fast I didn't even see it. Do it again so I can watch." She stayed, watching, while Charles did the puzzle again, responding to a call from another child but not moving away. The following day he again asked a teacher to look, and teachers began to turn to find him looking at them while using a material. The second objective, that teacher attention become meaningful to Charles, had been achieved.

The third of the initial objectives set for Charles was that he respond to teacher language cues. Because he followed instructions well, although silently, and was quick to imitate a behavior that a teacher named for another child as the "right way," focus was placed immediately upon verbal behavior. Teachers asked directly for language from Charles in answer to a question. For instance, when Charles was standing before his locker, a teacher went to him and asked, "Do you need help?" This standard verbalization was used by teachers because it was applicable across routine situations and so should help Charles discriminate that a teacher was going to want a standard response. The standardized response (*yes/no*) was also minimal, one which teachers had heard Charles emit already in response to his mother. Thus when a teacher asked Charles, "Do you need help?" if he nodded (or shook his head) the teacher said, "Can you say, 'Yes' (or 'No')?" If the teacher waited, Charles always answered obediently, "Yes," or "No." He had already learned the question-answer relation, and, as in all other areas, he followed instructions.

Soon, therefore, teachers began to ask for more elaborate language. A teacher would ask, "Do you need help?" and when Charles nodded she would instruct, "You need to say, 'I need help'." Dutifully, Charles would say softly, "I need help." Teachers tried a next step, asking, "What do you need?" but Charles' silence sent them back to instructing him. Although he always answered when so instructed, the sometimes long pause, the soft voice, and the bent head kept teachers feeling that they had forced the response from him. Later, in fact, they decided that they had moved ahead with Charles prematurely here, because, many months later, even when he initiated, "I need help," he did so in the same grudging tone of voice.

Fortunately as Charles began to use a wider range of materials, and as teacher attention and approval became more important to him, teachers could reduce the amount of instruction. Once it was clear that they had met their first set of three objectives, that Charles was engaged with a variety of materials, that their attention was important to him, and that he did imitate when instructed to do so, they proceeded to implement a second set of objectives for elaborating Charles' language to more people and situations, and making it work better than silence.

The first step toward making language work better than silence for Charles was to differentiate the length of attention. Teachers began making their attention to silence discriminably briefer than their attention when Charles asked them to "Look." For instance, when Charles was busy with a puzzle, in silence, the teacher paused beside him. She watched for a moment, hoping that her nearness would draw some soft comment from him. If he did not speak, she commented, modeling what she would have liked him to say. For instance, she said, "That's an easy puzzle." Then she moved away to attend to other children. When Charles said, "Look," however, the teacher sat down beside him. As she sat down the teacher said, for example, "Yes, I'm glad you called me. I've been wanting to see you do that puzzle." She then stayed until Charles finished the puzzle. Usually, if he did not speak, she did not speak. When he finished the puzzle, however, and looked at her with his message, *I did it*, in his face, he was initiating a communication situation, and the teacher asked for language. She said, at first, "Are you going to do another one?" If Charles nodded, or moved to get another puzzle, the teacher said, "Good," and turned to another child who was talking. One day, Charles said, "Yes," to the teacher's question; the teacher said, "Great, I'm glad you told me. Now I get to see you do two puzzles." After several days, when Charles had responded "Yes" on two subsequent occasions to this teacher, she began asking when he finished a puzzle he had called her to look at, "Which one are you going to do now?" On the second occasion of her asking, Charles said, "This one." He seemed to have learned that he could hold a teacher near him with a verbal response as well as bring her to him.

Teachers had also begun to work on Charles' requesting behavior. Because direct instructions, such as *You need to say, "I want help,"* seemed to threaten him, a less direct approach was elected. When other children were present and asking for materials while Charles waited, the teachers began to turn to Charles with a question. For example, one day at the easel, Charles and two other children were getting ready to paint. The teacher had already dispensed paint to the two other children who had specified the colors they wanted. Charles was waiting as usual. The teacher turned to him and, holding the paint before him, asked, "What is this?" Charles looked at her in silence, but the children on either side chorused, "Paint." The teacher said, "That's right, it's paint," and dispensed paint to Charles. The next time Charles and other children were together at the easel, Charles very softly answered, "Paint," to the same teacher question, simultaneously with the other children. Teachers began using this method to prompt Charles to speak. It was as though, in the presence of other children, Charles wanted to let the teacher know that he too knew the name of a material.

The fact that Charles would display knowledge showed up in other situations also. One day, Charles came to the teacher with a pegboard full of pegs. He stood before the teacher in silence holding out the pegboard. The teacher looked also in silence. Finally, after what seemed a full minute, Charles said, "Look." The teacher smiled and said, "Wow! That's all colors of pegs." She began naming the colors of the pegs as she pointed to each row, "Blue, red, green, uh. . . ." She paused, her finger on the next peg. Charles said, "Yellow." The teacher said, "Hey, you know your colors!" Charles smiled. A child nearby said, "I know my colors, teacher," and began naming the colors of his beads. The teacher looked at the other child and confirmed, "That's right. Yellow, blue. . . ." Charles stood in silence, watching. When the other boy called an orange bead red and the teacher said nothing, Charles suddenly said his first spontaneous sentence, "That's orange!"

In their assessment of Charles' progress, teachers discussed the significance of these observations. It was as though, in Charles' world, needs were communicated by context, and language was reserved for displaying knowledge. Charles would stand before the easel, beside the stack of puzzles, or before his locker with his coat unzipped. When a teacher asked, "What do you want?" his answer might well have been, "Isn't it obvious?" For he had indeed arranged a context that communicated, and made his needs apparent. To get teacher attention and approval, he seemed to have a whole different class of behaviors, one which had perhaps been approved in the past. He began to display to teachers what he could do and what he knew. This teacher assessment corresponded well with comments made by Charles' mother during an initial conference. She had stated that she thought her mother and her physician were wrong, and that Charles would do all right in school because he knew a lot, all his colors, and how to count, for instance. She was quite satisfied with how much he talked.

At school, Charles had soon discriminated that language (*Look*) worked better than silence when he wanted teacher attention. This was the most important discrimination, in terms of teacher goals, for this discrimination enabled them to begin elaborating his requesting behavior. Teachers set out to differentiate for Charles those situations in which it was obvious what he needed and those in which additional information was required. For instance, in situations in which a teacher dispensed items to a group of children crowded around her, Charles was often passed over. On the first such occasion, the teacher had handed out balloons for a science experiment, the children chorusing, "I want one." Charles waited, as usual, in prim silence. The other children were blowing up their balloons when the teacher looked questioningly at Charles. "I didn't get one," he said reproachfully.

Teachers had to be very sensitive to circumstances in which waiting would work to draw language from Charles, that is, those in which the context would communicate to Charles that the teacher was going to miss him if he did not speak up. Unlike his home, at school there were many other persons and he needed language in order to assert himself. The difficulty for teachers was that Charles seemed resigned to being last or doing without. He gave way to any child who interrupted, and withdrew to watch, impassive, if another child started to use his materials. Charles did not move away to play with something else, however. He remained gazing fixedly at the interloper with that stony stare so familiar to any teacher who had waited for Charles to verbalize.

Initially, teachers found that Charles would assert himself in order to display his knowledge or skill. He would initiate in order to name a color or letter for a teacher if a nearby child hesitated or made a mistake. He would readily name a material if it seemed that another child did not know what it was. As teachers praised, over and over, his skill with puzzles, pegs, and all other materials involving eye and fine motor coordination, Charles began to say, when another child was having difficulty, "I can do that." A teacher could then ask him to help the other child. At first she always stayed to watch and comment on the interaction. Gradually she began to ask Charles to tell the other child what to do rather than just showing him.

As Charles began to compete with other children for both materials and teacher approval, teachers were able to begin waiting and asking him to elaborate. For instance, when Charles said, "Look," a second time while engaged in the same activity, the teacher said, "Look at what?" If she could, she said this before she looked. Otherwise she looked into Charles, eyes rather than at what he was doing and waited for him to name an item or an accomplishment.

Although Charles was now using a variety of materials, he still had his favorites, puzzles and painting. Teachers began prompting him to request these favorite materials whenever other children were nearby. When Charles went to wait by the manipulative shelf, for instance, and several other children were engaged with materials nearby, the teacher went to Charles and asked, at first, "What are those?" as she touched the stack of puzzles. If Charles did not answer she could turn to the other children and repeat her question. After the children answered, the teacher again asked Charles, "What are they?". Soon the teacher began asking, "What do you want?" in the similar situation. Charles abruptly quit waiting and began verbalizing his requests for materials. One morning he was standing looking at a teacher, resting his hand on a nesting tower, when another child said, "You gotta ask." After a pause the child said, "It's a nesting tower," and a moment later said, "Say 'Teacher, can I play with the nesting tower'." In the face of Charles' continued silence, the other child stood up and attempted to take Charles by the hand, saying, "Come on, I'll help you. Teacher . . . . Charles wants a nesting tower." Charles pulled away and went to the creative area where he said to the teacher as soon as she looked at him, "Can I paint?"

Charles had been in the program for three months before teachers decided that their initial objectives had been met. Charles was regularly engaged with materials, he was initiating in order to call attention to his accomplishments, he was requesting materials and using language with other children. Teachers moved on to set long-range goals, defining objectives for increasing Charles' rate of talking, for increasing the volume of his speech, and for elaborating both his language and his play behaviors with children and materials. They worked on volume by occasionally waiting for Charles to call to them more loudly; primarily, though, they tried to attend differentially to his use of a louder tone. Charles did speak loudly at times when he was involved in a gross motor game with other children, and teachers could then attend both to the voice level and to the play in a context in which volume was entirely appropriate. Such situations also provided opportunities for teachers to prompt more elaborate language and more skillful interaction with children, but the teachers' emphasis was always on making whatever language Charles did use work effectively with the other children. A teacher repeated, often more loudly, Charles' statement to another child, and called on the child to listen. It was particularly important to teachers that Charles use language in this way, to influence the actions of others, because, although Charles now commented fairly often and initiated in order to display knowledge and accomplishments, he tended to use silence to communicate wants and to influence the actions of others. Increasing Charles' use of language as a means of affecting persons and events around him might have benefits both for the elaboration of his language and for how he operated on his environment. Teachers felt that Charles needed to be more assertive; silence already was not working very well as a way of dealing, for instance, with the incursions of other children on his play. To increase Charles' rate of using language to influence his environment, teachers focused on making his language effective whenever he stated a want or need, as when he told another child to stop or to move, and on arranging situations so as to increase the probability that Charles would verbalize. For example, teachers arranged many and various choice situations in which it was natural to ask, "Which do you want?" rather than, "What do you want?"

Teachers could be sure that if they watched him use a material without themselves verbalizing, he would comment eventually in order to draw their specific approval. Once he commented, teachers could try to begin a conversation. For example, a teacher watched as Charles played with dough. After considerable rolling Charles said of a long piece of dough, "A snake." The teacher said as she pointed, "A snake, that's his head." Charles said, "Snakes bite you." The teacher asked, "Did you ever get bitten by a snake?" Charles said, "Jody did," and began to describe the event.

Interaction with Charles became much easier when teachers were able to converse. When Charles himself brought up a topic for discussion, he seemed to do so in order to hold the teacher's attention and communicate something of concern to himself, and the teacher could ask with natural interest for elaboration. However, even after Charles had been in the program for a year, such conversations were not frequent. Teachers still had to remind themselves to include Charles in a group discussion. Charles still did not assert himself in such group situations, but, if the teacher did the interrupting and focused on him in a group, Charles usually responded with speech, although minimal and very soft. After a year in the program, Charles did use language for many different purposes on many different occasions. He was still by no means talkative, but neither was he deviant.

CASE STUDY 2

When four-year-old Louis came to the nursery school he talked enthusiastically, but none of what he said was intelligible to the teachers. The first and immediate problem was his disruptive play behavior. He was already receiving help from a speech therapist a half-hour each day. However, he did not generalize his speech skills to the nursery-school setting. He was especially inappropriate in talking with teachers and children during play activities. He had been operated on for "tongue tie" and often drooled or spit during rapid speech. His major communication problems included comprehensibility, attention and listening, and social and play skills. In the speech therapy sessions he had learned to imitate verbal patterns and to articulate comprehensibly in that situation.

In the classroom Louis moved from one activity to another almost as fast as he spoke. A teacher would hear him shout as he took a material or verbalized excitedly to another child. As she moved toward him he would often leave the material or throw it at the child. The teacher would have to go and bring him back from engagement with a second material in order to clean up the first material. While the teacher pointed out that he should listen to the other child's protests concerning interference, Louis was likely to be talking volubly to her about something that had apparently happened at home.

He seemed to comment on everything in the environment. Even while engaged in activity, Louis noticed if an insect crossed his path and ran to bring a teacher to see. Often he would loudly interrupt another child, jostling the child aside if necessary, in order to stand with his face directly before the teacher's, talking in a lengthy, voluble, incomprehensible stream, his face animated. Another child who interrupted was likely to be pushed away roughly. If the teacher turned away she was likely to be followed.

Louis initiated equally often to children. The other children protested about his abrupt interference in their play. They commented with distaste that he spat all over them when he talked to them. A child who refused to share the materials he was using or protested Louis's interference in his play was met with a stream of excited speech. Further protest from the child often resulted in physical aggression by Louis. If the child cried or called a teacher, Louis retreated to stand momentarily absolutely still. Then he would say almost clearly, "I sorry," and a moment later be back in the same activity from which the other child had tried to exclude him.

Verbal behavior seemed to function, for Louis, to avoid unwanted consequences. Teachers could be distracted from making him comply if he just kept talking. When teachers asked him for information or explanation, his answer was likely to be completely unrelated to the question. Either he changed the subject and began to comment, or he said something irrelevant. For instance, a teacher asked as he looked at a book, "What's the monkey eating?" Louis began to describe something about his mother and his shoes. When the teacher repeated her question, Louis said (it seemed), "It's a birthday cake."

The first objective for Louis, therefore, was to bring his behavior, verbal and otherwise, under instructional control. As in the therapy sessions, he had to begin to listen to the verbal behavior of others. This was a necessary step toward the second objective, which was to make approval as well as attention meaningful to Louis. To proceed with further instruction, teachers needed to make their approval discriminative for the materials, activities, and attention that Louis enjoyed. They needed to be able to use, for instance, "That's right, you cleaned up," as a necessary, mediating condition between Louis using one material he enjoyed and going to the next. Used in this manner, often, their "That's right" would come to have meaning for Louis; thus, they could use it to strengthen other behaviors such as slow and careful enunciation and cooperation with children. But first he had to be listening when they said it rather than talking himself in order to avoid their instruction.

Thus, the first program for Louis involved assigning a teacher, whenever available, to follow Louis from material to material so as to be there when he took the material. (The goals for the other children meant that a teacher could be assigned to follow Louis for only a half-hour or less per day. At other times the teacher assigned to an area just tried to catch him as often as possible and apply the agreed-on procedures, as below.) The teacher assigned to Louis put her hand on any material Louis began to take and interrupted his verbalizing to instruct, "You need to say, 'I want the car (or whatever material he was touching)'." If Louis did not say some approximation of her sentence, the teacher reduced the prompt to the name of the material, as, "Say 'car'." She required Louis to say the name of the material before she released it. Only when Louis imitated, or said an approximation to what she had said, could the teacher be sure he had attended to her verbalization. Getting Louis to talk was no problem. The speech therapy sessions had shown that he could imitate. In the classroom the task was to bring his speech under stimulus control. So the teacher held the material and repeated her instruction, as, "Say 'car'," until she got a corresponding response from Louis, a one-word response topographically similar to hers.

On the first occasion when the teacher insisted that he name an item, Louis moved, hardly pausing, to take a different material. When the teacher followed and again insisted, Louis moved on again. As soon as it became apparent that an entertaining game of "catch me" could ensue, the teacher led Louis to a chair at the edge of the play area and seated him. She put his hands in his lap. Holding them there she told him, "You need to sit here and watch how the other children ask for the toys they want."

She went with Louis back to the shelf. When he put his hand on a car she put her hand on it, too, and said, "Say 'car'." Tearfully, Louis said, "Ga." The teacher said, "That's right, car. That's good, Louis." The teacher sat down beside Louis and watched him run the car, plus several others, across the floor, talking volubly all the while. Shortly after Louis began to follow a teacher's instruction and name a material he wanted to use, teachers began intervening at the point of cleaning up a previously used material. For instance, when Louis ran to the manipulative shelf and grabbed the beads, the teacher put one of her hands on the beads and the other on Louis' hand. She said, "You need to say, 'I cleaned up my blocks'." Louis turned to the block area, looking startled. "Yes, you're right," the teacher said (because Louis' turning was an indication that he had been listening); "Say, 'clean up'." When Louis imitated her with an approximation to *clean up*, the teacher said, "That's right, clean up. I'll help you." Then, and later, when Louis imitated 'clean up,' and did so, he was always encouraged to take the next material without asking for it. Also, teachers gave Louis specific instructions only once or twice an hour, and only in very clear-cut situations. They did not want to depress his rates of using materials or of verbalizing. They knew it would require many occasions before he learned to refocus his attention. They tried to make the requirement on each such occasion as clear as possible; that is, the requirement was that Louis listen to what the teacher said. His imitation needed to be only close enough for the teacher to be certain he was following her instructions. So she never asked for a repetition, expansion, or a more clearly enunciated response when Louis imitated, and she instructed him only in the two contexts, of requesting materials and cleaning up. Louis' eagerness to use materials maximized the probability of his meeting any requirement and put teacher approval in the mediating relationship that would be needed later in order to strengthen other behaviors.

If Louis did not imitate as the teacher asked him to, she took his hand in order to lead him to the chair at the edge of the play area. Often Louis would then quickly say what he had been asked to say. Teachers learned to take Louis' hand first, before presenting the request for imitation. Taking his hand as if to lead him became a way of getting him to pause momentarily and attend briefly. Within two weeks, Louis would pause, momentarily immobile, looking at the teacher whenever she put one hand on a material and took his hand with her other hand. Soon teachers began prefacing their instruction with a question. For instance, a teacher put one hand on the blocks, took Louis' hand in hers, and said, "What do you want? Say, 'I want a block'." Or, "What do you need to do? Say 'clean up'." When Louis said an approximation to *block* or *clean up*, the teacher always presented confirmation, approval, and permission to use the material or help in cleaning up.

Teachers gradually reduced their behavior of going to Louis, taking his hand, and presenting only the question, "What do you want?" or "What do you need to do?" They instructed him in what to say only if he did not respond to the question with an approximation to *clean up* or the name of a toy. Then they began asking the question from a distance, going to Louis only if he did not pause and turn toward them. After Louis answered, teachers made sure that their approval ("That's right") was the signal to Louis that he could now take a material he wanted to use.

After several weeks, teachers began to look for indications that their approval was meaningful to Louis. When both Louis and another child were putting away blocks, for instance, and the teacher said to the other child, "That's exactly the right way to stack the blocks, one on top of each other," the teacher looked to see whether Louis would also begin stacking his blocks so that she could comment similarly to him. If he did not, she would have to instruct him as usual. On one such occasion, a teacher noticed that Louis, having jumbled a variety of blocks together on the shelf, paused and looked over to her. She looked at him without speaking or moving. Louis raked the jumbled blocks back onto the floor and began stacking them. The teacher immediately went to help him and to confirm his behavior. "Yes, you're stacking them," she said. "That's exactly the right way to put the blocks back on the shelf."

Once teachers had a means of getting Louis to listen to them and their approval was becoming meaningful to him, their first objectives had been met. They were ready to define new objectives for language and for interaction with children and materials. Louis needed to listen to other children as well as to teachers, he needed to speak more slowly and carefully, and he needed to explore materials with greater elaboration. It was decided that the three objectives could be met within a single program.

First, a teacher continued to be assigned to follow Louis for a half-hour each day, at different times on different days in order to discourage his discriminating teacher availability. With a stopwatch the teacher waited at first until Louis had been engaged with a material for five seconds (half his average engagement time per material). Then she went and sat down with him to watch, listen, and comment as long as he remained engaged with the material. Gradually, as his average attention span per material lengthened second by second, she waited a second longer before joining him.

While with Louis, the teacher worked on language. When she joined him, she introduced a topic of conversation, modeling what she would have liked him to say. Louis tended to comment almost exclusively on topics other than his ongoing activity. Therefore, the teacher always modeled a statement concerning his current behavior or material. She said, for instance, "You're working a puzzle," or, "You're building with those blocks," hoping to draw an elaborating comment from Louis. Or, she said, "There's the dog in that puzzle," or, "You have a long string of beads," or, "Those pegs are blue." If Louis answered with a statement unrelated to the teacher's, she listened receptively, but kept her verbal behavior minimal. She did not want to discourage his talking, but neither did she want to encourage his already high rate of commenting on unverifiable stimuli and events. In order that the content of his language might become more appropriate for use with other children, it was important that Louis learn to describe what he was doing in ways that would provide structure to another child who might join him. At this point, another child never joined Louis' play. Either Louis joined others' play or he played in parallel.

When the teacher sat down with Louis, she introduced a topic, as by modeling, "You're working that puzzle." If Louis responded with, "Last night my daddy took me to the drive-in and I saw . . . (teacher translation to a point of incomprehensibility)," the teacher listened and nodded. As soon as Louis paused a moment, she said, pointing to the puzzle, "The boy goes right there." On one such occasion Louis said, also pointing to the puzzle, "That's a garbage truck." "That's right," the teacher said enthusiastically, "and there's the. . . ." Louis eagerly supplied, "Garbage man," and began to describe how he had seen a garbage man at his house. After a sentence, the teacher interrupted, placing her hand on Louis' hand and saying, "He had a truck just like that," pointing to the one in the puzzle. She wanted Louis to learn that he must pause so that an exchange of language can occur in conversation, and she wanted to redirect him to the present, tangible context that another child would need. Louis began to describe the differences between the garbage truck in the puzzle and the one he had seen. The teacher did not interrupt but picked up the puzzle piece of the garbage can. As Louis grabbed at the piece, the teacher asked, "Where does it go?" Louis said, "I know where it goes," and the teacher gave it to him, saying, "Where? Show me," and then confirming Louis both putting it in the puzzle and telling her so. She said, "That's right, it goes right there and you told me that."

This was the sort of exchange which teachers hoped eventually might occur between Louis and another child. Although rare, opportunities did arise when other children were present and could be drawn into this sort of teacher-guided conversation. The teacher could then focus on keeping Louis' comments related to the topic of the other child's comments, and on interrupting him, with a touch on the hand, in order to cue him that it was the other child's turn to speak. The teacher interpreted and summarized Louis' statements to the other child and supplied an answer for him if his was too far off the topic or addressed solely to her. The teacher's primary aim was to introduce Louis and the other child to positive interaction. So she tried to maintain the conversation until either child lost interest. These early conversations between Louis and another child were both rare and brief.

Whenever Louis exchanged language with another child, the teachers focused on trying to interpret his speech to the other child. They addressed the comprehensibility of his speech only when he was talking just to them. However, their goal in these one-to-one conversations with them was that Louis learn the communication pattern of shared language, the requirement for listening as well as talking. Therefore, they never instructed in that context. Rather, they prompted better enunciation by responding naturally to elements they could not understand. For instance, a teacher said, "Your mama gave you what? I didn't understand." Or, "Tell me that again, slower. What was it that happened to your daddy's car?" Louis seemed well aware that his speech was not comprehensible. After a short time in the program, when he was really involved in telling a teacher something, he began to spontaneously repeat himself, sometimes several times, slowing down and enunciating with care in order to get some important message across.

Teachers instructed Louis to improve his enunciation only when he requested materials and activities, when there was something tangible for which he could work. Because he was so eager to use materials, and because his attention span was so short, instructional occasions were numerous once Louis had learned to wait for teacher permission after asking to use a material. The teachers and the speech therapist drew up sets of words, phrases, and sentences for training over the school year in the therapy session and for practice in the classroom. The therapist selected an array of classroom materials for use in training sessions. A list of these materials was posted each week in the classroom in order to remind teachers to ask Louis for clear enunciation whenever he requested them. The teachers recorded for mention to the therapist often-used words and phrases that Louis enunciated particularly poorly. The therapist mentioned to teachers the sounds and sound combinations on which Louis currently needed most practice, and together they worked out specific words and occasions for practice. Along with regular consultation, teachers and therapist each observed Louis' behavior in the other's setting and made occasional tape recordings in order to verify progress.

In the classroom, in one of the early weeks, teachers and therapist assigned themselves to work on the initial sound /k/. The classroom offered a maximum of occasions for practice and feedback on "Can (I play with . . .)," and toy cars were Louis' favorite material for indoor play. The therapist showed the teachers the criterion response to be obtained and how to prompt the correct mouth and tongue movements. Then, in the classroom, teachers began to instruct Louis every time he asked for a material. When Louis reached for a material and verbalized, the teacher nearest to him squatted before him, put her hand on the material, and said, "Say, 'Can I'." On the first such occasion Louis protested volubly to the effect that he already had asked for the material as required. The teacher took his hand and repeated her instruction, "Say, 'Can I'." Louis said, "Can I." Although his enunciation was just as poor as before, the teacher said, "That's right, 'Can I.' Yes, you can. Here." Only after Louis was responding regularly and immediately to the teacher's frequent instruction to imitate did the teachers begin asking for clearer enunciation before releasing the material.

Soon, as the teacher approached Louis after he had verbalized while reaching for a material, he began to say spontaneously, "Can I." If his enunciation was close to criterion, the teacher confirmed, "That's right, Can I. You said it really clearly. You certainly can." If Louis' enunciation was poor in terms of his current level of performance, the teacher instructed him, "Say 'Can I'." If his enunciation on this try was better, the teacher told him so in her confirmation. If his enunciation was equally poor, the teacher might instruct him to try it again, one more time, depending on how many times he had practiced so far that day. Very early in the day, for instance, the teacher usually asked for a second try for improved enunciation. This seemed to clarify for Louis the standard teachers were going to want that day. At the end of the school day, after Louis might have practiced on several dozen occasions over the day, the teacher was much more likely to accept a very poor imitation and say, "OK, Louis, you can play with the blocks (or whatever)." She did not confirm the "rightness" of a poor response, however, and she did not remove her expectation, and instruction, for a clearer enunciation on his next request for a material.

Fairly soon, Louis began saying quite clearly, "Can I," as soon as the teacher turned to instruct him. (He said, "Can I," even if his initial request had begun, "I want.") Teachers had also been instructing improved enunciation whenever Louis asked to use toy cars. Now they began carrying a toy car with them, and intermittently they began asking Louis to name the car on occasions when he asked for other materials. His play with cars had become less frequent, but of longer duration, since teachers had begun asking for careful enunciation. As his attention span lengthened, fewer occasions arose for instruction. So when, for instance, Louis asked to paint and, then, as the teacher turned to him, carefully enunciated, "Can I," the teacher confirmed, "Right, you said, 'Can I' very clearly and you certainly can." Then, as she handed Louis a paint apron with one hand, she held the toy car out in the other and asked, "What's this? Say, 'car'."

If necessary, she instructed again, "Say, 'car'." Then, if Louis did not answer or began talking of something else, she moved away to prepare his or another child's paper and paint.

Shortly, teachers were able to drop the instruction and merely question Louis, "What's this?" or "What do you want?" Nearly always he answered willingly if the teacher was focused entirely on him. Teachers introduced pictures of a cat and a coat for Louis to name as well as the toy car. And when Louis initiated one of his narratives, teachers could interrupt to prompt a better /k/ sound ("Your daddy's what?"). On occasion, especially if the teacher's attention appeared to be wandering, Louis would pause in a narrative for a slow and careful initial /k/ on a word. Then Louis began to call out or come to a teacher to say one of "his" words in a sort of game of drawing instant teacher attention to himself, particularly when the teacher was involved closely with another child.

It was time to introduce a new sound. Initially /w/ was selected because of the utility in the classroom of words such as *want, wash, wagon,* and *water*. Teachers reinstated their previously used procedures: they put a hand on the material for which Louis asked and reached, and they instructed. They instructed, for instance, "Say, 'I want'," or, outside, "Say, 'wagon'," or, at the water table, "Say, 'water'." Instruction in the initial /w/ sound was introduced gradually, interspersed with continuing prompts for the /k/ sound. On the first day, a teacher offered, "I'll pull you in the wagon, Louis. Say, 'wagon'." Louis said, "Ca," as he sat down in the wagon. The teacher put down the handle of the wagon and squatted beside Louis, one hand on his, as she turned his face to hers with the other hand. She said, "Say, 'wagon'," and stroked his face as the therapist had shown her. When Louis make the /w/ sound, the teacher confirmed its correctness and began pulling him in the wagon.

Many occasions ensued when Louis, instructed to say /w/, said a word which began with a /k/ sound. Teachers made sure, as before, that Louis imitated the sound for which they asked before moving into activity. Just as important as practice in enunciation was practice in listening. Teachers tried to help Louis listen by pausing, waiting for eye contact or another indication of attention, before saying which of the sounds they wanted. For instance, when Louis entered the housekeeping area and said, "Can I . . . (unintelligible)," the teacher said, "Say. . . ." She paused for a moment, hoping that Louis' eyes would focus on her mouth. Then she said the word for imitation, "I want." As he moved away, Louis said clearly, "Can I." The teacher took his hand and led him to a chair at the edge of the area. As the teacher patted the seat of the chair to indicate that Louis should sit down, tears welled in his eyes. The teacher said, "I want. Say, 'I want'." Louis looked at the teacher quizzically a moment. She said, "I want." Louis said, "I want" (his version), and, as the teacher confirmed and praised his imitation, he returned to play. As before, the teacher always presented an entire word or phrase for imitation, but Louis was asked to make only the initial sound clearly.

From the outset, teachers presented an instruction to Louis only once within the free-play situation; if they had to repeat the instruction they removed Louis from play before they did so. This was the equivalent of the methods used by the speech therapist to ensure that Louis attended to her instructions. It was essential to teachers' long-term goals that Louis attend to their verbal behavior, and to even finer dimensions of it. The sequence of sounds to be worked on in the classroom necessitated that Louis' attending behavior reach criterion and be maintained at that level.

Therefore, each time a new sound was introduced, teachers always worked on Louis' listening first. If he said any approximation to the same word the teacher presented, the teacher confirmed and praised. A previously mastered sound such as the /k/ sometimes became less clear for awhile when a new sound was introduced, but very soon Louis began to look at the teacher's mouth when she paused after, "Say. . . ." Occasionally he would imitate her mouth movements, forming the sound simultaneously with the teacher. After Louis was saying the sound for which he was asked consistently, teachers began to ask for improved enunciation, both of the new sound and of all previously mastered sounds. Then they gradually began to drop the initial instruction and to ask only, "What is this?" or "What are you asking?" They added an instruction only if the initial enunciation was not up to standard.

As criterion was attained for each new sound, another was introduced. Each time, a similar succession of stages was followed. First came the focus on listening. Even late in the school year Louis had to be removed from play on occasion in order to remind him to attend the first time to a teacher verbalization introduced with, "Say. . . ." Second, focus was on improving enunciation of the new sound while maintaining and practicing the enunciation of all the old sounds. As an increasing number of sounds was introduced, the teachers cued themselves with color coding. They put a small blue square on certain materials to remind themselves to use a particular material to prompt clear enunciation of a particular sound. For instance, cars and cups were coded for prompting /k/, wagons for prompting /w/, pegs and puzzles for prompting /p/, the door to the outdoor play yard for prompting /d/. Whenever Louis asked for an item so coded, the teacher was thus reminded to ask, "What is this?" and to instruct if Louis' enunciation was not clear. In addition, whenever Louis learned the color coding such that he spontaneously produced, for instance, a clear "door" when he wanted to go outside, teachers added another classroom item to their coding, such as the dough.

After enunciation of a sound was established in requests for materials, teachers began prompting clearer enunciation in conversation, focusing on frequently used words of maximum meaning. Sometimes they could use their natural response to incomprehensibility and would ask for a repeat of a word they really did not understand. Usually, however, the words they did not understand involved sound combinations, such as blends, which Louis was not yet making even in therapy sessions. Teachers had come to understand most of what Louis said in the preschool context, but his spontaneous conversation was still almost as fast and voluble as before, and just as incomprehensible to an outsider. Teachers had worked from the outset to get Louis to slow down. They had begun by taking his hand, raising their eyebrows, and saying, "I'm listening, just to you. You don't need to hurry." Now Louis could be relied on to slow his speech when cued by a teacher's raised hand and raised eyebrows. Once slowed, teachers could concentrate less on merely understanding the message. They could pick out particular words for clarification within particular topics. If the conversation involved Louis' father, for instance, the teacher asked for improved enunciation of "Daddy" ("Who?"). If the topic concerned going somewhere, the teacher could ask for an improvement on "car." Most teacher effort, however, was concentrated on interactions relating to preschool materials and activities. Teachers found that only with the help of context would they understand Louis well enough, soon enough, to pick out specific words and ask in a natural way for a repeat within a conversation.

As they worked on Louis' speech, teachers also worked on his interactions with other children. The teacher initially assigned to follow Louis from one material to another and to instruct improved enunciation also followed his every interaction with a child. She interpreted Louis' speech and Louis' behavior to the other child and cued Louis' speech. Her initial focus was on getting Louis to ask another child, "Can I play with you?" (or with a material the child was using) before invading the other child's play, thus preparing the child for Louis' presence. When the teacher on assignment was following Louis, it was easy to take his hand so that he would pause before joining another child's play; the teacher could then instruct Louis in what he needed to say. When a teacher was not assigned to be right behind Louis, all teachers had to be alert to Louis' approach to others' play, and Louis moved so fast and so often that teachers could not always be there to help him. Thus, even as Louis was learning to pause and say, "Can I play?" children were responding as before and rejecting his presence. Teachers could sometimes persuade the child to include Louis, assuring the child that the teacher was going to stay right there. At other times the teacher brought or divided materials so that Louis could play in semiparallel. At first the teacher often had to help Louis accept the other child's rejection of his, "Can I play?" and play with Louis herself.

When a child did say, "Yes," to Louis' "Can I play?", the teacher remained close by. She prompted Louis to use the materials in ways similar to the other child, and described approvingly his actions that were corresponding or reciprocal to the other child's. She modeled statements describing and structuring the play, and she repeated the other child's statements, hoping that Louis would also imitate. She instructed Louis in giving simple directions, telling him, for instance, "Say, 'Move,' if he is in your way," or "Say, 'That's mine'," if you do not want him to take it." Louis needed such simple directions to other children to support his play. His tendency with children as well as with teachers was to talk a great deal, as though sheer quantity of verbal behavior would reduce the other person to compliance—as in fact it often did. Children, for instance, would give up before the onslaught of sounds and leave a material Louis wanted. When the teacher was assigned to Louis she interrupted Louis after he had said several sentences to another child who did not turn or look. The teacher touched Louis' hand to bring his attention to her. She said, "What?" in order to turn the conversation to her rather than to stop it.

The teacher assigned to Louis also instructed him in the use of materials, so that his play would not interfere with the other child's. She said, for instance, "Louis, put your pegs over here. Then those over there will be John's." Or, in the sandbox, "Louis, turn this way to dig, so your sand doesn't go on John." The teacher watched the interaction for signs that Louis was getting excited. When his gross motor movements became expansive and he began to swing his arms, for instance, or when he began to raise his voice in talking to the other child, the teacher asked him to come and play a different game with her. The teacher thus changed Louis' activity before it became inappropriate. When involved in play with other children, Louis often got excited and, shortly thereafter, aggressive. Teachers hoped that eventually both Louis and other children might notice and respond by changing activity to the signs of Louis' excitement and potential loss of control.

Louis became excited, and eventually aggressive, with other children, especially when he could not communicate with them. Each repetition of a statement to a child was louder than the one before. Louis soon was both shouting and grabbing the other child to get his attention. So grabbed, the other child was likely to pull away, saying, "Stop spitting on me!" Then Louis was likely to hit him. When a teacher was with Louis, she would call the other child to listen to Louis and interpret his statement if she understood it. If she did not understand, she could pull Louis out of play to have him clarify it to her before insisting to the other child. Often, however, when the teacher began to pull Louis from play, saying, "Come here and tell me that again. I didn't understand, and neither did John," Louis would shake his head and say something else, this time somewhat more comprehensible, slower and simpler.

The program for Louis during his first preschool year thus consisted of procedures for requesting situations and procedures for use in child and teacher interactions. In requesting situations when Louis wanted materials or access to activities, emphasis was on improving enunciation of specific sounds, words, and, late in the year, phrases. This aspect of Louis' speech improved markedly. He had soon discriminated the communicative context, that an attempt at clear enunciation would get him what he wanted. He also learned the cue to listen (the teacher's hand on his) and the relation (the need for listening in order to speak) in order to obtain a material. So well did he learn the context of requesting that Louis even began to use it to draw teacher attention. When the teacher regularly assigned to Louis was not available, for instance, Louis occasionally went from one material to another or said a sound other then the one the teacher instructed him to say. Teachers recognized Louis' need for attention, but the unavailability of the regular teacher usually meant that they were so busy that it was easy not to respond to this mode of attention seeking; they simply gave Louis permission to use a material immediately.

At the end of the preschool year, however, Louis had made considerably less progress in the communicative context of conversation. Teachers simply could not be with Louis consistently enough to ensure his use of a different communication pattern, and generalization from their teaching was very slow. Louis' initial style continued to work for him: children continued to give up in the face of verbal inundation, teachers continued to respond after Louis had talked so long that his volume had increased to a point of disruption. Only when a teacher was assigned to Louis could she ensure that he would be cued to pause for listener response after every statement or two, that he would be cued to slow down and simplify. After many instructions, Louis had learned to respond to a teacher's touch or raised eyebrows. Eventually, whenever a teacher was present, Louis adopted even with children a different communication style, one directed toward interaction rather than control or compliance. Louis began to look at the other person before he spoke, to point to or touch an object he was talking about, and to frown, pause, and repeat when the other person frowned or raised an eyebrow. Occasions of such seeming intent to communicate increased in frequency, but even after a year in the program Louis' old style was the most usual. In comparison to his peers, his attention span was still very short, his activity level very high. He still noticed every stimulus change and gravitated to possess it, verbally and physically. Any impediment to immediate possession served to heighten his activity level to the verge of uncontrollability. Louis' speech was an instrument for gaining possession of things and people, and teachers accepted that marked changes in his communication patterns were likely to occur only in conjunction with changes in his interaction patterns. Gradually bringing Louis to notice and to work to possess more subtle, less easily obtained aspects of his environment was a learning goal achieved only over considerable time.

REFERENCES

Bijou, S. W., and Baer, D. M. 1965. Child Development. Vol. 1. Appleton-Century-Crofts, New York.

Broen, P. A. 1972. The verbal environment of the language learning child. ASHA Monogr. 17.

Bruner, J. S. 1975. The ontogenesis of speech acts. J. Child Lang. 2:1–19.

Cataldo, M. F., and Risley, T. R. 1974. The Resident Activity Manifest: Handbooks for Observers (I. Measuring environmental stimulation, II. Measuring interaction, III. Measuring participation in activities). Center for Applied Behavior Analysis, Lawrence, Kan.

DeLaguna, G. 1972. Speech: Its Function and Development. Yale University Press, New Haven.

Hart, B., and Risley, T. R. 1975. Incidental teaching of language in the preschool. J. Appl. Behav. Anal. 8:411–420.

McCarthy, D. 1954. Language development in children. In L. Carmichael (ed.), Manual of Child Psychology, pp. 492–630. John Wiley & Sons, New York.

McNeill, D. 1970. The Acquisition of Language. Harper & Row, New York.

Morehead, D. M. 1975. The study of linguistically deficient children. In S. Singh (ed.), Measurement Procedures in Speech Hearing and Language, pp. 19–53. University Park Press, Baltimore.

Quilitch, H. R., and Risley, T. R. 1973. The effects of play materials on social play. J. Appl. Behav. Anal. 6:573–578.

Schiefelbusch, R. L., and Lloyd, L. L. 1974. Introduction. In R. L. Schiefelbusch and L. L. Lloyd (eds.), Language Perspectives—Acquisition, Retardation, and Intervention, pp. 1–15. University Park Press, Baltimore.

chapter 6

Parent as Intervention Agent

From Birth Onward

Jean Bragg Schumaker

Department of Human Development
and Family Life
University of Kansas
Lawrence, Kansas

James A. Sherman

Department of Human Development
and Family Life
University of Kansas
Lawrence, Kansas

Most child-care books for parents treat language development as something that often happens independent of parent involvement. They emphasize descriptions and timetables for the cooing of the infant, the babbling of the toddler, and the speech of the young child (e.g., Better Homes and Gardens 1943; Ilg and Ames, 1955; Brazelton, 1969, 1974). Benjamin Spock (1946), author of the most widely distributed child-care book, says that the rate of language development is a matter of personality or temperament, with the quiet child taking longer than the outgoing child. He describes the nervous, silent mother or the fussy mother as having detrimental effects on her child's language development, but offers few suggestions for parents who wish to enhance their children's language development. Spock, along with others (e.g., Fromme, 1956; Chess, Thomas, and Birch, 1972), does offer suggestions to parents of children who show slow language development or speech defects. "Treatments" include having the child play with other children, giving him[1] more experiences and adventures, using comfortable affection, encouraging the child to name things, protecting him from the remarks of insensitive adults, and getting therapy for breathing and psychological problems. Some authors (e.g., Better Homes and Gardens, 1943; Fromme, 1956; Gordon, 1970; Church, 1973; U.S. Department of Health, Education, and Welfare, 1973) offer a list of suggested "do's" and "don'ts." The suggestions range from "setting a good example" to how to talk to the child (softly, lovingly) to encouraging parents to imitate the child's sounds. But many authors contradict each other in their suggestions. Some suggest that it is important to imitate the infant's sounds. Others warn against ever doing so. Some emphasize the importance of not using "baby talk." Others entreat parents to use short, simple phrases. Thus, although a few child-care books describe procedures for parents to follow during their child's language development, the procedures are often contradictory, and there is no research to substantiate the effectiveness of the different procedures. Also, in most of these books, discussions of language development are limited to a few scattered paragraphs.

Thus, there is a need to provide parents with more information. Parents who are concerned about doing the best for their child might be helped by data compiled on language development and by a set of step-by-step procedures suggested by research findings. Such information, if used successfully by parents, may prevent speech deficits. Parents who suspect a speech problem, or who detect a lack of language development in their child, can use such information for remedial purposes.

Finally, there is some agreement by educators that proficiency in language is the basis for success in academic pursuits (e.g., Weikart,

---

[1] Masculine pronouns are used throughout for the sake of grammatical uniformity and simplicity. They are not meant to be preferential or discriminatory.

1966). Reading, writing, and working with numbers are tasks based on language skills. If parents had more information about their roles in language development, perhaps their children would be less likely to reach school with language deficits that cause them to fall behind other children in acquiring academic skills. Baer (1970, 1972) has suggested that development may be a process that depends on many factors of "heredity" and "environment." Although factors of heredity are presumably set once the child is conceived, the environment can be manipulated so that behavior-changing (developmental) processes are enhanced. Baer argues that we should not gamble that desirable behavior-change processes are present in the environment by chance. We should discover what they are and program their presence within the environment. Horowitz and Paden (1973) present an excellent review of such programming and the concomitant changes in development that are produced in the fields of emotional, physical, and intellectual functioning. Such programming could also be valuable in language development.

A review of the relevant literature on parents' roles in the development of productive (or spoken) language may help us arrive at some suggestions for parents. An attempt is made here to integrate normative and experimental research to determine what information is available. Because there are many studies to cover, no attempt is made to detail each study's inadequacies. Many of the studies are inadequate in various respects. Some have failed to include information about the reliability of data collected by observers. Others have not included important experimental controls. The conclusions of some go considerably beyond the results obtained. But, in most areas, the sheer volume of studies with similar results lends credibility to those results. Although many procedures are not totally supported by research, we have selected procedures that are at least suggested by research, that seem to involve no risk of detrimental effects, that are practical for parents to use as an integrated part of the child's language environment, and that we hope will be enjoyable for both parents and children.

THE LANGUAGE ENVIRONMENT

The Effects of Sensory Deprivation on Language Development

The language environment, according to Cazden (1972), consists of the language a child hears, the interactions in which he engages, and the arrangement of his physical setting. Research is making increasingly apparent the notion that the general language environment plays an important role in the language development of children. Indeed, it appears that if a child is deprived of various aspects of a language environment his speech may be retarded or nonexistent (e.g., Singh and Zingg, 1966; Lane, 1976).

Some of the earliest studies were conducted to determine the possible effects of the environment on a child's overall development. They stemmed from a controversy over the merits of adoption and foster care versus institutionalization of an infant. Because some theorists held that development is an innate process, it was thought that little harm would be done by placing a child in an institution. Others felt that institutional life lacked the stimulation usually provided by parents (the mother, in particular) and that development would be retarded in such a setting. Indeed, several studies (e.g., Ripin, 1933; Goldfarb, 1943a, 1943b, 1945; Freud and Burlingham, 1944; Spitz, 1945, 1946; Brodbeck and Irwin, 1946) have supported the latter hypothesis. They found that children raised by consistent mother figures (whether in foster homes, natural homes, or by their mothers in prison) scored significantly higher on IQ tests and verbal tests than children raised in orphanages or institutions without consistent mother figures, even though their scores were similar in the first few months of life. Furthermore, many of the institutionalized children had serious speech problems. Brodbeck and Irwin (1946) found significant differences between the types of sounds made by children raised in orphanages and those raised by families, as early as when the children were two months old. They reported that the family children exhibited vocalization patterns that continued to increase in frequency and variety with age, whereas orphanage children hit a plateau between two and six months.

Because most of these studies emphasized the role of the mother figure in providing the stimulation for a child's natural development, Rheingold (1956) decided to become a "mother" for eight institutionalized children for eight weeks. She found no initial differences between her "mothered" infants and a group of unmothered infants before her intervention began, but considerable differences in several areas (e.g., "mothered" infants were higher in social responsiveness, fine motor control, gross motor development, and frequency of vocalization) during and after intervention. When Rheingold and Bayley (1959) tested the same infants one year later (after they had all been placed in foster homes), they found that the "mothered" group vocalized more frequently than the "unmothered" group.

Although all these studies point to the importance of a single mother figure in the development of a child, Tizard and his colleagues have recently concluded that other environmental variables are also important. In comparing different environmental characteristics of several institutions, Tizard et al. (1972) found that institutions in which child language development levels were highest were characterized by age mixture of the residents, greater staff stability, greater staff autonomy, access of children to outside experiences, and the quality of adult utterances (e.g., informative statements, and answering children's utterances) aimed at the children.

In a later study, Tizard and Rees (1974) conducted follow-up observations of children who were initially retarded in language development and who lived in an institution that had been changed (as a result of their earlier study) to provide mixed age groupings, high staff autonomy, generous portions of toys, books, and outings, low child/staff ratios, and greater staff stability. They found no evidence of retardation in these children. Tizard and Rees conclude that, although these children were retarded in expressive language skills at age two, they had been able to "catch up" to the norm by age four after their environmental conditions had changed. Further, Tizard and Rees state that close personal relationships between staff and children had been discouraged in this institution. For this reason, they argue that a close personal relationship is not necessary for normal language development.

In summary, early studies of institutionalized children indicated the severe retardation effects that institutionalization can have on a child's language development. Several authors concluded that the most important factor in this retardation was the lack of a consistent mother figure. However, more recently it has been suggested that other environmental conditions can be equally important in affecting language development. However, the studies reviewed are not without their methodological problems. For example, the groups in the studies were not assigned randomly to foster homes versus institutions or to one institution versus another. Initial bias might therefore be present. In some of the studies, the authors relied on caseworkers' reports as one of their major sources of data. In others, persons were employed to test the infants in their institutions, foster homes, etc. It would be fairly safe to assume that the testers were not blind to the conditions surrounding the infants in most cases, and no reliability measures were provided for the reports of caseworkers or testers.

Nevertheless, sociolinguistic research lends support to the contention that the amounts and types of speech directed at children might have a profound effect on their language development.

Parental Influence: Correlates of Varied Stimulation

Some sociolinguists have concentrated their research on the analysis of maternal behavior and its correlation with the test scores and school success of their children. In order to study the nature of mothers' interactions with their children, Hess (1969) and Hess and Shipman (1965, 1967, 1968) asked mothers to teach their children simple sorting tasks and, through a cooperative effort with their child, to copy a sketch with an Etch-a-Sketch toy. In early studies they found that maternal teaching styles (using praise, rationales and descriptions of consequences for actions, larger amounts of speech, more words of abstract quality, and instructions versus commands) were more predictive of a child's performance on intelligence tests than an index of maternal IQ and social class combined. Later, Hess (1969) found that specificity of directions (positively related) and imperative statements (negatively related) were more highly correlated with preschool measures of a child's performance (standard achievement tests and teacher's ratings) than a combined index of child's IQ, mother's IQ, and social class.

Stodolsky (1965) studied 56 of Hess and Shipman's subjects in elementary school and found the variable that most highly correlated with a child's score on the Peabody Picture Vocabulary Test was his mother's vocabulary score on the Wechsler Adult Intelligence Scale. The aspects of maternal teaching style that most highly correlated with the child's vocabulary score were the amounts of positive feedback delivered by the mother and the extent to which the mother described task-specific elements in the environment. Similarly, Bing (1963) observed that mothers of children with high verbal test scores used different teaching styles than mothers of children with low verbal test scores. They were more active in giving help to their children when it was requested, they gave more feedback, and they used more verbal and physical interaction with their children.

It appears that the language environments of children with low verbal test scores are different from those of children with high verbal test scores. The mother's use of speech, more specifically, her use of vocabulary, praise, corrective feedback, prompts or help, instructions, and rationales concerning consequences of actions, is highly predictive of children's scores on IQ tests and language tests. It is important to note that the studies reviewed in this section were correlational and did not demonstrate functional or causal relationships between parent and child behavior. Nevertheless, they lay the groundwork for many of the studies reviewed in later sections.

The Relationship Between Receptive and Productive Language

The direct effects that the general language environment may have on productive (or spoken) language development have been examined above. The language environment may also have an indirect effect on productive language through its effects on the development of receptive language. Some theorists have hypothesized that a child must comprehend or understand speech before he can use it. Several authors (e.g., Gesell and Thompson, 1934; McCarthy, 1954; Lenneberg, 1962; Fraser, Bellugi, and Brown, 1963) have reported that they have observed children to comprehend specific language structures before spontaneously producing them. If children must comprehend before they can produce language, they are very dependent on persons around them to provide necessary stimulation to make comprehension possible.

Research on the possible interactions between receptive and productive language is rather limited and in some cases contradictory. Some researchers have concentrated on how receptive language skills relate to the productive articulation of language. Pimsleur (1963), for instance, reported that receptive discrimination training facilitated the learning of French pronunciation. Winitz and Preisler (1965) found similar results when training children with speech defects. All of the children in the study pronounced the word /srəb/ (shrub) as /skrəb/ (scrub). One group was trained to discriminate receptively between the two pronunciations as another person spoke them. The other group was trained to discriminate receptively between two other words, /sliyp/ and /ʃliyp/. Most of the group that was trained to discriminate between the words /srəb/ and /skrəb/ learned to pronounce the words. Children in the other group did not.

In a later study, Mann and Baer (1971) taught four preschool children to point to (receptively identify) objects in response to nonsense words. After two weeks of daily sessions, the children were asked to imitate these nonsense words (experimental words) and another group of nonsense words (control words) they had never heard. The researchers found that the children articulated the experimental words more accurately than the control words. Thus, it appears that receptive exposure to language can facilitate appropriate articulation of that language.

Some other researchers have wondered whether learning receptive language skills helps children learn to use productive language rules. Guess (1969) trained retarded children to identify (receptively) singular objects from plural objects. For example, when the experimenter said "pencil," the child was to point to the pencil. When the experimenter said "pencils" the child was to point to a pair of pencils. In tests after this receptive training, the children were asked to verbally label the singular and plural objects. They used only singular labels. Then Guess trained the children to verbally label the singular and plural items. Next, he taught the children to point to the pairs in response to a singular label and to the single object in response to the plural label. When he tested the subjects on the expressive labeling, he again found no transfer from receptive to expressive language. In a follow-up study, Guess and Baer (1973) found that only one subject of four showed any transfer of receptive training to productive use of singular and plural forms. It is possible that the retarded children in these two studies had some difficulty in generalizing from one sensory modality to another. Replication of these procedures with normal children will be necessary to obtain more information, but the one case showing generalization from receptive to productive language suggests that such a process is possible.

Several researchers have investigated whether receptive skills concerning sentence structure have any relation to the production of sentences. Shipley, Smith, and Gleitman (1969) found evidence that children comprehend sentence structures before they produce them. They studied two groups of children: one group, the "telegraphic" group, was using utterances ranging in mean length from 1.4 to 1.85 words; the other group, the "holophrastic" group, was using only one-word utterances. In the experiment, mothers presented their children with three types of commands: full-length commands (e.g., *Throw me the ball*); telegraphic commands (e.g., *Throw ball*); and holophrastic commands (*Ball*). The experimenters recorded "relevant responses" to the commands, which were defined as any physical contact with the object of the command (touches), looking at the object, verbally replying to the command, or imitating the command. The "telegraphic" group responded to the full-length commands more frequently than to the telegraphic and holophrastic commands. For the "holophrastic" group, the telegraphic and holophrastic commands were more effective in eliciting relevant responses than the well-formed commands. However, some authors (e.g., Nelson, 1973; Bloom, 1974) have criticized this study because the results do not show that the children comprehended the commands. They claim that the relevant responses recorded in this study do not necessarily reflect comprehension.

Nelson (1973) conducted a comprehension test similar to that of Shipley, Smith, and Gleitman with 17 children ranging in age from 13 to 17 months. However, she scored the children's responses differently; children who followed through on the whole request received a higher score than children who acted on the object and an even higher score than children who looked at or touched the object in the request. She found that the children's scores increased as the length of the request increased up to five words. She also found that the children's comprehension scores were highly correlated (0.77) with number of vocabulary words they had used productively. In addition, when she correlated their scores with their vocabulary level two months after the comprehension testing, the correlation was essentially the same (0.75). Because the comprehension scores were also highly correlated with other measures she used (e.g., acquisition rate or words acquired per month, age at 10 phrases, and mean length of utterance at two years), Nelson suggests that comprehension is related to subsequent development of productive speech.

In another study, Gaer (1969) found that children understood three types of sentence forms (active, interrogative, and passive) before they produced these sentence forms. The children seemed to produce the negative sentence form before they could understand it, but Gaer suggests this is an artefact of the procedure used. He explains that when a picture was shown to the children, the experimenter presented a negative statement like "The boy is not pushing the girl." The child was to answer "Yes" if the picture illustrated the sentence and "No" if the picture did not illustrate the sentence. But Gaer hypothesizes that the children became mixed up in these responses because of the negative nature of the presented stimuli.

Fraser, Bellugi, and Brown (1963) studied the relationship between receptive speech and two kinds of productive speech, imitation and spontaneous production. They presented 12 three-year-olds with pictures, sometimes asking them to imitate sentences about the pictures, sometimes asking them to point to the correct picture after listening to a sentence, and sometimes asking them to produce sentences about the picture after listening to the experimenter's sentences. Ten different language constructions (e.g., mass nouns and count nouns, singular and plural nouns, singular and plural subject-verb agreement, verb tenses, etc.) were included in the sentences that were presented by the experimenter. In general, Fraser et al. found that the children imitated a particular construction before they comprehended it and comprehended a particular construction before they produced it. Lovell and Dixon (1967) used essentially the same procedures with two-year-olds and replicated Fraser et al.'s results.

However, two authors (Baird, 1972; Fernald, 1972) have critiqued Fraser et al.'s methods of scoring correct and incorrect responses. They have shown that, because of the scoring method, the children had a higher probability of being successful by chance on the comprehension tasks than on the production tasks. Fernald (1972) replicated Fraser et al.'s study using two sets of scoring procedures: the original set used by Fraser et al. and a revised set that equated the chance rate of success between the comprehension and production tasks. Fernald found that his results replicated Fraser et al.'s when he used their scoring procedure. However, when he used the revised scoring procedure, the results showed no significant differences between the children's scores on the production and comprehension tasks.

Bloom (1974) further questioned Fraser et al.'s procedures by asking whether the production task was really an imitation task since the verbal stimuli presented to the child at the beginning of each production trial contained all the information the child would need to produce the sentences (e.g., *Here are two pictures, one of a boy pushing a girl, the*

other of a girl pushing a boy. Make a sentence about this picture.).
Bloom reasons that the children might have had more difficulty with this
task than the imitation task and the comprehension task, not because
they could not produce the sentences but because they were trying to
imitate sentences whose length exceeded their memory span.

Keeney and Wolfe (1972) conducted a study comparing the
comprehension, imitation, and production of subject-verb agreement.
Avoiding the problems Fraser et al. encountered with their production
task, Keeney and Wolfe taped samples of the children's spontaneous
speech. They found that although the children used subject-verb
agreement in their spontaneous speech, imitated sentences containing
subject-verb agreement, and corrected sentences containing incorrect
subject-verb agreement, they did not perform significantly better than
chance on the comprehension task. Because of this, Keeney and Wolfe
wondered whether their comprehension task (pointing to one of two pictures after hearing a sentence) was a valid test of the children's
comprehension, particularly since the children did not seem to inspect
the pictures carefully before choosing one, and they often pointed to one
section of a plural picture (e.g., pointed to one bird in a picture of two
birds) in response to a singular sentence (e.g., *The bird is singing*).

In another study reporting production before comprehension,
Chapman and Miller (1973) tested production and comprehension of
sentences containing a subject, verb, and object using a toy-manipulation
task. For the production task, the experimenter acted out a sentence
(e.g., boy doll pushes a toy truck) and asked the child, "What is happening?" For the comprehension task, the experimenter presented a sentence
(e.g., *The boy pushes the truck*) and asked the child to act out the
sentence using the toys. The children preserved subject-object order more
often in the production task than in the comprehension task. Nevertheless, a question remains as to whether "acting out" skills are substantially the same as comprehensive skills and whether they can therefore reflect a child's level of comprehension.

In a more recent study related to the interaction between
comprehension and production of language, Bohannon (1975) concluded
that receptive discrimination preceded accurate imitation. He asked 54
first, second, and fifth graders to imitate two types of sentences:
sentences formed with grammatical word order, and sentences in a
scrambled word order. Several months later the children were asked to
receptively discriminate between the two types of sentences. Children
who discriminated between the two sentence types imitated the normal
sentences significantly better than children who did not discriminate.

Taken collectively, the results of studies investigating the relationship between receptive and productive speech do not allow unambiguous

conclusions. On one hand, several studies that have taught certain types of auditory discriminations have found that subsequent speech articulation is improved. On the other hand, the two studies that involved teaching children to discriminate receptively among singular and plural objects found little transfer (except in one subject) to productive use of singular and plural labels. Furthermore, the studies investigating the possible developmental sequence of receptive and productive speech for certain language forms (i.e., those employing imitation-comprehension-production tests) have produced contradictory results. Perhaps these contradictory results are caused by the use of inappropriate methodology and measures of speech comprehension and production that do not reflect children's actual language skills.

Despite our inability to make definite general conclusions about the positive effects of receptive language learning upon productive speech, no studies have indicated that receptive speech skills adversely affect production. Thus, even though it continues to be important to determine whether receptive language facilitates subsequent production in normal language growth, it seems safe to say that providing children with opportunities to discriminate differences in words and sentence forms cannot hurt and, in some cases, may well foster productive language acquisition.

In conclusion, there are many direct and indirect effects that the general language environment may have on children's development of productive language. Research conducted with children, who have in some way been deprived of a natural language environment, indicates that adults need to be present and regularly speaking to a child in order to prevent profound language retardation. Correlational research suggests that the language environments of children who obtained low scores on language tests are different from the environments of children obtaining high scores on language tests. Studies also indicate that specific mother behaviors are correlated with children's verbal test scores. Finally, some of the research on the relationship between receptive and productive language was reviewed and the suggestion made that the general language environment may have an indirect effect on productive language through its influence on the development of receptive language.

The following sections include research that suggests functional relationships between parent behaviors and child language development in various stages of that development. More specifically, the emphasis is on research that illustrates a relationship between two aspects of the general language environment—the language children hear and the interactions in which they engage—and their language development.

PARENT ROLES IN THE
DEVELOPMENT OF SOUNDS AND WORDS

The research already reviewed indicates that events occurring in a child's natural environment can have detrimental as well as beneficial effects on the child's language development. For the most part, this research was general and correlational. Experimental evidence reviewed below suggests that specific types of environmental stimuli can have specific outcomes for the production of sounds and words.

Conditioning Vocalizations in Infants

In the development of the earliest approximations to language, "shaping" is thought to play an important role (e.g., Fry, 1966). Parents theoretically take part in this shaping process by attending to their infants' vocalizations in ways that increase the frequency of vocalizations and also by differentially attending to their infants' vocalizations to produce (or shape) closer and closer approximations to their native language. This theory is based on three propositions: 1) that infant vocal behavior is operant behavior and can be conditioned, i.e., rates of vocalization can be changed, 2) that certain infant vocal behaviors can be strengthened (in terms of future probability of occurrence) while other vocal behaviors are weakened or extinguished, and 3) that parents deliver stimulation contingent on their infants' vocalizations in the natural environment.

Several investigators have attempted to demonstrate the operant nature of infant vocal behavior by using a standard reversal design (see Baer, Wolf, and Risley, 1968), by first measuring the on-going rates of vocalization ("baseline"), then applying consequences to infant vocalization to see if the rate of that behavior would increase ("conditioning" or "treatment"), and then withdrawing the consequences to see if the rate would decrease ("return-to-baseline" or "post-treatment baseline"). In research by Rheingold, Gewirtz, and Ross (1959), for example, the experimenter was present but motionless during baseline, a broad smile, three "tsk" sounds, a light touch applied to the infant's abdomen immediately followed all vocalizations during conditioning, and the experimenter remained present but motionless during a return-to-baseline. Their results showed a significant increase in vocalization rate from baseline to treatment and a significant decrease from treatment to the post-treatment baseline. However, although they controlled for the possibility that the experimenter's presence might elicit more vocalization (by having the experimenter present during all conditions), they did not control for the possibility that smiling, touching, and "tsking" might elicit vocalizations rather than condition them. Todd and Palmer (1968), using a similar design, found that rates of infant vocalization increased when a woman's voice was made contingent on (immediately followed) vocalization, and that the rates decreased when the woman's voice was no longer contingent on vocalization. Like Rheingold, Gewirtz, and Ross, they also failed to control for the possible eliciting effects of their independent variable, the woman's voice. Wiegerink et al.'s (1974) research had substantially the same problems. In determining whether or not developmentally delayed infants (MDI on the Bayley Infant Intelligence Test was below 50 for all infants) could be conditioned to vocalize, they used the consequences of a smile, praise (e.g., *Good girl*), and a light touch on the chin or abdomen during conditioning. Their results replicated those of Rheingold, Gewirtz, and Ross and Todd and Palmer and also extended the findings of these studies by indicating no differences in conditioning effectiveness between an infant's mother and a stranger. Nevertheless, as in the Rheingold, Gewirtz, and Ross and Todd and Palmer studies, there were no controls for the eliciting effects of the consequences (smile, praise, and touching).

In an effort to eliminate the type of confounding that results from lack of control over the eliciting qualities of social stimulation, Weisberg (1961) used several reversal designs to compare the effects of noncontingent and contingent, social (smile, praise, and touching) and nonsocial (a door chime) stimulation on infant vocalization. The group results show the only group to increase significantly in vocalization rate from baseline to treatment and to decrease significantly from treatment to the post-treatment baseline was the group receiving contingent social stimulation during treatment. However, because the individual data indicate that not one of the infants clearly shows this conditioning pattern, the conclusion needs to be qualified somewhat.

In a slightly different attack on the same problem, Ramey and Ourth (1969) compared the effects of 0-second delay, 3-second delay, and 6-second delay in the delivery of social consequences using three groups of infants in parallel reversal designs. The 0-second delay group was the only group showing conditioning effects. Because the design controlled for possible eliciting effects of the social consequences (if the stimuli were elicitors, all three groups should have shown the effects), these data support the proposition that infant vocalization is operant behavior. The data also indicate that stimulation must be delivered immediately after a child's vocalization to produce increased vocalization rates.

Sheppard (1969) chose a different type of experimental design to demonstrate the operant nature of vocalization. He taught his infant to kick her legs when a red light was on and to vocalize when the light was off. Flashing lights paired with a tape of the mother's voice were the consequences applied to the behaviors in the respective conditions. Although Sheppard studied only one infant, his results lend support to the idea that infant vocalization can be conditioned.

Other investigators have concentrated on demonstrating the second proposition: that specific vocal behavior of infants can be strengthened or weakened differentially, depending on the presence or absence of rewarding consequences. Their designs have been basically similar. Two or more vocal responses have been chosen, and, after baseline rates have been recorded, social consequences have been made contingent on one of the responses. If the rate of that vocal response increased while the rates of others remained stable or decreased, the investigators concluded that infant vocal behavior was under the control of differential reinforcement.

For example, Wahler (1969) used a pair of vocalizations within each of four reversal designs. Mother attention was made contingent on both sounds during baseline conditions and only on one sound during the treatment condition. In three out of four pairs of sounds, the vocalization receiving contingent mother attention increased in rate from baseline to treatment and decreased in rate from treatment to post-treatment baseline. The response that did not receive contingent attention during treatment decreased in rate from baseline to treatment and increased in rate from treatment to post-treatment baseline.

In a similar use of reversal designs, Routh (1969) had three groups of infants receive varying treatments. The consequences (a smile, three "tsk" sounds, and a touch to the abdomen) were delivered contingent on vowel sounds for Group I, consonant sounds for Group II, and all sounds for Group III during the treatment conditions. For all groups during baseline and post-treatment baseline conditions, an expressionless and nonresponsive experimenter sat in front of the infant. The mean results show significant increases in the rates of target responses (those followed by consequences) for each group from baseline to treatment and no increases in the rates of the other responses.

Hursh and Sherman (1973), using a multiple baseline design (see Baer, Wolf, and Risley, 1968) across responses for each of three children, also obtained results that support the proposition that infant vocal behavior can be brought under differential control. They systematically applied a treatment package of parental modeling of a vocal response, contingent praise, and parent imitation of the infant's sounds to each of three vocal responses in succession. In all three children an increase in the rate of a particular response occurred only when the parent modeled the response and praise and imitation were applied to that response. Meanwhile, the rates of other responses remained at baseline levels.

Since the studies by Wahler (1969), Routh (1969), and Hursh and Sherman (1973) support the proposition that individual vocal responses can be strengthened and weakened according to the consequences applied, they also support the proposition that vocal behavior can be conditioned in general. All three studies controlled for the eliciting effects of social stimulation. If social stimulation causes a general increase in vocalization, all the sounds would have increased in rate. Because only the sound that was receiving treatment in each case showed rate increases, it can be concluded that the social stimulation was serving a rewarding function in the process.

From the above discussion it appears that specific vocal behavior can be differentially strengthened through consequences applied by adults. Nevertheless, the third proposition (that parents deliver stimulation contingent on their infant's vocalizations) remains to be supported. Few researchers have set out to determine whether parents engage in social behaviors (that might serve as reinforcers) in their interactions with their children, whether they use these behaviors contingent on their infants' vocalizations in general, and whether they make the behaviors differentially contingent on vocalizations that approximate sounds in their native language. In somewhat related research, Hursh and Sherman (1973) asked parents to increase their children's (age 15–20 months) output of certain vocal sounds, and measured what the parents did. They found that the parents modeled the sounds almost exclusively and did not provide systematic consequences for the responses. However, Hursh and Sherman did not measure motor behaviors (such as smiling, touching, proximity to the child) that may act as reinforcing consequences in the natural environment. The children were older than one year of age, and it could be that parent-teaching behaviors at this age heavily rely on models whereas at an earlier age they may rely solely on rewards. Finally, the parent behavior they measured was contrived. It may be that parents do something entirely different when they have not been instructed specifically to increase the rate of a particular sound.

In another study touching on the problem of whether parents provide contingent social stimulation for sound production, Lenneberg, Rebelsky, and Nichols (1965) measured the vocalizations of infants born to deaf and to hearing parents. They found that there were no differences between the two groups of infants in the frequency of sounds produced, the time of emergence of cooing, and the frequency of cooing, even though there were marked differences in the quantity and quality of noise levels in the two groups' homes. Lenneberg, Rebelsky, and Nichols also looked at the relationship between the number of voices close to the child during the day and the amount of cooing by the child. They found no correlation. They concluded that cooing is not a socially reinforced behavior but a manifestation of an internal state. There are several problems with this conclusion. First, these researchers assumed that, since deaf parents cannot hear their children's cooing, the children did not receive any of the stimulation that the children of hearing parents receive. However, all the infants of the deaf parents had hearing visitors who may have provided such stimulation. In addition, the deaf families had voice-activated red lights in most rooms to indicate when the infants were making noise. Because the red lights were within the infants' sight, they may have functioned as rewarding stimuli to maintain the infants' vocalization rates at normal levels.

It is also possible that there were differences between the two groups of infants that were not detected because of the insensitive observation code used by Lenneberg et al. They recorded whether or not an infant made a sound in a six-minute time block. Thus, an infant who made only one sound in six minutes would appear similar to one who made 10 sounds in six minutes. In addition, the quality of sounds produced by the infants was not measured or compared. It may be that there were quantitative and qualitative differences between the two groups' production of sounds but that because of the insensitivity of the observation system these differences were not detected. Because of the problems described here and the fact that this technique does not measure the relationship between frequency of cooing and parent-presented stimulation immediately following cooing, it is unclear whether the conclusions in this study were justified.

Further research is needed before the third proposition concerning parents' use of consequences on infant vocalization can be supported. This research would involve "invasion" of the natural environment (the home) by observers and equipment to record instances of infant vocal behavior and the parent behaviors surrounding that vocal behavior in time. From these records it would be possible to determine whether infant vocalization is followed by social stimulation like or unlike that used in the laboratory studies. In addition, it would be possible to answer some practical questions about how often parents apply these rewards to vocalization, what parent behaviors are used as consequences more frequently than others, which sounds parents are more likely to follow with social stimulation than others, and whether parents discriminate between infant vocal responses that sound like and unlike their native language in applying their consequences.

Once this descriptive research has been conducted, investigators might concentrate on how often parents should apply consequences and what parent behaviors are more effective than others. The research to date has concentrated on the latter of these two issues. Haugan and McIntire (1972) compared the effectiveness of three different consequences on the rate of vocalization of 24 institutionalized infants. The children were three to six months old and were eligible for adoption. The three consequences compared were: 1) food (a spoonful of fruit pudding), 2) vocal imitation by an adult of the same sound and of the same duration as the infant's sound, and 3) tactile stimulation or stroking of the infant's face, neck, or arms for two seconds. Three groups of infants, each receiving one of the consequences during treatment, were run through parallel reversal designs. All of the groups showed conditioning effects, but the group receiving vocal imitation showed significantly greater effects than the other two groups.

Hursh and Sherman (1973) conducted a component analysis of their package of modeling the sound, praise, and vocal imitation of the sound to determine which single component or which combination of components was most effective in increasing the child's rate of emitting a particular sound. The mean results for three children indicate that the total package was most effective in increasing the rate of a particular sound, modeling alone was second most effective, and praise alone and praise plus vocal imitation were equally least effective (although all combinations produced some change). Although these results might be seen as contradictory to Haugan and McIntire's results, it is important to note that the children involved in this research were 15 to 20 months old, or one year older than the infants studied by Haugan and McIntire. In addition, Hursh and Sherman did not compare the effectiveness of the parent behaviors that Haugan and McIntire used, such as touching, to the components of their package. Thus, it remains unknown what parent behaviors are the most effective in conditioning vocalization at various ages.

It seems, therefore, that a great deal of research is still required to provide parents with the information they need to efficiently encourage vocalization in their infants. Even when this information has been provided, a question of the relation of vocalization to future language development will remain. Intuitively, it seems that more practice making sounds will lead to earlier word and sentence formation. Indeed, some language-training programs (e.g., Lovaas et al., 1966) for developmentally retarded children begin with increasing the child's rate of sound production. Yet whether early sound production has a function in the language development of a normal child is still a controversial subject.

Jakobson (1941), for example, has suggested that babbling is discontinuous with later language development. He held that babbling is unrestricted and not governed by the phonological restraints of the languages of the world. Jakobson (1971) further noted that an infant produces many different types of sounds during babbling and that most of these sounds are eliminated when the child proceeds to using words. Even sounds the child will later use in his native language are dropped out for a time. Jakobson's claims of a discontinuity between babbling and later language may have produced a hiatus in research on the topic, although recently the issue has been revived. Oller et al. (1974), for example, studied the sound production of eight infants under the age of 13 months. They audiotaped 30-minute samples of each child's babbling, and two independent observers listened to the tapes and transcribed each utterance. They found that the infants used many more singleton consonants than consonant clusters (two or more consonants in combination, e.g., sc, tr, st) and at least twice as many initial consonants (those coming at the beginning of a sound) than final consonants (those coming at the end of a sound). Both these characteristics have been documented to be present in early child speech. Additionally, they found that the infants used many of the same substitutions that young children use in their early speech. They concluded that babbling seems to be governed by phonological universals and is continuous with meaningful child speech. However, the authors did not address themselves to the possible effects that practice in the early sound-production stage has on later language development.

In conclusion, research concerning the shaping theory has suggested that the rate of infant vocalizations can be increased, that specific vocalizations can be strengthened while others are weakened, and that parent behaviors can play a role in such a process. It is improbable that the shaping process accounts for all of a child's language development because it is unlikely that parents shape every verbal response of their children. This would require a dedicated and knowledgeable effort by all persons in the child's environment. Perhaps the shaping process is involved only in the initial elaboration of an infant's vocalizations. Additional research is needed to determine just how often parents attend to their infants' vocalizations, to answer several practical questions about the most effective parent techniques, and to determine the relationship between early vocalizations and later language development.

The Role of Imitation

In the previous section, the role parents play in elaborating the variety and increasing the number of vocalizations of their children was emphasized. This represents only part of the developing vocal competence of the child. At some point in language development, children begin to imitate others. At first, this may involve matching the intonation patterns of parental utterances or sounds in isolation. Later, it may involve matching approximations to words, entire words, and even phrases. Many feel that the development of imitative skills is critical to adequate language development because, through an imitative process, children may learn the intonation and stress patterns, the sounds, words, phrases, and perhaps even the grammatical structure of a language (Sherman, 1971).

How does imitation develop in children and what role do parents play in that development? Unfortunately, there are no clear answers to these questions. Observers of child language generally agree that utterances by parents can serve as models for their children. Beyond this, there is little agreement, although several authors have proposed plausible theories about how children's imitation might develop and about the roles parents might play in the process.

Mowrer (1960), for example, has emphasized the role that imitation might play in the initial elaboration of sounds and then words. Mowrer sees parents playing a less active role in this process than they would in a shaping process. In fact, he theorizes that it is the positive value of parents' voices that takes on the important role. More specifically, he suggests that parents' voices take on rewarding value for an infant by being paired with the "good" things in the infant's life (warmth, dryness, food, comfort, etc.). When the infant begins making his own sounds, Mowrer hypothesizes, those sounds that are similar to sounds his parents have made will have similar rewarding value. Thus, the child will continue to repeat those sounds and will also make sounds that are gradually more and more like his parents'. Through this process the child will eventually say words.

To substantiate Mowrer's theory it would be necessary to demonstrate that: 1) parents speak to infants while they are feeding, clothing, and comforting them, 2) parents' voices become rewarding to infants because of the association with feeding, comfort, etc., 3) infants can discriminate one sound from another, and 4) an infant's sounds that approximate parent sounds are more reinforcing to the infant than those sounds that do not approximate parent sounds.

Little research has concentrated on these issues. Casual observation indicates that parents do speak to their young infants during feeding, changing, and bathing. However, there is little information available as to how much they talk to them, what kinds of things they say, and the voice tones they use.

There is some information available about the rewarding value of parent's voices. Friedlander (1968) placed two identical toys in three 11–13-month-old infants' playpens. Manipulation of one toy activated a tape of the child's mother's voice, whereas manipulation of the other toy activated a tape of Bach organ music. By comparing the number of times each tape was activated, he found that the infants played more with the toy that was paired with the mother's voice than with the toy paired with the organ music. When Friedlander used the same method to compare the effects of a stranger's voice to the music, no clear preference emerged. When he compared the effects of the mother's voice using flat inflection and unfamiliar words with the stranger's voice using bright inflection and familiar words, he found no preference in one infant (the youngest of three subjects) and a preference for the flat mother's voice in the other two infants. This research indicates that mothers' voices do have some greater reward value than other types of sound stimulation in the environment. However, it does not indicate how that rewarding nature comes about. Because at least some of the infants seemed to prefer the mother's voice over the stranger's, even when the stranger used phrases previously used by the mothers, it would seem that something in the child's history of interaction with the mother enhanced the value of the mother's voice. Whether or not this "something" was a pairing of the mother's voice with the "good" things in life remains unknown.

Other research has been aimed at evaluating whether infants can discriminate sounds. Eimas et al. (1971) used an habituation paradigm to determine that infants can discriminate between two sounds (/b/ and /p/) as young as one to four months old. These researchers first recorded ongoing rates of sucking. Then, while an infant was sucking, they played a tape of a voice repetitiously emitting one sound. This resulted in an increased rate of sucking compared to the original rates. Gradually, the rate of sucking began to decrease. When the sucking rate approached the original level, the tape was switched to a voice emitting the other sound. Eimas et al. found the infant's rate of sucking increased again corresponding in time with the change. Control subjects did not receive this switch and showed no change. Their sucking response rate continued to decline. Eimas et al. concluded that the infants receiving both sounds could discriminate between the two sounds even though they were closely related (both sounds are produced similarly except the /b/ sound is voiced and the /p/ sound is voiceless).

Moffitt (1968) and McCaffrey (1969) reported similar results using heart rate as their dependent variable. Moffitt indicated that 20–24-week-old infants could discriminate between /b/ and /g/ sounds. McCaffrey reported that 11–28-week-old infants could discriminate between the consonants /p/ and /t/ and that 4–15-week-old infants could discriminate between the vowels /a/ and /i/. These findings lend some credibility to the idea that infants can discriminate between sounds. Whether they can discriminate between sounds that are similar and

dissimilar to sounds their parents make and whether they can discriminate between sounds they make themselves are two questions
requiring further research.

The final issue relevant to Mowrer's theory is whether an infant's
sounds that are similar to parent sounds are more rewarding to the infant
than are sounds that are unlike parent sounds. There is apparently no
research available to answer this question. However, it would seem feasible to record an infant's sounds and to divide them into two tapes: one
tape containing sounds similar to sounds parents make and the other
containing sounds unlike parent sounds. Then the same method as that
used by Friedlander could be employed to determine which tape the
infants preferred.

In summary, there is some (although not overwhelming) evidence that
Mowrer's self-shaping theory may describe some of the processes taking
place in early language development. Until further research has been
conducted, we can do little more than guess at how parents' voices become
rewarding for children. Since several researchers (see Kelleher and Gollub,
1962; and Fantino, 1977 for a review) have shown that previously neutral
stimuli can take on reinforcing properties through association with
primary reinforcers (food, for instance), it appears that this could be the
process taking place. On the other hand, it may be that a mother's voice
becomes reinforcing even before birth. Sheppard (1969) reports the frustration of his child (as shown by loud crying) each time he stopped a tape
recording of the mother's beating heart. If a newborn child is familiar with
the mother's heart beat, the child may also be familiar with the mother's
voice as it resounds through her body.

As we have seen, Mowrer has proposed a relatively nonactive role
for parents in the process of a child's sound and word development. The
parent simply needs to talk to the child while feeding, comforting, and
bathing him. The child does the rest. He essentially teaches himself.
Risley (1966), however, proposes that parents play a supportive role in
this process. He suggests that parents generally attend to infant vocalizations (by picking them up, talking to them, smiling at them, etc.) and
that this general attention enhances the self-shaping process. Risley theorizes that such enhancement might take place because self-reinforcement
processes are weak in comparison to reinforcement provided by others.
If parents' general attention is enough to reinforce general vocalization,
Risley reasons, any additional self-reinforcement may be enough to
increase the production of certain sounds to the exclusion of others.
Most of the research reviewed in this chapter so far lends some credibility to such a proposal.

Another theorist, Fry (1966), sees the parent's role in the imitation
process to be even more active than do Mowrer and Risley. According to

Fry, the development of sounds and words proceeds as follows. First, the parent presents a model of a word (e.g., *dog*) in the presence of the proper object. If the child imitates that model with an approximation (e.g., *da*), the parent praises the child and may repeat the model (e.g., *That's right! Dog*). In later instances, the parent praises the child if he makes closer approximations to the model. Soon the child is producing the whole word in imitation of the parent. Eventually, when the child sees the object, he produces the word for that object without waiting for the parent's model. Other people, in addition to the parents, take on the rewarding function; when the child's speech becomes clearer, they begin to speak to the child in response to his speech.

Fry's theory depends on four major assumptions: 1) parents present models to their children, 2) parents respond with some sort of reinforcing stimulation when their child makes an attempt to imitate them; 3) parents begin to respond differentially to encourage their child to make closer and closer approximations to their models, and 4) such a process teaches a child to use words spontaneously and appropriately. Thus, in contrast to Mowrer's theory, which strongly relies on the child's refinement of his own speech, Fry's theory places a heavy emphasis on the parents' use of feedback to refine the child's speech. The remainder of this section is devoted to reviewing the research that has a bearing on Fry's theory.

As with Mowrer's theory, the research relating to Fry's theory is limited. Normative (nonmanipulative) research gives us some indication that mothers do present models for their children. For example, Broen (1972) found that 15% of mothers' speech to their 18–28-month-old children is composed of one-word utterances. These short utterances might function as models. In addition, 30% of the mothers' speech is short declarative sentences (e.g., *That's a car, There's the truck, Here's a purse*). These might also serve as models because specific objects are being labeled in relatively brief utterances.

Moerk (1972), who also observed the interactions between mothers and children, reported that parents provide models for their children. According to Moerk, parents not only provide models but instruct their child to try to imitate the model (e.g., *Tape recorder* (said slowly, short pause). *Can you say it?* or *Say refrigerator*). In addition, he reports that the parents he observed were constantly translating their own actions and characteristics of the environment into words for their children (e.g., *First, I'll wash your hands and your face. Let me wash your legs. Now get your slipper on your right foot*). Because all of these statements were paired with appropriate actions and objects, Moerk calls these statements "models."

Moerk's research also has some bearing on the question of whether parents provide rewarding feedback to the child after the child attempts to imitate. In many of the examples he cites in his article, the parent provides some kind of positive acknowledgment of the attempt (e.g., *Yeah. Oh, that's good. That's right, tape recorder, yeah. That's better. Very good. Yeah, refrigerator*). In fact, some of his examples indicate that parents withhold their praise until the child emits a closer approximation to the word than the child's first effort provided.

> Mother: *Can you say soldier?*
> Child: *Sold.*
> Mother: *Can you?*
> Child: *Sold—Soldier.*
> Mother: *That's better.*

However, although these examples are indicative of the presence of parent models, praise, and differential praise in parent-child interactions, we know very little about these parent behaviors. Such necessary information as to how frequent these interactions are, at what age or stage of language development they begin, how much time elapses or how many trials take place before the parents expect closer and closer approximations, and what benefits result from such interactions has not been covered in Moerk's or any other research to date.

Several investigators have shown that an imitation process similar to the one proposed by Fry can be used successfully to teach speech-deficient children to produce sounds and words. In one of the earliest studies in this area, Lovaas et al. (1966) established vocal and, eventually, verbal imitation in several children. The children involved in this study, all mute schizophrenics, were taught to imitate by first rewarding them (with praise and food) for any vocalizations they produced. Then they were rewarded for all vocalization following an adult's vocalization within six seconds and finally for vocalizations that followed the model within six seconds and that more and more closely matched the model. After 26 days, the children were imitating not only sounds but words. As training progressed and the children learned to imitate several sounds and words, the probability that they would imitate novel words increased sharply. When rewards were delivered noncontingently rather than contingently, imitative behavior deteriorated. During later sessions, Lovaas et al. interspersed some Norwegian words with the English words. They found that the children's accuracy of imitation improved on the Norwegian words, even though they were never rewarded for imitating those words (rewards for imitating English words had continued throughout this latter phase, however).

Subsequent studies have replicated and extended these effects. Brigham and Sherman (1968) found that initially inaccurate imitations of words improved as long as the children in the study were rewarded for their accurate imitation of other words, even though such improvement was not required or rewarded. Garcia, Baer, and Firestone (1971) taught two retarded children to imitate short vocal sounds. As more short vocal sounds were trained, the frequency of imitating untrained sounds gradually increased. However, Garcia et al. found this generalization of training limited to the imitation of short vocal sounds; the children did not imitate longer vocal responses that had not been trained. Schroeder and Baer (1972) taught two retarded girls to imitate words. Half of the time they taught three words simultaneously to criterion (concurrent procedure). The other half of the time they taught each of three words separately to criterion in a series (serial training). After several alterations of these procedures, they found that there were no differences between the procedures in the number of training trials to reach criterion for each group of three words. Yet they found that imitative accuracy on untrained words and phrases was higher immediately after concurrent training than after serial training.

Risley and Reynolds (1970) extended this research on imitation training to investigate the effects of emphasis in a model's voice on a child's imitation. Three five-year-old disadvantaged children were asked to imitate sentences that contained a varied number of phrases, but they were always given candy regardless of their imitative accuracy. The adult stressed (by raising her voice) certain words as she read each sentence. The results indicate that stressed words were more frequently imitated as long as the number of stressed words in the sentence was low (one word in a sentence). When the number of stressed words was increased to 16% or 32% of the words in the sentence, the number of stressed words that were imitated decreased. These results indicate that it is possible for sentences or long phrases to function as models for the child who is currently at the one-word utterance stage, as long as the parent stresses a small number of words in each sentence. Whether or not parents provide this stress is currently uninvestigated.

These five studies thus provide us with the information that the process of rewarding closer and closer approximations to a model's sounds is useful in teaching vocal and verbal imitation. They also indicate that when rewards no longer immediately follow imitations, a child no longer imitates. However, according to the results, rewards do not have to follow *every* imitation. Even though the children were never rewarded for their imitations of some words, their accuracy of imitating these words continued to increase. In addition, according to Schroeder and Baer's results, it is possible to teach several words simultaneously through imitation. Not only is the simultaneous training of several words possible, it also seems to enhance the children's attempts at imitating new words. This simultaneous learning of several words is a likely set of circumstances for the natural environment. Finally, the Risley and Reynolds study provides information that sentences (which make up the majority of parent speech according to Broen, 1972) can function as models as long as parents provide stress on a small number of words. Nevertheless, these studies have their limitations. Because they were all conducted in laboratory settings and because most of them used candy as a reward for the children, they might say little about how functional the imitation process is in the natural environment, the child's home.

The evidence available for the functioning of imitative processes in home environments is limited. Two studies have been conducted in which parents were specifically asked to provide models for their children. In one, the previously described study by Hursh and Sherman (1973), parents were requested to model sounds (e.g., *dee*) systematically and then to praise and repeat the sound if their child said it (e.g., *Good, you said "dee"*). The results showed that models, praise, and imitation of a particular sound by parents increased the frequency with which the children uttered those particular sounds. Furthermore, the combination of modeling, praise, and repetition produced greater increases than any of the components applied alone or in pairs. In another study, by Whitehurst, Novak, and Zorn (1972), the subject was a 40-month-old child with severely retarded speech development. The authors asked the child's mother to vary her use of conversation (statements such as *We're having hamburgers tonight*) and imitative prompts (such as, *Can you say "house?"*). They found that if the level of conversation or if the level of imitative prompts were separately raised above baseline levels, the child steadily began to use more new words and phrases. The highest rate of new-word usage occurred when both conversation and imitative prompts were at high levels.

Two additional studies have looked at naturally occurring amounts of imitation in young children in the home. Bloom, Hood, and Lightbown (1974) conducted extensive observations of the spontaneous and imitative speech of six children in their natural homes during the time that the mean length of the children's utterances increased from one to approximately two morphemes per utterance (ages 18 to 25 months). They found that there was a considerable amount of variability in the amount of imitation exhibited by the children. Some children apparently imitated adult utterances very little (e.g., only 4–6% of utterance types were imitative), whereas other children seemed to imitate adult utterances a great deal (e.g., 30–40% of utterance types were imitative). Their data also suggest that the children tended to imitate words that they did not produce spontaneously and vice versa, whether these words were used in isolation or as part of a phrase. Furthermore, in the case of several of the children observed, there seemed to be a developmental trend from imitation to spontaneous usage; that is, utterance types that initially were used imitatively, later stopped being used imitatively and instead were exhibited spontaneously.

Schumaker (1976) also recorded the speech of six children (ages 19 to 23 months) in their homes as their mothers went about their daily activities as they normally did. Schumaker reported frequency of all imitations in contrast to Bloom et al., who reported number of different utterance types imitated. Nevertheless, the results of the two studies are in considerable agreement in that Schumaker also found that the children varied considerably in the amount that they imitated the utterances of their mothers. For some children as little as 3% of their utterances were imitative, whereas for other children 25% of their utterances were imitative.

The results of the study by Hursh and Sherman (1973) and Whitehurst, Novak, and Zorn (1972) suggest that models systematically provided by parents can have substantial effects on the utterances of their children. The results of the studies by Schumaker (1976) and Bloom, Hood, and Lightbown (1974) indicate that in the natural home situation children vary considerably in the extent to which they imitate the utterances of their parents. If the data obtained in the latter two studies are representative of normally occurring amounts of imitation of young children 18 to 24 months old, they suggest that high levels of imitation are not always required at this age for normal language development. However, the data of Bloom et al. indicate that when high amounts of imitation do occur the process appears to be developmentally progressive from imitative to spontaneous speech.

There is a clear need for additional research in this area. If, at any point in language development, imitation is helpful (if not necessary), we need to study, normatively and experimentally, more about how parent utterances interact with those of their children to foster language development. It would seem useful, for example, to determine what parent utterances function as models, how often these models are and should be presented, how often parents give their children positive feedback for imitating or attempting to imitate, whether parents withhold positive feedback until the child makes a closer approximation to their model, how often and when this occurs, and whether this whole process has any relation to the spontaneous use of words by the child.

This section has been devoted to the discussion of three main theories of the development of sounds and words in children's language. According to the conditioning theory, parents may provide contingent social stimulation for their children when the children vocalize. Sounds more and more like the native language are then shaped by the parents' differential application of social contingencies. Mowrer's theory emphasizes the rewarding value that parent's voices take on through their pairing with food, warmth, dryness, etc. The child eventually shapes his own sounds to be like his parents' because those sounds similar to parents' sounds are more reinforcing than others. Like Mowrer, Fry proposes the important role of parents as models in the imitation process. However, he also emphasizes the active role of parents as providers of differential consequences for closer and closer imitations of their models.

None of the three theories has been totally substantiated, although some research has been conducted that speaks to each theory's propositions. It is quite plausible that none of them truly accounts for what is happening in the process of a child's language development. It is possible that some or all of these processes work in combination with each other or with other undiscovered processes.

FROM WORDS TO SENTENCES AND CONVERSATION

Natural Observations of Rule-Governed Language

When children progress from the holophrastic stage, i.e., the stage of one-word utterances, they begin to chain words together. This happens somewhere between 18–24 months of age (Nelson, 1973). Brown and Fraser (1964) and Brown and Bellugi (1964) call this the stage of telegraphic speech. Here, the child is using phrases containing two or more words but does not include parts of speech such as articles, auxiliary verbs, and inflections. Brown and Fraser note that children at this stage seem to use only those words with high information content. Through normative research of children in their natural environments, some investigators (e.g., Brown, 1973; Bloom, 1974) have shown the versatile nature of the two-word utterance stage. For instance, children's speech at this stage shows attributive relations (with adjectives and nouns, *Big boat*),· possessive relations (e.g., *Mommy coat*), locative relations (e.g., *Sweater chair, Walk street*), agent-action (e.g., *Mommy put*), agent-object (e.g., *Mommy sock*), and action-object relations (e.g., *Put book*). From this telegraphic stage, children gradually add more and more words and word forms to their utterances until they are effectively communicating with full sentences.

In this progression from single-word utterances to sentences, children seem to acquire two sets of complex grammatical rules: rules of syntax and rules of morphology (also called rules of accidence by Wilkinson, 1971). Rules of syntax are those concerning word order (e.g., in questions the auxiliary verb *be* comes before the subject—*What is he doing?*—whereas in statements it comes after the subject—*He is swimming*). In addition, rules of syntax include rules of co-occurrence and rules of substitution. Rules of co-occurrence indicate which types of words can be placed next to each other. For example, we can say *the ferocious lion* (determiner, adjective, noun) but not *the ferocious ate* (determiner, adjective, verb). Rules of substitution indicate that words fall in several categories (count nouns, mass nouns, transitive verbs, intransitive verbs, etc.) and can only be substituted within those categories. For instance, in the sentence *The ferocious lion ate his trainer, devoured* (another transitive verb) can be substituted for *ate* but *growled* (an intransitive verb) cannot.

The other set of rules children acquire, rules of morphology or accidence, include all those rules having to do with changing the form of individual words. These rules enable speakers to use singular and plural forms of words (e.g., *dog* versus *dogs*), to form possessives (*Mommy's coat* versus *This coat belongs to Mommy*), to use number and tense in verbs (e.g., *he talks, they talk, he talked, they talked, he's talking, they're talking*), to adjust the case of pronouns to be subject, objects, or possessives (e.g., *he, him, his*), to indicate degree of comparison in adjectives and adverbs (e.g., *prettier* versus *prettiest*) and to add prefixes and suffixes to words (e.g., *pre-, un-, re-, -ment, -some, -ness, -ly*).

Evidence Available for Children's Use of Rule-Governed Language

There is considerable evidence available to support the notion that children use "rules" when speaking. Smith's (1933) and Brown and Fraser's (1964) normative research reveals that children make certain systematic errors in their speech. For example, a child may make the error of pluralizing the word *foot* to get *foots*. Brown and Fraser suggest that a child smooths language into a more regular system. The child "overgeneralizes" the pluralization rule he has found to be generally successful in creating plurals (namely, "add an /-s/ to the singular form of a word ending in an unvoiced sound") for all words that might fit the rule. Brown and Fraser claim that errors of this sort are frequent in children's speech and reflect their attempts to use a set of general rules.

Berko (1958) conducted some research that also indicates the use of rules of morphology in children's speech. Using a set of nonsense words to control for the possibility that the child may have "memorized" forms of familiar words, she presented a picture to the child saying, for example, "This is a wug." Then, after adding a similar picture, she said, "Now there is another one, there are two of them. There are two _____." The child was asked to complete the sentence in each case. Berko tested 12 adults, 19 preschoolers, and 61 first graders on their use of plurals, possessives, verb tenses, and comparatives and superlatives.

The answers of the adults served as a "standard" for evaluating the children's responses. Berko found that the children produced adult-like regular forms of the words in response to her questions, and that the older children produced more adult-like forms than did the younger children. Berko concluded that the children were using rules to produce these forms because it was unlikely that they had prior experiences with these nonsense words.

Brown and Berko (1960) extended this research to cover rules of syntax or, more specifically, rules of substitution. They gave 20 children from each of the first three grades and 20 adults a word-association test and a word-usage test. In the word-association test, the subjects were asked to say a word that they associated with a word that the experimenter presented. Words in six parts-of-speech categories were presented: count nouns, mass nouns, adjectives, adverbs, transitive verbs, and intransitive verbs. In the word usage test, the experimenter presented a nonsense word in one of six parts-of-speech slots in a sentence. For example, when presenting the nonsense word as a count noun the experimenter said, "Do you know what a *wug* is? This is a picture of a little girl thinking about a *wug*. Can you make up what that means?" The children were required to repeat or paraphrase one of the sentences using their own word in place of the nonsense word (e.g., "She is thinking about a *dog*"). When presenting the nonsense word as a transitive verb, the experimenter said, "This is a woman who wants to *wug* something. Can you make up what that means?" An appropriate reply might be, "She wants to *send* something." Brown and Berko's results show that the adults reliably used words that fit in the same parts-of-speech categories as the nonsense words on both tests. The children's results demonstrate that their scores increased (reflecting adult parts-of-speech usage) as their age increased and that their scores on the word-association and sentence tests were closely related. Brown and Berko suggested that this gradual increase in scores reflects the children's gradual organization of words into syntactic classes and, therefore, their gradual acquisition of syntactic rules.

Thus, it appears that children do use rules of syntax and morphology. Although several investigators have been able to document when the use of these rules appears in children's speech and the order in which they appear (e.g., Braine, 1963; Miller and Ervin, 1964; Cazden, 1968; Klima and Bellugi-Klima, 1969; Menyuk, 1969; Ervin-Tripp, 1970; and Bellugi, 1971), little is known about the method by which children acquire these rules. It is probable that these rules are learned through children's experiences with their language environments. Yet this remains a speculation in the absence of specific research designed to evaluate what environmental variables affect children's acquisition of language rules in the natural environment.

Experimental Production of Rule-Governed Language

The Role of Models and Reinforcement   Several investigators have attempted to teach rule-governed language to children with language defects. The success achieved in the studies suggests that similar variables might be responsible for natural language learning. The basic strategy of these researchers has been to teach children to use specific language responses exemplifying a particular rule and then to determine the extent to which the children will begin to produce, on their own, new language forms that also exemplify the rule.

A study by Guess et al. (1968) provides an excellent example of this type of research. A 10-year-old retarded girl was presented with a random sequence of one object or two objects to label. She was asked, "What do you see?" and if she replied with the appropriate single label (e.g., *cat*) or plural label (e.g., *cats*), she was given a bite of food. If she did not reply correctly, a model of the correct response was presented by the experimenter. Then, after 10 seconds, a new trial commenced. After training the child on two singular-plural discriminations, Guess et al. found that she formed the plural correctly on the first trial of all the new items that were subsequently presented to her. In a second condition the rule was reversed; she was given plural models for singular objects and singular models for plural objects. After training on six item-discriminations the girl again began using the required label (according to the reversed rule) on the first trial an item was presented. In a final condition, she was given models for normal plural usage. A singular model was presented for singular objects and a plural model was presented for plural objects. The child immediately began to generate plural labels for plural items and singular labels for single items on the first trial with each new set of stimuli.

In addition to these findings, Guess et al. found that the child labeled uncommon plural forms according to the rule of adding an /-s/ allomorph, which she had learned in training (e.g., she produced the form *mans*). She also used the /-s/ allomorph to pluralize words requiring a /-z/ allomorph (e.g., words like *shoes, bananas, dogs*). The authors theorized that since the first six words she learned to pluralize required an /-s/ ending, she had generalized this form to all other plurals she was asked to provide. Sailor's (1971) results support this hypothesis. When he taught children to pluralize words requiring an /-s/ ending (words ending in unvoiced sounds), they also used this ending on words requiring a /-z/ ending (words ending in voiced sounds). Similarly, when he taught them to pluralize words with a /-z/ ending, they also used the /-z/ ending to pluralize words requiring an /-s/ ending. This phenomenon of "overgeneralization" (Brown and Fraser, 1964; Schumaker and Sherman, 1970), or the use of a rule learned for certain language instances for other similar but inappropriate language instances, characterizes the many errors that children make at this stage of language development.

Several other researchers have taught language-deficient children the generative use of rule-governed language. Under the category of syntactic rules, Wheeler and Sulzer (1970) and Bennett and Ling (1972) taught children the generative use of articles and auxiliary verbs; Hart and Risley (1968, 1974) taught generative use of adjective-noun combinations; Twardosz and Baer (1973) taught the generative use of a simple question; and Hart and Risley (1974) and Stevens-Long and Rasmussen (1974) taught the generative use of compound sentences. Under the category of morphological rules, Guess (1969) and Guess and Baer (1973) were successful in teaching the generative use of plurals; and Schumaker and Sherman (1970) and Clark and Sherman (1975) were successful in teaching the generative use of verb tenses. Still others have taught a combination of syntactic and morphological rules. Garcia, Guess, and Byrnes (1973) and Lutzker and Sherman (1974) taught children the generative use of singular and plural sentences requiring noun-verb agreement. Sheldon (1974) successfully taught the generative use of verb tenses within chained sentence responses to pictures and conversational speech.

All studies cited in the previous paragraphs involved exceptional children (e.g., retarded children, autistic children, perceptually handicapped children) who were deficient in language skills. In two studies, Whitehurst (1971, 1972) provided some verification that the same procedures are successful with normal children. In both studies, Whitehurst used nonsense words to teach two-year-old children the generative use of adjective-noun combinations.

It is important to recognize that all studies used some combination of imitation and reinforcement in teaching the first few examples of a rule; that is, a language form was modeled for the child, and the child was reinforced for imitating the model. This successful use of reinforcement and imitation procedures has led some researchers (e.g., Sherman, 1971) to suggest that imitation and reinforcement might play a role in the normal child's acquisition of grammatical rules.

In summary, the body of research just described indicates that children can be taught through imitation and reinforcement to produce novel forms of plurals, verb tenses, adjective-noun combinations, and sentences that have never been modeled for them during training. It appears that, when children learn a rule concerning one language class, they also use that rule for other similar language classes. It is not until they receive corrective feedback (i.e., are trained on a discrimination between language classes) that they generate new uses of a rule only within the appropriate language class (e.g., Schumaker and Sherman, 1970; Sailor, 1971). However, it is important to note that all these studies took place under laboratory conditions and, with the exception of Sheldon's (1974) study, did not approximate normal conversational usage of the particular forms taught. Whether similar processes of imitation and reinforcement are at work in the natural environment of the normal child remains to be determined.

The Role of Prompts   Another process that may be involved in complex language development is prompting. Prompting is a method of cueing a person into action. It has been used in several studies to give children cues about the verbal responses required in a particular situation. In these studies, prompts have taken the form of questions requiring some verbal response from the child. Prompting has usually been used in combination with reinforcement. Sometimes it is used in combination with both modeling and reinforcement. Reynolds and Risley (1968), for example, used prompting in combination with teacher praise to increase the verbal responses of a four-year-old child. Each day, observers recorded three five-minute samples of the child's verbalizations during free play. After a stable baseline record was obtained, the teacher began asking the child a few questions each time the child requested materials. These questions concerned the characteristics of the materials, additional materials needed, and projected uses of the materials. If the child answered the questions, she received praise and the requested materials. Throughout the day spontaneous verbalizations were praised as well. During this condition the child's total number of verbalizations, imperative sentences, and verbalizations directed at the teacher increased. When the teacher discontinued her question-prompts and attended to the child only when she was silent, the child's verbalizations returned to baseline levels. When teacher prompts and praise were made contingent on verbalizations, the child's verbalizations again rose. In a final analysis, Reynolds and Risley had the teacher discontinue her prompts but continue her praise for verbalizations. Frequency of verbalizations gradually decreased during this condition. When prompts were reinstated, the child's verbalization frequency again rose. Reynolds and Risley concluded that prompts were an important part of their procedure.

Hart and Risley (1968) also used prompts, but this time the target response was a particular language class—adjective-noun combinations—and 15 children were involved. Again, a 15-minute sample of each child's speech was recorded daily until a stable baseline was obtained.

When use of materials was made contingent on a child asking for the materials with a color adjective-noun combination, the child's use of these combinations increased in spontaneous speech. Prompts (e.g., *What color of a car?*) and models (e.g., *a red car*) were presented the first few days of this condition. When materials were no longer contingent on adjective-noun combinations, the children's use of them in spontaneous speech returned to baseline levels.

In a further extension of this procedure, Hart and Risley (1974) used a four-level prompting procedure to increase preschool children's use of nouns, then adjective-noun combinations, then color adjective-noun combinations, and finally compound sentences in their spontaneous speech. When a child indicated that he wanted to use a particular preschool material, the teacher first waited 30 seconds to see if he would utter the required response. Then, if the child had not uttered the response, the teacher asked him two levels of questions (e.g., when the adjective-noun combination was required, the teacher first asked, "What kind of a car do you want?" and then asked, "I have red cars and blue cars, big cars and little cars. What kind of a car do you want?"). Finally, if the child still had not uttered the correct response, the teacher presented an imitative prompt (e.g., "Say the whole thing, 'a red car'."). Spontaneous frequency of each of the target responses increased only when the prompting procedure was implemented and materials were made contingent on such responses.

In summary, these three studies indicate that prompting can function as a device to teach children to use particular language forms in their spontaneous speech. Since the research was conducted in a preschool setting, it appears that the procedures can work in a relatively natural environment for children. Whether prompting functions as a procedure used by parents in their interactions with children is another question.

Thus, from the research conducted to develop procedures for teaching handicapped or disadvantaged children the complex rules of language, three successful procedures have emerged: modeling, reinforcement, and prompting. To determine whether these processes have any relation to the development of generative rule use in normal children, it will be necessary to find out whether parents use these processes and, if they do, whether they have any functional relationship with the normal child's learning of the generative use of language rules.

Evidence for the Existence of Models in the Natural Environment

Subjectively, one might claim that parents provide models. Anything they say within earshot of the child can function as a model. An objection to this notion might be that adult speech is so complex and irregular that it confuses a child. Recent research (e.g., Maclay and Osgood, 1967; Goldman-Eisler, 1968) indicates that, indeed, adult language is rapid, has many pauses unrelated to grammatical structure, and contains frequent disfluencies and broken sentences. But, according to some sociolinguists, these characteristics are present at their extreme only when an adult is addressing another adult. Researchers are finding that when an adult addresses a child various adjustments are made. Baldwin and Frank (1969), for instance, reported that lower and middle class black mothers in Harlem as well as white mothers from Washington Square reduce the grammatical complexity of their utterances when talking with their three-year-old children in comparison to their speech directed at adults.

These findings were supported by Snow (1972), who asked mothers to complete each of two tasks (telling a story and teaching a categorization task) in four situations: 1) when a two-year-old was present, 2) when a 10-year-old was present, 3) when making a tape to be played for the two-year-old, and 4) when making a tape to be played for the 10-year-old. Snow found, regardless of whether the child was absent or present, a significant difference between the ways mothers spoke to two-year-olds and 10-year-olds. For the two-year-olds, the lengths of utterances and preverb lengths (number of words present before the verb) were shorter. There were fewer subordinate clauses, compound verbs, and third-person pronouns. Sixteen percent of all utterances directed at the younger child were simple phrases without verbs. Repetition of whole sentences was four times as frequent as for the 10-year-olds. In addition, paraphrasing or semantic repetition was three times as frequent for the younger as for the older children. Presence of the child resulted in more simplification in the mother's speech than when the mothers made the tapes. When Snow tested college women (who were not mothers) in the same situations, she reported substantially the same results.

Broen's (1972) data also support the notion that the language directed at children consists of simplified, organized, and redundant utterances. Broen measured the speech of 10 mothers of two children in five situations: 1) while in free play with the younger child (18-28 months); 2) while in free play with the older child (over 45 months); 3) while telling a story to the younger child; 4) while telling a story to the older child; and 5) while speaking to the experimenter. In order for a family to participate in the study, the oldest child had to score not more than 0.5 standard deviations below the mean on three tests of verbal ability. This measure was used to indicate that the mothers involved in the study were good "teachers" of language. Broen found significant differences between the speech directed at the younger and older children and also between the speech directed at the older children and the experimenter. As the age of the speaking partner increased, the rate of speech (words per minute) increased, the number of different words increased, and the number of disfluencies (irrelevant repetitions, interjections of words, sounds or phrases and broken sentences) also increased. In addition, Broen found that about 15% of the mother's speech to the younger child consisted of single-word utterances. The number of single-word utterances decreased as the speaking partner's age increased. Broen also studied the location of pauses in the mother's speech and found that 98.6% of all the pauses in speech directed at the younger child followed sentences or single-word utterances (those utterances that were not grammatically related to previous sentences), whereas only 89.3% and 53.9% of the pauses in speech directed at the older child and the adult followed sentences. Broen concluded that, as the age of the speaking partner increases, the location of pauses shifts from sentence boundaries to other positions.

Broen also studied the types of sentence structures used by the mothers with their younger child. She found that 15% of the sentences were grammatically incomplete; the mothers used many sentences in which they had left out some form of the verbs *do* or *be* (e.g., *Want her hat on?* instead of *Do you want her hat on?* or *You gonna hug her?* instead of *Are you gonna hug her?*). Questions accounted for 37% of the sentences, imperatives for 24% of the sentences, and declaratives for 30% of the sentences.

This research was extended by Phillips (1973) by measuring mothers' speech to eight-month-old boys, 18-month-old boys, 28-month-old boys, and adults. She also found significant differences between maternal speech directed at the children and that directed at adults. Although there were no differences between speech directed at the eight-month-olds and 18-month-olds, there were significant differences between the speech directed at the 18-month-olds and the 28-month-olds in five out of nine measures; fewer words, modifiers, verbs, and verb forms per utterance, and fewer different words were directed at the 18-month-olds than at the 28-month-olds. Phillips replicated these procedures with female infants and obtained similar results with additional significant differences in the proportion of function words directed at 18- and 28-month-olds. She concludes that mothers speak more and more adult-like as a child grows older and that this process may start while the child is between the ages of 18 and 28 months.

Fraser and Roberts (1975) have done a similar study. Mothers' speech to 18-month-old, 30-month-old, four-year-old, and six-year-old children was recorded while the mothers and children were engaged in a model-building task and in a storytelling task. Fraser and Roberts found significant differences between the speech directed at the children at each age level, with the most marked differences occurring when the mothers spoke to the 30-month-olds and the 18-month-olds. The mothers spoke more in longer utterances and used more grammatically complex utterances and wider vocabularies as the age of the child increased.

To summarize these findings, it appears that mothers do not direct the same complex, irregular speech they use with adults toward their children. In fact, mothers seem to regularly adjust their speech to the age of the child they address. These adjustments are made in several areas: the lengths of utterances, the location of pauses, the number of disfluencies or broken sentences, the rate of speech, the vocabulary breadth, the complexity of sentence structure, and the frequency of repetitions. Whether all parents automatically make these adjustments and whether these adjustments function as models that are important to the language development of children remain to be determined.

The Function of Models in the Natural Environment

Besides the question of whether parents' utterances are systematic enough to plausibly serve as models for their children, there is the question of whether models are imitated by normal children and utilized in their progress from single-word utterances to conversation. Several methodologies have been used to answer this question, but, generally, the findings have been contradictory.

One of the methodologies has involved observations of children in their natural environments. Typically, samples of each child's spontaneous and imitative speech are collected and transcribed. Then a grammar, or set of rules, is written for each child's spontaneous speech and the imitative utterances are compared to this grammar. It has been theorized that, if the imitative utterances are more advanced than the grammar, then imitation might function as a grammatically progressive device for the child.

Ervin (1964) conducted this type of research. First, she recorded the spontaneous and imitative utterances of five children. After writing a grammar for their spontaneous utterances, she found, for four of the five children she studied, about equal proportions (about 80%) of their imitated and spontaneous utterances could be accounted for on the basis of rules written for the spontaneous utterances. Because both imitations and spontaneous utterances could be accounted for by the same grammar, Ervin concluded that imitations were not grammatically progressive and that, thus, there was little evidence that imitation played a role in grammatical progress. However, Sherman (1971) has questioned the grammar Ervin devised. If, for example, the grammar she produced for spontaneous utterances was too general, it would predict both spontaneous utterances and imitative utterances—essentially any utterance the child might make. Brown, Fraser, and Bellugi (1964) have indicated that, because there are many arbitrary decisions made when forming a grammar, it is necessary to test the grammar once it has been formulated. They claim that a good quality grammar is predictive of everything a child might say but does not predict what the child does not say. Sherman states that since Ervin did not report testing her grammar it is impossible to tell whether it was specific enough to detect possible differences between spontaneous and imitative utterances. An additional critique of Ervin's conclusions might suggest that the imitative utterances that did not fit the grammar may have been more adult-like than the spontaneous utterances. She reports studying the imitative utterances that did not fit the grammar devised for one child's spontaneous utterances. Ervin found that this child's imitative utterances were not accounted for by the grammar because they were less adult-like than the spontaneous utterances. However, she does not report a similar analysis of the other four children's imitative utterances that were not accounted for by their grammars. Even a small percentage (which in this case could be up to 20% of the imitative utterances) of more adult-like utterances could be a sufficient percentage to aid grammatical progress.

A second type of methodology used to investigate the function of verbal models for normal children is closely related to Ervin's methodology. Here, researchers have specifically asked children to imitate them and then have compared the children's imitations to their spontaneous utterances. The rationale behind these studies is that, if imitation fosters more adult-like speech, the children should correctly imitate utterances that they do not display in their spontaneous speech. Brown and Fraser (1964), for example, asked children to imitate sentences of varying grammatical types modeled by an adult. They found that the children imitated only parts of the sentences. In fact, the mean lengths of the children's imitations were about equal to the mean lengths of their spontaneous utterances.

Menyuk (1963) presented nursery school and kindergarten children with a list of sentences to imitate. She had previously constructed a grammar for the children from samples of their spontaneous speech. Although the younger children did not imitate as well as the older children, all of them produced imitations grammatically superior to their spontaneous speech.

Thus, the results obtained from this methodology of asking children to imitate and comparing their imitations to some measure of their spontaneous speech are somewhat contradictory. There are at least two explanations for these differences. First, it may be that some of the measures used were too general to detect any differences, whereas others were specific enough to detect the differences. Brown and Fraser's method of comparing mean lengths of utterances may not have been specific enough to detect use of different word orders, or different forms of new vocabulary. Menyuk's grammar may have been constructed to detect small differences between imitated and spontaneous utterances. Second, it is possible that, by asking a child to imitate, one might distort the natural process that usually produces grammatical progress. For example, Slobin and Welsh (1971) reported that they waited for a child to spontaneously utter a long sentence. They then asked her to imitate it at two different times: immediately and 10 minutes later. They found that she imitated the sentence correctly immediately after she had uttered it, but she did not imitate it correctly when the model was presented later. Bloom (1974) found similar results when asking a 32-month-old boy to imitate utterances he had made on the previous day. Concluding in both studies that the child did not do as well when the utterance was out of context, the authors stated that results of elicited imitation tests should be regarded as conservative estimates of a child's spontaneous and imitative competence.

A third methodology used to study the function of models with normal children involves the presentation of models and then an opportunity for the children to use the model in their subsequent utterances. The researchers have measured whether or not the children utilized the model in forming their own utterances, under the assumption that if children utilize models in their natural environments they will use them in the experimental situation.

Bellugi (1971) noted that a child did not invert subject-verb order when asking questions. She presented him with several models of questions where the subject-verb order had been correctly inverted and asked the child to repeat them. For example, the child was asked to say, "Where can he put them?" She reports that the child said, "Where he can put them?" Thus, regardless of the models presented to him, the child produced questions that did not include an inverted subject-verb order. Because the child did not imitate exactly, one might conclude that models may not be functional in complex language development.

Gleason (1967) reports similar results. She gave a model (e.g., talking about a bell, she said, "Yesterday it rang") and then asked children to produce the same form (e.g., "What did the bell do yesterday?"). Only 50% of the first graders she tested produced the correct form. She concluded that, since many children did not imitate her models, the plurals and tenses children use are products of their own linguistic systems and not imitations of adults. It is possible, however, that children may not readily imitate a stranger and this testing situation did not typify a natural interaction between child and adult.

Some other researchers have reported more positive results. Bloom, Hood, and Lightbown (1974), for example, audiorecorded speech samples of four children whose imitative utterances comprised more than 15% of their speech. They categorized all of the children's utterances that occurred five or more times into what they called "semantic-syntactic categories" and then compared the imitative and spontaneous utterances within these categories. Bloom et al. found that the children imitated utterances from categories in which they also emitted a few spontaneous utterances. The children rarely imitated utterances from categories in which they did not produce any spontaneous utterances or from categories in which they produced many spontaneous utterances. They concluded that the children were imitating utterances in categories they were in the process of learning and that, as the children learn a category, they shift gradually from many imitated utterances and a few spontaneous utterances in that category to more and more spontaneous utterances.

Bloom, Hood, and Lightbown compare their results to the results obtained by Ervin (1964), discussed earlier, and conclude that the differences in the results are because of the different categories used in the two studies. Ervin categorized according to rules of word order, and Bloom et al. categorized according to semantic-syntactic guidelines. Bloom et al. note that no differences appear between spontaneous and imitative utterances in their data when they used rules of word order to categorize the children's utterances. They conclude that analyses using word order as a basis of comparison are not sensitive enough to detect differences, whereas analyses using semantic-syntactic categories are sensitive enough.

Additionally, Bloom et al. found some interesting results when comparing the mean length of spontaneous utterances to the mean length of imitative utterances. In those speech samples in which imitations comprised more than 15% of a child's speech, they found the mean length of imitations to be greater than the mean length of spontaneous utterances. In those samples from the same children in which imitations comprised less than 15% of a child's speech, the mean length of spontaneous utterances was consistently greater than the mean length of imitations. Bloom et al. state that these data, combined with the above described results, indicate that in order to claim that imitation has an important function in language development one needs to concentrate on the semantic-syntactic differences rather than differences in word order and length of utterance.

Using a variation of this methodology, Lahey (1971) found changes in Head Start children's language when a model's descriptions of toys in a box were alternated with the children's descriptions. For one group of children, the model included descriptive adjectives. For a control group, the model included no adjectives. For only the children in the first group did the frequency of descriptive adjectives increase. In a later study,

Lahey and Lawrence (1974) reported similar results. Again, the children were asked to describe pictures in alternation with an adult model. The model used descriptive adjectives in one condition but not in another. No instructions were given except to describe the pictures and no reinforcement was provided. The authors report clear effects with second- and fourth-grade children and weaker effects with preschool children, especially with those from low income families. When the model used descriptive adjectives, the children's use of them increased. When no adjectives were used by the model, few were used by the children.

Other researchers have also reported obtaining effects when modeling was instituted. In one study, Odom, Liebert, and Hill (1968) included three groups of second-grade children. One group was exposed to a model that used sentences containing grammatical prepositional phrases (preposition-article-noun) and were rewarded for the production of such sentences. The other group was exposed to a model using sentences that contained ungrammatical prepositional phrases (article-noun-preposition), and they were rewarded for producing such phrases in their sentences. The third group was a control group that received no prepositional models. Both experimental groups showed an increased use of grammatical prepositional phrases in contrast to the control group. In a second experiment, the experimental children were specifically instructed to imitate the model. Still, both experimental groups showed increases in grammatical prepositional phrases, regardless of the form modeled to them.

In a follow-up study, Liebert et al. (1969) replicated the procedures once more with five-, eight-, and 14-year-old children. The children were again asked to imitate the model's sentences as well as to produce their own. In the youngest children, both groups increased their use of grammatical prepositional phrases over baseline levels. However, in the older groups, those receiving ungrammatical models began using ungrammatical prepositional phrases. The authors concluded that use of new language rules may be influenced through modeling and reinforcement and that the degree of influence may increase with increasing age. However, because their study took place under laboratory conditions and the children involved were somewhat older than what is considered to be the age of language-developing children, their findings might not apply to younger children.

Others have reported similar success in affecting children's language through the use of models. Bandura and Harris (1966) tried various combinations of modeling, reinforcement, and instructions with 100 second graders. They found that a combination of reinforcement and instructions increased the use of prepositional phrases but that modeling, reinforcement, and instructions were the most effective combination in increasing the use of passive voice. Because the children had not exhibited the use of passive voice but had used some prepositional phrases before the study began, the authors concluded that modeling enhanced the production of a new language form, whereas modeling was not necessary to increase the frequency of a previously used form.

Rosenthal and Whitebook (1970) reported that third and fourth graders exposed to a model of a particular sentence pattern began to use that pattern, whereas children in a control group who were not exposed to that pattern did not begin using it.

Rosenthal, Zimmerman, and Durning (1970) investigated the influence of a model on sixth-grade children's formulation of questions. Of five groups, one received no models, and the others received models of questions asking for physical attributes, pragmatic functions, causal relationships, and judgments of value or preference on some of the trials. On other trials, all the children had to invent their own questions. Rosenthal et al. found that the experimental children's questions were similar to the modeled questions to which they had been exposed and concluded that rule-governed behavior is subject to vicarious modification through models.

In summary, most studies that have systematically provided certain types of language models to children have found that the models affected the children's productions. A few studies have not found this effect, which may be the result of using single models of varying structures in contrast to using many models with the same structure. It may be that children must be presented with many models of a particular language form and have many opportunities to imitate that form before they will use it on their own. Indeed, Slobin (1968) reports, after inspecting several transcripts of children's language, that a given language construction appears as an imitation and then does not appear in a child's spontaneous speech until weeks or months later. Another possible reason for the contradictory nature of these studies could be the age of the subjects selected for study. Positive effects were obtained with older children, and weak or no effects were obtained with younger children. Older children may need fewer practice trials than younger children before making use of a new skill in their spontaneous speech.

Using a fourth methodology—one closer to the natural environment of the language-developing child—Brown, Cazden, and Bellugi (1969) looked at the frequency of occurrence of particular features of maternal speech and correlated these with children's acquisition of those features. Out of 1,253 utterances, Eve's mother used 31 possessives, while Adam's mother used 24 and Sarah's mother used six. Eve happened to use possessives more frequently than Adam, and Adam used them more frequently than Sarah. When Eve was 18 months old, her mother used the prepositions *in* and *on* three times as much as the prepositions *with, of, for,* or *to.* When Eve was 24 months old she used *in* and *on* correctly 90% of the time, whereas she used the others only 67–77% correctly. However, while looking at the same data, Brown (1973) related the frequency of parent modeling of 14 morphemes (e.g., articles, possessives, number, tense) to the order in which the children acquired those morphemes. He found no relationship. For example, articles were modeled the most frequently by parents but were acquired later than seven other morphemes. He concludes that frequency of modeling of morphemes has no effect on order of acquisition of the morphemes (which, by the way, was very similar for all three children). These two studies do not demonstrate a functional relationship between models and production, but they do introduce a methodology that might be employed in combination with an experimental methodology to determine the function of models. Parents might be asked specifically to model a particular language construction, say a particular preposition. Then, after noting the influence of this model on the child's speech, a new preposition could be modeled and the resulting effects measured, and so on.

To conclude this discussion of the function of models in the natural environment, the results of the research have not been entirely consistent. The four methodologies used to study the question have yielded varying results. When the word order of spontaneous imitative utterances has been compared to the word order of spontaneous utterances through a grammar written for the spontaneous utterances (e.g., Ervin, 1964), there seems to be no difference. However, when spontaneous and imitative utterances are compared through the use of semantic-syntactic categories (e.g., Bloom et al., 1974), the results show that lexical and grammatical imitation can precede spontaneous usage. When elicited imitations were compared to spontaneous utterances, some researchers (e.g., Brown and Fraser, 1964) found no differences, whereas others (e.g., Menyuk, 1963) found that imitations were grammatically superior to spontaneous speech. These conflicting results may be caused by the different comparison procedures. For example, Brown and Fraser compared mean lengths of utterance and Menyuk compared the utterances through the use of a grammar. Menyuk's method may have been specific enough to detect the differences, whereas Brown and Fraser's method may have been too general. In most studies in which models were presented systematically to children, their subsequent spontaneous productions were affected. In a few studies, however, no effects were seen. This may have been because of different amounts of models used and the differing ages of the children. Finally, children's order of acquisition of some language forms was correlated with their mothers' use of those forms.

Evidence for the Existence of Prompts in the Natural Environment

There is little information about parents' use of prompts. A prompt is a method to cue someone into action. Thus, in relation to language development, a prompt can be any parent behavior that requires a verbal response on the part of the child. For the purpose of this analysis, two types of parent-presented prompts are of interest: 1) questions that require an answer other than *yes* or *no*, and 2) direct requests for the child to imitate. There has been no research reported on whether parents prompt, the frequency with which they prompt, the types of prompts they use, or the circumstances under which they prompt. However, the reports of theorists and the transcripts included in the reports of normative researchers are somewhat instructive.

Wilkinson (1971) reports that mothers supply direct language instruction for their children. For example, they might say, "It's a ball. What is it?" They might also present their children with fill-in-the-blank type questions like, "This is a _____?"

Brown, Cazden, and Bellugi (1969) found that, when mothers did not understand their children's utterances, they prompted the children to repeat the utterance more clearly. For example, if the child said, "I want milk," the mother would prompt by saying, "You want what?" In addition, if the mothers asked their child a question like, "Where will I put it?" and the child made no response, the mothers reformulated the question, if the mothers asked their child a question like "Where will I put completion format similar to the fill-in-the-blank format reported by Wilkinson (1971).

Moerk (1972) also reports that mothers instruct children through "question and answer games." He states that, when a mother notices some lack of proficiency in her child's language, she begins a circular teaching episode that may involve several questions by the mother and answers by the child. Some examples of parent prompts are illustrated in Moerk's article. According to his tables, mothers ask questions like. *What's this?, What's that?, What's all over your face?, What's the rabbit doing?, What did Mrs. Williams say?, What color is this?,* and *What is Aida doing?* They also ask their children to imitate complex phrases or sentences. A few examples that appear in Moerk's article are *Say: I haven't had my chocolate milk* and *Can you say "paint brush"?* In addition, there are a few examples in Moerk's article of fill-in-the-blank prompts: *That's the _____, Who was supposed to land on the moon?, Flowers in a what? We put flowers in _____?, With a _____?,* and *There goes a what?*

An inspection of examples of mothers' speech reported by Broen (1972) also indicates that mothers use many questions that could be considered prompts. Broen reports that about 37% of mothers' speech to young children are questions and 24% of all questions are those requiring more than a *yes* or *no* answer. Examples of these questions are *What's this?*, *What's that?*, *What do you think?*, *What happened?*, and *What do you want?*

Although the above information indicates that mothers do use prompts, there are many remaining questions about the nature of the prompts parents use, the frequency of these prompts, and the functional relationship of such prompts to the development of rule-governed language. Further normative and experimental research appears warranted to answer these questions.

Evidence for the Existence of Reinforcement in the Natural Environment

For the imitation-reinforcement model to be plausible as an account of the learning of complex rule-governed language, reinforcement must be present in the natural environment. Whether or not it is remains an unanswered question, but several studies have provided some information about parent behaviors that act as reinforcers for their children's language.

Brown, Cazden, and Bellugi (1969) recorded adult expressions of approval and disapproval immediately following child speech in the natural environments of three children. They reported that there was no evidence that expressions of praise (*that's right, very good,* or *yes*) were contingent on syntactic correctness. Disapproval (*that's wrong, no*) was only contingent on gross errors of word choice. They also reported that in all their tapes of parent-child interactions there was not a single correction of syntactic errors.

In a later study, Brown and Hanlon (1970) investigated the possibility that differential communication might act as a reinforcer for child utterances. They categorized adults' responses to children's questions into sequiturs (clearly relevant and understanding answers) and nonsequiturs. Nonsequiturs were defined as queries, irrelevancies, misunderstandings, and no response from the parent. The results showed no evidence that there was differential responding by parents to grammatically sophisticated versus grammatically primitive questions.

A study by Nelson (1973) indicated that about 7% of behavior (verbal and nonverbal) of young children was followed by some sort of approval or acceptance from mothers, and only 4% was followed by rejection. In a more recent study, Schumaker (1976) studied the verbal interactions between six mothers and their children (19–23 months old) in their natural environments. She found that 2–6% of child utterances were followed by praise or approval and less than 1% by corrections from the mother.

These studies suggest that parent approval and disapproval do not often occur and that when they do they are not contingent upon grammatical correctness or complexity in children's speech. Thus, parents may not respond in ways that reinforce more adult-like utterances. It is possible, however, that parents may differentially respond to their children's speech in more subtle ways that do produce more complex language. For example, parents may look at, smile at, or physically touch the child more often after grammatically correct utterances than after primitive utterances. Since Hart and Risley (1968, 1974) found preschool materials to be reinforcers for children's utterances, it is plausible that objects in the home environment serve much the same purpose. Perhaps clear, well-formed utterances more frequently lead to the acquisition of requested objects (e.g., food, toys, clothes) than do poorly formed utterances.

Another possibility is that particular forms of parent statements that immediately follow child utterances serve as reinforcers. For example, the use of direct imitations of a child's utterances may serve as reinforcers for those utterances. There is no language development research to substantiate this proposition, but a recent study in the field of motor imitation suggests its plausibility. Gladstone and Cooley (1975) found that preschool children increased their responses when the experimenter exactly imitated the children's behavior. For example, when a child rang a bell and the experimenter imitated that response, the child's rate of bell ringing increased while her rates of other responses decreased. Then, if the experimenter only imitated the child's horn-blowing responses, her horn-blowing rate increased and the rates of other responses decreased. These results indicate that behavioral similarity can function as a reinforcer for motor behaviors. Whether it functions as a reinforcer for complex verbal behaviors remains unknown. In a descriptive account of verbal interactions between six mothers and their children, Schumaker (1976) found that about 4% of the children's utterances were followed by direct imitations by the mothers. Research addressing the issue of whether these imitations function as reinforcers appears warranted.

Other types of parent statements that might act as reinforcers for complex rule-governed verbal behavior are "expansions" and "extensions." Expansions are statements made by an adult contingent on a child's utterance, which take the child's words in the same order but add enough to make the child's utterance into a grammatical sentence (Brown and Bellugi, 1964). For instance, if a child said, "Look, dog," an adult might expand by saying, "Look at the dog." Extensions are similar to expansions in that they, too, are contingent on a child's utterances. However, extensions do not involve the same words as the child's utterance. They add to the child's utterance with completely different words (Cazden, 1972). If a child said, "Look, dog" an adult might extend this by saying, "He is running fast." Both expansions and extensions seem to occur immediately after a child's utterance; thus, in addition to their possible roles as reinforcers, they might also act as models while the child's attention is focused on a given situation. This seems plausible because, if expansions and extensions only functioned as reinforcers, children would continue repeating their short, non-adult-like utterances. In order for expansions and extensions to have a grammatically progressive role in language development, they must function as reinforcers for verbalizations in general as well as models for future verbalizations.

Cazden (1972) has theorized that expansions might be important because they are well-formed models that are paired with meanings a child can understand and is attending to at a particular moment. She has also emphasized the possible role of expansions as corrective devices. If, for example, a child emits a poorly formed utterance and the parent expands it with correct grammar, Cazden claims that the parent is warmly focusing on the child's achievement as well as providing models for further improvement.

There is a little information about the frequency of parent expansions and even less on extensions. Slobin (1968) reports that parents of 18-month- to three-year-old children expand 30% of their children's utterances and that some expansions are said in a declarative tone and others are said in a questioning manner. Also, according to Slobin, children imitate 10% of parents' utterances and 15% of these imitations directly follow expansions. About half of these expansion-imitations (or approximately 0.75% of a child's utterances) are more complex than the child's original statement. Slobin hypothesizes that these expansion-imitations might aid a child's grammatical development. He notes that, as children grow older, parents expand less and converse more. For example, Nelson (1973) reports very low amounts of expansions by mothers of 24-month-old children.

Schumaker's (1976) results replicate and extend those of Slobin. She found that about 28% of the children's utterances were followed by expansions and about 1% of the children's utterances were followed by extensions. The mothers used several types of expansions including expansion-questions, expansion-commands, and expansion-corrections. In addition, they used what Schumaker called "one-word" and "two-word" expansions. In the case of a one-word expansion, if a child emitted an approximation to a word (e.g., *ba*), the mothers sometimes expanded with the full word (e.g., *ball*). If a child approximated a two-word utterance (e.g., *Dada ca*), the mothers sometimes formed a two-word expansion (e.g., *Daddy's car*). The expansions provided by the mothers appeared to serve as models for the children in that about 24% of the mothers' expansions were imitated by the children. Ten percent of these imitations were exact replications of the mothers' expansions. Because an exact replication of an expansion represents improvement over the child's original utterance, it follows that expansions can serve as models for improving child language. The mothers appeared to be very attentive to their children's imitations of expansions; 82% of this type of imitation was immediately followed (within 10 seconds) by another utterance by the mothers. A relatively large percentage (36%) of these following utterances was another expansion; a smaller percentage (7%) was praise.

There have been some studies that have investigated the general functional relationship between expansions or extensions and the development of rule-governed language. Cazden (1965) used three groups of black preschool children to compare the effects of expansions and extensions. The children in one group received individual attention by a trained adult who expanded all their utterances for 40 minutes daily over a period of three months. Children in the second group received the same attention, but the adult followed all their utterances with an extension. Children in the third group (control group) received no special treatment. The dependent variables were the children's scores on a sentence-imitation test, plus measures of their mean length of utterance, noun-phrase index (the mean number of elements per noun phrase, including plurals and possessives), a verb-phrase index (mean number of verb elements per verb construction), an index of auxiliary verbs, and a sentence-type index. These measures were obtained from tapes of each child's speech before and after the experiment began. Cazden reports no differences between the control group and extension group and only slight differences between the expansion group and extension group in favor of the extension group. However, these differences showed up only in the sentence-imitation test, and here the extension group's performance was equivalent to the control group's and the expansion subjects had the lowest mean score of the three. She hypothesizes that perhaps when a variable like expansions is taken out of its natural context (i.e., is used more frequently than it is naturally used by parents), something of its function might be lost. For instance, if every utterance of a child is expanded, the probability of misinterpreting the child's meaning may increase and a poor expansion may interfere with learning. Furthermore, she wondered whether the artificial elevation of expansion or extension rate may decrease the attention level of the child. Finally, she states that the dialect differences between the children and the experimenters may have interfered with the learning process. It is also possible that the language-teaching devices used by adults (parents, relatives, preschool teachers, etc.) outside the experimental setting were sufficient to offset any effects that might have been obtained from the research, especially since such general measures were used to indicate any changes in language development, measures that may not be sensitive enough to show clearly the effects of the manipulations.

Cazden (1972) also correlated three children's acquisition of specific grammatical forms (like inflections) with the rate of mothers' expansions that included those specific forms. Again, she reported somewhat negative results. Although the general rate of mothers' expansions correlated with the children's general rate of language acquisition, the rate of noncontingent models of specific grammatical forms correlated more highly with the order of acquisition of those forms than did the rate of expansions of those specific forms.

Malouf and Dodd (1972) report another test of expansions with 84 first graders. Their task involved a simple declarative sentence that described "wugs" (imaginary bugs) along three body dimensions: body coverings, limbs, and antennae. An arbitrary syntactic rule was established by the experimenters specifying that the order of the adjectives describing these three dimensions must be: 1) body covering, 2) limbs, and 3) antennae. The children received training trials on this order of the adjectives combined in pairs: body covering–limbs, limbs–antennae and body covering–antennae. They did not receive training on the three adjectives combined in one sentence. After they had learned a sentence for each of the pairs of adjectives, they received a test trial in which the description required all three adjectives. One group of children (the control group) received no training, just test trials. Another group, the "input" group, listened to a recorded sentence on each training trial. Children in a third group, the "imitation" group, listened to the recorded sentence and were then asked to describe the wug. The fourth group, called the "expansion" group, was asked to describe the wug and then to listen to a recorded sentence. The data showed that the expansion and imitation groups were superior to the input and control groups in producing the correct order of the three adjectives, but the expansion and imitation groups' performances were not significantly different from each other. One possible explanation for these results may be that the two treatments (imitation and expansion) were not that different from each other. The expansion treatment probably did not involve "true" expansions on every trial. After a child receiving the expansion treatment described the wug, he listened to a recording of the correct sentence. This would not necessarily be an expansion of the child's utterance. In most cases, it was probably either a contingent imitation of the child's correct utterance or a contingent correction of the child's incorrect utterance. Only in cases in which the child uttered only part of the sentence and had begun the order of adjectives correctly would the recorded sentence be an expansion of the child's utterance. Thus, Malouf and Dodd may have really been comparing models presented before a child utterance with models presented after a child utterance rather than testing the function of expansions.

Nelson, Carskaddon, and Bonvillian (1973) compared the effects of expansions to extensions. They employed a control group design with three groups of 14 preschool children. Each experimental child met individually with an experimenter twice a week for sessions lasting 20 minutes for 11 weeks. For one group, the experimenter expanded all their incomplete utterances and "recast" all their complete utterances. The authors defined "recasting" as saying the child's utterances in a different form. They provided an example of a recast of *The bunny chased fireflies* as *The bunny did chase fireflies, didn't he?* Whenever possible, as each sentence was expanded or recast, the experimenters placed an emphasis on forming predicate (verb clause) expansions rather than subject expansions. For the second group, all utterances were followed by extensions. The control group did not receive the special sessions.

Nelson et al. used much the same dependent measures as Cazden (1968). The results showed significant differences between the "expansion-recast" group and the control group on most posttest measures but no significant differences between the "expansion-recast" group and the extension group and none between the extension group and the control group. However, the differences between the expansion group and the extension group approached significance in the use of verb phrases and auxiliary verbs with the expansion group using more than the extension group. Because Nelson et al. concentrated on expansions of the predicate (verb forms), their results reflect this concentration to some degree. Nevertheless, their results do not clearly show a differential effect of expansions.

Two recent studies have yielded the most positive results regarding the role of expansions in language development. Both studies employed manipulation of mothers' interactions with their children in the natural home setting. In the first study (Schumaker, 1976), four mothers were asked to expand some of their children's (18–20 months old) utterances and not to expand others while each mother-child pair looked through a book of pictures. The results indicated that as the mothers began to use a particular expansion the children imitated the expansion and then began to spontaneously use the same expansion phrase. In addition, the children used the expansion phrase with words the mothers had not previously included in their expansions as well as with the words that had been previously included in the expansions.

In a similar study, employing the picture-book method, Hovell, Schumaker, and Sherman (1978) investigated the effects of parent models and expansions on four two-year-olds' spontaneous use of color and size adjective-noun combinations. For some pictures the mothers modeled one adjective-noun combination (e.g., said, "blue ball" before the child said anything); for other pictures they expanded the other adjective-noun combination (e.g., after the child said, "car," the mother expanded with, "big car"); for other pictures the mother neither modeled nor expanded. The results showed that increased rates of the children's spontaneous use of target adjective-noun combinations were related to the parents' use of both models and expansions. However, the expansions produced stronger effects than the models. These results, combined with those from the Schumaker (1976) study, indicate that expansions can function as models for spontaneous child speech and may play an important role in normal language development.

Thus, the parent behaviors that may function as reinforcers for the development of rule-governed language are still relatively unknown. Some studies have indicated that parents rarely praise or correct child language or respond differentially to grammatically sophisticated versus unsophisticated questions. Instances in which parents do correct their children are those in which a child has used an incorrect word. Some research has indicated that direct imitation as well as the acquisition of desired objects might serve as reinforcers but these have not been tested in the natural environment. Finally, several recent studies suggest that parent utterances, like expansions that are contingent on child utterances, serve as reinforcers as well as models for future child speech.

SOME SUGGESTIONS FOR PARENTS

The research covering parent roles in language development has been reviewed. Although this research is not definitive, a number of suggestions can be offered for parents. These suggestions are not intended to build parent interactions with their children but rather to enrich existing interactions in ways that facilitate language development. Parents should incorporate these suggestions into normal activities with their children. Although the suggestions are based on research, many have not been specifically tested by parents. None of the suggested activities seems to involve any risk to a child's welfare, and most should be enjoyable for both parents and children.

All the suggested activities should be used within incidental teaching episodes. These are normally occurring situations in which a child indicates an interest in interacting with an adult. Through incidental teaching episodes, the adult can capitalize on a situation or event to which the child is attending. By using incidental teaching episodes, parents need not schedule language-training sessions that halt other daily activities. They simply proceed through their normal daily activities and simultaneously intersperse incidental teaching episodes in these activities. Incidental episodes can be effective and enjoyable as well as practical. Several studies (e.g., Hart and Risley, 1968; Reynolds and Risley, 1968; Hart and Risley, 1974; Montes, 1974) have shown incidental teaching episodes are effective in teaching language skills to preschool children engaged in free play. Hart and Risley (1968) found that formal language training in a lesson-like format had little effect on children's spontaneous use of language. However, when incidental teaching episodes were interspersed throughout naturally occurring events, they found large and durable changes in the children's spontaneous language. Furthermore, they later showed that the children consistently chose play materials that were always paired with incidental teaching episodes in preference to materials that were not paired with such episodes. Hart and Risley (1974) suggest that the children found the incidental learning episodes enjoyable. The following suggestions, then, should enrich children's language environments. The suggestions can be easily incorporated into the ongoing activities of the home, thereby requiring a minimum of extra effort by parents. For the most part, the suggestions are designed to be used in interactions initiated by the child.

Parents Should Talk to Their Children

Parents' language appears to serve some very important functions in a child's language development. Parents' speech provides models for children to imitate, and the stimulation needed for language comprehension, which some theorists propose comes before language production. Finally, parent voices or the specific things parents say may function as rewards for child language.

When to Begin   Children should be exposed to a language environment as soon as possible. The research supporting Mowrer's hypothesis of self-shaping indicates that, the sooner a parent's voice becomes rewarding, the sooner language development begins. It is important to begin speaking to infants soon after birth.

When to Talk   Opportunities for talking to infants include such activities as bathing, dressing, diaper changing, feeding, comforting, and playing. If parents speak to infants during such activities, the infants' language exposure is naturally interspersed throughout the day and language is paired with relatively pleasant happenings in the child's life.

What to Say   Parents may wonder what they should say to a very young infant, since the infant will not understand speech at a very early age. It is probably not important what parents say as long as they say something. However, it is just as well for parents to talk to their newborn infants as if they do understand, because they soon will understand. It is important to talk about the people, actions, and objects to which the child is attending. This helps the child begin to pair words with the appropriate people, objects, and events. Before the infant begins to speak, the parent should carry on a one-sided conversation. Thoughts can be verbalized, no matter how complicated they might be. The infant should be treated as someone who understands whatever the parent might say. For example, as the parent debates about what to have for dinner, this debate should be verbalized for the child.

A little time each day can be devoted to reading to the infant. Even very young infants enjoy hearing parents read nursery rhymes and poetry, perhaps because of the rhyming words and interesting tempos. The incorporation of a reading time in the daily life of a child from infancy can help enhance language development. As the child begins to attend more and more to the pictures on the pages and the story, there will be many opportunities for incidental teaching. When choosing a picture book for an infant, select one with large, colorful pictures with only one object depicted on a page. If the pictures are large and colorful, the infant may be more attracted by them and may be more likely to associate the words the parent uses with the pictures.

Here are examples of things parents can say to their infants:

1. When dressing:
   "Here is your foot (hand, head, ear, nose, etc.)."
   "Where's your foot? Here it is!"
   "Let's put your arm through the sleeve."
   "Now we'll put your shoes (socks, pants, shirt, etc.) on."
   "There's a duck on your dress. See the duck? The duck says quack, quack, quack!"
   "Your pants are green. My pants are blue."
   "Let's comb your hair. It's getting so long."
   "You look *so* nice!"
   "Are you wet? Is your diaper wet? It sure is! Let's make you dry."
2. When feeding:
   "Here's some applesauce."
   "Isn't that good?"
   "Oh, you've got some cereal on your cheek."
   "Let's get you cleaned up."
   "Oh, you're such a mess!"
   "First, I'll wash your face. Now I'll wash your hands."
   "Here comes the spoon."
   "Open your mouth wide."
   "Now we'll have some peas."
   "Mmmm. It's so good!"

While bottlefeeding or nursing there will be few objects or events in sight for the child. In such a situation, endearing statements, like "You're such a good baby," can be used. If the parent runs out of things to say while nursing or bottlefeeding, a magazine or book can be read out loud to the infant or songs can be sung.

3. When playing:
    "See the ball (block, doll, truck, etc.)."
    "Touch the ball (block, doll, truck, etc.)."
    "Let's shake your rattle."
    "Let's push the truck."
    "Pull the string."
    "See the dolly's eyes? Now they're open. Now they're closed."
    "Here's a ring (block, ball, doll, etc.)."
    "Where's Johnny? (When playing peek-a-boo) There he is!"
    "Look in here."
    "What's in the box? It's Jack!"
    "Hug the dolly."
    "The dog is so soft. Feel how soft he is."
    "Do you want the bell? Here it is!"

How to Speak to an Infant   To make speech as pleasant to an infant as possible, parents should use a calm and pleasant tone of voice and should speak to the infant so that the infant can see the parent's face easily. If this is done consistently, the infant may quickly learn the association between movements of the parent's mouth and speech.

To enhance the modeling function of parent speech, words should be pronounced clearly (so that each sound can be heard) and statements made slowly (so that words do not run together). Research has indicated that mothers of children who score in the average or above average ranges on a verbal test speak differently to their younger children than to their older children and adults. They speak slowly and often repeat whole sentences to the younger children. They use a narrower vocabulary with the younger children. In addition, they use short statements of three or four words and often use one-word utterances. As the children grow, the lengths of the mothers' utterances increase. The mothers pause at the end of each utterance to their young children, clearly delineating the end of one sentence and the beginning of another. All these adjustments serve to simplify language models for young children. Because it is not known whether all parents automatically make these adjustments, parents would be wise to determine whether they are making them and, if they are not, to concentrate on making them.

Summary of Suggestions on General Speech

1. Speak to the infant as often as possible, especially when engaged in pleasant activities.

2. Talk about people, objects, and events that are immediately present or occurring in the infant's environment and to which the infant is attending.
3. Set aside a short time each day (10–15 minutes) to read to the infant. Choose interesting things to read such as nursery rhymes and poetry. When selecting picture books for the young infant, choose those with large colorful objects depicted.
4. Use a pleasant tone of voice.
5. Speak slowly and clearly so that each sound is pronounced and words do not run together.
6. Use sentences of one to four words.
7. Repeat sentences often.
8. Pause between sentences to delineate the end of one sentence and the beginning of another.
9. As the child begins to speak, gradually increase the lengths of your utterances, use a wider vocabulary, use less repetition, and begin to speak a bit faster.

Increasing Vocalization in Infants

Vocalizations can be defined as any sound a child makes with the vocal apparatus, excluding crying and reflexive coughs, sneezes, and hiccups. The vocalizations of an infant may be the precursors of speech, but there is no research available to support this notion except the reports of Lovaas et al. (1966), who taught language-deficient children to speak by first increasing their rates of spontaneous vocalization. Yet, the notion is a logical one, and there seems to be no risk involved in increasing a child's rate and variety of vocalizations.

In increasing vocalizations in an infant, the parent should wait until the infant makes a vocal sound other than a cry, cough, sneeze, or hiccup. It is not clear when infants make these first vocalizations. Some may vocalize as they are lying on their backs after feeding. Others may vocalize in the time immediately before feeding or immediately before crying. To account for these individual differences, parents must patiently listen to determine the times when their infant vocalizes.

When the first vocalizations are heard, the parent should immediately go to the infant, place his face in plain view of the infant, smile, say something in a praising tone of voice (e.g., "You said 'ah'" (or whatever sound the child made). "You're talking to me!" "Good girl!" "Good boy!") and provide some tactile stimulation (e.g., rub the infant's cheek, stomach, arm, or leg, or pat the infant's head). When another sound is emitted by the infant, the parent should again smile, say something, and touch the infant.

At first, the infant may make only one sound. This is all right. The parent should wait 15–20 seconds, and if no additional sound is made the parent can return to whatever activity was interrupted by the original sound. If the infant does make an additional sound or sequence of sounds, the interaction can be repeated as many times as is enjoyable to both parties. When the infant is very young, his attention may last only through two or three exchanges. However, Wolff (1961) reports that when an infant is only 28–37 days old it is possible to have 10 to 15 exchanges between parent and child.

One key to this procedure is for the parent to listen for sounds the infant is making. Thus, it is better if the parent is not talking constantly to the infant. The infant should be given a chance to "talk." It is important that the parent attention *immediately* follow the sound. If the parent cannot immediately give the child attention, then it is better to wait for another vocalization rather than provide late attention. The immediacy of attention is important here: attention must be closely paired in time with the vocalization if the attention is to help the frequency of vocalization increase. A third key to the procedure is that parents should try to provide equal attention to a variety of sounds. Some of the research reviewed indicated that, if one sound receives attention to the exclusion of others, the frequency of that sound will increase while the others decrease. Because language is based on a variety of sounds, the child must have more than one sound in his repertoire. Thus, whenever the parent hears the child making a new sound, the parent should try to immediately give the child attention to encourage the use of that sound in the future. The new sound can be strengthened by attending to the child each time it occurs while only attending to older vocalizations intermittently. Then, as the child uses the new sound more and more frequently, it can be attended to intermittently as well.

How Often Should These Interactions Occur? At first, the infant will be making few sounds and it will be wise to attend to as many as possible. Later, as the child begins to make many vocalizations, it will be impossible for the parent to attend to all of them. At this stage it is important to intersperse such interactions throughout the day and engage in them whenever the parent is already doing something with the child or whenever the situation allows the parent to drop the task at hand and attend to the child. Eventually, the parent may not need to be in the immediate vicinity of the child to keep an interaction going. Talking to the child across a room, for instance, may be enough to maintain an interaction.

Summary of Suggestions for Increasing Vocalizations

1. Wait until the infant emits a vocal sound *other* than a cry, cough, sneeze, etc.

2. Go to the infant and place yourself where the infant can easily see your face; smile, say something pleasant, and touch the infant.
3. Wait for the infant to make another sound.
4. Again, get in close proximity, smile, say something pleasant, and touch the infant.
5. This exchange can be repeated several times, as long as it is enjoyable for parent and child.
6. Parents should attend to their infant's vocalizations several times a day, spaced throughout the day.
7. Attention should be provided for a variety of sounds.

Teaching the Infant to Imitate

Imitation appears to be important for the language-developing child. Through imitating the language he hears, the child can learn to make relevant sounds, to form words, and to communicate in well-formed sentences. Research has shown that children do imitate their parents, that prior imitations later become spontaneously used utterances, that they can learn complicated grammatical structures and rules through imitative processes, and that they can use these rules to form their own spontaneous utterances. Thus, it may be helpful in enhancing a child's language development to begin encouraging the imitative process as soon as possible.

Teaching the Temporal Relationships of Imitation   Once the infant is vocalizing frequently and making a variety of sounds, the next step is to teach the infant to imitate simple sounds. According to Piaget (Morehead and Morehead, 1974), language imitation begins with an episode initiated by the infant. The infant makes a sound, the parent imitates that sound, and then the infant makes another sound. Such interactions can occur as early as two to four months old. Thus, the key to beginning imitation training is for the parent to imitate the child's sound first. This initiates a chain of interactions with the parent imitating the child and the child imitating the parent. At first, it is important only that the child make a sound after the parent makes a sound. The child's sound need not match the parent's sound. The parent, on the other hand, should try to match the child's sound. This makes it more likely that the child will make the same sound again and will thus match the parent's sound. As long as the child is making a sound soon after the parent makes a sound, the child will be learning the *temporal* relationship between the parent's model and his own sound production.

Once the infant begins to respond readily to these imitative interchanges, the parent should try to initiate the exchange. Instead of waiting for the infant to make a sound, the parent should choose a sound the child has frequently made (and preferably has been the target of several previous imitative interchanges) and should model that sound for the child. At a time when the parent is in close proximity to the child, and the child is quiet, the parent should place his face so that the child can see it easily and can utter the model (e.g., "ah") *once*. If the child makes any sound within 10 seconds of the model, the parent should smile, touch the child, and say the sound again. The exchange can be repeated several times. If the child makes no sound within 10 seconds, the parent should not be upset but should continue on with the task at hand (feeding, changing, bathing, etc.). After a few minutes, another model can be presented and the procedure repeated. Several such imitative exchanges can take place in a day. Parents should also continue attending to the infant's general vocalizations throughout the day to maintain the general level of vocalization.

Teaching the Topographical Relationship of Imitation   When the infant is reliably making any sound within 10 seconds of the parent's model, the parents can begin presenting their smile, touch, and praise only when the child utters a sound that is similar to the model. To begin an exchange, the parent should wait until the child is quiet. The parent should then utter the model once in close proximity to the child so that the child can see the parent's face and clearly hear the sound. If the child makes the same sound as the parent's model within 10 seconds of the model presentation, the parent should smile, say the sound again, and touch the infant. If the child makes no sound or a *dissimilar* sound, the parent should continue on with the task at hand (feeding, dressing, etc.) and plan another model in the next few minutes.

It is extremely important for the parent to present the model only once and then wait for the child to respond. If the model is repeated several times, the child will have little chance to make a sound. In fact, the child may never make a sound at such a time because so much attention is being paid to his silence. It is also very important that attention not be presented for silence or dissimilar sounds after the model. The goal is to teach the infant to imitate a model. This requires close temporal proximity as well as similar topography. In other words, if the child does not produce a similar sound immediately, attention should not be presented. Attention at this time only serves to confuse the child and to make the learning process longer.

Introducing More Sounds   Once the infant begins to produce regularly a sound similar to the model, a different model can be introduced. Again, it will be helpful if the sound chosen for the second model is one that the child has been known to produce during spontaneous vocalizations and one that has been the target of imitative exchanges initiated by the child. The parent should wait until the child is quiet and present the new model so that the parent's face is within easy view of the infant. If the infant makes a sound similar to the model, the parent can provide attention. If the child makes another sound or no sound at all, the parent should withdraw quietly and wait for another opportunity to present a model.

When the infant reliably imitates the second sound, models of the first sound and the second sound can be alternated. When the infant is reliably imitating each sound presented, a third sound can be introduced. After the child learns to imitate this third sound, the three sounds can be presented in a mixed sequence. Then a fourth sound can be introduced and so on.

Throughout the imitative learning process, the parent should expect that progress will be slow and highly variable. Thus, a child may begin to imitate a sound one day but fail to imitate it again for a week. A child may learn to imitate two new sounds in 10 minutes yet not learn to imitate any new ones for five days. Parents should not become worried or anxious about their child's progress. Progress will be made, although slowly and in an irregular way. The important thing is to make the imitative exchanges enjoyable for both parent and child.

A Note About the Types of Sounds to Use as Models   The types of sounds parents use as models are very important. If they are too complex, there will be little chance for the child to imitate them at an early age. Parents should begin by modeling very simple sounds and progress gradually to more complex sounds. The suggestion for parents to initially model sounds that the infant has been known to emit spontaneously is an important one. These sounds will be the easiest for the child to learn to imitate since he has learned to produce them already. Some normative researchers (see McCarthy, 1954, for a review) have indicated that vowel sounds are the first types of sounds uttered by infants. Thus, parents might model individual vowel sounds (e.g., ă, ŏ, ĕ, ō) for the infant, at first. Then, some consonants like g, k, r, x can be modeled. These also appear to be among the first sounds uttered by infants (McCarthy, 1954). Next, consonant-vowel combinations like mă, mō, bă, bō, and bē, and double consonant-vowel combinations like mă-mă, nă-nă, bī-bī and dă-dă can be modeled.

Teaching the Labeling Concept between Words and Objects or Events   When the child is readily imitating consonant-vowel combinations it will be time to start teaching the relationship between words and objects or events. Parents can begin to use real words for their models, but it will be necessary for the words to be paired with their appropriate objects or events. For example, the parent should hold a ball within easy sight of the child and present the model "ball." At this stage, the parent should provide attention for any approximation to the model. In this case, the child might say "bă" and the parent should smile, enthusiastically saying something like, "Great! You said ball!" and touch the child.

According to some normative researchers (see McCarthy, 1954, for a review) the first words used by children are usually monosyllables formed out of a consonant-vowel combination (e.g., bă). Thus, although parents can model simple one-syllable words with final consonants, they should not at first expect the child to produce the final consonant. Praise should be provided for imitations that approximate the total word. Researchers (e.g., McCarthy, 1954; Guillaume, 1971) have also noted that children readily use double consonant-vowel combinations (e.g., mă-mă, dă-dă). Thus, parents can model words with two syllables and allow such double combinations. Later, they can model words that have two different monosyllables. Examples of these are baby (bā-bē) and teddy (tĕ-dē). Here is a list of words that parents can model and the imitations or approximations to imitations they might expect their child to produce.

Models	Possible imitations or approximations
more	mō
boat	bō
ball	bă
bee	bē
mine	mī
duck	dū
bath	bă
dog	dŏ
light	lī͞
moo (sound cow makes)	mo͞o
beans	bē
peas	pē
key	kē
car	că
tree	tē
bus	bŭ
spoon	po͞o
block	bŏ
boy	bō-ē
eat	ē-ē
knee	nē
eye	ī
nose	nō
mouth	mow
toe	tō
meat	mē
hat	hă
hot	hŏ
ma-ma	mă-mă
da-da	dă-dă
night-night	nī-nī
bye-bye	bī-bī
banana	nă-nă

no-no	nō-nō
pee-pee	pē-pē
cracker	că-că
ba-ba (sound sheep makes)	bă-bă
honey	hŏ-nē
tummy	tă-mē
belly	bĕ-lē
elbow	el-bō
body	bŏ-dē
cookie	k͞oo-kē
puppy	pŭ-pē
teddy	tĕ-dē
umbrella	bĕ-lă
kitty	kĭ-tē
lady	lā-dē
baby	bā-bē
potty	pă-tē
dolly	dă-lē
coffee	cŏ-fē
doggie	dă-gē
mommy	mă-mē
daddy	dă-dē
tick-tock	dē-dă
choo-choo	t͞oo-t͞oo

In a study of the first 50 words children learn, Nelson (1973) concluded that children tend to learn first the names of things that move or act on their own (e.g., people, pets, vehicles) and things upon which they themselves can act (e.g., toys, foods, certain clothing like shoes). Words that name objects that are static or with which the child does not interact (e.g., house, kitchen, sky) are later acquisitions. Bloom (1974) notes that words labeling events in the child's environment (e.g., *more, gone, up,* and *no*) are also early acquisitions. The parent should thus concentrate at first on modeling the names of those objects and events in the child's immediate environment to which the child is attending or with which the child is interacting. Of course, the parent should continue conversing with the child. The presentation of models should not preclude ongoing conversation.

When a child is learning his first words, parents should use the same word for the same person, object, or event over and over again. Switching to different words will confuse the child and will make the process of learning to label a longer one.

Thus, throughout this period of teaching labeling skills, the parents should be presenting models for the child at every opportunity. During play, toys should be labeled. During feeding, foods can be labeled and the words *more, please,* and *thank you* modeled appropriately. During each departure, the word *bye-bye* can be modeled. While "reading" picture books, the names of objects in a picture can be modeled as each object is pointed out. An individualized picture book can be made by the parent by cutting pictures out of magazines and glueing them and pictures of family members to pages that are placed in a loose-leaf notebook. This book can contain pictures of people and objects with names the child can imitate easily. The book can be "read" several times a week with the parent presenting a model for each picture. New pictures can be added gradually.

Again, if the child imitates the model exactly or with an approximation, the parent should smile, and say something like, "Good, you said _____!" or "Yes, it's a _____!" If the child says nothing or makes some other sounds unlike the model, the parent should wait a few minutes before presenting another model. Here are some other examples of the parent attention that can be provided for correct imitations:

> Hugging
> Tickling
> Laughing
> Patting the child's head
> Smoothing hair
> Saying, "Wow, you said _____!"
> Saying, "Fantastic, you said _____."
> Saying, "That's right, you said _____."
> Bouncing the child on knee
> Holding the child up in the air above head

It may not be necessary to touch the child or imitate the child' utterance during every teaching episode. However, Haugan and McIntire (1972), and Hursh and Sherman (1973) indicate that this parent attention is powerful in teaching language. Tactile stimulation will not always be possible if the parent is engaged in an activity several feet away from the child. In such situations, praise and imitation of the child's utterance may be sufficient.

Summary of Procedures for Imitation Training

1. When teaching the temporal relationship between models and imitations, listen for the child to make a sound. Immediately get near the child so he can see your face. Then imitate the child's sound once. If the child makes any sound during the next 10 seconds, smile, imitate the child's sound, and touch the child. Continue this exchange several times.
2. Once the child is participating readily in imitation exchanges, try initiating the exchange with a sound used in previous exchanges. The parent should be in close proximity to the infant and model the

sound once. If the infant responds with any sound within 10 seconds, smile, say the sound again and touch the infant.

3. When teaching the topographical relationship between models and imitations, present the model once. If the child makes a sound similar to the model, provide attention. If the sound is not similar to the model or no sound is made by the child, return to some other activity and present another model in a few minutes.

4. Once the child reliably produces an imitation of the model, new models can be introduced. Start by choosing other simple sounds the child has produced spontaneously in the past. Model one sound until the child imitates it reliably, then mix models of the new sound with other sounds the child already imitates. Then introduce another new sound, and so on.

5. When teaching the relationship between words and people, objects, or events, models of words should be presented in combination with the people, objects, or events the words name. Attention should be provided for imitations that approximate the words. Start with words requiring only a consonant-vowel combination. Then, introduce words with double consonant-vowel combinations and then words with two different consonant-vowel combinations.

Prompting Spontaneous Word Usage

In many cases, the child will utter a word before the parent presents the model. This will probably happen after the word and object (or event) have been paired many times by the parent. If the child does produce a word spontaneously, the parent should give praise immediately and imitate the child's word. If the child uses an appropriate approximation to a word, the parent should not imitate the approximation but should say the whole word clearly in a supportive way. Thus, if the child says "bă" for ball, the parent should say something like, "Right! It's a ball."

Parents can also enhance spontaneous word use by using two additional procedures. The easiest thing for the parent to do is to remain silent and wait to see if the child will produce the word. For example, after having the child imitate the word *ball* many times after showing the child a picture of a ball, the parent might show the picture of a ball and wait 15–20 seconds to see if the child will say "ball" or an approximation without a model. If the child does, the parent can then smile and say something like, "Right! Ball!" If the child says nothing, the model can be presented and attention provided for correct imitation of the model.

The other way of prompting spontaneous use of a word is to ask the child a question such as, "What's this?" "What's that?" "What do you want?" If the child does not answer within a few seconds, the model should be presented and attention provided for correct imitation of the model. If the child does answer the question, however, the parent should smile and say something like, "That's right, it's a ball." When using a question-prompt, the parent should be careful to say the question only once and then wait quietly for at least 15 seconds for the child to say something. Then the model can be presented. If the question is repeated several times, the child will not have a chance to speak and may not learn to answer the question.

When the parent asks "What do you want?" he should be careful that the child labels the object either spontaneously or in imitation before giving the object to the child. However, this question should not be asked until the child has imitated the name of the object many times. This will increase the chances of the child either naming the object spontaneously or in imitation when the question is asked and will decrease the chances of having to delay temporarily the child's access to the object because he has not named it. Opportunities for this kind of prompt will arise many times a day. The child will initiate the teaching episode by pointing to something or otherwise indicating that he wants something. It will be the parent's chance to enhance the child's language development by spending a few minutes in an incidental teaching episode.

If the child makes an error and spontaneously uses an incorrect word for something, the parent should be as supportive as possible while providing a correct model. Thus, if the child says "doggie" when seeing a horse, the parent might cheerfully say, "Well, it's kind of like a doggie, but he's a horse. Can you say 'horse?'"

Summary of Suggestions for Prompting Spontaneous Word Use

There are two types of prompts to use after a child has partially or fully imitated a particular word several times.

1. When the object or picture is in the child's presence, wait a few seconds before presenting a model. If the child says the word spontaneously, smile, praise, say the word, and touch the child. If the child says nothing, present the model and wait for the child to imitate before smiling and praising.
2. When the object or picture is in the child's presence, ask a question to prompt the child's use of the word without a prior model. Questions like, "What's this?" "What's that?" and "What do you want?" are appropriate here. Say the question once and wait for a response. If the child says nothing, present a model and provide attention to the child if it is imitated.
3. If the child spontaneously uses an incorrect label, the parent should be supportive while providing the correct label for the child to imitate.

Expansions

Some research indicates that things parents say in response to their child's speech serve as models for the child's future speech. Some of these parent responses are called "expansions" and have been shown to follow as many as 30% of a child's utterances. An expansion is a parent utterance that uses what the child has said to form a more adult-like utterance. For instance, if the child said, "Ball," the parent might expand by saying, "Yes, it's a ball." It may also be possible that one-word parent utterances also function as expansions. For example, if the child says, "dŏ," in the presence of a dog, the parent might expand by saying, "Dog." In other words, an expansion might be any parent utterance that adds something to the child's utterance to create a more precisely pronounced word or a more grammatical sentence. In most instances, the parent uses the actual or presumed environmental context of the utterance to make an expansion that could be said to closely approximate what the child might be intending to say. For example, in one context, *Daddy car* could be expanded to, *Yes, that's Daddy's car.* In another context, it could be expanded to, *Daddy is driving the car.*

Expansions can be easily used by parents in responding to their children's speech. Expansions enable the parent to present positive attention for spontaneous language use and simultaneous models for future utterances. In addition, expansions may be the forerunners of true conversation. Whenever a parent hears the child spontaneously produce a word, the parent should try to respond to the child with an expansion. Some examples of expansions follow:

	Child utterance	Possible parent expansion
One-word expansions	dă	dog
	bō	boat
	ōō	shoe
	hă	hat
	hŏ	hot
Two-word expansions	dădă că	Daddy's car
	bōō bō	blue boat
	thă bă	that ball
General expansions	ball or bă	Yes, it's a ball.
	shoe	We'll tie your shoes.
	că	Here are two cats.
	bye bye	Bye-bye Daddy.
	i ceam	The ice cream is cold.
	Here man	Yes, here's the mailman.
	Look truck!	Yes, look at the big truck!
	Mommy tea	Mommy is having tea.

Expansion questions	ēē	Do you want to eat?
	car	Where is the car?
	dolly	Do you want the dolly?
	See Bobby	Shall we go see Bobby?
	Susie toe	What about Susie's toe?
	Milk all gone	Is the milk all gone?
Expansion requests	dŏ	Bring the dog over here.
	bŏ	Show me the book.
	spo͞o	Don't throw the spoon.
	mō mil	Give the kitty more milk.
Expansion corrections	dŏ	It's bigger than a dog, but it's a horse.
	cǎ	Cars are little. That's a truck.
	pea	Peas are green. That's yellow corn.
	Daddy shoe	That's not Daddy's shoe! It's Mommy's shoe.
	He brang two balls	Right, he brought two balls to our house.

It is important, at first, to limit the expansions to one to four words more than the child has used in order to enhance their function as models for the child.

Summary of Expansions

1. When the child produces a word or a few words spontaneously, the parent can expand on the utterance by adding more sounds to correctly pronounce the word or by adding more words to make a grammatical sentence.
2. Expansions should be produced by the parent immediately after the child has said something spontaneously.
3. Expansions should be utterances of few words (at least at first) in order to enhance their modeling function.
4. An expansion should pertain specifically to the environmental context to which the child is attending when he makes the original utterance.
5. Expansions can be used frequently. Research has shown parents using expansions following 30% of a child's utterances.

Extensions

Extensions are similar to expansions in that they are uttered immediately after the child's spontaneous utterance. Thus, like expansions, extensions might function as attention for the child's spontaneous utterances and might encourage such utterances in the future. In addition, extensions might serve as models for future spontaneous utterances. However, extensions are different from expansions in that they do not include words from the child's utterance. They involve the addition of some information and often substitute a pronoun or synonym for the word the child used. For example, if the child said, "dog," the parent might make an extension by saying, "He is running," or, "The puppy is brown." Unfortunately, there is no evidence available to support the contention that extensions function to teach language to children. Nevertheless, normative research has shown that parents do use extensions. Schumaker's (1976) data show, for example, that 1% of mothers' speech to 19–23-month-old children consists of extensions. It may be that, as children grow older and more conversation takes place, extensions become more frequent in parents' speech. Hopefully, future research will identify the types of extensions parents use, the frequency with which they use extensions corresponding to different child ages, and the function of extensions. Below are some examples of extensions parents might use. Note that extensions, like expansions, should pertain to the actual or presumed environmental context to which the child is attending.

Child utterance	Possible parent extension
ball	Let's bounce it.
shoe	Put it on and we'll tie it.
Big doggie	Yes, he sure is huge.
Bye-bye	We'll see you later, daddy.
Mmm, ice cream	It sure tastes good!
Mailman	He's bringing our mail.
Mine	Oh, is that yours?
Look truck	I see it.
See flowers	They sure are pretty.

Summary of Extensions

1. When the child produces a word or words, parents can follow these utterances immediately with extensions by substituting a pronoun or synonym for the word(s) the child used and adding other words to form a more adult-like utterance.
2. Extensions should pertain to the environmental context to which the child is attending.

Prompting Spontaneous Utterances of Several Words

Another thing parents can do once their child is spontaneously emitting one-word utterances is to prompt multiword utterances. This can be done using a procedure similar to the one used by Hart and Risley (1974) that involves several levels of prompts. For example, if the parent wished to

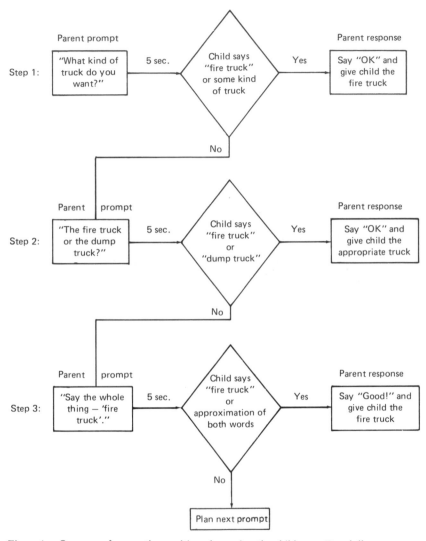

Figure 1.   One way of prompting multiword use after the child says, "truck."

promote the child's use of adjective-noun combinations, he might ask, "What kind of a cookie do you want?" or "How many cookies do you want?" when a child says "cookie." If the child said, "chocolate cookie" or "two cookie," respectively, in response to the questions, the cookies should be delivered. If the child says nothing or repeats, "Cookie," then the parent should initiate the next level of prompts and say, "I have chocolate cookies or vanilla cookies. What kind do you want?" or "You may have one cookie or two cookies. How many do you want?" If the child answers the question appropriately, the parent should deliver the cookie or cookies. If the child still says nothing, the parent should say the question once more, model an answer (e.g., "Say, 'Two cookies'") and wait for the child to imitate before presenting the cookies. In the case of difficult words like *chocolate* or *vanilla* any approximation should be acceptable (at first) as long as two words are attempted by the child. Later, the parents can require closer and closer approximations to the model before presenting the requested material. The diagrams in Figures 1 and 2 show two ways of using several levels of prompts when a child uses a one-word utterance.

Many of these episodes can occur in one day. To increase the frequency of such episodes, parents might place certain desired items on the top shelf or out of reach of the child to necessitate the child's asking for them.

Of course, there are many other types of two-word combinations besides the adjective-noun variety that we have covered. Brown's (1973) research shows that children also combine two words to form possessive relations, locative relations, agent-action relations, agent-object relations, and action-object relations. Some ways that these kinds of two-word utterances can be prompted follow:

Initial child response	Parent prompts	Hoped-for child response
For Possessive Relations		
"Book"	Step 1: "Whose book is that?"	"Johnny book."
	Step 2: "Is it Mommy's book or Johnny's book?"	"Johnny book."
	Step 3: "Say, 'Johnny's book'."	"Johnny book."
For Locative Relations		
"Book"	Step 1: "Where is the book?"	"Book chair."
	Step 2: "Is book in chair or is book on table?"	"Book chair."
	Step 3: "Say, 'Book in chair'."	"Book chair."
For Agent-Action Relations		
"Mommy"	Step 1: "What's Mommy doing?"	"Mommy push."
	Step 2: "Is Mommy pushing or is Mommy patting?"	"Mommy push."
	Step 3: "Say, 'Mommy push'."	"Mommy push."
For Agent-Object Relations		
"Book"	Step 1: "Who's reading the book?"	"Mommy book."
	Step 2: "Is Mommy reading book or is Susie reading book?"	"Mommy book."
	Step 3: "Say, 'Mommy book'."	"Mommy book."

Initial child response	Parent prompts	Hoped-for child response
For Action-Object Relations		
"Book"	Step 1: "What are you doing with the book?"	"Read book."
	Step 2: "Are you reading book or are you eating book?"	"Read book."
	Step 3: "Say, 'Read book'."	"Read book."
"Door"	Step 1: "What should I do with the door?"	"Open door."
	Step 2: "Should I open door or close door?"	"Open door."
	Step 3: "Say, 'Open door'."	"Open door."

Another procedure parents can use to encourage their child to use multiword utterances is to ask a question and then model the utterance they wish the child to produce. If the child asks for more water by saying, "Water," the parent might ask, "What do you want?", provide the model, "More water," and wait for the child to imitate before providing the water. Later, after the child spontaneously says, "More water," "More milk," etc., you might provide a three-word model like, "More water, please." Later still, a longer model like, "May I have more water, please?" can be used. This is a gradual building process and requires spontaneous use of a phrase before each new model is presented by the parent and a longer phrase is required of the child.

Summary of Suggestions on Prompting Two or More Word Utterances

1. Parents who wish to encourage multiword utterances can ask questions of the child and provide models for the child to imitate in answering the question.
2. Some models might provide the child with two options from which to choose, as with the model, "Do you want a blue ball or a red ball?"
3. Some models might require that the sentence be broken into a series of shorter models. In later attempts at the same sentence, the models can be made progressively longer until the child can imitate a model of the whole sentence. Then the parent can leave out the model and simply ask the question.

Concluding Comments

The emphasis throughout this section has been to capitalize on child-initiated utterances to further expand the child's developing language repertoire. When children are labeling or commenting actively about the world around them, they are perhaps most receptive to enthusiastic praise, expansions and extensions of their utterances, and questions from

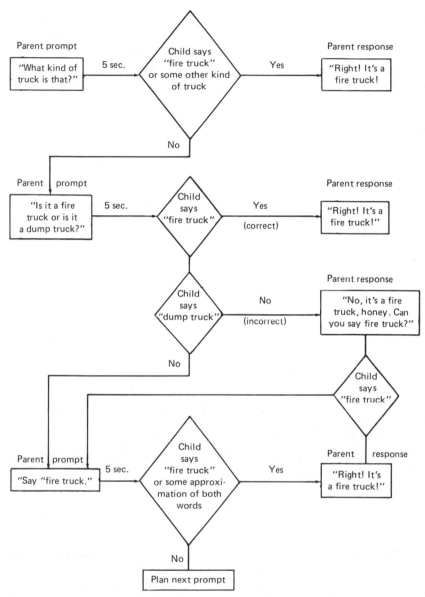

Figure 2.   Another way of prompting multiword use after the child says, "truck."

the parent. These are things that most parents already do, at one time or another. Perhaps the major value of this section is to suggest additional opportunities for, and a greater frequency of, such parent-child language interactions. We do not mean to imply that parents should speak to their children only when the child has spoken. A significant part of language learning may occur as a result of parents providing a variety of experiences for their children and commenting on these experiences by labeling objects, actions, and people, and by describing the characteristics of the environment around the child. This language input is also a normal and very desirable part of most parent-child interactions. At the same time, we regard parent-child language interactions as a type of rudimentary "conversation" in which two people attempt to communicate with each other. In any conversation, both people need to have an opportunity to speak, and each person needs to respond to the other in ways that maximize the likelihood of future conversations and mutual satisfaction. It is hoped that the suggestions offered will do that for both parents and their children.

ACKNOWLEDGMENTS

The authors would like to thank Drs. Melissa Bowerman, Frances D. Horowitz, Todd R. Risley, and Joseph E. Spradlin for their many helpful suggestions in the revision of this manuscript.

REFERENCES

Baer, D. M. 1970. An age irrelevant concept of development. Paper presented to the 74th Annual Convention of the APA, Washington, D.C., 1966. Subsequently published under the same title in the Merrill-Palmer Q. Behav. Dev. 16:238–245.

Baer, D. M. 1972. The control of developmental process: Why wait? In J. R. Nessleroade and H. W. Reese (eds.), Life-Span Developmental Psychology: Methodological Issues. Academic Press, New York.

Baer, D. M., Wolf, M. M., and Risley, T. R. 1968. Some current dimensions of applied behavior analysis. J. Appl. Behav. Anal. 1:91–97.

Baird, R. 1972. On the role of chance in imitation-comprehension-production test results. J. Verb. Learn. Verb. Behav. 11:474–477.

Baldwin, A. L., and Frank, S. M. 1969. Syntactic complexity in mother-child interactions. Paper presented at Meeting of Society for Research in Child Development, March, 1969, Santa Monica, Cal.

Bandura, A., and Harris, M. B. 1966. Modification of syntactic style. J. Exp. Child Psychol. 4:341–352.

Bandura, A., and Walters, R. H. 1973. Social Learning and Personality Development. Holt, Rinehart and Winston, New York.

Bellugi, U. 1971. Simplification in children's language. In R. Huxley and E. Ingram (eds.), Language Acquisition: Models and Methods, pp. 95–119. Academic Press, New York.

Bennett, C. W., and Ling, D. 1972. Teaching a complex verbal response to a hearing-impaired girl. J. Appl. Behav. Anal. 5:321–327.

Berko, J. 1958. The child's learning of English morphology. Word 14:150–177.

Better Homes and Gardens Baby Book. 1943. Bantam Books, New York.

Bing, E. 1963. The effect of child rearing practices on the development of different cognitive abilities. Child Dev. 34:631–648.

Bloom, L. Talking, understanding and thinking. 1974. *In* R. L. Schiefelbusch and L. L. Lloyd (eds.), Language Perspectives—Acquisition, Retardation, and Intervention, pp. 285–312. University Park Press, Baltimore.

Bloom, L., Hood, L., and Lightbown, P. 1974. Imitation in language development: If, when and why. Cog. Psychol. 6:380–420.

Bohannon, J. N. 1975. The relationship between syntax discrimination and sentence imitation in children. Child Dev. 46:444–451.

Braine, M. D. S. 1963. The ontogeny of English phrase structure: The first phrase. Language 39:1–13.

Brazelton, T. B. 1969. Infants and Mothers. Dell Publishing Co., New York.

Brazelton, T. B. 1974. Toddlers and Parents: A Declaration of Independence. Delacorte Press, New York.

Brigham, T. A., and Sherman, J. A. 1968. An experimental analysis of verbal imitation in preschool children. J. Appl. Behav. Anal. 1:151–158.

Brodbeck, A. J., and Irwin, O. C. 1946. The speech behavior of infants without families. Child Dev. 17:145–156.

Broen, P. A. 1972. The verbal environment of the language learning child. ASHA Monogr. No. 17.

Brown, R. 1973. A First Language: The Early Stages. Harvard University Press, Cambridge, Mass.

Brown, R., and Bellugi, U. 1964. Three processes in the child's acquisition of syntax. *In* E. Lenneberg (ed.), New Directions in the Study of Language, pp. 131–161. MIT Press, Cambridge, Mass.

Brown, R., and Berko, J. 1960. Word association and the acquisition of grammar. Child Dev. 31:1–14.

Brown, R., Cazden, C. B., and Bellugi, U. 1969. The child's grammar from I to III. *In* J. P. Hill (ed.), 1967 Minnesota Symposium on Child Psychology, pp. 28–73. University of Minnesota Press, Minneapolis.

Brown, R., and Fraser, C. 1964. The acquisition of syntax. *In* U. Bellugi and R. Brown (eds.), The Acquisition of Language. Monogr. Soc. Res. Child Dev. 29:43–79.

Brown, R., Fraser, C., and Bellugi, U. 1964. Exploration in grammar evaluation. *In* U. Bellugi and R. Brown (eds.), The Acquisition of Language. Monog. Soc. Res. Child Dev. 29:79–92.

Brown, R., and Hanlon, C. 1970. Derivational complexity and order of acquisition in child speech. *In* J. R. Hayes (ed.), Cognition and the Development of Language, pp. 11–53. John Wiley & Sons, New York.

Cazden, C. B. 1965. Environmental assistance to the child's acquisition of grammar. Unpublished doctoral dissertation, Harvard University, Cambridge, Mass.

Cazden, C. B. 1968. The acquisition of noun and verb inflections. Child Dev. 39:433–448.

Cazden, C. B. 1972. Child Language and Education. Holt, Rinehart and Winston, New York.

Chapman, R. S., and Miller, J. F. 1973. Early two and three word utterances: Does production precede comprehension? Paper presented at the Fifth Annual Child Language Research Forum, April, 1973, Stanford University, Stanford, Cal.

Chess, S., Thomas, A., and Birch, H. 1972. Your Child Is a Person: A Psychological Approach to Parenthood Without Guilt. Viking Press, New York.

Chomsky, N. 1965. Aspects of the Theory of Syntax. MIT Press, Cambridge, Mass.

Church, J. 1973. Understanding Your Child from Birth to Three: A Guide to Your Child's Psychological Development. Random House, New York.

Clark, H. B., and Sherman, J. A. 1975. Teaching generative use of sentence answers to three forms of questions. J. Appl. Behav. Anal. 8:321–330.

Clarke-Stewart, K. A. 1973. Interactions between mothers and their young children: Characteristics and consequences. Monogr. Soc. Res. Child Dev. 38:6–7.

Eimas, P. D., Siqueland, E. R., Jusczyk, P., and Vigorito, J. 1971. Speech perception in infants. Science 171:303–306.

Ervin, S. M. 1964. Imitation and structural change in children's language. In E. H. Lenneberg (ed.), New Directions in the Study of Language, pp. 163–189. MIT Press, Cambridge, Mass.

Ervin-Tripp, S. 1970. Discourse agreement: How children answer questions. In J. R. Hayes (ed.), Cognition and the Development of Language, pp. 79–107. John Wiley & Sons, New York.

Fantino, E. 1977. Conditioned reinforcement: Choice and information. In W. K. Honig and J. R. Staddon (eds.), Handbook of Operant Behavior, pp. 313–339. Prentice-Hall, Englewood Cliffs, N.J.

Fernald, C. D. 1972. Control of grammar in imitation, comprehension and production: Problems of replication. J. Verb. Learn. Verb. Behav. 11:606–613.

Fraser, C., Bellugi, U., and Brown, R. 1963. Control of grammar in imitation, comprehension, and production. J. Verb. Learn. Verb. Behav. 2:121–135.

Fraser, C., and Roberts, N. 1975. Mothers' speech to children of four different ages. J. Psycholing. Res. 4:9–16.

Freud, A., and Burlingham, D. 1944. Infants Without Families. International Universities Press, New York.

Friedlander, B. Z. 1968. The effect of speaker identity, voice inflection, vocabulary, and message redundancy on infants' selection of vocal reinforcement. J. Exp. Child Psychol. 6:443–459.

Friedlander, B. Z. 1970. Receptive language in infancy. Merrill-Palmer Q. 16:7–51.

Fromme, A. 1956. The ABC of Child Care. Pocket Books, New York.

Fry, D. B. 1966. The development of the phonological system in the normal and deaf child. In F. Smith and G. A. Miller (eds.), The Genesis of Language, pp. 187–206. MIT Press, Cambridge, Mass.

Gaer, E. P. 1969. Children's understanding and production of sentences. J. Verb. Learn. Verb. Behav. 8:289–294.

Garcia, E., Baer, D. M., and Firestone, I. 1971. The development of generalized imitation within topographical determined boundaries. J. Appl. Behav. Anal. 4:101–112.

Garcia, E., Guess, D., and Byrnes, J. 1973. Development of syntax in a retarded girl using procedures of imitation, reinforcement, and modelling. J. Appl. Behav. Anal. 6:299–310.

Gesell, A., and Thompson, H. 1934. Infant Behavior: Its Genesis and Growth. McGraw-Hill Book Co., New York.

Gladstone, B. W., and Cooley, J. 1975. Behavioral similarity as a reinforcer for preschool children. J. Exp. Anal. Behav. 23:357–368.

Gleason, J. Berko. 1967. Do children imitate? Paper read to International Conference on Oral Education of the Deaf, Lexington School for the Deaf, June, 1967, New York, N.Y.

Goldfarb, W. 1943a. Infant rearing and problem behavior. Am. J. Orthopsychiatry April:249–265.

Goldfarb, W. 1943b. The effects of early institutional care on adolescent personality. J. Exp. Educ. 12:106–129.

Goldfarb, W. 1945. Effects of psychological deprivation in infancy and subsequent stimulation. Am. J. Psychiatry 102:18–33.

Goldman-Eisler, F. 1968. Psycholinguistics: Experiments in spontaneous speech. Academic Press, New York.

Gordon, I. J. 1970. Baby Learning Through Baby Play: A Parents' Guide for the First Two Years. St. Martin's Press, New York.

Guess, D. 1969. A functional analysis of receptive language and productive speech: Acquisition of the plural morpheme. J. Appl. Behav. Anal. 2:55–64.

Guess, D., and Baer, D. M. 1973. An analysis of individual differences in generalization between receptive and productive language in retarded children. J. Appl. Behav. Anal. 6:311–329.

Guess, D., Sailor, W., Rutherford, G., and Baer, D. M. 1968. An experimental analysis of linguistic development: The productive use of the plural morpheme. J. Appl. Behav. Anal. 1:297–306.

Guillaume, P. 1971. Imitation in Children. (E. P. Halperin, trans.). University of Chicago Press, Chicago.

Hart, B., and Risley, T. R. 1968. Establishing use of descriptive adjectives in the spontaneous speech of disadvantaged preschool children. J. Appl. Behav. Anal. 1:109–120.

Hart, B., and Risley, T. R. 1974. Using preschool materials to modify the language of disadvantaged children. J. Appl. Behav. Anal. 7:243–256.

Haugan, G. M., and McIntire, R. W. 1972. Comparisons of vocal imitation, tactile stimulation and food as reinforcers for infant vocalizations. Dev. Psychol. 6:201–209.

Hess, R. D. 1969. Parental behavior and children's school achievement: Implications for Head Start. In E. Grotberg (ed.), Critical Issues in Research Related to Disadvantaged Children, pp. 1–76. Seminar #5. Educational Testing Service, Princeton, N.J.

Hess, R. D., and Shipman, V. 1965. Early experience and the socialization of cognitive modes in children. Child Dev. 36:869–886.

Hess, R. D., and Shipman, V. 1967. Cognitive elements in maternal behavior. In J. P. Hill (ed.), Minnesota Symposium on Child Psychology, Vol. 1, pp. 57–81. University of Minnesota Press, Minneapolis.

Hess, R. D., and Shipman, V. 1968. Maternal influences upon early learning. In R. D. Hess and R. M. Baer (eds.), Early Education, pp. 91–103. Aldine, Chicago.

Horowitz, F. D., and Paden, L. Y. 1973. The effectiveness of environmental intervention programs. In B. M. Caldwell and H. Ricciuti (eds.), Review of Child Development Research, Vol. III, Chap. 6.

Hovell, M. F., Schumaker, J. B., and Sherman, J. A. 1978. A comparison of parent models and expansions in two year old children's acquisition of color and size adjectives. J. Exp. Child Psychol. 25:41–57.

Hursh, D. E., and Sherman, J. A. 1973. The effects of parent presented models and praise on the vocal behavior of their children. J. Exp. Child Psychol. 15:328–339.

Ilg, F. L., and Ames, L. B. 1955. Child Behavior: From Birth to Ten. New York: Harper & Row.

Jakobson, R. 1941. Kindersprache, Aphasie und Allgemeine Lautgesetze. Almqvist and Wiksell, Uppsala.

Jakobson, R. 1971. The sound laws of child language and their place in general phonology. *In* A. Bar-Adon and W. F. Leopold (eds.), Child Language: A Book of Readings, pp. 75–82. Prentice-Hall, Englewood Cliffs, N.J.

Keeney, T. J., and Wolfe, J. 1972. The acquisition of agreement in English. J. Verb. Learn. Verb. Behav. 11:698–705.

Kelleher, R. T., and Gollub, L. R. 1962. A review of positive conditional reinforcement. J. Exp. Anal. Behav. 5:543–597.

Klima, E. S., and Bellugi-Klima, U. 1969. Syntactic regularities in the speech of children. *In* D. A. Reibel and S. A. Schane (eds.), Modern Studies in English: Readings in Transformational Grammar. Prentice-Hall, Englewood Cliffs, N.J.

Lahey, B. B. 1971. Modification of the frequency of descriptive adjectives in the speech of Head Start children through modelling without reinforcement. J. Appl. Behav. Anal. 4:19–22.

Lahey, B. B., and Lawrence, J. H. 1974. An analysis of the effects of modelling on morphemic and syntactic features as a function of family income and age. (Abstract only). J. Appl. Behav. Anal. 7:482.

Lane, H. 1976. The Wild Boy of Aveyron. Harvard University Press, Cambridge, Mass.

Lenneberg, E. H. 1962. Understanding language without ability to speak: A case report. J. Abnorm. Soc. Psychol. 65:419–425.

Lenneberg, E. H., Rebelsky, F. G., and Nichols, I. A. 1965. The vocalizations of infants born to deaf and to hearing parents. Hum. Dev. 8:23–37.

Lewis, M. M. 1969. Language and the Child. King, Thorne, and Stace, Ltd., England.

Liebert, R. M., Odom, R. D., Hill, J. H., and Huff, R. L. 1969. Effects of age and rule familiarity on the production of modelled language constructions. Dev. Psychol. 1:108–112.

Lovaas, I. O., Berberich, J. P., Perloff, B. F., and Schaeffer, B. 1966. Acquisition of imitative speech by schizophrenic children. Science 151:705–707.

Lovell, K., and Dixon, E. 1967. The growth of the control of grammar in imitation, comprehension and production. J. Child Psychol. Psychiatry 8:31–39.

Lutzker, J. R., and Sherman, J. A. 1974. Producing generative sentence usage by imitation and reinforcement procedures. J. Appl. Behav. Anal. 7:447–460.

McCaffrey, A. 1969. Speech perception in infancy. Personal communication. As reviewed in Friedlander, 1970.

McCarthy, D. 1954. Language development in children. *In* L. Carmichael (ed.), A Manual of Child Psychology, pp. 492–630. 2nd ed. John Wiley & Sons, New York.

Maclay, H., and Osgood, C. E. 1967. Hesitation phenomena in spontaneous speech. *In* L. A. Jakabovits and M. S. Miron (eds.), Readings in the Psychology of Language. Prentice-Hall, Englewood Cliffs, N.J.

Malouf, R. E., and Dodd, D. H. 1972. Role of exposure, imitation, and expansion in the acquisition of an artificial grammatical rule. Dev. Psychol. 7:195–203.

Mann, R. A., and Baer, D. M. 1971. The effects of receptive language training on articulation. J. Appl. Behav. Anal. 4:291–298.

Menyuk, P. 1963. A preliminary evaluation of grammatical capacity in children. J. Verb. Learn. Verb. Behav. 2:429–439.

Menyuk, P. 1969. Alternation of rules in children's grammar. *In* D. A. Reibel and S. A. Schane (eds.), Modern Studies in English: Readings in Transformational Grammar, pp. 409–421. Prentice-Hall, Englewood Cliffs, N.J.

Miller, W., and Ervin, S. 1964. The development of grammar in child language. *In* U. Bellugi and R. Brown (eds.), The Acquisition of Language. Monogr. Soc. Res. Child Dev. 29:9–39.

Moerk, E. 1972. Principles of interaction in language learning. Merrill-Palmer Q. 18:229–257.

Moffitt, A. R. 1968. Speech Perception by Infants. Unpublished doctoral dissertation, University of Minnesota, Minneapolis. As reviewed in Friedlander, 1970.

Montes, F. 1974. Incidental teaching of beginning reading in a day care center. Unpublished doctoral dissertation, University of Kansas, Lawrence.

Morehead, D. M., and Morehead, A. 1974. From signal to sign: A Piagetian view of thought and language during the first two years. *In* R. L. Schiefelbusch and L. L. Lloyd (eds.), Language Perspectives—Acquisition, Retardation, and Intervention, pp. 153–190. University Park Press, Baltimore.

Mowrer, O. H. 1960. Learning Theory and the Symbolic Process. (Chapter 3: Learning theory and language learning.) John Wiley & Sons, New York.

Nelson, K. 1973. Structure and strategy in learning to talk. Monogr. Soc. Res. Child Dev. 38(149).

Nelson, K. E., Carskaddon, G., and Bonvillian, J. D. 1973. Syntax acquisition: Impact of experimental variation in adult verbal interaction with the child. Child Dev. 44:497–504.

Odom, R. D., Liebert, R. M., and Hill, J. H. 1968. The effects of modelling cues, reward, and attentional set on the production of grammatical and ungrammatical syntactic constructions. J. Exp. Child Psychol. 6:131–140.

Oller, D. K., Wieman, L. A., Doyle, W. J., and Ross, C. 1974. Child speech, babbling and phonological universals. Stanford Papers Rep. Child Lang. Dev. 8:33–41.

Phillips, J. R. 1973. Syntax and vocabulary of mothers' speech to young children: Age and sex comparisons. Child Dev. 44:182–185.

Pimsleur, P. 1963. Discrimination training in the teaching of French pronunciation. Mod. Lang. J. 47:199–203.

Ramey, C. T., and Ourth, L. L. 1969. Effects of delayed reinforcement on infant's vocalization rates. Paper presented at Society for Research in Child Development, March, 1969, Santa Monica, Cal.

Reynolds, N. J., and Risley, T. R. 1968. The rate of social and material reinforcers in increasing talking in a disadvantaged preschool child. J. Appl. Behav. Anal. 1:253–262.

Rheingold, H. L. 1956. The modification of social responsiveness in institutional babies. Monogr. Soc. Res. Child Dev. 21:5–48.

Rheingold, H. L., and Bayley, N. 1959. The later effects of an experimental modification of mothering. Child Dev. 30:363–372.

Rheingold, H. L., Gewirtz, J. L., and Ross, H. Q. 1959. Social conditioning of vocalizations in the infant. J. Comp. Physiol. Psychol. 65–72.

Ripin, R. 1933. A comparative study of the development of infants in an institution with those in homes of low socio-economic status. Psychol. Bull. 30:680–681.

Risley, T. R. 1966. The establishment of verbal behavior in deviant children. Unpublished doctoral dissertation, University of Washington, Seattle.

Risley, T. R., and Reynolds, N. J. 1970. Emphasis as a prompt for verbal imitation. J. Appl. Behav. Anal. 3:185–190.

Rose, J. B., and McLaughlin, M. M. (eds.). 1949. A Portable Medieval Reader. Viking Press, New York.

Rosenthal, T. L., and Whitebook, J. S. 1970. Incentive versus instructions in transmitting grammatical parameters with experimenter as models. Behav. Res. Ther. 8:189–196.

Rosenthal, T. L., Zimmerman, B. J., and Durning, K. 1970. Observationally induced changes in children's interrogative classes. J. Personal. Soc. Psychol. 16:681–688.

Routh, D. K. 1969. Conditioning of vocal response differentiation in infants. Dev. Psychol. 1:219–226.

Sailor, W. 1971. Reinforcement and generalization of productive plural allomorphs in two retarded children. J. Appl. Behav. Anal. 4:305–310.

Schroeder, G. L., and Baer, D. M. 1972. Effects of concurrent and serial training on generalized vocal imitation in retarded children. Dev. Psychol. 6:293–301.

Schumaker, J. 1976. Mothers' expansions: Their characteristics and effects on child language. Unpublished doctoral dissertation, University of Kansas, Lawrence.

Schumaker, J., and Sherman, J. A. 1970. Training generative verb usage by imitation and reinforcement procedures. J. Appl. Behav. Anal. 3:273–287.

Sheldon, J. W. 1974. "Once upon a time . . ," or How to teach retarded children to tell stories—towards conversational speech. Unpublished doctoral dissertation, University of Kansas, Lawrence.

Sheppard, W. C. 1969. Operant control of infant vocal and motor behavior. J. Exp. Child Psychol. 7:36–51.

Sherman, J. A. 1971. Imitation and language development. In H. W. Reese and L. P. Lippsitt (eds.), Advances in Child Development and Behavior, pp. 239–272. Academic Press, New York.

Shipley, E., Smith, C., and Gleitman, L. 1969. A study of the acquisition of language: Free response to commands. Language 45:322–342.

Simeonsson, R. J. 1973. Contingent social stimulation of infant vocalizations: Developmental delay and mother-infant interaction. Paper presented at the Biennial Meeting of the Society for Research in Child Development, Philadelphia.

Singh, T. A. L., and Zingg, R. M. 1966. Wolf Children and Feral Man. The Shoe String Press, Hamden, Conn.

Slobin, D. I. 1968. Imitation and grammatical development in children. In N. S. Endler, L. R. Boulter, and H. Osser (eds.), Contemporary Issues in Developmental Psychology. Holt, Rinehart and Winston, New York.

Slobin, D. I., and Welsh, C. A. 1971. Elicited imitation as a research tool in developmental psycholinguistics. In C. S. Lavatelli (ed.), Language Training in Early Childhood Education, pp. 170–185. University of Illinois Press for the ERIC Clearinghouse on Early Childhood Education, Urbana.

Smith, M. E. 1933. Grammatical errors in the speech of preschool children. Child Dev. 4:183–190.

Snow, C. E. 1972. Mothers' speech to children learning language. Child Dev. 43:549–565.

Spitz, R. A. 1945. Hospitalism: An inquiry into the genesis of psychiatric conditions in early childhood. Psychoanal. Study Child 1:53–74.

Spitz, R. A. 1946. Hospitalism: A follow-up report on the investigation described in Vol. 1, 1945. Psychoanal. Study Child 2:113–117.

Spock, B. 1946. Baby and Child Care. Pocket Books, New York.

Stevens-Long, J., and Rasmussen, M. 1974. The acquisition of simple and compound sentence structure in an autistic child. J. Appl. Behav. Anal. 7:473–479.

Stodolsky, S. S. 1965. Maternal behavior and language and concept formation in Negro preschool children: An inquiry into process. Unpublished doctoral dissertation, University of Chicago, Chicago.

Tizard, B., Cooperman, O., Joseph, A., and Tizard, O. 1972. Environmental effects of language development: A study of young children in long-stay residential nurseries. Child Dev. 43:337–358.

Tizard, B., and Rees, J. 1974. A comparison of the effects of adoption, restoration to the natural mother, and continued institutionalization on the cognitive development of four-year-old children. Child Dev. 45:92–99.

Todd, G. A., and Palmer, B. 1968. Social reinforcement of infant babbling. Child Dev. 39:591–596.

Twardosz, S., and Baer, D. M. 1973. Training two severely retarded adolescents to ask questions. J. Appl. Behav. Anal. 6:655–661.

U.S. Department of Health, Education, and Welfare. 1973. Infant Care. Award Books, New York.

Wahler, R. G. 1969. Infant social development: Some experimental analyses of an infant-mother interaction during the first year of life. J. Exp. Child Psychol. 7:101–113.

Weikart, D. P. 1966. Results of preschool intervention programs. Paper presented at the symposium on the Education of Culturally Disadvantaged Children, University of Kansas, Lawrence.

Weisberg, P. 1961. Social and non-social conditioning of infant vocalizations. Child Dev. 34:377–388.

Wheeler, A. J., and Sulzer, B. 1970. Operant training and generalization of a verbal response form in a speech-deficient child. J. Appl. Behav. Anal. 3:139–147.

Whitehurst, G. J. 1971. Generalized labeling on the basis of structural response classes by two young children. J. Exp. Child Psychol. 12:59–71.

Whitehurst, G. J. 1972. Production of novel and grammatical utterances by two-year-old children. J. Exp. Child Psychol. 13:502–515.

Whitehurst, G. J., Novak, G., and Zorn, G. A. 1972. Delayed speech studied in the home. Dev. Psychol. 2:169–177.

Wiegerink, R., Harris, C., Simeonsson, R., and Pearson, M. E. 1974. Social stimulation of vocalizations in delayed infants: Familiar and novel agent. Child Dev. 45:866–872.

Wilkinson, A. 1971. The Foundations of Language: Talking and Reading in Young Children. Oxford University Press, England.

Winitz, H., and Preisler, L. 1965. Discrimination pretraining and sound learning. Percept. Mot. Skills 20:905–916.

Wolff, P. H. 1961. Observations on the early development of smiling. In B. M. Foss (ed.), Determinants of Infant Behavior II. Methuen, London, John Wiley & Sons, New York.

chapter 7

Application of Miniature Linguistic System or Matrix-Training Procedures

Bruce Wetherby

John F. Kennedy Center for Research on
Education and Human Development
and
Psychology Faculty
George Peabody College for Teachers
Nashville, Tennessee

Sebastian Striefel

Exceptional Child Center
and
Psychology Department
Utah State University
Logan, Utah

A previous chapter by the first author (Wetherby, 1978) has suggested that a large portion of past and present language research can be conceptualized within a miniature linguistic system framework originally developed by Esper (1925). That chapter also discussed the significance a miniature linguistic system analysis of language may hold for those interested in a functional analysis of verbal behavior. Specifically, the notions of sequence, class, and generalization, which constitute three of the major characteristics of language, were said to be addressed by a miniature linguistic system analysis of language.

A miniature linguistic system can be defined as a stimulus-response matrix system in which responses controlled by one class of stimuli are taught to occur in sequential order with responses controlled by another class of stimuli, with the end result being that the subject responds correctly to new or untrained combinations of stimuli from these two classes. Specifically, this paradigm, as shown in Figure 1, suggests that language is composed of sequentially produced responses that are members of a particular class of potential (and substitutable) stimuli that are combinable with each other. Corresponding to this analysis of the potential combinations of language responses available, a miniature linguistic system analysis suggests that specific environmental stimuli control the production of specific responses and that the multitude of stimulus combinations available in the environment will control the potential production of a multitude of language responses. In this light, traditional analyses of generalized language in terms of primary stimulus generalization, abstraction, and response-class approaches are seen as insufficient because they do not provide an appreciation of the stimulus control relations inherent in language (Wetherby, 1978).

Experimental data are available to support a miniature linguistic system conceptualization of language. A review of a number of miniature linguistic system experiments (e.g., Esper, 1925; Braine, 1963, 1965; Foss, 1968; Smith, 1966a, 1966b; Guess et al., 1968; Premack, 1970; Whitehurst, 1971; von Glasersfeld, 1977; Striefel, Wetherby, and Karlan, 1976) has indicated that methodological procedures have existed for a number of years that can be used either 1) to demonstrate the orderly and systematic nature of language or 2) to establish generalized language responses in children or animals deficient in such skills (Wetherby, 1978). A general rule common to all of these studies, as shown in Figure 1, has been that, as portions of various dimensions or classes of responses are taught to occur with members from another class, novel combinations of

The preparation of this chapter was supported, in part, by a predoctoral research traineeship awarded to the senior author through National Institute of Child Health and Human Development Research Service Award HD 07066 to the Kansas Center for Mental Retardation and Human Development, University of Kansas. Appreciation is expressed to Drs. Kenneth F. Ruder, Richard L. Schiefelbusch, and Joseph E. Spradlin for their support and encouragement.

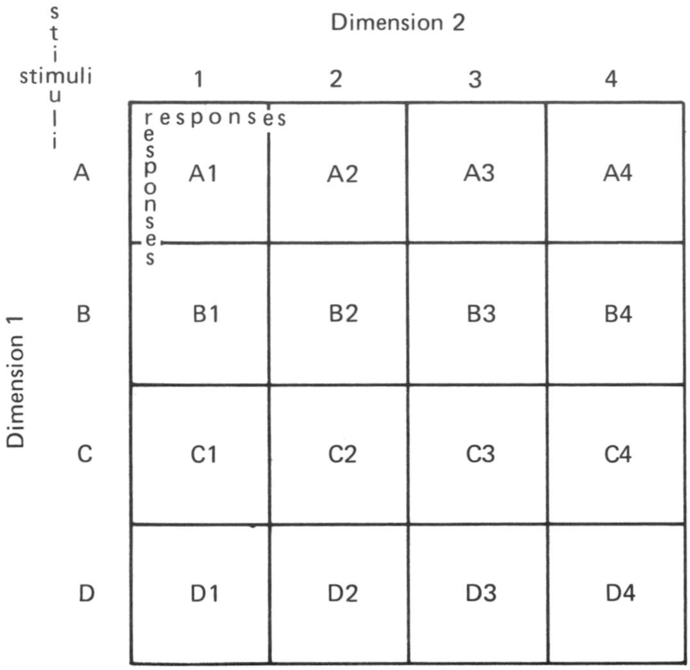

Figure 1. The basic miniature linguistic system or matrix-training paradigm. Letters and numbers outlining the matrix refer to dimensions of discriminative stimuli, while letter-number combinations within each box of the matrix refer to corresponding response combinations.

stimuli will be responded to correctly without direct training. This result implies that the language response, as an organism output, is only as systematic as the arrangement of stimuli controlling the response as input.

As mentioned, a miniature linguistic system analysis of language has implications for individuals interested in establishing generalized language in language-deficient individuals. The purpose of this chapter is to illustrate how a miniature linguistic system analysis of language can be used to guide the training of a generalized receptive or productive language repertoire, and to eventually isolate what appear to be some of the critical features involved in the acquisition of generalized language by language-deficient individuals.

DEVELOPMENT OF
GENERALIZED RECEPTIVE LANGUAGE SKILLS

The first illustration of the development of generalized receptive language with miniature linguistic system or matrix-training procedures will be the establishment of generalized instruction-following behavior. Instruction-following behavior can be defined as the compliance of an individual to the spoken requests of another. This behavior is important for remediation because it is a skill that is very functional for growth and development, and it is also a subset of a large repertoire of behavior called receptive language. The development of generalized instruction-following behavior is also an area the current authors have researched (e.g., Striefel and Wetherby, 1973; Striefel, Wetherby, and Karlan, 1976, 1978). As such, research conducted by the authors can be used to illustrate how one may establish generalized receptive language skills with miniature linguistic system or matrix-training procedures. Research conducted in this area is reviewed in detail in this chapter to provide a perspective on what seem to be some of the critical variables involved in the development of generalized receptive language.

The Need to Establish Generalized Instruction-Following Skills

A primary characteristic of all language-remediation attempts is to justify the need for such interventions. In terms of instruction following, as mentioned above, it is obvious that a large portion of our day-to-day activity is spent responding to the directives of other individuals and that such a skill facilitates our survival (Striefel, Wetherby, and Karlan, 1978). Consequently, it is important that all individuals be given the chance to develop a large and functional instruction-following repertoire.

The development of such a skill should not be specific to only those instructions that have been taught directly. A functional instruction-following repertoire exists when an individual can respond to many combinations and variations of instructions *the first time one is confronted with these new requests*. Such a generalized skill allows the expansion of adaptive skills and provides a means for more quickly learning the receptive rules of new situations. Thus, it is important that the parameters governing the development of a generalized instruction-following repertoire be pinpointed.

Relative to its importance in our everyday lives, the experimental analysis of instruction-following skills has been minuscule (Garcia and DeHaven, 1974; Harris, 1975; Snyder, Lovitt, and Smith, 1975). To this date, only a handful of studies have been published that are concerned with the determination of factors involved in the development of instruction-following skills (e.g., Zimmerman, Zimmerman, and Russel, 1969; Whitman, Zakaras, and Chardos, 1971; Striefel and Wetherby, 1973; Scheuerman et al., 1974; Striefel, Bryan, and Aikins, 1974; Smeets and Striefel, 1976a, 1976b; Striefel, Wetherby, and Karlan, 1976, 1978), and only a subset of these have demonstrated the development of generalized instruction-following skills. Even in a related literature, the development of generalized receptive grammatical skills, there has been relatively little interest (e.g., Baer and Guess, 1971; Baer, Guess, and Sherman, 1973; Frisch and Schumaker, 1974).

Various reviews of the cited work on establishing instruction-following skills have pointed to a lack of understanding about the processes involved in developing a generalized repertoire of such skills (e.g., Garcia and DeHaven, 1974; Harris, 1975; Snyder, Lovitt, and Smith, 1975). Although all the instruction-following studies referenced above established specific instructional skills with their respective studies, some did not establish generalized responding to untrained instructions. These inconsistent findings, however, besides questioning the various instructional or experimental techniques of some of the studies, call attention to the methodological procedures necessary for teaching or establishing generalized language. Thus, a historical review of some of this research should serve to illustrate how a miniature linguistic system analysis of language can be used to understand and develop generalized language.

Initial Attempts to Establish Generalized Instruction-Following Skills

One of the first experiments to investigate the establishment of generalized instruction-following skills was that of Whitman, Zakaras, and Chardos (1971). These investigators, citing the need to establish instruction-following skills and to determine if reinforcement and physical guidance procedures could be used to teach this skill, taught two severely retarded children to follow instructions. They then assessed generalization to other instructional stimuli. Training and generalization items are shown in Figure 2 for each subject.

The essense of the Whitman et al. (1971) training procedure is the application of a fading technology. In this procedure the subject is instructed to perform a specific response, for example, *point to your nose*, and, if the subject does not perform this response within a specific time period, the subject is put through the total response manually by the experimenter; that is, when confronted with no response or an incorrect response to the above instruction, the experimenter takes the subject's hand, forms it into a pointing fist, and then moves the hand and finger until they point at or touch the subject's nose, at which point the subject is reinforced for the complete response. On the next and successive trials, however, the experimenter provides gradually less help in performing the terminal response until the subject performs the total response alone.

Results of the Whitman et al. (1971) study indicated that both subjects gradually learned to respond to a majority of the trained instructions and that, correspondingly, most of the generalization items were also produced, although the latter were never taught or reinforced. The number of correct responses to the unreinforced generalization items, however, was slightly less than that for the trained items. These results

Training Items	Generalization Items

Subject 1

1. Sit down	1. Come here
2. Stand up	2. Hold my hand
3. Look at me	3. Put your hands on the table
4. Point to your nose	4. Point to your ear
5. Pick up the cup	5. Point to your mouth
6. Give me the pencil	6. Point to your arm
7. Put the pencil in front of the box	7. Give me the cup
8. Clap your hands	8. Give me the jacket
9. Put your hands under the table	9. Pick up the pencil
10. Point to your eye	10. Put the pencil in the box
11. Pick up the jacket	11. Put the pencil behind the box

Subject 2

1. Look at me	1. Pick up the block
2. Point to the window	2. Give me the block
3. Pick up the pencil	3. Put the block in the box
4. Give me the pencil	4. Put the block next to the box
5. Put the pencil in the box	5. Look at the lamp
6. Put the pencil next to the box	6. Touch your leg
7. Pick up the cup	7. Pick up the toy
8. Give me the cup	8. Give me the toy
9. Touch your arm	9. Point to the door
10. Go to the door	10. Go to the window

Figure 2. Training and generalization items for the two subjects reported by Whitman, Zakaras, and Chardos (1971).

were interpreted by the authors to suggest that fading and reinforcement techniques may be used to teach instruction-following skills to severely retarded children, and that the use of these skills may generalize to other instructions not trained directly.

One problem with accepting the above conclusion, however, concerns the possibility that the Whitman et al. (1971) subjects may have known the generalization instructions before training, and that the generalization effect reported may not have been caused by the training procedures. This possibility, which is fully acknowledged by the authors, suggests that the screening procedures incorporated to determine whether or not subjects responded to verbal instructions may have been inadequate. Specifically, Whitman et al. selected their subjects on the basis of teacher reports indicating that the children could, but did not currently, respond to the training and generalization items. Thus, the possibility exists that the subjects did not perform the instructions for motivational reasons, and that simple reinforcement of a subset of the total instructions was sufficient to motivate the subject to respond to the remaining instructions, which just happened to be those used to assess generalization effects.

This motivational possibility was addressed in a subsequent study by Striefel and Wetherby (1973). These investigators, citing the need to determine the stimulus-control parameters of instruction-following behavior and to replicate the procedures of Whitman et al. (1971) systematically, while controlling for motivational factors, taught a profoundly retarded child to follow instructions and assessed for generalization effects. Unlike the previous study, these investigators reinforced the appropriate use of any instruction performed correctly during part of their initial baseline, and used a multiple baseline design across instructions (Baer, Wolf, and Risley, 1968) in order to directly assess the effects of their training procedures on the acquisition of each instruction. Striefel and Wetherby's (1973) training and generalization instructions are shown in Figure 3. As can be seen, the generalization items were direct recombinations of the training instructions in order to maximize the possibility of generalization. Striefel and Wetherby's (1973) training procedures also incorporated fading and reinforcement procedures but used a number of

Training Items	Generalization Items
1. Stand up	1. Point to hair
2. Sit down	2. Brush shoe
3. Brush hair	3. Lift ear
4. Drink from glass	4. Push block
5. Raise your hand	5. Blow on ball
6. Clap your hands	6. Drop feather
7. Eat with spoon	7. Wave scissors
8. Drop ball	8. Hold out hand
9. Push car	9. Touch cheek
10. Touch your knee	10. Rub knee with washcloth
11. Fold your arms	
12. Lift block	
13. Open your mouth	
14. Blow on feather	
15. Hold out scissors	
16. Fold hands	
17. Put on glove	
18. Wave your hand	
19. Rub cheek with washcloth	
20. Point to ear	
21. Point to shoe	
22. Point to nose	
23. Nod your head "yes"	
24. Shake your head "no"	
25. Stick out tongue	

Figure 3. Training and generalization items for the subject reported by Striefel and Wetherby (1973).

steps taken from a predetermined task analysis for teaching each instruction. Additional procedures included interspersing all trained instructions with other learned instructions to ensure that each item was learned. Generalization items were interspersed throughout the training of instructions, with these probes, similar to the Whitman et al. (1971) procedures, unreinforced.

Unlike the findings of Whitman et al. (1971), Striefel and Wetherby (1973) found that, although the subject acquired the training instructions when they were taught, the subject did not exhibit correct responding to the generalization items. Rather, Striefel and Wetherby found that "the subject always performed the behavior that had been associated with the noun during training, regardless of the action specified by the verb in the generalization item" (p. 669). That is, when presented with the generalization item, *push block,* which was a recombination of the trained instructions, *lift block* and *push car*, the subject would lift the block. This finding indicated that the subject had learned to perform specific responses to specific commands and that he could not generalize the use of components from any two instructions to a new instruction containing these components.

This hypothesis was further supported by additional data collected by Striefel and Wetherby (1973). After training was accomplished, the subject was provided with a series of "instructions" that presented portions of the original instructions or those instructions in a different order. Results of this probing indicated that specific portions of a trained instruction, but not the whole instruction, controlled an appropriate response. For example, when presented with *drop* or *ball,* as components of the trained instruction, *drop ball*, the subject may have provided no response for the verb and performed the total behavior of dropping the ball when presented with the noun.

Realizing the need to replicate Striefel and Wetherby's (1973) findings, Striefel, Bryan, and Aikins (1974) systematically replicated the former author's general procedures with three other severely retarded children. This experiment was identical to Striefel and Wetherby's (1973) in all areas except in the use of a transfer of stimulus-control training procedure that used time-delay principles (Touchette, 1971). The essence of this technique, in contrast to the fading and shaping procedure, is to take advantage of a subject's ability to imitate an experimenter model of a behavior. Then, after a particular behavior is modeled and paired with a verbal instruction depicting this activity, the instruction is presented slightly before the experimenter models the behavior. Gradually, over trials, this delay between presentation of the instruction and a model is increased to the point that the subject eventually (and usually) will transfer stimulus control of the imitative response from the experimenter's model to the spoken instruction. An advantage a time-delay procedure has over a fading procedure for establishing compliance to verbal instructions seems to be the ease with which it can be implemented, and the degree to which it avoids the need to develop a task analysis for each instruction.

Similar to Striefel and Wetherby's (1973) findings, Striefel et al. (1974) found that, although training procedures were responsible for subject compliance to instructions trained directly, generalization items were not performed correctly. Analysis of these incorrect responses by Striefel et al. also revealed error patterns identical to those reported by Striefel and Wetherby (1973).

Together, the findings of Striefel and Wetherby (1973) and Striefel et al. (1974) suggest that the Whitman et al. (1971) findings of generalized responding to new instructions were an artifact of their subject selection procedures and that generalized instruction-following behavior is not an automatic result of teaching a severely retarded child to follow a set of instructions. In fact, considering that Striefel and Wetherby taught more than twice as many instructions as Whitman et al. and still did not obtain generalized instruction following, one is compelled to conclude that it is not *how many* instructions one trains that determines generalization but *how* one trains these skills that determines the development of such a repertoire.

Development of Generalized Instruction-Following Skills

This issue of how to establish generalized instruction-following skills was addressed by Striefel, Wetherby, and Karlan (1976) using training procedures that can be described within a miniature linguistic system framework. These authors used the transfer of a stimulus-control procedure developed by Striefel et al. (1974) to establish generalized verb-noun instruction-following skills in two severely retarded children. Characteristic of a miniature linguistic system approach to language, their procedures relied on the repetition of specific instructions within each language class with members from another class to establish a generalized repertoire of language skills.

Striefel et al. (1976) taught each child to respond with a specific motor action to each named object when a verb-noun instruction was provided. Once this training occurred for the first verb with each noun, the subjects received training on the next verb with each noun, and so on for each verb. Throughout training, to ensure that the subjects learned to respond to both aspects of the verb-noun instructions, each learned instruction was intermixed with previously learned items. This forced the subject to pay attention to both components of the verbal instructions, a prerequisite the authors felt necessary for establishing generalized instruction following.

The hypothesis of the Striefel et al. (1976) experiment was that the training sequence used may be an appropriate one for establishing generalized instruction-following skills with severely retarded children. To measure adequately the occurrence of this potential finding, the authors incorporated a multiple baseline design across each verbal instruction. This design consists of probing each verbal instruction over time while a specific verbal instruction is being trained. Thus, if the manner in which the instructions are being trained is the critical variable for establishing generalized instruction following, the exact point at which generalized responding occurs should be pinpointed with the multiple baseline design. To ensure that this indeed was the case, Striefel et al. (1976) reinforced all correct responses (i.e., training item or probe) throughout the study to encourage the subjects to respond correctly at all times and to avoid the potential discrimination of probe items. A reinforced baseline was also conducted before training to ensure that the majority of instructions incorporated within the matrix were not previously learned.

The paradigm and results for the Striefel et al. (1976) experiment are shown for each subject in Figures 4 and 5. Combinations of 12 verbs and 12 nouns were used, for a total of 144 instructions. After the verbs and nouns had been trained to occur with each other for a small percentage of the total number of instructions, results indicated that the remaining instructions for both subjects were responded to correctly without direct training. Specifically, Subject 1 responded to 113 of the 144 instructions correctly without training (78%), while Subject 2 responded to 82 of 132 instructions correctly (62%). A smaller number of total instructions was reported for the second subjects because this individual demonstrated knowledge of one verb with each of the nouns before training of this verb occurred.

The finding of a large percentage of generalized (or untrained) responding in the Striefel et al. (1976) experiment contrasts markedly with the previous findings of Striefel and Wetherby (1973) and Striefel et al. (1974). Striefel et al. remarked on this occurrence and suggested that generalization in their study appeared "to reflect the relative significance of current training procedures" (p. 258). Put another way, their findings indicate that the manner in which specific verb-noun instructions are taught is the ultimate determinant of whether generalized responding can be obtained and that training procedures that do not take such factors into account will result in a lack of generalization.

A point should be made about the type of generalization obtained in the Striefel et al. (1976) experiment. Specifically, the generalization obtained is a form distinguishable from primary stimulus generalization. A primary-stimulus generalization analysis of generalized responding specifies that a new or novel response can be operationally defined as the

Noun

	1	2	3	4	5	6	7	8	9	10	11	12
A	T	T	T	T	T	G	G	G	G	G	G	G
B	T	T	T	T	T	T	T	T	T	T	G	G
C	T	T	T	G	G	G	G	G	G	G	G	G
D	T	T	T	G	G	G	G	G	G	G	G	G
E	T	T	G	G	G	G	G	G	G	G	G	G
F	T	G	G	G	G	G	G	G	G	G	G	G
G	T	T	G	G	G	G	G	G	G	G	G	G
H	T	G	G	G	G	G	G	G	G	G	G	G
I	T	G	G	G	G	G	G	G	G	G	G	G
J	T	G	G	G	G	G	G	G	G	G	G	G
K	T	G	G	G	G	G	G	G	G	G	G	G
L	T	G	G	G	G	G	G	G	G	G	G	G

Verb (vertical label at left)

Figure 4. Paradigm and results for Striefel, Wetherby, and Karlan's (1976) first subject. Instructions indicated by "T" were trained (see text for details), while those indicated by "G" were responded to correctly without direct training.

production of an already learned response to a stimulus that is physically similar, but not identical, to the discriminative stimulus originally taught to control the production of this response (e.g., Miller, 1951). Defined as such, generalization of the use of a word would be governed by the physical similarity a particular stimulus demonstrated with the original discriminative stimulus. Previous research has already determined that the closer a stimulus resembles the original discriminative stimulus or standard, the higher the probability that the conditioned stimulus will also control the response.

The generalization obtained in the Striefel et al. (1976) experiment, on the other hand, is different from primary stimulus generalization because the factors that determine its occurrence are based upon a different set of principles; that is, transfer in this situation is based upon a response being provided to the same stimulus, with a generalized response simply being one for which appropriate responses are sequenced to a new combination of two stimuli. Consequently, the exact response that is conditioned to occur in the presence of a particular stimulus is not produced to a new stimulus that is physically similar but, rather, with a different stimulus that also controls the production of a particular response. Thus, generalization in the Striefel et al. (1976) experiment is best described as a "combinative" form of generalization to distinguish

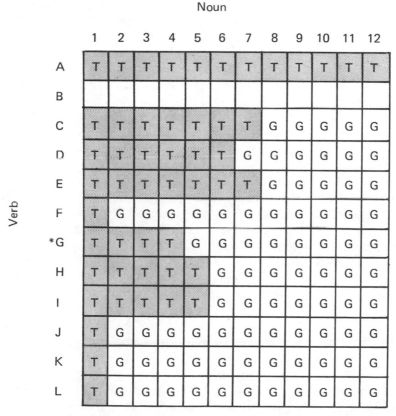

Figure 5.   Paradigm and results for Striefel, Wetherby, and Karlan's (1976) second subject. Instructions indicated by "T" were trained (see text for details), while those indicated by "G" were responded to correctly without direct training. The asterisk signifies the point at which a new trainer started to work with this subject, while the spaces for Verb B indicate that these instructions were performed correctly during the initial baseline.

it from the primary-stimulus generalization form of generalized responding.

The above analysis of a combinative form of generalization in the Striefel et al. (1976) experiment does not preclude the occurrence of primary stimulus generalization in language. One can determine easily that, although a specific stimulus controls a specific response in the combinative generalization situation and although these stimuli can be combined with other stimuli controlling different responses, the ultimate use of specific words in combination with each other will be determined by the stimuli present. Thus, to the degree that various environmental stimuli controlling the production of a specific response differ from one another, the occurrence of a specific labeling response across all these stimuli can only be made as a function of primary stimulus generalization. Together, however, primary stimulus generalization processes and a combinative form of generalization seem to account for the realm of generalized responding contained in the miniature linguistic system.

One question that can be raised about the miniature linguistic system training procedure developed by Striefel et al. (1976) concerns the degree to which the generalized skill developed while learning the system can be extended to new verbs and/or nouns not originally taught within this context; that is, one may ask whether, upon learning a new set of verbs and nouns, the use of these language constituents can be combined with those constituents already trained.

This question was addressed by Striefel, Wetherby, and Karlan (1978) in their monograph exploring the development of generalized instruction-following skills in severely retarded individuals as a function of miniature linguistic system learning. Two studies were reported that explored the generalization of new exemplars within a class to previously trained members from a second class, with both studies assessing the degree of generalization exhibited when one new component is added. The first study explored the generalization that occurred when the names of new objects were learned in isolation and then combined with previously trained verbs, and the second study explored the generalization of newly acquired verbs with instructions using previously trained nouns. The paradigm is shown in Figure 6.

Subjects in the first experiment were Subject 1 from the Striefel et al. (1976) experiment and two additional severely retarded adolescents, who had previously been taught a generalized 12 (verb) × 12 (noun) instruction-following skill by the authors. The training procedures (described previously) included the use of a time-delay transfer of stimulus-control procedure. Six verbs, taken from each subject's list of previously learned verb-noun instructions, were combined sequentially with 14 new nouns that could be broken down into one of three types.

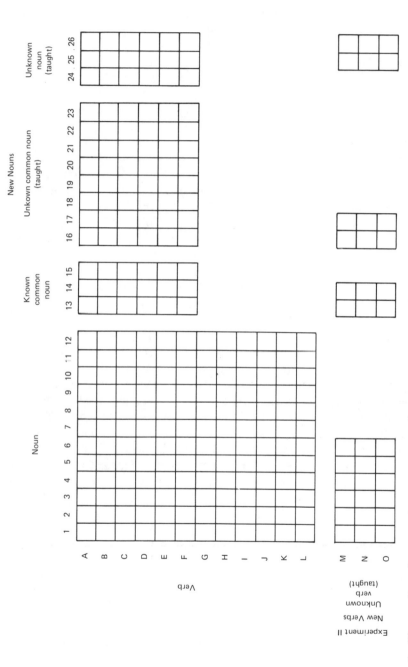

Figure 6. The paradigm of two experiments (see Striefel, Wetherby, and Karlan, 1978) designed to explore the generalization of previously trained verb and noun components to newly trained verbs and nouns.

The first type of noun assessed for generalization to previously known verbs was that which the subject already knew. Knowledge of these nouns was assessed by asking the subject to point to a particular item from a set of common nouns most likely in the subject's repertoire already. Three nouns of the first type were selected for combination with previously learned verbs. The second type of noun assessed for old verb–new noun generalization was a common object, but one for which the subject did not know the referent until it was taught by the experimenter. Thus, in this situation, eight objects were selected for labeling one at a time, and then combined with previously known verbs as each was learned. The third type of noun was also unknown to the subject before labeling and subsequent generalization assessment but was not a common noun. Rather, physical referents for these nouns were random shapes cut from $1/4$-inch Masonite. The three objects of this kind were labeled with nonsense names similar to those used in Berko's (1958) experiment investigating grammatical rule usage in children.

Results of this first experiment indicated that all three subjects were readily able to extend the use of previously trained verbs to the majority of 14 nouns not originally trained in combination with these verbs. These findings indicated that subjects who have been trained to develop a generalized verb-noun instruction-following skill with miniature linguistic system or matrix-training procedures can extend the use of previously trained verbs to other known or trained nouns with relative ease.

A second study by Striefel et al. (1978) was designed to determine if newly trained verbs would generalize to previously trained nouns. Four adolescents, the three from the previous study and one other severely retarded individual, who also had been taught a generalized verb-noun instruction-following skill, served as subjects. In short, training procedures consisted of teaching the subjects to respond to verb labels with an action not previously part of their instruction-following repertoire. This training was accomplished by instructing the subject to perform a designated action (verb) without specifying a noun referent. Four arbitrary Masonite shapes were used at random as training referents for each verb. These referents were not similar to those trained as objects in the previous experiment. A multiple baseline design was used to demonstrate the acquisition of each verb as it was trained. Twelve previously trained nouns were used to assess generalization after each verb was learned: six from the original verb-noun repertoire each subject had learned, and two from each of the three portions of the previous experiment. Because one individual had not participated in the previously cited experiment, only six nouns were used to assess verb generalization with this subject.

Generalization results for the newly acquired verbs indicated that three of the four subjects readily extended their use to previously trained nouns; that is, these subjects were able to perform actions acquired with nonspecified referents with other nouns the subject already had in his repertoire. For the remaining subject, generalization of newly acquired verbs did not occur until the first verb was trained directly to occur with one of the nouns. Even after this point, however, the subject did not generalize as extensively as the three other subjects.

Overall, the results of this study systematically replicate the results of the previous experiment by indicating that the use of newly trained verbs may generalize to previously trained nouns just as new nouns may generalize to previously trained verbs. Together, such findings indicate that language-deficient individuals can be taught skills that will enable them to add newly acquired words about the nature of the environment to previously existing language repertoires. As summarized in Figure 6 for the above two experiments, severely retarded subjects can be taught to generalize the use of components of a previously acquired verb-noun instruction-following skill to new components acquired within a different context. These data suggest that subjects trained to generalize responding to a matrix of 12 verb $\times$ 12 noun verbal instructions can extend the use of either constituent to new members of the other class rather easily.

The results of the above two studies reported by Striefel et al. (1978) indicated that the components of an established verb-noun instruction-following skill can be extended readily to include additional verbs and nouns that are trained in isolation (i.e., outside of the verb-noun context). These findings imply that matrix-training procedures may be incorporated to develop generalized language responding beyond that which is trained directly. The type of generalization exhibited in the previous two experiments, however, was between one previously learned component and one newly acquired component. One may question whether the generalization obtained would occur if two new components were added to a subject's repertoire at the same time.

This question was addressed in a third study by Striefel et al. (1978) using a diagonal training approach across a four verb $\times$ four noun training matrix that incorporated all new stimuli. This paradigm is shown in Figure 7. The items marked T_1–T_4 were trained initially. The assumption behind training on the diagonal in this particular study was that, if subjects had acquired a purely generalized strategy for dealing with new instances of verb and noun classes, they then would be able to generalize to the remaining 12 boxes in the matrix on the basis of the minimal information provided by training on the diagonal; that is, after having learned the four items shown, theoretically the subject has received all the information

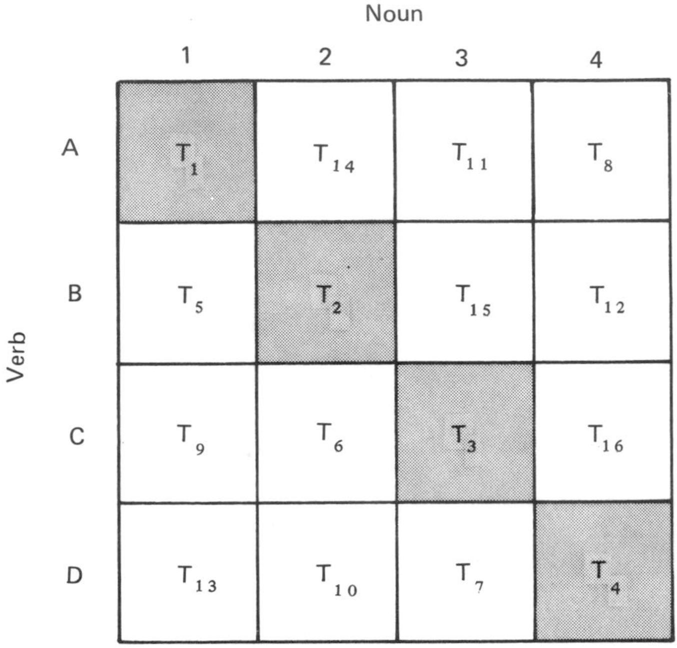

Noun

	1	2	3	4
A	T_1	T_{14}	T_{11}	T_8
B	T_5	T_2	T_{15}	T_{12}
C	T_9	T_6	T_3	T_{16}
D	T_{13}	T_{10}	T_7	T_4

Verb

Figure 7. Diagonal verb-noun training strategy.

necessary to perform the rest of the matrix, and, if previous verb-noun training has suggested that there are verb and noun components to a verbal instruction, the subject should be able to respond appropriately to the remaining combinations of these components.

Three severely retarded adolescents were selected as subjects. As in the previous two experiments, all subjects had been taught previously to respond with a generalized skill to combinations of instructions incorporating 12 verbs and 12 nouns (Striefel et al. 1976, 1978). Procedures consisted of training the verb-noun combinations in the order shown, with a multiple baseline design incorporated to determine the occurrence of generalization to the as-yet-untrained instructions and the effectiveness of training procedures. As mentioned, if the three subjects had acquired a maximal instruction-following skill, they should have been able to generalize their responding to the full matrix after having been trained to follow the first four instructions.

Results indicated, to the general surprise of Striefel et al. (1978), that Subjects 1, 2, and 3 needed to be trained on 6, 11, and 12 verb-noun instructions, respectively, before generalization occurred to the remaining instructions. This finding suggested that the subjects had not learned a generalizable skill in their previous verb-noun training that would enable them to respond to new instances of verbs and nouns together. An explanation of these findings seemed warranted.

In a subsequent review of miniature linguistic system research, Wetherby (1978) found one other study that required the differential response to two different dimensions of stimuli while training along the diagonal. This study (Foss, 1968) indicated that the Striefel et al. (1978) finding of minimal generalization while training along the diagonal may not be so strange, and that an additional training strategy may have to be incorporated to facilitate generalization with a minimal amount of training. Specifically, Foss (1968) found that adults, who have already established repertoires of generalized language, did not generalize when required to learn a miniature linguistic system by exposure to the diagonal items. He found, in contrast, that a stepwise training strategy, or one in which an item from one dimension is trained with two from the second before proceeding to the second item in the first dimension, was the most efficient training sequence for producing generalized responding. This strategy, shown in Figure 8, suggests that training procedures incorporating a stepwise or overlap function should be used to establish generalized responding to verb-noun components that are both new.

This implication was addressed in a fourth study reported by Striefel et al. (1978). Two severely retarded adolescents were incorporated as subjects. Subject 1 had acquired a generalized instruction-following skill previously, and Subject 2 had not worked with the current experimenters previously. Similar to the procedures reported in the previous experiment, subjects were presented with a specified training sequence, and generalized responding to the remainder of the matrix was monitored with a multiple baseline design across instructions. The general training sequence is shown in Figure 8. The first subject was trained on a three verb × four noun matrix, while the second subject received training on a 12 verb × 12 noun matrix.

Results of the experiment, incorporating a stepwise training strategy across the verb-noun matrix, revealed that both subjects demonstrated generalized responding to the majority of items in the matrix with the minimal amount of training this strategy requires. These findings suggest

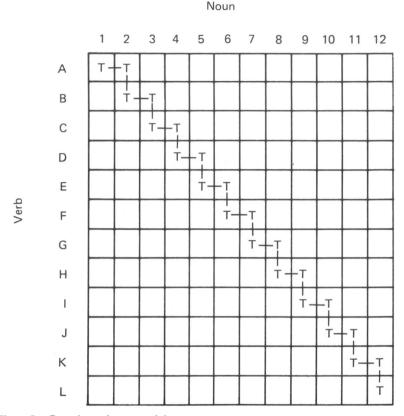

Figure 8.   Stepwise verb-noun training strategy.

that the lack of generalized responding reported in the previous experiment with the diagonal training strategy need not occur, and that a matrix-training strategy that introduces new verb and noun components in a stepwise fashion may be more efficient for established generalized instruction-following skills. These results also indicate that such a strategy may even be a more appropriate training strategy than the matrix-training procedures originally developed by Striefel et al. (1976).

What could account for the difference in exhibited verb-noun generalization between the diagonal and stepwise training strategies? It appears that the manner in which the verb-noun information is introduced in the two respective strategies is what is responsible for the different generalization effects. Specifically, in the diagonal approach, it appears that, although the subject is presented with potential information to provide a correct verb-noun response, the subject is not forced to discriminate and respond differentially to both components of the instruction in order to respond correctly; that is, like the subjects in the Striefel and Wetherby (1973) and Striefel, Bryan, and Aikins (1974) experiments, a subject confronted with this training strategy may focus upon either the verb or the noun and still perform the terminal response specified (theoretically) by both components.

On the other hand, the subject who is presented with the stepwise training strategy across verb-noun instructions is required, upon the addition of each instruction, to discriminate and respond differentially to each component of the instruction. This strategy seems to take advantage of the basic parameter of generalized language within a miniature linguistic system—overlap of the components—in order to facilitate the development of such a skill. The degree to which such a training strategy may be incorporated to develop generalized instruction-following skills in severely retarded children is unknown at this time, and would seem to warrant additional study.

A word of caution before interpreting the results of the Striefel et al. (1978) fourth experiment as suggesting that a stepwise training strategy may be more efficient for developing generalized verb-noun instruction-following skill than the procedures developed by Striefel et al. (1976). Although Striefel et al. (1978) results suggest that a subject, who does not know the training instructions, can be taught a generalized instruction-following skill with a stepwise training procedure, *it is not known whether such a procedure would work with individuals who do not know how to follow any instructions*. That is, Foss (1968) reported his findings of generalization with a stepwise training strategy using normal adults as subjects. There is no doubt that these subjects have a long history of putting language constituents together. By the same token, the language history of one of the two subjects in the Striefel et al. (1978) fourth experiment included participation in previous studies by these authors concerned with establishing generalized instruction following. In this light, and because it was virtually impossible to determine what, if any, instructions the second subject (who had not previously participated) may have known before the stepwise training was implemented, it would be safe to conclude that, until future research can examine the relationship between prior language learning and the use of a stepwise training strategy, one should use (or be prepared to revert to) matrix-training procedures similar to those reported by Striefel et al. (1976) to establish instruction-following skills in individuals suspected to be lacking in this area.

Development of More Complex Generalized Instruction-Following Skills

Up to this point, various experiments conducted by the authors and associates (Striefel et al., 1976, 1978) have focused on the develop-

ment of generalized verb-noun instruction-following skills using miniature linguistic system or matrix-training procedures. These experiments
have indicated that severely retarded children can be taught generalized
receptive language skills by training in an orderly and systematic fashion,
and that such skills may even be accomplished more efficiently if care is
taken to force the subject to discriminate and differentially respond to
each new component of a verbal instruction. Additional results have indicated that the use of a generalized verb-noun instruction-following skill
may be extended to new verb or noun components not originally trained
within the verb-noun context. These results indicate that severely and
profoundly retarded individuals can be trained to approximate the receptive language skills of normal individuals.

Despite the gains shown by these individuals, the acquisition of a
generalized verb-noun instruction-following repertoire represents but a
small portion of the instructions potentially available. If language-deficient individuals are to better approximate the language of normal individuals, additional instruction-following skills need to be acquired. The
form of this additional training may be the establishment of a greater
two-word receptive vocabulary, or it may be an increase in the syntactic
complexity of the provided instructions.

One way to increase the syntactic complexity of instructions taught
to severely retarded individuals is to add an adjectival component to
those skills already learned. As adjectives refer to characteristics of a
noun, the establishment of a generalized verb-adjective-noun instruction-
following repertoire would be a logical next step in increasing the
syntactic complexity of a receptive language. The training of such a
repertoire would also provide an enlarged arena for testing the adequacy
of miniature linguistic system or matrix-training procedures for establishing generalized language in language-deficient individuals.

Striefel et al. (1978) reported an experiment designed to establish
generalized verb-adjective-noun skills in retarded children. This study
attempted to establish color adjective usage within a verb-adjective-noun
context, and also attempted to assess the degree of generalization
obtained. A review of this study would seem to be useful for understanding the framework from which a miniature linguistic system or matrix-
training procedure may approach the remediation of language deficiencies.

The Striefel et al. (1978) experiment had some basic characteristics. First, it attempted to establish verb-adjective-noun instruction-
following skills in severely retarded adolescents who either 1) had been
trained previously to follow verb-noun skills in a generalized manner, or
2) had possessed these skills without having been trained by the current
authors. Second, original training procedures consisted of attempts to

train the verb-adjective-noun skill by specifying the total response chain; that is, a subject who did not know colors was instructed, for example, to *push white car*, and was expected to pick up proper adjective usage within this context. Third, the experiment used the time-delay transfer of stimulus-control procedure described previously (Striefel et al., 1974) and also incorporated a multiple baseline design across all or part of a representative sample of the total number of instructions in order to determine the point of generalization and the efficacy of current training procedures. Finally, the experiment made variations in the original training procedure in order to facilitate the acquisition of a generalized verb-adjective-noun instruction-following skill.

As mentioned, Striefel et al. (1978) attempted to establish verb-adjective(color)-noun instruction-following skills. The four subjects in this experiment were presented with the task of learning a subset of an eight verb × eight adjective × eight noun matrix of instructions and probed for generalization to the remaining items. As shown in Figure 9, there was a total of 512 instructions, of which 148 were trained directly. Because 512 instructions would present a difficult monitoring problem for the multiple baseline design, a representative sample of the total number of instructions was designated as the items to be probed. This modification allowed the experimenters to probe at least one instance of each verb, adjective, and noun every few days and, consequently, to better monitor the development of the subject's generalized instruction-following skill. The multiple baseline probes are shown by circles in Figure 9.

Results of this first attempt to train verb-adjective-noun instructions with four severely retarded children indicated that only one subject was able to acquire the use of color adjectives within the verb-adjective-noun context. This subject, who had learned to perform the verb-noun components of the three-word instructions outside of the Striefel et al. (1978) laboratory, acquired and generalized the use of three colors to the instructions that were probed, and demonstrated a generalized knowledge of three other colors before these instructions were trained by the experimenters. The remaining two instructions were not accounted for because the subject was removed from the hospital for an extended home leave. In contrast, results for the three remaining subjects indicated that these individuals had an extremely difficult time learning to respond differentially to the adjectives specified; that is, these three subjects were unable to respond differentially to instructions containing either the first or second color, with their performance at about chance level.

Striefel et al. (1978) interpreted these results to indicate that it may be very difficult to establish an adjective component between an already existing verb-noun skill, and that procedures that teach adjec-

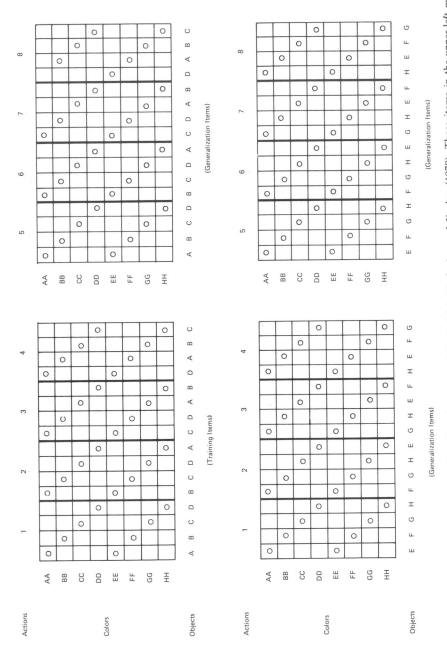

Figure 9.   The 512 verb-adjective-noun combinations incorporated by Striefel, Wetherby, and Karlan (1978). Those items in the upper-left matrix were trained, with the remaining items assessed for generalization.

tives in isolation may have to be used to establish verb-adjective-noun skills. The Striefel et al. rationale for this conclusion was based on their conceptualization that a progressive receptive grammar could be seen as chunked or sequential phenomena and that an effort to teach such a receptive skill should attempt to start at either end of the chain, but not in the middle. To test this hypotheses, Striefel et al. (1978) designed a second experiment in which the adjective component was taught alone and the use of this adjective was probed with verb-adjective, adjective-noun, and verb-adjective-noun instructions.

Procedures for this study consisted of training the adjectives with the time-delay transfer of stimulus-control procedure. One obvious difference between the current training procedures and those reported by the previous attempt to teach adjectives, besides the fact that only one word (the color adjective) was specified, was that the object the experimenter used to model the adjective was *different* from that responded to by the subject. This modification was made in order to help encourage the subject to focus upon color as the relevant dimension. Similar to the previous experiment, all probe items were conducted after each color adjective was taught.

Results of the Striefel et al. (1978) attempt to establish verb-adjective-noun instruction-following skills, by teaching the color adjectives alone with previously learned nouns as referents, indicated that only one subject was able to acquire adjective usage within this context. The use of these adjectives, however, in the form of verb-adjective, adjective-noun, and verb-adjective-noun generalization was minimal. Results for the remaining two subjects indicated a general lack of progress in performing the conditional discrimination required between the first two trained colors.

The lack of acquisition and/or generalization obtained by teaching adjectives alone with previously learned objects as referents was puzzling. Striefel et al. (1978) speculated that, although training adjectives alone should have focused the subject's attention upon color as a relevant cue, something about the manner in which the adjectives were trained may have interfered with the acquisition of color words. For example, when the experimenter says *red* and then touches a red object for which the subject already has a label in his repertoire (e.g., ball), the subject may have thought that the experimenter was interested in relabeling the object. Consequently, the inability of the subjects to acquire and/or generalize the use of receptive color adjectives may have been due to their failure to focus upon color as the correct stimulus dimension. This potential finding suggested to the authors that future attempts to teach receptive color adjectives in isolation should take advantage of a subject's ability to attach receptive words to shape as a physical dimension in order to establish differential responding to color.

This suggestion was addressed in a third study designed to establish verb-adjective-noun instruction-following skills in the two remaining severely retarded adolescents. The training and generalization probing procedures were similar to those reported in the previous experiment, except that stimuli the subject had not been previously required to identify were used as the training stimuli. In addition, one characteristic of these stimuli was that they were made out of paper, and, as such, were readily modifiable. Procedures consisted of teaching the two remaining subjects who had not acquired color adjective usage to respond to an object of one shape and color when one label was presented and then to respond to a second color and shape item when a second label was heard. After these differential responses were established, stimulus control over responding was shifted to the color characteristic of these items by fading the physical differences between these stimuli. Such a fading sequence is shown in Figure 10.

The purpose of the fading sequence was to encourage the subject to respond to a specific color when a specific adjective was spoken by the experimenter. Once such responding was established for each color, the subject was presented with previously learned objects to determine if color identification would occur with these items before generalization probes of verb-adjective, adjective-noun, or verb-adjective-noun instructions were provided.

Results of the Striefel et al. (1978) attempt to teach adjective responding using physical shaping procedures indicated that these procedures were successful with one of the two remaining subjects. Specifically, this subject acquired each of the eight colors in a minimal time, generalized the receptive identification of the colors to objects, and (except for one color) demonstrated substantial generalization to verb-adjective, adjective-noun, and verb-adjective-noun instructions. The final subject, perhaps thoroughly confused by all the procedure changes, did not make it through all of the fading sequence steps, and was subsequently unable to relearn the prefading discrimination.

These results indicated to Striefel et al. (1978) that procedures designed to establish receptive color adjective responding should incorporate objects as training stimuli that the subject has not previously learned or identified. In this manner, one may establish receptive adjective responding with relatively little interference from previously learned skills, and, as shown by one subject's extensive generalization to verb-adjective, adjective-noun, and verb-adjective-noun instructions, may encourage the generalization of color adjectives to larger components of instructions.

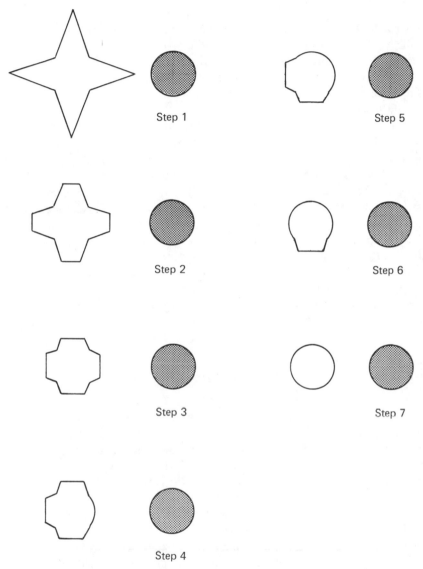

Figure 10. The fading sequence used by Striefel, Wetherby, and Karlan (1978) to teach differential responding to color.

The results of the Striefel et al. (1978) attempt to add an adjective component to the verb-noun instruction-following skills of severely retarded adolescents have indicated that miniature linguistic system or matrix-training procedures may be incorporated in order to establish systematically larger sequences of receptive language skills. Specifically, their results indicate that by training a subset of verb-adjective-noun instructions with each adjective, or by training an adjective in isolation, one may establish generalized verb-adjective-noun instruction-following skills. Because the parameters of this generalized responding are not completely known, the exploration of training procedures designed to facilitate the development of larger sequences of generalized language would seem to warrant additional study.

Overall, the research conducted by Striefel and Wetherby (1973), and Striefel et al. (1974, 1976, 1978) suggests that the development of generalized instruction following is not an automatic outcome of teaching a language-deficient individual to follow a number of instructions. Rather, their research has determined that the systematic teaching of a smaller number of instructions may facilitate the development and generalization of instruction-following behavior. As a subcomponent of a larger repertoire of behavior that we call receptive language, the successful development of a generalized instruction-following skill in severely retarded adolescents suggests that they can be taught to approximate the receptive language capabilities of normal individuals. However, the extent to which such intervention strategies will prove successful for the majority of receptive language deficiencies remains to be studied.

DEVELOPMENT OF
GENERALIZED PRODUCTIVE LANGUAGE SKILLS

A second general repertoire of verbal behavior that may be addressed by miniature linguistic system or matrix-training procedures is productive language. This repertoire of behavior, like the development of receptive language skills, is very functional for survival. Factors involved in productive language have also been of interest to a large number of experimenters (see Garcia and DeHaven, 1974; Harris, 1975).

Wetherby (1978) has reviewed a number of productive language studies, some of which were taken from nonremediational literatures, and has suggested that a large portion of these experiments can be analyzed within a miniature linguistic system framework. As such, Wetherby suggested the implications of the procedures held in common by these studies may be addressed for establishing generalized productive language in language-deficient individuals. What follows is a short review of three studies that have dealt with the establishment of generalized productive language skills from a miniature linguistic system or matrix-training framework.

One of the first experiments to address the systematic development of functional productive language was conducted by Guess et al. (1968). These experimenters, using imitation and reinforcement procedures, taught a severely retarded and nonverbal child the productive use of the plural morpheme. The Guess et al. (1968) paradigm and results are shown in Figure 11. By systematically teaching the retarded child to produce the correct singular label for a single instance of a corresponding object, and by establishing the correct label plus the plural morpheme ending /s/ when two objects were present, Guess et al. demonstrated that additional pairs of objects the subject knew would be pluralized correctly without direct training. This finding suggested to the authors that the subject had developed a language performance that could be characterized as "generative" in nature, and that such procedures may be used to remediate the productive language deficiencies of retarded children. Guess et al. (1968) supported this latter conclusion by demonstrating that the subject's use of the productive plural morpheme could be changed by reversing the reinforcement contingencies.

A second study using procedures similar to those advocated by a miniature linguistic system or matrix-training approach to the remediation of language deficiencies was conducted by Lutzker and Sherman (1974). In contrast to the previous study, Lutzker and Sherman (1974) taught the generalized use of two-sentence forms corresponding to correct subject-verb agreement with three moderately retarded and two normal, preschool-age children. Their paradigm and results can be conceptualized as shown in Figure 12. These authors used reinforcement and imitation procedures to teach a basic class of sentences, and then incorporated a multiple baseline design to determine the generalization of trained sentence forms to untrained combinations of pictures depicting a particular action by one or two people, animals, or things. Lutzker and

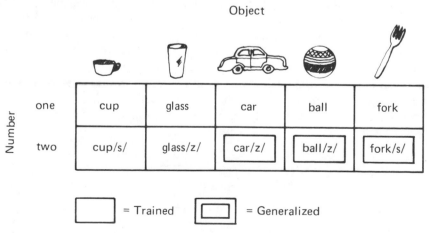

Figure 11.   The matrix paradigm of Guess et al. (1968).

Picture

picture of _____ running   picture of _____ sailing   picture of _____ riding

•	The boy is running	The boat is sailing	The bear is riding
• •	The boys are running	The boats are sailing	The bears are riding

Number

Figure 12.   The matrix paradigm of Lutzker and Sherman (1974).

Sherman (1974) found that, as a function of training, the subjects learned to respond with appropriate sentences to corresponding pictures, and that they eventually produced these responses without the need for training. Overall, the results of Lutzker and Sherman indicate that miniature linguistic system or matrix-training procedures can be used to establish generalized sentence usage in language-handicapped or normal preschool children.

A third and final example of a language-training experiment that used miniature linguistic system or matrix-training principles was conducted by Schumaker and Sherman (1970). These investigators were also interested in the appropriate development of verb tense, and they designed an experiment to demonstrate the acquisition and generalization of the verb endings /ed/ and /ing/. Using imitation and reinforcement procedures, Schumaker and Sherman (1970) taught three institutionalized retarded children the task shown in Figure 13. In short, similar to the findings reported by Guess et al. (1968), by Lutzker and Sherman (1974), and by others using the miniature linguistic system or matrix-training paradigm (see Wetherby, 1978), Schumaker and Sherman (1970) found that, as training progressed for each ending across a number of verbs, the subjects eventually generalized the use of the verb endings appropriately to instances of new verbs. The authors concluded that their procedures were responsible for this development.

However, Schumaker and Sherman (1970) were quick to point out that, although their subjects behaved in a generalized manner that was consistent with that obtained for the use of verb inflections in the normal

	paint	skate	smile	play
Now the man is _____ ing. Yesterday he _____ .	painted	skated	smiled	played
Yesterday the man _____ ed. Now he is _____ .	painting	skating	smiling	playing

Figure 13.   The matrix paradigm of Schumaker and Sherman (1970).

environment, "the verb inflections were taught in response to verbal cues ('Now' and 'Yesterday'), not in response to temporal cues" (p. 286), which would have been required and natural in a normal language environment. Nevertheless, despite the natural handicaps that experimental investigations like Schumaker and Sherman's must address, their results greatly advance our understanding of what parameters are involved in the development of generalized speech and language in language-deficient individuals.

Combined, the results of Guess et al. (1968), Lutzker and Sherman (1974), and Schumaker and Sherman (1970) serve to indicate that productive language repertoires may be developed systematically using miniature linguistic system or matrix-training procedures, and that such procedures may be used to remediate the productive language handicaps of language-deficient individuals. These results also systematically replicate the findings of research conducted by Striefel et al. (1976, 1978) and suggest that similar processes are involved in the development of generalized behavior within both productive and receptive language repertoires.

At this point, a general listing and discussion of the basic parameters of the miniature linguistic system or matrix-training approach to developing generalized language is appropriate for those interested in establishing such behavior in the receptive and productive communication repertoires of language-deficient individuals.

TRAINING PRINCIPLES INVOLVED IN ESTABLISHING GENERALIZED LANGUAGE WITH MATRIX-TRAINING PROCEDURES

As reflected in Figure 1, the basis of current experiments addressed to the remediation of receptive and productive language deficiencies has been the miniature linguistic system. The basic parameters of the miniature linguistic system include the differential labeling or response to instances of discriminative stimuli that can be broken down along at least two dimensions, the combinations of which constitute the language system to be learned. Subsequently, as a function of training on a subset of these items, a subject exposed to learning the miniature linguistic system will demonstrate a high probability of exhibiting generalized and appropriate sequences of responses corresponding to the stimulus combinations present. The end result of learning such a system is an individual who exhibits appropriate, novel, and rule-governed behavior in line with the language system to be learned.

Wetherby (1978) has suggested that the miniature linguistic system has some important implications for those interested in conceptualizing and providing an experimental or functional analysis of language. By the same token, the current authors have attempted to demonstrate in this chapter how the miniature linguistic system can be used for the remediation of receptive or productive language deficiencies. The matrix-training approach for the remediation of language deficiency through the development of generalized language has some specific implications for those interested in language remediation. These implications can be broken down into nine general categories of what one must do in order to train or establish generalized language.

1. *Emphasize repetition by training a matrix.*   The first thing one must do to encourage generalized language is to ensure that each class of potential response (e.g., adjectives, verbs, nouns) is taught so items from each class occur many times in combination with items from the other class or classes during training. The result of this procedure should be a subject who learns: 1) the referent for each item in each class, 2) that particular items from a class may occur with items from other classes, and 3) that a specified response sequence is required.

2. *Teach each language class until generalization occurs to new members.*   Training a matrix will not result automatically in generalized language. The only way to ensure that the subject has learned a receptive or productive language is to train combinations of items until the subject begins to respond to untrained items with the same sequence rule that was taught. This criterion should be the functional definition of when one has established a generalized language repertoire. It is of minimal value for an individual to have learned a subset of specific responses without being able to capitalize on what was trained previously by applying it in new situations. As demonstrated by the first two experiments in the Striefel et al. (1978) monograph, the development of a generalized language repertoire should extend to other items not originally trained by the trainer.

3. *Use concurrent training procedures.*   Schroeder and Baer (1972) have suggested that improved verbal imitation scores may be obtained in retarded children if verbal imitation procedures taught more than one imitative response at once rather than in succession. The essence of the argument behind such a procedure is that a subject learns to discriminate differences between each stimulus-response contingency more efficiently, and that untrained stimuli and responses are better discriminated and, consequently, less likely to interfere with learning. The same holds true for the learning of language with miniature linguistic system or matrix-training procedures; that is, the generalization of responses in a matrix-learning situation is dependent upon the discrimination of each verb and noun from other members *within* each of these classes. Unless a subject is required immediately to respond differentially

to each trained item by intermixing this response with those previously trained, the subject will have had little practice at discriminating the conditions for potential responses, and may not respond or generalize appropriately.

4. *Determine the discriminative stimuli for each language response.* One factor that will serve to facilitate the development of generalized language in language-deficient individuals is to be aware of the discriminative stimuli that control each component of a language response; that is, in the miniature linguistic system or matrix-training situation, it is important to determine that each component of a language response is controlled by a specifiable discriminative stimulus (e.g., Shape 1 is *ball*, Shape 2 is *car*, etc.). This is important because such knowledge will allow the trainer to determine whether or not a particular response is appropriate given the stimulus conditions present.

A second reason it is important to determine the discriminative stimuli that control responding is that such knowledge will allow the trainer to determine if what has been trained is significant and/or whether it constitutes a complete language system. To illustrate, Baer and Guess (1973), working from a response class analysis of language, established the use of generalized language in language-deficient individuals using imitation and differential reinforcement techniques. Specifically, as shown in Figure 14, they taught four severely retarded children the generalized use of the noun suffix, /er/. This was demonstrated by the children's acquired ability to label new nouns with the suffix without direct training. As a control, Baer and Guess discontinued differential reinforcement for the noun + /er/ response sequence and initiated training for a noun + /ist/ response sequence. In general, the results indicated that the subjects provided whichever ending was being reinforced and that they

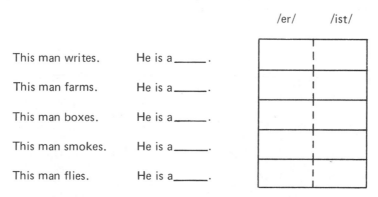

Figure 14.   The matrix paradigm (almost) of Baer and Guess (1973). The dashed line signifies that /er/ and /ist/ were trained in succession and not concurrently.

continued this ending spontaneously with nouns that had never been trained to occur with this particular suffix. Although these results indicate that generalized noun + /suffix/ responding can be established in severely retarded children, as shown by the dotted lines in Figure 14, it is doubtful if the subjects would have retained the use of either ending, because the conditions that call for their appropriate use were never discriminated; that is, the subjects provided either /er/ or /ist/ in response to differential reinforcement, *but not because they discriminated prior discriminative stimuli that signified the appropriate and differential use of these endings.* As indicated by Wetherby (1978), one will need to train at least two dimensions of stimuli that each contain at least two discriminative stimuli requiring differential responses in order to demonstrate the acquisition of a particular linguistic structure.

A third reason why it is important to determine the discriminative stimuli for each language response is that this knowledge will better allow one to determine whether all the components of the language system can be allowed to occur or can be trained together. Not all components of a matrix, especially if the matrix contains utterances larger than two word, require that they should be potentially combinable with each other. For example, Wetherby (1978) has reported that components of a four-word miniature linguistic system that Premack (1970) taught to his chimpanzee, Sarah, were not completely substitutable. Specifically, as shown in Figure 15, Premack found that, given the nature of the direct object in a subject-verb-object-direct object matrix, the particular verb(s) that may be selected for use will vary. Consequently, it is very important to know the discriminative stimuli that control language responding in order to determine what may be a permissible sequence of responses.

5. *Retain all that is trained.*   Related to the need to establish generalized responding is the obvious fact that what generalizes is

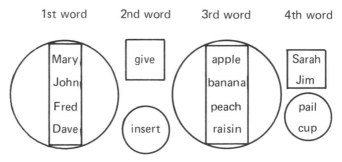

Figure 15.   The substitutable nature of the subcomponents of a larger miniature linguistic system taught to a chimpanzee by Premack (1970).

dependent upon what the subject knows. Thus, if one wishes to establish a generalized language system, all previously learned responses need to be reviewed periodically in order to ensure that the subject will retain a corresponding knowledge of what language generalization rules are being reinforced. It does not help to test a subject for knowledge of a rule that is not being maintained currently.

6. *Determine the extent of the matrix system that is being trained.* Related to the importance of determining what discriminative stimuli control each language response is the induction that one should always be aware of the size and/or extent of the language system being taught. This knowledge should help the therapist to determine: 1) what needs to be reviewed and retained, and 2) what needs to be trained.

7. *Reinforce all correct responses during assessment and training.* A simple point, but one often overlooked by many language trainers and/or experimenters, is the importance of reinforcing all correct language responses during assessment and training conditions. The underlying assumption of all language remediation attempts is that it is reinforcing for one to be able to respond appropriately in the receptive language situation and to produce grammatically correct utterances in the productive language situation. To fail to provide such reinforcement for a correct language response in any situation is handicapping to the individual being trained because the individual may discriminate the conditions of nonreinforcement and, consequently, not demonstrate what he already knows. For example, Whitman, Zakaras, and Chardos (1971), discussed earlier, reported the development of generalized instruction following, whereas Striefel and Wetherby (1973), using essentially the same training procedures, did not. This difference can be accounted for reasonably by the differences in initial language-assessment procedures (i.e., Striefel and Wetherby used a reinforced initial baseline while Whitman et al. did not).

The above discussion, however, is not meant to detract from the importance of providing an intermittent schedule of reinforcement, which suggests that any response will be more resistant to extinction if it is not reinforced every time it is presented. Rather, the point is that reinforcing all acquired language repertoires will serve: 1) to encourage the subject to perform what he knows, 2) to avoid unnecessary training, and 3) to facilitate the generalization of language. An intermittent schedule of reinforcement is best used to maintain the use of an already established language repertoire.

8. *Use systematic training procedures to establish individual stimulus-response relationships.* Language represents the sequential arrangement of at least two responses controlled by a corresponding number of discriminative stimuli. We either produce language or we

respond to it. In either case, however, an initial stimulus-response relationship must be established before this response can be used in a generalized manner with novel arrangements of stimuli. Care must be taken to ensure that systematic and effective procedures are derived through which the trainer may establish stimulus-response relationships with relative ease.

One such method that has worked well for establishing stimulus-response relationships is the time-delay transfer technique. First demonstrated by Touchette (1971) and subsequently adopted by Striefel, Bryan, and Aikins (1974) for teaching receptive language skills, this procedure transfers stimulus control over an imitative response from the modeled response to other (and more appropriate) stimuli in the environment (e.g., words spoken by the trainer). The essence of this procedure is to increase the time delay between the modeled response (as a stimulus) and the presentation of the stimulus for which stimulus control is desired. Used by Striefel et al. (1974) and Striefel et al. (1976, 1978), the procedure has the advantages of being easily adaptable to the language-learning situation and being effective in transferring stimulus control.

Overall, the primary advantage of establishing a systematic stimulus-response training procedure is that it shortens the time spent training language constituents and lengthens the time spent teaching other responses that subsequently will facilitate the development of generalized language. Effective language therapists seek consistent means for facilitating the acquisition of additional response repertoires.

9. *Include different people as part of one stimulus class.*   Directly related to the need for establishing generalized language is the need to include different trainers (i.e., people) as a stimulus class in the training matrix. We do not provide appropriate productive utterances to just a few people. Rather, we speak freely and openly to any individual who becomes a part of the class of people to which we speak. This is not an accident, however. To establish language generalization to other individuals effectively the trainer must include each of these individuals as part of the language matrix. For example, Premack, whose work Wetherby (1978) discussed as an example of how miniature linguistic system or matrix-training procedures could be used to establish generalized language in a chimpanzee, included the names of the trainers as one dimension (i.e., class) of sequenced responses with a stimulus class of objects and their corresponding names. In short, generalization to other individuals is not something that is hoped for; it is something programmed to occur.

The combined use of the above nine recommendations for teaching generalized language to language-deficient individuals, as derived from a miniature linguistic system or matrix-training analysis of language, should serve to provide the speech and language therapist with a general set of rules for approaching the remediation of language deficiency. Although these principles are derived primarily from experimental investigations of the parameters governing the linguistic development of severely retarded adolescents or children (e.g., Guess et al., 1968; Schumaker and Sherman, 1970; Lutzker and Sherman, 1974; Striefel, Wetherby, and Karlan, 1976, 1978), the findings of these studies, combined with the results of other miniature linguistic system experiments conducted with different procedures and subject populations (see Wetherby, 1978, for a review), suggest that matrix-training procedures are quite reliable for establishing a "combinative" form of generalized receptive or productive language. Indeed, most successful language intervention and/or language remediation programs reported in current literature already contain many of the above nine training components. Consequently, this chapter should serve to integrate a line of research with current practice—something that does not always occur.

REVIEW AND CONCLUSION

The purpose of this chapter is to examine the implications that a miniature linguistic system or matrix-training approach to the study of language has for the remediation of language deficiency. To accomplish this goal, experimental matrix research conducted within both receptive and productive language modalities was reviewed to demonstrate how the major product of this paradigm—the development of generalized language—can be established in language-deficient persons. From this review, a set of nine training principles was derived for use by therapists interested in the establishment of generalized language skills.

Within the receptive language paradigm, a line of research concerned with the establishment of generalized instruction-following behavior using matrix-training procedures was illustrated. This research, exemplified by the work of Striefel and Wetherby (1973), Striefel, Bryan, and Aikins (1974), and Striefel, Wetherby, and Karlan (1976, 1978), indicates that generalized receptive language skills can be established in severely retarded adolescents, and this skill can be extended to new language elements without further training. Additional findings indicate the possibility that more efficient matrix-training procedures may be developed, and that larger sequences of language responses can be established systematically in the repertoires of severely retarded adolescents.

Within the productive language paradigm, research conducted by Guess et al. (1968), Lutzker and Sherman (1974), and Schumaker and

Sherman (1970) was reviewed as exemplifying miniature linguistic system or matrix-training procedures. This research indicates that, using such procedures, grammatical development and productive sentences can be trained to occur and generalize to new combinations of controlling stimuli.

A final section of this chapter addressed what seem to be some basic training principles involved in an attempt to remediate language deficiency using miniature linguistic system or matrix-training procedures. These nine principles point out the need for a language therapist to: 1) emphasize training a matrix, 2) teach until generalization occurs, 3) use concurrent training procedures, 4) determine the discriminative stimuli for a trained language response, 5) retain all that is trained, 6) determine the size of the matrix trained, 7) reinforce all correct language responses during assessment and training, 8) use systematic training procedures for establishing individual stimulus-response relationships, and 9) include a stimulus class of other people within the matrix to facilitate generalization of learned language repertoires to many individuals. The utilization of such principles should serve to facilitate the establishment of generalized language in language-deficient individuals.

In conclusion, miniature linguistic system or matrix-training procedures, as derived from a wide diversity of research concerned with the experimental development of language (Wetherby, 1978), seem to be suited for the establishment of generalized receptive and productive language skills in language-deficient individuals. To the degree that the utilization of such principles may be integrated into the language-training repertoires of various professionals, the language handicaps of many persons may be overcome. To this end, the remediation of language deficiency seems to vary commensurately with the development of research concerned with generalized language processes. This relationship should continue.

REFERENCES

Baer, D. M., and Guess, D. 1971. Receptive training of adjective inflections in mental retardates. J. Appl. Behav. Anal. 4:129–139.

Baer, D. M., and Guess, D. 1973. Teaching the productive use of noun suffixes to mental retardates. Am. J. Ment. Defic. 77:498–505.

Baer, D. M., Guess, D., and Sherman, J. A. 1973. Adventures in simplistic grammar. *In* R. L. Schiefelbusch (ed.), Language of the Mentally Retarded, pp. 93–105. University Park Press, Baltimore.

Baer, D. M., Wolf, M. M., and Risley, T. R. 1968. Some current dimensions of applied behavior analysis. J. Appl. Behav. Anal. 1:91–97.

Berko, J. 1958. The child's learning of English morphology. Word 14:150–177.

Braine, M. D. S. 1963. On learning the grammatical order of words. Psychol. Rev. 70:323–348.

Braine, M. D. S. 1965. The insufficiency of a finite state model for verbal reconstructive memory. Psychon. Sci. 2:291–292.

Esper, E. A. 1925. A technique for the experimental investigation of associative interference in artificial linguistic material. Lang. Monogr. No. 1.

Foss, D. J. 1968. An analysis of learning in a miniature linguistic system. J. Exp. Psychol. 76:450–459.

Frisch, S. A., and Schumaker, J. B. 1974. Training generalized receptive prepositions in retarded children. J. Appl. Behav. Anal. 7:611–621.

Garcia, E. E., and DeHaven, E. D. 1974. Use of operant techniques in the establishment and generalization of language: A review and analysis. Am. J. Ment. Defic. 79:169–178.

Guess, D., Sailor, W., Rutherford, G., and Baer, D. M. 1968. An experimental analysis of linguistic development: The productive use of the plural morpheme. J. Appl. Behav. Anal. 1:297–306.

Harris, S. L. 1975. Teaching language to nonverbal children—With emphasis on problems of generalization. Psychol. Bull. 82:565–580.

Lutzker, J. R., and Sherman, J. A. 1974. Producing generative sentence usage by imitation and reinforcement procedures. J. Appl. Behav. Anal. 7:447–460.

Miller, G. A. 1951. The role of learning. In G. A. Miller (ed.), Language and Communication. McGraw-Hill Book Co., New York.

Premack, D. A. 1970. A functional analysis of language. J. Exp. Anal. Behav. 14:107–125.

Scheuerman, N., Cartwright, S., York, R., Lowry, P., and Brown, L. 1974. Teaching young severely handicapped students to follow verbal directions. J. Spec. Educ. 8:223–236.

Schroeder, G. L., and Baer, D. M. 1972. Effects of concurrent and serial training on generalized vocal imitation in retarded children. Dev. Psychol. 6:293–301.

Schumaker, J., and Sherman, J. A. 1970. Training generative verb usage by imitation and reinforcement procedures. J. Appl. Behav. Anal. 3:273–287.

Smeets, P. M., and Striefel, S. 1976a. Acquisition of sign reading by transfer of stimulus control in a retarded deaf girl. J. Ment. Defic. Res. 20:197–205.

Smeets, P. M., and Striefel, S. 1976b. Acquisition and cross modal generalization of receptive and expressive signing skills in a retarded deaf girl. J. Ment. Defic. Res. 20:251–260.

Smith, K. H. 1966a. Grammatical intrusions in the free recall of structured letter pairs. J. Verb. Learn. Verb. Behav. 5:447–454.

Smith, K. H. 1966b. Grammatical intrusions in the free recall of structured letter pairs: Mediated transfer or position learning? J. Exp. Psychol. 72:580–588.

Snyder, L. K., Lovitt, T. C., and Smith, J. O. 1975. Language training for the severely retarded: Five years of behavior analysis research. Excep. Child. 42:7–15.

Striefel, S., Bryan, K. S., and Aikins, D. A. 1974. Transfer of stimulus control from motor to verbal stimuli. J. Appl. Behav. Anal. 7:123–135.

Striefel, S., and Wetherby, B. 1973. Instruction-following behavior of a retarded child and its controlling stimuli. J. Appl. Behav. Anal. 6:663–670.

Striefel, S., Wetherby, B., and Karlan, G. R. 1976. Establishing generalized verb-noun instruction-following skills in retarded children. J. Exp. Child Psychol. 22:247–260.

Striefel, S., Wetherby, B., and Karlan, G. R. 1978. Developing generalized instruction-following behavior in the severely retarded. *In* C. E. Meyers (ed.), Quality of life in severely and profoundly mentally retarded people: Research foundation for improvement. Monogr. Am. Assoc. Ment. Defic. No. 3.

Touchette, P. 1971. Transfer of stimulus control: Measuring the amount of transfer. J. Exp. Anal. Behav. 15:347–354.

von Glasersfeld, E. 1977. The yerkish language and its automatic parser. *In* D. M. Rumbaugh (ed.), Language Learning by a Chimpanzee: The Lana Project. Academic Press, New York.

Wetherby, B. 1978. Miniature languages and the functional analysis of verbal behavior. *In* R. L. Schiefelbusch (ed.), Bases of Language Intervention, pp. 397–448. University Park Press, Baltimore.

Whitehurst, G. J. 1971. Generalized labeling on the basis of structural response classes by two young children. J. Exp. Child Psychol. 12:59–71.

Whitehurst, G. J. 1972. Production of novel and grammatical utterances by young children. J. Exp. Child Psychol. 13:502–515.

Whitman, T. L., Zakaras, M., and Chardos, S. 1971. Effects of reinforcement and guidance procedures on instruction-following behavior of severely retarded children. J. Appl. Behav. Anal. 4:283–290.

Zimmerman, E. H., Zimmerman, J., and Russel, C. D. 1969. Differential effects of token reinforcement on instruction-following behavior in retarded students instructed in a group. J. Appl. Behav. Anal. 2:101–112.

chapter

8

Programming for Language and Communication Therapy

Gerald M. Siegel

Department of Communication Disorders and
Center for Research in Human Learning
University of Minnesota
Minneapolis, Minnesota

Joseph E. Spradlin

Bureau of Child Research
University of Kansas
Lawrence, Kansas

LANGUAGE AND COMMUNICATION THERAPY

At the end of each calendar year, the *Journal of Speech and Hearing Disorders* and the *Journal of Speech and Hearing Research* publish a cumulative index for that year in which the papers are classified according to their major category or topic. It is interesting to compare the pattern of publication for these two major journals for the years 1966 and 1976 (see Table 1). The table is ours, but the categories are a selection from those included in the cumulative indices. Of the topics we selected—stuttering, articulation, voice, and language—language clearly dominates both journals in 1976. The trend in the table is a reflection of trends in the field. Language has become the major preoccupation of speech clinicians and many others working with handicapped children. Moreover, the table is only a partial reflection of the increased interest in language. Not represented is the proliferation of books, chapters, and articles in other journals read by speech and language clinicians. Clearly, language is at the tip of almost everyone's tongue in the field of communication disorders.

Although fields with a strong clinical commitment such as communication disorders are invariably influenced by the shifting tides and fashions in related disciplines, the current intense interest in language disorders does not seem to be temporary. Fundamental changes have occurred in the public schools and in society as a whole that have left indelible marks on the professions devoted to the care and education of children. In numerous states there are now "right-to-education" laws that place the responsibility for educating and serving even the most profoundly impaired or handicapped children in the public schools. Virtually all children are now viewed as educable to some degree, regardless of their measured IQ, physical dexterity, social graces, or toilet habits. Practically the only functioning criterion for whether or not a child should be included in a school program is the tenacity and aggressiveness of the child's advocates, usually his[1] parents. If the parents want their child in a school program, chances are some such program will have to be devised.

The consequences of these changes are evident as we observe both the school and the residential institution. Institutions for the mentally retarded are often at one-third of their former size, and the residents who remain have the most profound and disabling problems. Teachers and clinicians working in institutional settings have some radical rethinking and adjusting to do. The same is true in the public schools. The current generation of professionals working in both environments generally have not been educated academically or by experience to handle the children

---

[1] Masculine pronouns are used throughout for the sake of grammatical uniformity and simplicity. They are not meant to be preferential or discriminatory.

Table 1.   Classification of articles published in JSHR
and JSHD in 1966 and 1976

	JSHR		JSHD	
	1966	1976	1966	1976
Articulation	5	2	7	10
Voice	1	1	5	3
Stuttering	11	14	5	6
Language	13	20	6	27

and the problems they now confront daily. In almost every instance, in addition to problems in general management, motivation, ability to attend to a task, coordination, and so on, there is some major difficulty in communication—in language. Speech and language clinicians are faced with the urgent need to discover and develop new clinical techniques appropriate for children from whom we have been largely insulated in past decades. Perhaps more important is the task of recalibration. Clinicians must rethink what it is they ought to be doing, and with whom. There was a time when labeling a child as retarded was tantamount to excluding him from speech therapy because the potential gains were considered minimal. Now we must again ask who really needs our services, and what constitutes a legitimate allocation of our skills.

Every profession has implicit standards that define successful performance by its members. At one time clinicians took pride in the size of their caseload. Now a large caseload suggests that the clinician must be doing trivial work, spending time on minor, unimportant speech variations, and ignoring profoundly handicapped children. If dismissal rate was once worn as a badge of success, this too must be reevaluated. The children now in speech therapy are not likely to be dismissed after a brief stint. Indeed, it may be more normal for these children to remain in therapy throughout their school life. In some of these children the hoped for increments are miniscule compared to the expectations built up with past generations of speech-handicapped children. In addition to the continuing need to accumulate new knowledge and techniques, clinicians have the added problem of reevaluating their expectations so they can assess their own accomplishments and achievements realistically.

This is a fluid and exciting time for child-centered professions. To a significant degree, and much more quickly than most had anticipated, the dream of clinicians working in the schools has been realized. There is certainly no justification now, if ever there was, to distinguish between speech therapy in clinical and in school environments. Clinicians in the schools are working with the full range of handicaps, and the notion that the school clinician requires less knowledge and education than a hospital clinician is simply and patently false. The challenge in the school is of the highest magnitude, and that is clearly "where the action is."

The more profound and complex the problems the child presents, the more difficult it becomes to maintain traditional discipline boundaries. Severely handicapped children present an aggregation of problems that tax the resources of classroom teacher, special learning teacher, physical and occupational therapists, school social worker, speech and hearing specialist, and other service professionals. There was much written about the desirability of a team approach in the past. Now it is an inevitability. The need is to find effective ways to coordinate the activities of the various professionals who will be working with the child. No one profession is adequate to deal with the full range of behavioral, emotional, educational, sensorimotor, and communicative disabilities of these children. There must be a reasonable division of responsibility lest we get tangled up in each other's test kits, but professional efforts must be coordinated so that each child receives a coherent program of instruction and therapy.

The form of this coordination is necessarily determined by the structure of the system providing service to the child rather than by some universal administrative formula. In some cases it will be most reasonable for the speech and language clinician to take a lead role in mediating among the professionals working with the child and in ensuring some integration of programming. In other cases, it will be a special learning teacher or the classroom teacher. The form of integration should flow from the characteristics of the service system surrounding the child. Coordination does not necessarily imply the imposition of a single approach to therapy and teaching, but it does involve sharing insights and knowledge about the child and an appreciation of the varying ways the child is being educated through the special programs he experiences. It does not seem crucial that the child be treated with absolute consistency across all disciplines serving his needs. He need not have the same reinforcers, the same schedules, or, indeed, be subjected to behavior modification in every setting in which he works. Children are typically far more adjustable and less fragile than we expect. Part of their learning to cope with the world is learning that different situations typically involve different expectations and patterns of behavior.

A Working Definition of Language

The eventual goal of the communication therapist is to abet the child's communication skills through attention to his speech, language, hearing, and interpersonal reactions. This does not define a very narrow province within which to work. Communication is so basic a human endeavor that it underlies or at least influences most affective, intellectual, and interpersonal behaviors. Although each discipline must be aware of "the whole child," we cannot truly assume responsibility for every aspect of his performance and abilities. Instead, each discipline must determine some area of professional competency that will contribute to the child's welfare, and stake out the parameters of that area. This is no simple task. In the area of language and communication, for example, there are no ready, neat definitions. In a recent publication, Siegel and Broen (1976) urged that it is the responsibility of each clinician to develop a framework—a working definition—for conceptualizing what is meant by language, rather than mindlessly accepting the definition or framework that may be implicit in some language test that may be convenient and available. This is what every test-maker must do to determine what behaviors or skills to tap in the formulation of the test. The clinician can do no less.

When one buys a particular assessment instrument, one also buys into the author's conceptualization of what is important in language, and authors will differ on this. Some tests are loaded with irregular forms of the plural (for example, the Grammatic Closure subtest of the Illinois Test of Psycholinguistic Abilities (ITPA); Kirk, McCarthy, and Kirk, 1968) while others, such as Carrow's (1973) Test for Auditory Comprehension of Language (TACL), probe the child's understanding of the rules underlying regular pluralization forms. The first test looks at pluralization as an automatic, rote memory process, the second as the expression of a grammatical rule. The competent speaker learns rule and exceptions, but neither test is designed to fill out the whole picture. Similarly, the ITPA probes the child's knowledge of prepositions fairly deeply, while Lee's (1974) Developmental Sentence Scoring (DSS) procedure does not score prepositions. Again, the two tests will yield a different view of linguistic ability and of what is necessary to be an adequate communicator. The ITPA tends to encourage simple, single-word responses; the DSS is based on an analysis of sentences.

In short, language tests do not all measure the same behaviors and, thus, for practical purposes, the tests define language in different ways. Because no single definition is entirely adequate, the clinician must have some personal view or model for language. It need not be an elegant and logically flawless definition. It is a working hypothesis as to the skills that are important for the child's communication development. It is a map that lays out the areas of the clinician's concerns. To have such a definition seems crucial, both to aid in evaluating and working with the child, and also as a scheme for evaluating the usefulness of the myriad tests and language kits that continually compete for the clinician's attention.

Siegel and Broen (1976) suggested four areas for consideration in language assessment. These seem equally appropriate as a framework for language therapy:

1. Phonological performance, including the child's categorization and discrimination of speech sounds, as well as their production
2. Grammatical performance, including understanding and production of the morphology and syntax of the language
3. Knowledge and use of vocabulary and concepts
4. Interpersonal, communicative use of language as a means of acquiring and ordering knowledge and of purposefully operating on the environment

Just as a language test serves, in practice, to define the domain of language, so too does a language instruction procedure. The caveat offered by Siegel and Broen concerning assessment applies even more forcefully to therapy. Language programs will vary in approach, in teaching strategy, and in the aspects of language they emphasize. Language therapy programs can be extremely helpful and efficient, but it must be recognized that each tends to define language, and thereby the clinician's concerns, in a particular way.

Language and Communication Disorders

The increasing emphasis on disorders of language has resulted in a new point of balance for much of the basic academic work and clinical preparation of students in communication disorders. At one time, articulation disorders served as a kind of prototype for a good part of the discipline. Students were introduced early to processes of normal articulation development, and it was in this context that broad questions concerning development, variability, individual differences, methods of assessment, clinical judgments were first raised. Similarly, the first sheltered exposure of a student clinician to therapy was likely to be with a misarticulating client. It was through such experience that the student built up the basic clinical skills that would later be adapted to the variety of clients requiring service. In a similar way, research in articulation disorders was prototypical for much of the research in other areas of the field. It seems now that language has displaced articulation, and even, in some instances, preempted it, so that questions previously framed in terms of articulatory performance are now approached from the perspective of phonology, linking it formally to issues in linguistics.

If this analysis of the shifting center of the discipline is correct, it suggests that future generations of clinicians will be very conversant with research and theory relating to language and its development, and very attentive to changing orientations and new developments in these areas. This will constitute the primary basic science for the field, just as anatomy, physiology, and acoustic sciences were for so long dominant. It seems likely that this is not a passing phenomenon but rather a fundamental restructuring. It is from such a knowledge base that clinicians will continue to evaluate the variety of approaches and products relating to language assessment and therapy that will be thrust at them, both in the literature and by commercial vendors. Speech and hearing specialists, and especially those working in school environments, have tended to resist a high degree of specialization—for good reason. Few schools could afford to hire different specialists to work with the stutterers, cleft palate, voice, articulation, hearing-impaired children that might make up the typical roster of children being seen for therapy, especially when caseloads were often between 90 and 120 children per clinician. In recent years caseloads have been reduced dramatically, while the number of clinicians hired has proportionately increased; thus, it may be more feasible to contemplate specialization, especially in urban school systems. Even so, it is likely that all speech and hearing personnel will continue to share a common set of academic experiences, that these will have psycholinguistics and language development at their core, and that this will also provide the basis for communicating across disciplines to colleagues in the fields of special education, learning disabilities, mental retardation, autism, and the like.

A Sampling of Language Therapy Programs

In a recent book, Fristoe (1976) reviewed 39 commercially available therapy kits. There are many more that have been described or at least mentioned in the literature. This volume contains programs or approaches to language therapy that provide a fair sampling of the available systems. Hart and Rogers-Warren (Chapter 5) are dealing with active, basically normal young children. Guess, Sailor, and Baer (Chapter 3) seem to have developed procedures with a view toward severely retarded adolescents or older children who are at least capable of vocal imitation. Hollis and Carrier (Chapter 2) present methods for children who are so severely impaired they may never acquire vocal skills. Waryas and Stremel-Campbell's (Chapter 4) procedures would seem to be targeted for retarded children whose speech already displays considerable linguistic structure. Schumaker and Sherman (Chapter 6) are concerned with the contributions of the parents to language development, starting with prelingual interactions between the parent and the babbling infant. Wetherby and Striefel (Chapter 7) offer the miniature language framework as a point of departure for analysis and intervention in instances of disordered languages.

These approaches may be taken as exemplars. They differ in a number of ways. For one, the authors reveal their own theoretical biases in the language they use to describe their work. The authors clearly work from different theoretical backgrounds or models. The approaches differ also in terms of the population of children for whom they are appropriate. They are not interchangeable. Regardless of theoretical vantage point, there would be little reason to use the Guess, Sailor, and Baer program for the relatively advanced children treated by Hart and Rogers-Warren. The differences do not rest entirely with the relative language level of the children. The procedures have been devised for children who may be very different in age as well, and this, too, is relevant to their appropriateness.

In this chapter issues are raised that seem relevant to the general process of language therapy rather than to a particular approach. The issues addressed are:

1. What assumptions underly the development and use of a language therapy program?
2. Should language therapy programs be based on normal developmental order, or on some kind of explicit task analysis?
3. What is the relationship between communication disorder and language disorder?
4. Under what circumstances is it appropriate to design nonspeech methods as the basic communication modality?
5. What is the significance of differential diagnosis for language therapy procedures?
6. What is the place of the operant imitation paradigm in language therapy?
7. What is the relationship between reception (comprehension) and expression (production)?
8. How does the clinician achieve transfer from the clinic or laboratory to the child's wider environmental interactions?

THE USE OF LANGUAGE PROGRAMS

Perhaps the most compelling reason for turning to an available language therapy program is that it brings order to the confusing variety of claims and definitions that surround the concept of language. It provides the clinician with a framework within which to work. Language becomes the set of behaviors to which the program is addressed. Specialists in communication disorders have always disagreed about how best to approach problems such as stuttering, articulation, and voice, but there has at least been some general agreement about the problem domain, enough so that the clinician could proceed to plan a therapy regime. Not so in language. The problem area is so encompassing and definitions are so abstract and vague that there are no clear agreements about what constitutes a language disorder or whose definition of language to use in therapy. Should therapy be based upon earlier definitions in which language was viewed in terms of length of response, size of vocabulary, type-token ratios, egocentric remarks? Or is language best thought of as input and output hierarchies such as those incorporated into the ITPA model? Shall language be thought of as an interpersonal device, or in terms of its formal, structural properties? If language is defined in psycholinguistic terms, whose psycholinguistics should we accept: Transformational or case grammar? Syntax, semantics, or pragmatics?

Given the disparity of approaches and orientations to language, and the fact that many persons now working as clinicians have not been educated in modern psycholinguistics, the clinician may despair of ever making a reasoned decision about the nature of language therapy, and, instead, may select a program arbitrarily, perhaps one that is being used by a colleague or that has some national acclaim. The program provides a beginning. For those who feel overwhelmed by shifting and competing theories and by the enormity of the task, a well-designed therapy program has great appeal. Nonetheless, there are important questions that must be raised when this approach is used.

The clinician must decide which of the available programs is best designed for his clients. To do so, he must determine what definition of language has been incorporated into the various programs under consideration. It would be helpful if programs were very explicit about their underlying rationale and model, but they often fall short. The clinician's first responsibility in selecting a program, then, is to determine the definition of language or communication that is the basis for the program. Does it focus on syntax or semantics? Is it concerned with teaching the child how to manipulate the environment, or how to manipulate sentences? Is it appropriate for children who already have some vocal communication skills, or is it designed for the instatement of rudimentary tokens of communication? Does it teach only vocal forms of verbalization, or does it allow for alternative forms of communication? Because programs do not always make explicit their orientation to language, the clinician may have to make this determination on the basis of a study of the program itself. This clearly involves more than passively selecting and applying a particular approach.

Another important question concerns the degree of flexibility that is built into the alternative programs. Underlying the use of programs is the general implication that there is a universality of effectiveness in the implementation of language teaching. Most programs provide a well-charted, systematic sequence of steps. This seems to embody a rather powerful assumption about the nature of language and language learning. In short, Jimmy, Johnny, Sarah, and Scott, all of whom are language deficient, should learn the same sequence of language skills, in essentially the same way. As discussed in more detail below, there is some disagreement concerning the basis for mapping the necessary sequences, but the general notion of universality underlies all programs to a lesser or greater degree. A question to be asked of any program is how flexible it is. Does the program have built-in options that allow systematic individualization? Is the logic of the program sufficiently explicit that the clinician can make meaningful alterations in the procedures? There are important compromises or trades to be negotiated. The more specific or inflexible a program is, the less the clinician need be concerned about making individual decisions. The child is "plugged into" the program, and the clinician then becomes a tool of the program, rather than the program a tool of the user. Clearly, this is a very efficient arrangement. The question is whether such efficiency is equally useful to all of the children undergoing therapy. Whatever conclusion the clinician comes to, it is important at least to recognize that, by definition, a language therapy program provides an approach to therapy that implies a universality of effectiveness for all children being treated. Guess, Sailor, and Baer (Chapter 3) pose this question:

> If useful language communication is indeed the end result of a sequence of instruction in the elements of language, then by what curriculum could such instructions best proceed? In other words, which elements should be taught in what order, for maximal results from minimal teaching?

Perhaps it is implicit in that statement, but to make our concerns more obvious, we might offer the modification, ". . . which elements should be taught in what order for *which children* for maximal results?"

DEVELOPMENTAL VERSUS REMEDIAL LOGIC

Guess, Sailor, and Baer (Chaper 3) contrast *developmental* and *remedial* bases for developing language intervention strategies. They state the difference:

> Developmental logic supposes that the best way, or perhaps the only effective way to teach language to a deficient child, is in the sequence in which normal children learn language. If language has a complex structure, such that parts of it depend for their function on other parts of it already being mastered, then the normal developmental sequence must represent at least one effective sequence of learning these interdependencies. Conceivably, there is no alternate sequence in which language can be learned, at least by children learning it at the usual stages of their

development. This possibility is bolstered by the reported uniformity with which children acquire language. . . .

Remedial logic, by contrast, supposes that children being taught language relatively late in their lives, because they have failed to acquire it adequately in their earlier experiences, no longer possess the same collection of abilities and deficits that normal children have when they begin to acquire language. . . . Remedial logic, then, will not ask in what order the retarded child needs to learn language but rather in what order the language taught most quickly will accomplish some improvement in the child's communication. . . . Thus, a program based on remedial logic will try to establish first the most useful elements of language that the child might need. What these are will depend on the child's environment.

Remedial versus developmental logic, which is the more appropriate basis for designing a language instruction program? Intuitively, it is appealing to argue that the sequence in which skills emerge in normal development is the sequence in which it should be taught to defective children. Waryas and Stremel-Campbell (Chapter 4) and Miller and Yoder (1974) urge such an approach. This is not an unfamiliar argument to speech clinicians. Not many years ago there was a similar division in articulation therapy, with some clinicians proposing that the normal developmental pattern of phoneme acquisition ought to be used as the basic design for the child with multiple articulation deficits and with others suggesting that a behavioral index, such as stimulability, might be more useful. In the case of articulation therapy, the argument really disappears under careful scrutiny because it is based on some unfounded assumptions. The very concept of a normal developmental progression in articulation mastery is a loose theoretical construct. Generally, the basis for the developmental model has been the data of Templin (1957) or some of the earlier cross-sectional studies of acquisition (Wellman et al., 1931; Poole, 1934). These data are noteworthy for their enormous variability. The fact is, as is well indicated in Winitz (1969), these theoretical models of acquisition are very poor representations of the course of development in individual children, and there is no reason to presume that a single progression is the best or easiest for a specific normal child, to say nothing of deviant speakers. Thus, at close range, the very construct of a single developmental progression for normal children becomes illusory.

What of other aspects of language? To what extent is syntactic or semantic development identical across children? There is no clear answer. It depends on what is being studied, and why. Under the influence of Chomsky's (1957) early discussion of "linguistic universals," there was a major interest in discovering commonalities in development across children and, indeed, cultures (Slobin, 1970). Once the point had been made that such universals can be found, it was tolerable to notice that there are also local exceptions. Bloom (1970), for example, has shown that there are important differences in development even among the small set of children she has studied intensively. She noted early that some children's first combinations were of the noun plus noun variety, while others made use of a relational structure involving words like *more* or *all gone* in combination with a substantive. It is not clear why the children differed at this early stage of two-word combination, and all of the children went on to develop adequate language usage. But the differences are there. Similarly, she noted that there are differences in the single-word utterances of children (Bloom, 1973), and in the way children exploit the possibilities that inhere in spontaneous imitations as a means of bridging the gap between partial understanding and mastery of various grammatical forms (Bloom, Hood, and Lightbown, 1974). Braine (1976) recently presented an exhaustive analysis of the available corpora of word combinations for children with mean utterance length of up to about 1.7 morphemes. He concluded that previous research has tended to emphasize the similarity of developmental patterns and to describe early speech in terms of generalizations that have often obscured the substantial differences in the corpora of the children studied.

Thus, depending on one's orientation, it is possible to find impressive evidence for both the universality and the diversity of language development. Of course, there must be some level at which all children proceed according to the same plan. It would seem quite safe to argue that all children learn easy forms before difficult ones, but it does not necessarily follow that what is easy for one child will be simple for all others. The complexity of language is determined in part by its internal structure, as might be revealed by a transformational analysis, but it is also determined by the complexity of the ideas to be communicated, by the child's cognitive and perceptual attributes, by the child's experiences, and so on. To make the strong case for a single developmental continuum is to argue for a universality of language development that is unaffected by personal and experiential factors. The idea of a developmental sequence is useful as a guidepost in research on language development, but it ought not to be taken as a foregone conclusion about the process itself.

Related to the idea of a universal developmental progression is a terribly simplistic view that has dogged the area of language development since the early days of count-and-tally research in child development. This is the notion of a developmental chart for language that is similar to the kinds of charts physicians and others use for describing height, weight, and stages of physical maturation. Why not have a chart that places babbling at one end and mature language at the other, with the intervening steps interpolated to define the progression so that we can know at a glance where the child is, where he has been, and where he must next proceed to develop normally? It is an attractive but unworkable model. There simply is no such continuum that can be developed for behavior as multifaceted and as complex as language. One can create a continuum, such as vocabulary size, or mean length of utterance, but these do nothing to reveal the complexities of the skills involved in language and communication mastery. What would be needed to fit such a model to the realities of language acquisition would be an indefinite number of specific continua, each defining some aspect of language, and then still others to interdigitate the first set.

For example, children typically are observed to pose yes/no questions before Wh-questions (Dale, 1976). Similarly, Brown (1973) has described a universal acquisition sequence across some 14 morphological forms, and Bloom's (1970) data indicate that children first learn to express denial, then rejection, and finally nonexistence in the acquisition of negation. But these sequences account for only a fraction of what is involved in language development. Furthermore, there is no scheme that integrates across these categories of development. How do the 14 morphemes interdigitate with question acquisition and use of negation? Each new developmental pattern would have to be located with respect to all of these others for anything like a complete developmental scheme to emerge. Within particular dimensions of language, such schemas do occur with some consistency, but not necessarily for all children. Across categories, language seems too complex to be captured by a developmental progression.

This is not to argue that the search for universalities of language use and development is unwarranted. Such research may prove very useful to the clinician. In evaluating an apparent developmental pattern, important insights about the structure of language are obtained. This is as helpful to the practitioner as it is to the theoretician. But the promise of language programs based on normal developmental data seems to emanate from too simplistic a view of the nature of language and of language learning.

The remedial approach, as described by Guess, Sailor, and Baer (Chapter 3), has the advantage of encouraging the clinician and teacher to be attuned to the needs of the child in the particular environments in which he functions rather than to some hypothetical universal program. However, it is also beset by some of the same difficulties that inhere in the developmental approach. The remedial programs developed by Guess et al. are appropriate for severely retarded children with minimal communication skills. It is not apparent how to proceed once the child has gone beyond this preliminary stage of communication; that is, the decision rules are not obvious for determining which higher level linguistic skills would prove most functional for the child. Nor is it immediately evident how to define the properties of these skills in behavioral terms. To what extent, for example, should the concept of a linguistic transformation be incorporated into a specific training sequence? Should therapy designed to teach questions or negation stay close to the surface structure representations, or should it build these sentence forms as variations of a declarative "deep structure"? Part of the problem rises from the fact that behavior modification is now seen as a form of behavioral engineering rather than a theoretical system. Rather than generating a specific content, it looks to other disciplines, such as psycholinguistics, for the specification of the relevant content. This has proved quite adequate for the analysis of various morphological forms, but it is not clear if more abstract linguistic formulations, those involving transformations or other transductions of rules into surface manifestations, can be treated by a behavioral analysis.

Perhaps the question of whether language training should be predicated on developmental or remedial orientations presumes too much. It presumes that these two approaches are sufficiently well developed that a choice is possible. It seems more likely that both are at a relatively rudimentary stage of refinement and that the literature is too scant at this moment to foster a choice. What is necessary, instead, is to exploit both approaches where possible. On some points the two approaches will converge. At others they will hopefully contribute unique insights into the structure of language and communication. If a development inquiry pulls language apart to reveal its inner organization, this may be invaluable in language teaching. If a task analysis exposes the organization of behavior in a different way, this, too, can be exploited in the development of a program. At some points it will certainly be the case that an analysis of the behavior in question is not yet available, and the existing developmental understandings may constitute the best model for the manner in which the behavior should be dissected and taught. In any case, the clinician's prospects for creative application of a program are enhanced when the rationale underlying any program is made explicit and when the clinician is equipped to understand and evaluate both the rationale and the extent to which it is properly represented in the program. This again implies a knowledgeable clinician who does more than passively administer a predetermined program.

LANGUAGE AND COMMUNICATION DISORDERS

Hollis and Carrier (Chapter 2) propose (citing Cherry, 1961) the following definition of communication: "In the broad sense, communication is a social affair in which one individual attempts to transmit an idea or thought to another individual." In the same chapter they define language as ". . . *a set of semantic and syntactic rules that allows A and B to correlate their environmental maps or distinctions and symbols*" (italics theirs). What sense can be made of disordered language and communication from these definitions? It would seem from this framework that language is in the service of communication—it is the device that provides the structure for the transmission of ideas and thoughts between individuals. Language is defective, then, when it is ineffective in facilitating such transmission. But not all communication disorders are the product of language deficits. The deaf receiver may function quite well when the transmission system is visual but be totally handicapped when forced to deal with spoken language. It is not the listener's language that is at fault in this instance but the match between his receiving capabilities and the transmission mode.

On the other hand, there are many "disorders of communication" that do not seem to fit the Hollis et al. framework. Martin and Haroldson (1969) found that severe stutterers were no less effective in transmitting complex messages than were normal speakers in a situation that required listeners to solve problems on the basis of spoken instructions; that is, transmission of ideas and thoughts was no problem for the most severe stutterers although there would be little disagreement that they had manifest "communication disorders." Thus, at least from the vantage of speech pathology, successful communication is not synonomous with accurate transmission of information. The same can be said to be true of other "communication disorders." There are some situations in which a breathy or hoarse voice may interfere with transmission, but these are probably rare. Similarly, it is only the most severe articulation defect that is likely to interfere with successful communication as traditionally defined. At least in our culture, a communication disorder also exists when ordinary listeners find the speaker's style of transmission unpleasant, regardless of whether the message gets across.

By the same token, it is not entirely clear what parameters determine degree of language disorder. Chomsky (1957) made the distinction between "grammaticalness," the extent to which a sentence can be accounted for by application of a grammatical rule system, and "acceptability," the speaker/hearer's willingness to tolerate such sentences in spoken conversation. There are instances of formally grammatical sentences that contain so many levels of embedding as to be unintelligible, and not at all communicative. Other sentences may fail to mark important grammatical distinctions but be readily interpretable. When the promise of linguistics for language disorders first became evident, many of us heeded Bellugi and Brown's (1964, p. 6) admonition that to understand what this newly discovered discipline had to offer, "no baptism short of total immersion would suffice."

We surfaced, with skin wrinkled by this and numerous previous baptisms, to find that not even total immersion in linguistics would assuage the problems in defining disordered communication. The linguists do not choose their models or explanatory devices in order to satisfy the needs of those working with disordered or retarded language. It remains to be determined how well the descriptions of the linguist will fit the requirements of the clinician, and it seems that it is the clinicians and teachers who will have to make that determination. Linguists have shown no such disposition. Thus, we find studies of the sort reported by Leonard (1972) in which the attempt is made to discover which of the linguist's descriptions most closely correlate with clinical judgments of deviancy. Much remains to be done in searching for such correlations, and there is little reason to suspect that the two systems will map onto each other precisely. Having discovered, for example, that a given child has a number of specific grammatical differences, the clinician will still have to make a judgment as to which of these most clearly sets the child apart as language handicapped. The items that preoccupy linguists, the special cases that are useful for testing theories, may have little relevance for clinical language pathology. Children can get along very well without the passive construction and without making the distinctions embodied in sentences contrasting *tell, ask,* and *promise,* even though these special instances focus on important cases for the linguist.

In short, language and communication are two constructs that stand in uncertain and uneasy relation to each other. The constructs themselves are not sufficiently understood to make clear relationships. We need not await precise definitions. As clinicians, we are concerned with language and communication, with the transmission of information and ideas, and with the form in which the transmission is accomplished, and, beyond this, with the acceptability of the transmission style to the speaker's listeners and to himself. The degree of importance we ascribe to these various aspects of communication will depend on the child's level of functioning and his current circumstances. Clearly, the niceties of pear-shaped tones will have little value for a nonvocal child. The determination of what is important for the child is the responsibility of the clinician, in concert with the child, his parents, and other professionals whenever feasible. Once again, it should be pointed out that not all language programs will emphasize the same aspects of communication. The clinician must be aware of this as he goes about selecting a language program to be used as the vehicle for instruction. There is no way simply to select the "best" language program. The needs of the child and the characteristics of the program must be known and, to the extent possible, matched.

NONVOCAL COMMUNICATION

The child who cannot or will not communicate through conventional speech need not be cut off entirely from communication with others. One of the significant benefits to fall out from the new emphasis on psycholinguistics is the insistence on drawing a distinction between language, an underlying system, and speech, one means of realizing or expressing that system. Although speech is generally the most efficient method of putting language into palpable form, it is not the only system, and for some it may not be efficient at all. Of course, this is not a new insight. Teachers of the deaf have argued for decades about the relative merits and evils of oralism versus signing as the primary language medium for the deaf (Moores, 1974; Wilbur, 1976). What has changed is that psycholinguistic theory has added new legitimacy to the position that learning a language system, regardless of the expressive medium, is the first order of importance. The argument can now be made that, if the child knows something about the structure of language, however learned, this ultimately will facilitate vocal skills. Implicit in this position is the idea that signing is indeed a full-blown language (Wilbur, 1976), that it is easier for the deaf child to learn conventional spoken English as a second language than as a first language, and that, even if the oralists' worst fears are realized and the child who is taught signing later balks at learning spoken English, it is still to the child's advantage because signing represents the child's best chance to acquire a basic linguistic competence.

The desirability of teaching signing as the basis for later development is still in question. The claim that signing is no less a language than oral speech is being tested. The relationships among various forms of signing have yet to be charted fully. These issues remain. What has changed significantly in the wake of theoretical development is that it is now possible to contemplate testing these empirical issues. The world is no less flat or round than it was before, but we need not be quite so wary as we approach the edge. It is in this sense that theory, which sometimes binds us to a position or view of the world, also frees us to explore it.

Systems of nonvocal communication are now being explored with other populations of speechless children. Vanderheiden and Harris-Vanderheiden (1976) describe a variety of alternative communication systems, ranging from primitive indications of *yes/no* to rather complex electronic systems. In some instances the motivation for employing an alternative communication mode is obvious, as in the case of the severely paralyzed child who cannot control the vocal structures sufficiently to negotiate speech. In other cases it is puzzling why an alternative system seems to work—but it does. We are seeing a 10-year-old autistic child in our clinic who has a vocal repertoire that consists of little more than a handful of vowels and consonants that can be spoken only in isolation, and with great physical stress despite the lack of any apparent physiological or neurological impediment. After years of unsuccessful attempts to teach simple vocal patterns, a teacher discovered that the child would write readily. She now has a functional though limited ability to communicate through script. We are still mystified by the child's inability to learn simple speech production when she can master the complexities of script. Most important, we have a medium through which to teach.

One of the most fascinating new developments in nonvocal communication exemplifies the potential unity of research, theory, and clinical application. Premack began his research with chimps to test the claim that language is a uniquely human capacity. His first attempts (Premack and Schwartz, 1966) to teach the chimps an analog to adult phonology failed, but led to a detailed analysis of language in behavioral terms and to the development of a minilanguage using manipulable plastic forms that varied in shape and color (Premack, 1970, 1971; Premack and Premack, 1972). The success of this venture, and especially of Premack's conceptual analysis of language, stimulated Carrier (1974, 1976) to apply these methods as the basis for a nonspeech language-initiation program (Non-SLIP) to be used with severely retarded children. The approach has since been extended to autistic children (Premack and Premack, 1972; McLean and McLean, 1974), aphasic patients (Velletri-Glass, Gazzaniga, and Premack, 1973), and others (Carrier, 1976).

The crucial questions concerning clinical application of Non-SLIP are still only sparsely explored. In summarizing his cumulative experience with the program Carrier (1976) has written:

> In essence, it is reasonable to conclude at this time that Non-SLIP is ready for general clinical application. It is a tool that is an effective means of getting a large percentage (over 90% in available data) of children, with previously low likelihood of success, started in the process of learning communication skills (p. 542).

This is not to say, however, that Non-SLIP is intended as a communication system in its own right, to be used as an alternative to speech:

> There is one additional aspect of Non-SLIP that should be clarified. This training program is designed to teach a child a set of conceptual skills necessary to the acquisition of functional linguistic communication. Thus, it focuses on teaching a child tactics for learning language rather than teaching

a circumscribed set of "functional" communicative responses. As a result, the vocabulary, the grammar, and the specific sentences trained are quite unlike those traditionally viewed as appropriate for such children. . . . The role of Non-SLIP is not so much one of teaching functional communication responses as it is one of teaching tactics for acquiring these responses (p. 529).

The value of Non-SLIP, then, is not as a communication system, but as a means of effecting a transition to a conventional system, such as speech. Again quoting from Carrier (1976):

After the early research had indicated that children could learn communication skills using the nonspeech symbols and training procedures, an attempt was made to study the transition of children from nonspeech to spoken responses. It was discovered that all but a few children could at least partially make such a transition by the time they had finished training on prepositions. . . . It was thus concluded that children at this stage of skill acquisition were ready to move into more conventional training. They were now able to succeed in learning speech responses and various linguistic rules (p. 537).

The success of the Carrier programs, according to the author's own claims, is to be evaluated in terms of how readily children make the bridge from the arbitrary system of shapes and forms to more ordinary communication modes, such as speech or, perhaps, signing. Although Carrier seems optimistic about the prospects for Non-SLIP, the data relevant to this test are very sparse, consisting of the author's anecdotal reports (Carrier, 1976) and a number of unpublished papers. It should be noted that, because of its design, Non-SLIP must pass a sterner test than other nonvocal communication systems. Carrier does not offer Non-SLIP as a useful clinical program in its own right. The system is creditable only to the extent that it promotes communication in some other, conventional medium.

This is in contrast to the other nonvocal communication systems (Clark and Woodcock, 1976; Vanderheiden and Harris-Vanderheiden, 1976; Wilbur, 1976), whose primary purpose may be satisfied if they provide any means of communication, no matter how simplistic or primitive, to the child who is otherwise cut off from social communicative interaction. The effectiveness of the Bliss program, for example, is immediately demonstrated as soon as the previously noncommunicative child can signal an aide his desire for food, drink, or toilet. The child need only learn to point to the appropriate pictures on his board, all of which are reinforced with the printed word for the benefit of the aide so that only the child is required to master the meaning of the abstract symbols. Of course, there are some skills involved. The child must learn the symbols, know how to point, and have the presence to realize that the aide's attention must be drawn to the board. There is an element of role taking even in this relatively simple communication exchange, but little more is required of the system.

In summary, there are numerous approaches to nonvocal communication that vary according to specific modality, complexity, response requirements, etc. In addition, there is another important dimension along which they may differ. Some, such as Bliss, are designed primarily for the purposes of basic, functional communication. Some, like American sign language (Ameslan), attempt to teach an alternative language system, not just a means of communication. At least one other, Non-SLIP, is designed primarily as the substratum on which a more conventional communication system can be built. In selecting among or from these systems, it is important that the clinician be alert to the particular characteristics and terminal goals to which each program is directed.

The availability of systematic techniques for teaching alternatives to vocal communication greatly expands the potential contribution of the clinician to the child with a severe language handicap. At the same time, as so often seems to be the case, it adds a new dimension of concern. At what point should the attempt to teach standard speech be abandoned? How long should one persist in vocal training before attempting an alternative? When can the clinician or teacher feel assured that the child's failure to progress is attributable to the improbability of speech as a language vehicle for that child rather than some imperfection in the teaching program or the teacher's techniques? These are serious decisions, with important consequences, of the same order as those faced by families and teachers of the deaf. In the case of the profoundly retarded child, Guess, Sailor, and Baer (Chapter 3) indicate that an important prognostic sign for their program is the child's ability to perform vocal imitation. This is extremely important information. It requires that we count our failures as well as our successes, and that we try to make sense of both. Clearly, there is a need to identify additional criteria to be used as the base for decisions concerning whether a given child should be enrolled in speech or in some nonvocal communication program.

DIFFERENTIAL DIAGNOSIS

None of the language training chapters in this book devotes many pages to traditional diagnosis or evaluation. Although Hollis and Carrier (Chapter 2) and Guess, Sailor, and Baer (Chapter 3) do suggest adjustments in programming for the child who is deaf or has severe physical impairment of the speech mechanism, such terms as "brain injured," "autistic," or "congenitally aphasic" rarely occur. Is this omission justified? Can successful therapy programs be built without consideration of the particular populations of children with whom the programs will be attempted? More generally, do these diagnostic labels interact significantly with the kind of therapy that ought to be used? The use of traditional diagnostic categories is considered briefly below to determine what value they might have for the language programmer.

Most of the diagnostic labels used to classify children with communication problems were initially derived from medical models and, indeed, some were first promulgated by physicians. No doubt this is why these classifications tend to place great emphasis on etiology. For example, Rimland (1964) argues that autism is a genetically determined condition involving the reticular formation. Because there is no direct way to evaluate the biological aspects of autism, Rimland and his followers are forced to rely almost entirely on behavioral factors to distinguish between autistic and nonautistic children. Although the children are discussed as though they are biologically impaired, this is more a hypothesis concerning probable cause than it is a description of the children or their underlying deficit. The factors ultimately specified include aloofness from adults, average or better motor skills, unusual food preferences, rigidity in maintaining sameness in the environment, mute or echolalic speech, and stereotyped behavior. While this constellation of behavioral characteristics eventually may be linked to specific biological mechanisms, speculations concerning biological conditions have little significance for the treatment of autistic children, given our current state of knowledge concerning the form of these potential mechanisms and their poor predictive power for success or failure of educational endeavors (Lindsley, 1964). Regardless of etiology and classification, the language teacher must cope with and find ways to reduce stereotyped behavior, echolalic speech, and rigidity while encouraging the development of appropriate modes of language reception and expression. The instructional task seems to be the same, regardless of whether the child is labeled autistic, brain damaged, retarded, or congenitally aphasic.

There are several circumstances in which, at least in principle, it would be valuable to have diagnostic information based on the etiology or underlying cause of a speech and language disorder. If it were the case that careful differential diagnosis could, in fact, isolate clinical syndromes, the effort would be worthwhile if these three conditions could be met:

1. If there were some treatment method that could be aimed directly at the underlying biological condition; that is, if mental retardation were best treated by certain medical or pharmacological procedures

that are quite different from those that might be chosen for autism or aphasia

2. If knowing the underlying cause always led to different forms of behavioral therapy or instruction, even if no biologically oriented treatment program were possible

3. If differential diagnosis led to accurate predictions concerning the probable course of the behavioral disorders so that it would be possible to distinguish between the effects of therapy and the disease process itself

For the most part, none of these conditions can be met given our current knowledge in the field of behavior disorders. We do not yet have the information to allow a different frontal attack on the biological mechanisms underlying minimal brain damage, autism, mental retardation in most of its manifestations, dyslexia, and so on. Nor have powerful behavioral treatment methods been devised that are related specifically to underlying causal mechanisms. The programs described in this book deal with the organization of behavior, the structure of language and communication, and the analysis of environmental events, but not with specific syndromes. Finally, there are very few conditions in which a specific degenerative disorder can be identified that would severely impair progress in therapy or render a program of therapy useless. For most of the children seen in educational programs or speech and language programs, the condition exists as the expression of some unknown mixture of biological and environmental influences, and the best predictions concerning the child's developmental potential can be derived by analyzing the child's previous accomplishments and his response to therapy.

There is perhaps one last reason why differential diagnosis for communication handicaps seems somewhat futile. The minimal requirement for the application of diagnostic procedures would have to be that the clinical conditions or syndromes can be differentiated clearly. The problem here is that most of these syndromes are extremely fuzzy at best, as evidenced by the continuing attempt to find just the proper constellation of terms to describe the deficits. Autism has yielded recently to autistic-like. Minimal brain damage, dyslexia, congenital aphasia, aphasoid, exogenous and endogenous retardation are only a sampling of terms that give eloquent testimony to the fact that these diagnostic categories are very much in the eye of the beholders, and only equivocally in the behavior of the children.

There are, of course, some children whose problems emanate fairly directly from biological or neurological abnormalities. These include the cerebral palsied, the deaf, and the blind. Blindness, unless it is combined with some other handicapping condition, does not significantly affect the development of speech, language, or communication. Somehow these children learn to link their auditory experience with ongoing events and other verbalizations without the benefit of visual input. This is interesting to note in view of the strong bias in most programs to rely heavily on visual forms of stimulation. Cerebral palsy and deafness can have profound effects on a child's development of speech and functional communication. As Hollis and Carrier (Chapter 2) point out, both conditions require training procedures with special consideration to input and output modalities. For the deaf, language training may involve the use of the visual mode for input, and the sign language mode for output. For the cerebral palsied, the input modes are often disturbed, and it may also be necessary to develop alternative gross motor output modes that require less physical dexterity and control than vocal speech.

Even in the case of unequivocal deficits such as deafness or cerebral palsy, it is not the biological or the neurological aspects but rather the behavioral aspect of the condition that requires the modification of language-training procedures. Therapy for a deaf child takes note of the fact that he responds only minimally to auditory stimulation and hence fails to obtain, or to come into contact with, certain environmental stimuli required for the development of functional speech. Similarly, the cerebral palsied child shows limitations in the ability to generate certain conventional responses and thus may require alternative response modes.

If one interprets diagnosis very broadly, there are two types of behavioral diagnoses that could prove useful. One is a careful evaluation of a child's current behavioral status. The second is an evaluation of the rapidity with which a child learns new skills, or perhaps the power of the techniques required to teach a child new skills. The first type of evaluation would allow the language trainer to start at the correct point in training to avoid skipping vital steps or repeating training on behavior the child already exhibits. The first type of measure can be rather readily made through simple observation and testing. Methods for evaluating the rate of learning or the power of techniques necessary to ensure learning are not well developed. Yet, such evaluation could aid the language trainer in selecting the right program and in selecting children for training which would ensure some possibility of success. An example of a type of behavior that appears to predict subsequent progress in language training is vocal imitation. Lovaas and his colleagues (Lovaas et al., 1973) reported that autistic children who were echolalic progressed more rapidly in language learning than did mute autistic children. And Guess, Sailor, and Baer (Chapter 3) have indicated that vocal imitation is predictive of subsequent performance on their language program.

It is very likely that measures of both current behavioral skills and rate of learning will grow out of the procedures used in training. In view of the limited value of traditional diagnosis and the fact that development of useful behavioral diagnosis will be linked closely to language-program development, the current writers conclude that the neglect of differential diagnosis by the programs included in this book is an appropriate omission.

IMITATION AND LANGUAGE TRAINING

During recent years imitation has been the focus of discussions that have attempted to analyze the nature of imitation (Bandura and Walters, 1963; Baer, Peterson, and Sherman, 1967; Kuhn, 1973; Whitehurst, 1977), the role of imitation in language development (Ervin, 1969; Sherman, 1971; Slobin, 1971; Whitehurst, 1977), and the role of imitation in language training (Sherman, 1971). At first glance the nature of imitation may appear to be simple. A model exhibits some behavior and another person follows by emitting topographically similar behavior. However, not all topographically similar behavior is imitative. An airplane passes overhead, and first one person and then a second person look up. The two individuals perform topographically similar behavior in a sequence that is pertinent to imitation, but is this properly regarded as an instance of imitation? Not unless we can be sure that for the second person looking up was not under the control of the noise produced by the airplane. In order for the behavior of the second person to be imitative it must be under the control of the behavior modeled by the first person.

There is also a serious problem concerning how similar one person's behavior must be to the behavior of the second person before it is classed as imitative. Must it be similar on several dimensions or can it be similar on only one? The answers to these questions may determine how important imitation is to language acquisition. If one considers a response imitative only if it is an exact or nearly exact copy of the model's behavior, then imitation will not seem to be very important in language acquisition because few mother-child interchanges will satisfy this strict criterion. This seems to have been the view of some psycholinguists who have maintained that imitation is not very important in language acquisition (Ervin, 1969; Slobin, 1971). However, other writers (Ferster and Perrott, 1968; Whitehurst, 1977) have maintained that similarity between the behavior of two persons can be limited to a single dimension, provided that variations along that dimension are under the control of the model's behavior. From this point of view the critical element that defines imitation is functional control by a model's behavior along some dimension. This seems to be a reasonable way to define imitation because it is virtually impossible to obtain a response that matches that of a model on all dimensions. In Whitehurst's (1977) article, "dimension" is a very broad term that includes sentence complexity and sentence type. Given this broad definition, even most psycholinguists would agree that imitation plays a role in language acquisition. They would, no doubt, also argue that imitation, so defined, is not a simple response to a stimulus but a complex cognitive process.

Many attempts to analyze the nature of imitation do indeed consider it as a very complex problem. The child who imitates is assumed to observe the behavior of a model, perform some response, observe his own behavior, and make a comparison between his own behavior and that of the model. The comparison seems to be an extremely complex procedure because the stimuli produced by the model's behavior and the stimuli generated by the subject's own behavior are very dissimilar and may even fall into two different modes. In the case of vocal imitation, for example, the model's behavior is visual and auditory, while the child's behavior is auditory and kinesthetic. How is it that the child learns to make this magical comparison, especially with behavior he has never imitated previously? How does he recognize the similarity between his own behavior and that of the model?

Perhaps the analysis of imitation is more complex than it needs to be. Kuhn (1973) has suggested that children do not imitate behaviors not already in their repertoire. Is it also possible that generalized imitation does not really involve imitation of novel behavior but simply the rearrangement of components already learned? That is, the novel imitative response involves behavioral components already under the control of some stimulus component of the model's behaviors. What is learned and demonstrated in generalized imitation may be analogous to phenomena demonstrated by Striefel, Wetherby, and Karlan (1977) with verb-noun instruction-following. Striefel and his colleagues trained severely retarded children to respond correctly to a series of verb-noun instructions such as, *touch car, lift car, touch ball, lift ball.* They found that after a series of commands involving recombinations of verbs and nouns had been taught, the children would follow instructions involving new combinations of these same verbs and nouns. The children had been taught that each word controlled a particular component of the response. When components were recombined, the responses were appropriate. When training did not involve extensive recombination of verbs and nouns, generalization to new verb-noun combinations did not occur (Striefel and Wetherby, 1973). For a more complete discussion of this line of research see Wetherby (1978) and Wetherby and Striefel (Chapter 7).

Even a casual look at the items used for imitation training by Baer, Peterson, and Sherman (1967) suggests a great deal of component recombination among the various imitation items. For example, 21 of 130 items involve tapping either objects or body parts. After being trained to imitate tapping with many different objects, it would not be surprising if the child could imitate a new behavior involving tapping with some additional objects. No doubt combining and recombining of imitative units occur at a much more molecular level than that involved in the Baer, Peterson, and Sherman study. Is it possible that such recombinations are the essence of generalized imitation?

Such a component of imitation has implications for another baffling finding concerning imitation. Investigators (Lovaas, 1966; Brigham and Sherman, 1973) have found that not only do children attempt nonreinforced probe items but they actually improve in their productions of these items, despite the fact that differential reinforcement is never given for accurate response to the probes. One reason for increased accuracy in imitating the probes may be that the direct, reinforced imitative training sharpens the precision of the child's response to the elemental units that underly all of his imitative attempts—reinforced and nonreinforced. Thus, although a superficial analysis would suggest that the child is never reinforced for attempting the nonreinforced probe items, a closer analysis suggests that the crucial elements of these items are being shaped by the reinforcement given for the nonprobe items on the list. If, for some reason, imitation as a class of behavior is increased by training, all imitation should improve.

Note also that a component notion of imitation has practical implications. Such an analysis suggests that, if generalized imitation is to occur, behaviors involving recombinations of components should be used during training. Moreover, if the probe items involve components not occurring in the training items, generalized imitation should not occur. The component notion would give little reason to expect generalization from gross motor imitation to verbal imitation (Garcia, Baer, and Firestone, 1971), and the research indicates that such generalization does not occur readily (Baer, Peterson, and Sherman, 1967).

Regardless of the strict nature of imitation, or whether or not it is important to normal language acquisition, imitation seems to be relevant in two ways to the training of language-deficient children. First, presence of verbal imitation seems to be a predictor of subsequent language development when language-deficient children are put in language-training programs (Lovaas et al., 1973; Guess, Sailor, and Baer, Chapter 3). These findings suggest that it may be necessary to place a child, who does not have a verbal imitative repertoire, in a program that includes some nonspeech mode. Second, all language-training programs that use speech as the input-output mode rely very heavily on imitative procedures in nearly all phases of training.

The use of verbal imitation in language training can vary. Training can call for rote imitation in which the child is required to repeat a verbal utterance without being given any meaning or context for the utterance. This, of course, is the kind of training used by Lovaas and his colleagues (Lovaas et al., 1966) to establish imitative vocal responses in children who previously had shown no verbal imitation. Rote imitation may also be used in more advanced language training involving vocabulary or syntax training. However, there seems to be little reason not to provide the possibility for the child to learn the meaning or context during imitative training, and most language programs provide at least an appropriate picture as a stimulus in addition to the verbal model. There is some feeling that presenting the verbal stimulus alone in imitation training may actually interfere with subsequent receptive or productive training (Ruder, Hermann, and Schiefelbusch, 1977). The speech-based programs presented in this book all use imitation with context as a basic technique for teaching language. The programs by Waryas and Stremel-Campbell (Chapter 4) and by Guess, Sailor, and Baer (Chapter 3) present verbal models and pictures or objects to the student and require that the student imitate the model. This procedure is used both in improving articulation and in introducing new and more complex grammatical forms. Hart and Rogers-Warren (Chapter 5) suggest that, when a child makes a request for an object or activity, the teacher should provide models of grammatical form that are slightly more advanced than the language forms the child is using and that allow and encourage imitation of more advanced grammatical forms in their milieu form of teaching. However, if the child does not imitate the teacher's model, the teacher may still continue to acknowledge the child's request.

It is not surprising that imitation is ubiquitous in language training because modeling is certainly a quick and effective way of getting a close approximation to a target utterance from the child. In fact, with some children it may be the only way to obtain a close approximation to the desired utterance. However, when the child is reliably imitating a model, there is no guarantee that he is able to emit the utterance in appropriate context in the absence of the model. This means that once the child is reliably imitating the model there is a major step to be taken. That step is to get the child to use the linguistic form in nonimitative contexts. Several procedures have been used for establishing such nonimitative responding. Three suggested techniques are: 1) fading the verbal model (Lovaas et al., 1966; Risley and Wolf, 1967), 2) first presenting a picture or object and delaying the presentation of the verbal model (Risley and Wolf, 1967), and 3) presenting certain trials in which the verbal model is not presented (Whitehurst, 1977). Success has been reported with each of these methods, and no clear evidence exists that one is superior to the others. All of these procedures are used to varying degrees in the programs described in this book.

RECEPTIVE AND EXPRESSIVE TRAINING

The relationship between reception (comprehension) and expression (production) has been a topic of much recent discussion and disagreement (Bloom, 1974; Chapman, 1974; Ingram, 1974; Ruder and Smith, 1974; Guess, Sailor, and Baer, Chapter 3; Schumaker and Sherman, Chapter 6). Much of the disagreement seems to stem from a variety of conceptual and methodological issues. Early writers in the field of language readily accepted the proposition that language comprehension precedes language production (McCarthy, 1954; Lenneberg, 1962). However, recent conceptualizations of language have led to a reconsideration. Attacks on the proposition that comprehension precedes production come from two fronts: behavioral and cognitive psychology. From the point of view of behavioral psychology there is no reason to expect comprehension to be related in a specific way to production. Comprehension involves an implicit or explicit response to a linguistic utterance, whereas production involves a linguistic response to some situation or environmental context. Because different stimuli and responses are involved in the two performances, there is no reason to believe that the two could not develop quite independently and, hence, no reason to believe that comprehension must precede production.

Cognitive writers have suggested that both language production and comprehension are a reflection of underlying cognitive or linguistic competencies. Given this analysis, there is no reason to believe that comprehension should precede production. Thus, both behavioral and cognitive writers have suggested that the proposition that comprehension precedes production may not be true.

The concern with the relationship of comprehension to production led to a study by Fraser, Bellugi, and Brown in 1963. The results of this study seemed to support the proposition that comprehension preceded production. However, this study has since been criticized because the methods used to evaluate production and comprehension did not equate chance probabilities for being correct (Fernald, 1972). The contention is that, if these chance probabilities were corrected, there would not be differences in performance on comprehension and production tasks. The Fraser et al. (1963) study and the criticisms by Fernald (1972) are illustrative of the extreme methodological problem in conducting research on the relationships of reception and production. There is another issue involved in evaluating comprehension. Frequently nonlanguage context will allow a listener to respond appropriately to a linguistic utterance, while that context cannot aid the subject in producing a grammatically and semantically appropriate utterance if the speaker does not know the rules (Bloom, 1974). Thus, it is very difficult to determine exactly how much a listener comprehends. Note also that the use of context by the listener will lead to a systematic overestimation of the person's language comprehension.

A study by Chapman and Miller (1975) has opened the possibility that language production can precede reception. They found that some children used an appropriate form productively before they responded correctly to that form when it was presented in comprehension. The research alluded to above is but a small part of the research that has been conducted or is being conducted in an attempt to unravel the complexity of the development of production and comprehension. Nevertheless, it does illustrate the complexity of the issue and the lack of agreement that exists in the area.

The above research was primarily descriptive in nature. Perhaps research aimed at training production and comprehension would yield more orderly and consistent data concerning the relationship between comprehension and production. Certainly the results of training studies would seem relevant to a book on intervention. A few training studies are therefore examined below. Guess (1969) conducted a study in which two severely retarded adolescents were taught the receptive use of the plural morpheme. There was no generalization to the productive use of the plural morpheme. The subjects were then taught the productive use of the plural morpheme. Finally, the subjects were taught to respond to a single object when the plural of a noun was used, and to two objects when the singular form was used. In other words, the subjects were taught a reversed plural usage receptively. This training had no effect on the appropriate use of the plural morpheme in production. This study lead Guess to conclude that language reception and production could be disassociated from one another. A subsequent study by Guess and Baer (1973) has supported the notion that receptive and productive repertoires may function independently of each other.

Receptive training does not always fail to show generalization to production. Ruder and his colleagues (Ruder, Smith, and Hermann, 1974; Ruder, Hermann, and Schiefelbusch, 1977) have conducted a series of studies in which normal preschool- and school-age children were taught Spanish vocabulary items and structures in a comprehension task. The subjects were uniformly able to produce the vocabulary items or language structures under appropriate circumstances when they were given additional experience in imitating these vocabulary items or structures in the absence of any appropriate context.

Winitz and Reeds (1975) reported that when college students in a foreign language training program were given receptive training in a number of critical contrasts, correct production emerged without training. Once again, the Winitz and Reeds study and its accompanying rationale illustrate the complexity of the comprehension and production issue. Winitz and Reeds' research and their interpretation have raised again an issue that has occurred throughout this discussion of reception and production. What has the child discriminated or understood when he makes a correct comprehension response in a test situation, and how comparable are the tests for comprehension and production (Fernald, 1972; Bloom, 1974)? A child must ordinarily take into account many more contrasts to produce a word or sentence correctly than is usually required in comprehension tests. For example, to produce the word *dog* it is necessary for the child to take into account a variety of contrasts. However, if the child is required to point to a picture in response to *dog,* when presented with pictures of a dog and cat, the child conceivably could respond correctly without distinguishing between the phonemic contrasts involved in such words as *dog* and *hog, dog* and *doll* or, for that matter, *dog* and *bag.* Winitz and Reeds interpret their research as supportive of the notion that comprehension can precede production. However, it appears that their work could also support the notion that comprehension and production are developed simultaneously.

In the training studies just presented, the results have ranged from basic independence of productive and comprehensive repertoires (Guess, 1969) to complete emergence of production following comprehension training (Winitz and Reeds, 1975). While questions of whether comprehension always precedes production or whether production emerges without training may be important from a theoretical point of view, the critical issue for training is whether or not one sequence is more effective or economical than another. To our knowledge, this remains a relatively unexplored area of research.

One study (Miller, Cuvo, and Borakove, 1977) was conducted to teach retarded adolescents and adults the number of cents in various coins. They found that, while teaching reception did not affect expression, teaching expression resulted in almost complete transfer to reception. Surprisingly, there were no savings in trial to criterion on expression after having been trained on reception. This study suggests that training production first may be more efficient than training reception first. How the results from this task might relate to other language training remains to be determined.

As was the case with descriptive studies of normal language development, training studies also yield conflicting results concerning the relationship between production and comprehension. It is likely that some of the conflicting results come from the content taught or the procedures used. It is also likely that subjects at different levels of development yield markedly different generalization between the productive and receptive repertoires. Results with extremely young or severely handicapped persons may show little effect of training reception or production, whereas more sophisticated subjects such as college students may show marked transfer from comprehension to production.

All of the above studies were conducted in laboratory-like settings, and it is possible that this experimental procedure yielded findings that are not representative of the way reception and expression develop in the natural environment. The current writers hypothesize that there is a continual interaction between receptive and expressive skills. The child learns a limited meaning of the word: he uses the word in a number of contexts, sometimes inappropriately; through the use of the word the child is taught new meanings; now his reception has grown and he uses the word more appropriately. This sets the stage for more receptive learning. Needless to say, the theoretical and training literature presents the clinician with a perplexing and confusing picture with regard to the relationship of reception and expression: What should the language trainer do?

Guess, Sailor, and Baer (Chapter 3) have taken the position that verbal expression best allows the child to manipulate and control his environment, thus getting reinforcers from it. In this way they justify focusing training primarily on expression initially and then introducing tests and training procedures to ensure reception. No one would argue with the position that expression is important. However, the current writers do argue with the notion that expression is more important than reception in getting reinforcers from the environment. The failure to understand what others are saying is likely to cause the child to lose the opportunity for many reinforcers, including those involved in the mere inclusion in a social group. Language reception is an important skill, and it seems unlikely that one can justify focusing on expression training simply on the basis that expression has greater value for the individual than reception.

In view of the conflicting hypotheses and data concerning the relationship between reception and production, any suggestions to the clinician must be highly tentative. However, both production and reception are important. For this reason, it seems that both should be taught. We would recommend that they be taught in a concurrent fashion. Because both reception and expression are useful skills, the child who is taught both should profit greatly, whether receptive and expressive repertoires are independent or related in ways proclaimed by theorists. In either case, the child will end up with functional language behavior.

Suppose a child seems able to acquire a great amount of receptive language but he is unable to exhibit much, or perhaps any, expressive language. The child, when given concurrent training, will at least extend his receptive repertoire. If the child developed an extensive receptive repertoire but no productive repertoire, the teacher might wish to try another productive mode, as suggested by Hollis and Carrier (Chapter 2).

Suppose that for a given child and a given content, the finding of Miller et al. (1977) of generalization from expression to reception, but not from reception to expression, holds. In this case, the training may be slightly uneconomical, but both receptive and expressive repertoires will be achieved.

Finally, consider the possibility that the repertoires are initially independent, but through concurrent training the child gradually learns to use what is taught in one mode in the other. One could now introduce something in the receptive mode and the child would use it in the expressive mode or vice versa.

GENERALIZATION AND TRANSFER

The therapist or teacher who trains speech or language makes the assumption that his efforts will have an effect on the child's communication outside the training situation; otherwise, there would be no reason to engage in the training since it is usually an artificial intervention into the child's life, with no inherent value. The problem of training speech or language so that its use will generalize into natural settings raises many issues concerning the nature of teaching and of natural settings.

Perhaps the first need is to determine what language skills are likely to be useful in the natural environment. If the skills taught in the clinic are not commonly used in the child's natural environment, there is no reason to believe they will transfer or generalize beyond the confines of the clinic. If they do transfer, it is unlikely they will be maintained because these settings probably do not provide natural contingencies to reinforce them.

Three of the chapters in this book have as a major part of their rationale the selection of language skills that will be useful. Guess, Sailor, and Baer (Chapter 3) have ostensibly designed their language program so that the language taught will be functional in the child's natural environment. Waryas and Stremel-Campbell (Chapter 4) focus on the pragmatics of language. They attempt to teach linguistic units for use in those situations in which the child has shown an interest or in which the child already exhibits nonspeech communication. Hart and Rogers-Warren (Chapter 5) deal with the problem of transfer by doing the teaching in natural situations in which the child has a need to communicate, rather than in contrived clinical settings.

Each of these programs makes some attempt to create a bridge between the teaching and the natural environment in which the child's communication skills must function, but in no instance is there any demonstration of success in meeting this goal. Even Hart and Rogers-Warren focus their attention on a very specific setting, the preschool, and there is no guarantee that the behaviors that emerge in such a setting will also be appropriate and supported in the home or other settings in which the child is expected to perform. The possible failure of the natural environment to support the new language being taught is even greater in the programs of Guess et al. and Waryas and Stremel-Campbell. Many children to whom these programs are applied live in institutional environments where the functionality of language is questionable. All too frequently the routines and arrangements of the institution fail to make language useful and provide the children with infrequent opportunities to use their newly acquired language skills.

Given the strong possibility that the skills the child is learning in therapy do not generalize to his living environment, what changes should be made in the teaching and/or living environment to promote such generalization? The technology of such generalization is beginning to attract attention. Stokes and Baer (1977) abstracted several principles or procedures from their review of the literature. Among the procedures were: training across several settings, training many examples of the behavior, training "loosely," and training under contingencies similar to those found in the natural environment.

Training across settings involves teaching and reinforcing the child for emitting certain behavior in situation after situation until the child can demonstrate the skill in a situation never previously encountered, without additional training. This is the sort of procedure traditionally used by speech and language clinicians who first taught a specific skill to the child in an individual session in the clinic, then extended the skill to a group setting in the clinic, and then perhaps to the canteen or other setting. This form of carry-over training, although not unknown in speech and language therapy, has generally been unsystematic and not thoroughly monitored to determine if the target behavior has generalized into all appropriate settings. Even when such generalization training is programmed explicitly, the clinician accompanies the client from setting to setting. It is possible that generalization would be more satisfactory if different adults set up the occasions for the different settings in which the new skills should appear.

One of the most promising procedures in language training includes the use of multiple examples. This procedure has been widely used in establishing motor imitation (Baer, Peterson, and Sherman, 1967), morphological endings (Guess et al., 1968), and syntax (Wheeler and Sulzer, 1970) among language-deficient children. The procedure is as follows. Select a class of behaviors, such as using a noun and a verb to describe an animate object engaged in an action. After the children are trained with several examples of the use of this string, they can often use the string appropriately to describe new combinations of animate objects and actions. When this occurs, the children's use of noun-verb strings is considered generative, and the chances are increased that the child may encounter situations external to the training setting in which the use of such a string may be appropriate and hence reinforced.

Many training or clinical procedures for establishing speech and language are highly structured and there is a tendency to foster very stereotyped responses from trial to trial. Such training leads the client to use the language in very limited situations. Slight changes in the presentation of the stimuli may then fail to evoke the appropriate language response. In order to avoid such training effects, Stokes and Baer suggest the procedure of *training loosely*. The clinician varies the way the training is done from trial to trial and from session to session. In this way the clinician teaches the child to use the language response in the appropriate situation regardless of what other noncritical factors may be present or absent in the situation. Training loosely seems to be related to training many examples across multiple settings and should aid in increasing generalization into natural settings. Such training, it should be noted, is not equivalent to chaotic or haphazard instruction, although it is interesting to note that this seems to be a significant departure from the rigidly controlled stimulus-response sequences that were the hallmark of earlier behavior modification attempts. Perhaps Stokes and Baer are attempting to reintroduce the feature of flexibility, and even creativity, that was so important to traditionally educated teachers and clinicians.

Another issue in generalization and transfer is related to the kinds of artificial and contrived reinforcement methods and schedules frequently used in training. In the clinic it may be necessary to use powerful reinforcers with unvarying consistency to establish a repertoire of language responses, but this may contrast sharply with the reinforcement practices the child will experience in the natural environment. This problem can be overcome by gradually fading the frequency of reinforcement in the training session to the point where it more nearly matches the frequency of reinforcement for language use found in the natural environment. The type of reinforcers should also be shifted to those that occur in the natural environment. For example, while children may initially be given bites of ice cream for each correct description of a picture in the experimental setting, persons in the natural environment are more likely to reinforce such descriptions intermittently, by attending and talking to the child. For this reason, the therapist should attempt to use intermittent social reinforcers to maintain such describing responses in the training setting.

The contingencies of reinforcement may be very important in determining whether language skills generalize from the teacher to other persons in the environment and to other nontraining settings. Behaviorists often imply that to obtain generalization, all of the prevailing and antecedent stimulus conditions should be matched closely in the training and generalization situations. This would lead one to believe that generalization would occur best to persons who look like the trainer. If the trainer is a woman, more generalization should occur to women than men. However, stimuli need not look alike to have similar controlling properties (Spradlin, Cotter, and Baxley, 1973; Dixon and Spradlin, 1976; Spradlin and Dixon, 1976). If two stimuli can be substituted for each other without changing the reinforcement contingencies in the situation, they will be treated as similar. For example, the words *stone* and *rock* can be substituted in most verbal contexts without changing what would be an appropriate response to the context. Hence, they may be treated as similar when one is given a new function. To the extent that they have been treated as equivalent in a variety of old situations, they are likely to be treated as equivalent in new situations. This same kind of process no doubt happens to trainers and nontrainers. If the trainers reinforce some behaviors in the same manner as the child's parents, it is likely that other behavior will generalize from the training setting to the home; that is, if some responses are reinforced in both environments, other responses reinforced in only one environment may generalize into the environment in which it is not reinforced. The application of similar contingencies across situations provides a powerful mechanism of generalization, and is an argument for the inclusion of parents in therapy programs.

Parents or other persons working in the child's natural environment as cooperating teachers may solve a number of the problems of generalization and transfer automatically. Lovaas et al. (1973) found this to be true in the case of autistic children. MacDonald et al. (1974) report similar findings with Down Syndrome children. Parents as teachers in the home environment help make the clinic more similar to the home and increase the chance that similar reinforcement contingencies will be applied in both settings. Both of these outcomes should increase generalization.

CONCLUSION

The language therapy approaches included in this book provide a reasonable sample of the options available to the language teacher or clinician. The programs differ along a number of dimensions, perhaps most notably in terms of the children for whom they are intended. One of the clinician's first tasks in attempting to match a program to a child is to know for what population the program is suited, and the kinds of minimal skills the child must possess to perform in the program.

The programs also differ in the theoretical bases from which they were inspired, and this places an additional burden on the clinician. The clinician has some obligation to be informed about the underlying rationale of a program before selecting it and applying it in therapy. In the words of Waryas and Stremel-Campbell (Chapter 4), "when a decision is made to adopt one [or another] training procedure, the [language] practitioner is also making a judgment about the theoretical principles [upon which it is based]." It is perhaps not so much the theoretical principles as it is their translation into therapy activities and goals that must be of concern to the clinician. It is especially evident in the area of psycholinguistics that "theoretical principles" have a very high mortality rate, and each new psycholinguistic revolution leaves principles strewn about in its wake. Often, what appears to be a new psycholinguistic principle is more a change in the metalanguage with which basic data are represented. *Mommy sock* has been, in its short history, a "pivot plus open" construction, a noun plus noun construction, a genitive construction, etc. It is the task of language theorists to find general systems to account for the data of child language, but sometimes the useful insights are forfeited by the zeal with which the old is displaced by the new. It would be unfortunate, for example, if Chomsky's important revelations concerning the syntactic bases for language are lost in deference to the new enthusiasm for semantic and pragmatic aspects of language use.

Clinicians have an obligation to remain sufficiently knowledgeable and current in the literature to make informed evaluations concerning the claims of various treatment methods. If part of the attraction of a certain approach to therapy is that it is linked to a particular theory of language, the clinician had best be in a position to accept or reject that theory as an adequate characterization of the behaviors that appear in the clinic. Of course, the method or program must stand on its own merits as well, but if it incorporates a concept of language that is unacceptable to the clinician, there may be little reason to explore it further. Program designers also have an obligation to resist the temptation to exploit current fads, to be as descriptive as possible without indulging in the "change-its-name-but-not-its content" game, to acknowledge how a program is related to basic research or clinical experience, and to provide and generate data concerning the effectiveness of the methods proposed, their limitations, and the children for whom the program was developed. The program developer, it seems, must be forthcoming. There should be no mystery concerning the rationale underlying a program or the data that support it. The clinician should be an active partner in the task of evaluating an approach to therapy, of testing its limitations, and of modifying it to fit particular populations of children. As new understandings concerning the nature of language and communication occur, the clinician should be able to select from the old program those components that seem useful and to blend these with new insights that come from a current reading of the literature.

A program is a device, to be put at the service of a clinician, who, in turn, is at the service of a client in need of language therapy. It may be a simple-minded notion, but it is an important one nonetheless: the program should not dominate the clinician. The program should be a tool that he wields in the effort to find systematic and creative ways to work with a child. Program developers make significant contributions in that they help identify populations of children (those for whom the program is appropriate), they help define language in functional ways, they provide insights and speculations concerning the microstructure of behavior and the proper sequencing of a teaching schedule, and they give the clinician a set of options that can be incorporated into the therapy process. A good program is not designed, however, to replace a thinking clinician. Language programs are potentially most effective when they are sufficiently explicit that a creative and knowledgeable clinician can apply the program in a thoughtful way, building on the principles incorporated in the program in ways that make it increasingly appropriate for the problems presented by individual children. Conceptions of language and of effective ways to sequence and modify behavior will surely change with increasing information from applied and basic research, as well as with the stringent tests that occur daily in the clinic. What must be as constant as the northern star are the speech and language teacher's willingness and ability to mediate among these quixotic events and to use good clinical judgment, honed both by experience and information, to select for each child that approach to therapy that seems most appropriate for that child's unique needs.

REFERENCES

Baer, D. M., Peterson, R. F., and Sherman, J. A. 1967. The development of imitation by reinforcing behavioral similarity to a model. J. Exp. Anal. Behav. 10:405–416.

Bandura, A., and Walters, R. H. 1963. Social Learning and Personality Development. Holt, Rinehart and Winston, New York.

Bellugi, U., and Brown, R. (eds.). 1964. The acquisition of language. Monogr. Soc. Res. Child Dev. 29.

Bloom, L. 1970. Language Development: Form and Function in Emerging Grammars. MIT Press, Cambridge, Mass.

Bloom, L. 1973. One Word at a Time. Mouton, The Hague.

Bloom, L. 1974. Talking, understanding, and thinking. In R. L. Schiefelbusch and L. L. Lloyd (eds.), Language Perspectives—Acquisition, Retardation, and Intervention, pp. 285–311. University Park Press, Baltimore.

Bloom, L., Hood, L., and Lightbown, P. 1974. Imitation in language development: If, when, and why. Cog. Psychol. 6:380–420.

Braine, M. D. 1976. Children's first word combinations. Monogr. Soc. Res. Child Dev. 41.

Brigham, T. A., and Sherman, J. 1973. Effects of choice and immediacy of reinforcement on single response and switching behavior of children. J. Exp. Anal. Behav. 19:425–435.

Brown, R. 1973. A First Language: The Early Stages. Harvard University Press, Cambridge, Mass.

Carrier, J. K., Jr. 1974. Application of functional analysis and a nonspeech response mode to teaching language. In L. V. McReynolds (ed.), Developing systematic procedures for training children's language. ASHA Monogr. 18.

Carrier, J. K., Jr. 1976. Application of a nonspeech language system with the severely language handicapped. In L. L. Lloyd (ed.), Communication Assessment and Intervention Strategies, pp. 523–547. University Park Press, Baltimore.

Carrow, E. 1973. Test for Auditory Comprehension of Language. Urban Research Group, Austin, Tex.

Chapman, R. S. 1974. Discussion summary—Developmental relationship between receptive and expressive language. In R. L. Schiefelbusch and L. L. Lloyd (eds.), Language Perspectives—Acquisition, Retardation, and Intervention, pp. 335–344. University Park Press, Baltimore.

Chapman, R. S., and Miller, J. F. 1975. Word order in early two and three word utterances: Does production precede comprehension? J. Speech Hear. Res. 8:355–371.

Chomsky, N. 1957. Syntactic Structures. Mouton, The Hague.

Clark, C. R., and Woodcock, R. W. 1976. Graphic systems of communication. In L. L. Lloyd (ed.), Communication Assessment and Intervention Strategies, pp. 549–605. University Park Press, Baltimore.

Dale, P. 1976. Language Development: Structure and Function. 2nd ed. Holt, Rinehart and Winston, New York.

Dixon, M., and Spradlin, J. 1976. Establishing stimulus equivalences among retarded adolescents. J. Exp. Child Psychol. 21:144–164.

Ervin, S. M. 1969. Imitation and structural change in children's language. In E.

Lennenberg (ed.), New Directions in the Study of Language. MIT Press, Cambridge, Mass.

Fernald, C. 1972. Control of grammar in imitation, comprehension, and production: Problems of replication. J. Verb. Learn. Verb. Behav. 11:606–613.

Ferster, C. B., and Perrott, M. C. 1968. Behavior Principles. Meredith Corporation, New York.

Fraser, C., Bellugi, U., and Brown, R. 1963. Control of grammar in imitation, comprehension, and production. J. Verb. Learn. Verb. Behav. 2:121–135.

Fristoe, M. 1976. Language intervention systems: Programs published in kit form. In L. L. Lloyd (ed.), Communication Assessment and Intervention Strategies, pp. 813–859. University Park Press, Baltimore.

Garcia, E., Baer, D. M., and Firestone, I. 1971. The development of generalized imitation within topographically determined boundaries. J. Appl. Behav. Anal. 4:101–112.

Guess, D. 1969. A functional analysis of receptive language and productive speech: Acquisition of the plural morpheme. J. Appl. Behav. Anal. 2:55–64.

Guess, D., and Baer, D. M. 1973. An analysis of individual differences in generalization between receptive and productive language in retarded children. J. Appl. Behav. Anal. 6:311–329.

Guess, D., Sailor, W., Rutherford, G., and Baer, D. M. 1968. An experimental analysis of linguistic development: The productive use of the plural morpheme. J. Appl. Behav. Anal. 1:297–306.

Ingram, D. 1974. The relationship between comprehension and production. In R. L. Schiefelbusch and L. L. Lloyd (eds.), Language Perspectives—Acquisition, Retardation, and Intervention, pp. 313–334. University Park Press, Baltimore.

Kirk, S. A., McCarthy, J. J., and Kirk, W. D. 1968. Examiner's Manual: Illinois Test of Psycholinguistic Abilities. Rev. ed. University of Illinois Press, Urbana, Ill.

Kuhn, D. 1973. Imitation theory and research from a cognitive perspective. Hum. Dev. 16:157–180.

Lee, L. L. 1974. Developmental Sentence Analysis. Northwestern University Press, Evanston, Ill.

Lenneberg, E. H. 1962. Understanding language without ability to speak: A case report. J. Abnorm. Soc. Phychol. 65:419–425.

Leonard, L. B. 1972. What is deviant language? J. Speech Hear. Disord. 37:427–446.

Lindsley, O. R. 1964. Direct measurement and prosthesis of retarded behavior. J. Educ. 147:62–81.

Lovaas, O., Berberich, J. P., Perloff, B. F., and Schaeffer, B. 1966. Acquisition of imitative speech in schizophrenic children. Science 151:705–707.

Lovaas, O. I., Koegel, R., Simmons, J. Q., and Stevens-Long, J. 1973. Some generalization and follow-up measures on autistic children in behavior therapy. J. Appl. Behav. Anal. 6:131–166.

McCarthy, D. 1954. Language development in children. In. L. Carmichael (ed.), Manual of Child Psychology. John Wiley & Sons, New York.

MacDonald, J. D., Blott, J. P., Gordon, K., Spiegel, B., and Hartmann, M. 1974. An experimental parent-assisted treatment program for preschool language-delayed children. J. Speech Hear. Disord. 39:395–415.

McLean, L., and McLean, J. 1974. A language training program for nonverbal autistic children. J. Speech Hear. Disord. 39:186–193.

Martin, R., and Haroldson, S. 1969. The effects of stuttering on problem solving. Folia Phoniatr. 21:442–448.

Miller, M. A., Cuvo, A. J., and Borakove, L. S. 1977. Teaching naming of coin values—Comprehension before production versus production alone. J. Appl. Behav. Anal. 10:735–736.

Miller, J., and Yoder, D. 1974. An ontogenetic teaching strategy for retarded children. In R. L. Schiefelbusch and L. L. Lloyd (eds.), Language Perspectives—Acquisition, Retardation, and Intervention, pp. 505–528. University Park Press, Baltimore.

Moores, D. F. 1974. Nonvocal systems of verbal behavior. In R. L. Schiefelbusch and L. L. Lloyd (eds.), Language Perspectives—Acquisition, Retardation, and Intervention, pp. 377–417. University Park Press, Baltimore.

Poole, I. 1934. Genetic development of articulation of consonant sounds in speech. Elem. Eng. Rev. 11:159–161.

Premack, D. 1970. A functional analysis of language. J. Exp. Anal. Behav. 14:107–125.

Premack, D. 1971. Language in chimpanzee? Science 172:808–822.

Premack, D., and Schwartz, A. 1966. Preparations for discussing behaviorism with chimpanzee. In F. Smith and G. A. Miller (eds.), The Genesis of Language. MIT Press, Cambridge, Mass.

Premack, A. J., and Premack, D. 1972. Teaching language to an ape. Sci. Am. 277:92–99.

Rimland, B. 1964. Infantile Autism. Appleton-Century-Crofts, New York.

Risley, T. R., and Wolf, M. M. 1967. Establishing functional speech in echolalic children. Behav. Res. Ther. 5:73–88.

Ruder, K., Hermann, P., and Schiefelbusch, R. L. 1977. Effects of verbal imitation and comprehension training on verbal production. J. Psycholing. Res. 6:59–71.

Ruder, K. F., and Smith, M. D. 1974. Issues in language training. In R. L. Schiefelbusch and L. L. Lloyd (eds.), Language Perspectives—Acquisition, Retardation, and Intervention, pp. 565–605. University Park Press, Baltimore.

Ruder, K., Smith, M., and Hermann, P. 1974. Effects of verbal imitation and comprehension on verbal production of lexical items. In L. V. McReynolds (ed.), Developing systematic procedures for training children's language. ASHA Monogr. 18:15–29.

Sherman, J. A. 1971. Imitation and language development. In H. W. Reese (ed.), Advances in Child Development and Behavior, pp. 239–272. Academic Press, New York.

Siegel, G. M., and Broen, P. A. 1976. Language assessment. In L. L. Lloyd (ed.), Communication Assessment and Intervention Strategies, pp. 73–122. University Park Press, Baltimore.

Slobin, D. I. 1970. Universals of grammatical development in children. In G. B. Flores d'Arcais and W. J. M. Levelt (eds.), Advances in Psycholinguistics, pp. 174–186. American Elsevier, New York.

Slobin, D. I. 1971. Psycholinguistics. Scott, Foresman and Co., Glenview, Ill.

Spradlin, J. E., Cotter, V. W., and Baxley, N. 1973. Establishing a conditional discrimination without direct training: A study of transfer with retarded adolescents. Am. J. Ment. Defic. 77:556–566.

Spradlin, J. E., and Dixon, M. H. 1976. Establishing conditional discriminations without direct training: Stimulus classes and labels. Am. J. Ment. Defic. 80:555–561.

Stokes, T. S., and Baer, D. M. 1977. An implicit technology of generalization. J. Appl. Behav. Anal. 10:349–367.

Striefel, S., and Wetherby, B. 1973. Instruction-following behavior of a retarded child and its controlling stimuli. J. Appl. Behav. Anal. 6:663–670.

Striefel, S., Wetherby, B., and Karlan, G. 1977. Development generalized instruction-following behavior in the severely retarded. Am. Assoc. Ment. Defic. Monogr.

Templin, M. 1957. Certain Language Skills in Children. University of Minnesota Press, Minneapolis.

Vanderheiden, G. C., and Harris-Vanderheiden, D. 1976. Communication techniques and aids for the nonvocal severely handicapped. In L. L. Lloyd (ed.), Communication Assessment and Intervention Strategies, pp. 607–652. University Park Press, Baltimore.

Velletri-Glass, A., Gazzaniga, M., and Premack, D. 1973. Artificial language training in global aphasics. Neuropsychologia 11:95–104.

Wellman, B. L., Case, I. M., Mengert, I. G., and Bradbury, D. E. 1931. Speech sounds of young children. University of Iowa Studies in Child Welfare, 5.

Wetherby, B. 1978. Miniature languages and the functional analysis of verbal behavior. In R. Schiefelbusch (ed.), Bases of Language Intervention, pp. 397–448. University Park Press, Baltimore.

Wheeler, A. J., and Sulzer, B. 1970. Operant training and generalization of a verbal response form in a speech-deficient child. J. Appl. Behav. Anal. 3:139–147.

Whitehurst, G. J. 1977. Imitation, response novelty, and language acquisition. In B. C. Etzel, J. M. LeBlanc, and D. M. Baer (eds.), New Developments in Behavioral Research, pp. 119–137. Lawrence Erlbaum Associates, Hillsdale, N. J.

Wilbur, R. B. 1976. The linguistics of manual languages and manual systems. In L. L. Lloyd (ed.), Communication Assessment and Intervention Strategies, pp. 423–500. University Park Press, Baltimore.

Winitz, H. 1969. Articulatory Acquisition and Behavior. Appleton-Century-Crofts, New York.

Winitz, J., and Reeds, J. 1975. Comprehension and Problem-Solving as Strategies for Language Training. Mouton, Paris.

Discussion
and Summary

Richard L. Schiefelbusch

University Professor
and
Director, Bureau of Child Research
University of Kansas
Lawrence, Kansas

Language Intervention Strategies provides an overview of a number of important language intervention issues. Many of these issues are treated elsewhere, and those other sources are cited so that the reader can explore and select beyond what is documented here (McLean, Yoder, and Schiefelbusch, 1972; Schiefelbusch and Lloyd, 1974; Lloyd, 1976; Schiefelbusch, 1978). Helping the reader gather meaningful, practical information for intervention with special children is one of the purposes of this book.

To assist readers in using the information for their varied and complex purposes, the editor presents the following interpretative statement about each chapter of the book. The reader's task is to interpret this information and to map out a further plan to suit his[1] special needs.

In Chapter 1, "Identification of Children with Language Disorders," Rice notes that children with severe impairments can be identified readily but that for other children identification is not easy. Even for those referred and identified as having language or communication disorders there are still the problems of "what behaviors to look for" and "how to sample the behaviors." Rice does not duplicate the information presented by Miller (1978) but instead discusses the process of identifying behaviors and urges the clinician to work out procedures to fit his clinical objectives.

In brief, Chapter 1 provides a concise analysis of theoretical issues in language intervention, a review of the research literature that applies to identification, and a carefully prescribed set of characteristic behaviors that help identify language-impaired children. There is argument between Rice's recommendations and those presented by Siegel and Spradlin in Chapter 8, "Programming for Language and Communication Therapy," that each clinician must supplement professional knowledge with clinical judgment. Placing children in language programs may be a decision clinicians share with parents, the referral person, and the other instructional or clinical professionals who are accountable for the child's progress.

Hollis and Carrier, in Chapter 2, "Intervention Strategies for Nonspeech Children," describe "a basic communication system" to plan language intervention strategies for nonspeech children. Functional parts of the system are an environmental interaction model, a communicative channel model, an archetypal model, and a dual structure language model. The authors posit that for a nonspeaking child to learn functional language certain prerequisites are essential. The models aid in determining the prerequisites so the child can be assessed functionally and taught subsequently. For instance, what does the child know about his physical, spatial, and social environment? Does the child have a functional com-

---

[1] Masculine pronouns are used throughout for grammatical uniformity and simplicity. They are not meant to be preferential or discriminatory.

munication channel? What archetypal features (nonlinguistic cognitive map) does the child possess? What symbol modes (other than speech) does the child have, e.g., writing, manual signing, or gross motor movements? Does the child show knowledge of linguistic rules, perhaps in responding to differences in meanings?

The authors include a latticed design for teaching nonspeech language to impaired children. The lattice features environmental interaction, labeling, perception, vocal expression (if the child is able to speak in an advanced phase of training), and grammar. Although the training lattice provides only a general system, each program step can be divided into distinctive substeps for individual children.

This chapter provides an analysis of nonspeech aspects of language training. For instance, the authors separate the *symbol system* (individually selected to fit the child's functional attributes) and the *linguistic rules* that are taught. The design allows the two parameters to be taught independently. Thus, the nonspeech children may be taught the same linguistic rules as their speaking peers, but with alternative symbol modes.

The strategy of Guess, Sailor, and Baer in Chapter 3, "Children with Limited Language," is based on *remedial* rather than *developmental logic*. "Remedial logic . . . supposes that children being taught language relatively late in their lives . . . no longer possess the same collection of abilities and deficits that normal children have when they begin to acquire language. . . . Remedial logic, then, will not ask in what order the retarded child needs to learn language but rather in what order the language taught most quickly will accomplish some improvement in the child's communication" (pp. 105–106).

This approach was listed as a *functional strategy* under the heading of Design Strategies in the Introduction to this volume. The approach is indeed functional in that it defines the most important communication functions to be taught and the best operational system for teaching these functions. This effort calls for careful task selection and task analysis in long-term programming. It also calls for a data system that allows the clinician to refine procedures and to adapt the program to the child. The proof of the adaptation, of course, is the child's rate of progress.

The functional program that Guess, Sailor, and Baer have developed can be adapted to children of various age levels, but it is most functional for children who have not learned to use language during the normal acquisition years. It is designed to provide a complete instructional curriculum.

In Chapter 4, "Grammatical Training for the Language-Delayed Child: A New Perspective," Waryas and Stremel-Campbell describe a structured program that is also taught in a functional manner. However, their training approach is a reanalysis of the role of grammatical training for the language-delayed child from the perspective of recent advances in the study of child language. Rather than obviating the importance of structural training, new theoretical formulations of the semantic and pragmatic factors in language refocus the role of structure in language by placing it in the framework of the *how* of language which expresses the *what* (semantic functions) and the *why* (pragmatic functions). Language training is a process of teaching the child to "behave as if he knows the rules," producing congruence between the child's speech and his language community, so that communication results. In the process of this reanalysis of structure, specific reference is made to a language-training program for the language-delayed child. This demonstrates how some of these concepts are made real in the therapy setting. A general outline of procedures used within the program (as well as examples drawn from the development of one child receiving training) is presented.

This program may be especially useful to clinicians who favor a grammatical training strategy but who wish to incorporate the growing emphasis upon semantic and pragmatic features. The outstanding contribution may be that the authors have synthesized the three linguistic dimensions into a functional design for language instruction.

In "A Milieu Approach to Teaching Language," Chapter 5, Hart and Rogers-Warren describe the teaching of structure (grammatical and semantic training) and function (pragmatic training) in a manner strategically different from Waryas and Stremel-Campbell. Although Chapter 5 describes a formal "training environment" in which appropriate language forms, including phonetic, morphological, semantic, and syntactic features, are taught, their program is set in a contrastive informal "talking environment" in which the goal is simply the functional use of language. In the talking environment, the language-learning child must use language as a social communication tool. The environmental and instructional designing that Hart and Rogers-Warren advocate is labeled *the milieu teaching model.*

Their environmental emphasis is valuable for teachers of preschool and kindergarten children who wish to support language training. The two case studies at the end of their chapter tell the reader more about the complexities (and the simplicities) of teaching pragmatic functions of language than do any didactic explanations. Formal language rules, for each of the children, are a mere first step in the acquisition of functional language.

The combination of description and case illustration provided by Hart and Rogers-Warren establishes a design for combining preschool instruction and language training. The *milieu teaching model* may represent a functional advance in *context* or *incidental teaching* on the way to generalized language usage in the natural environment.

"Parent as Intervention Agent: From Birth Onward," Chapter 6 (the strategy of early intervention), was included among the strategies discussed earlier. However, parent intervention is more than a strategy. Parents occupy a position in language instruction that is considerably more important than the interventionist. The analysis of parental involvement provided by Schumaker and Sherman is extensive. They cover the issues of parental influences on language acquisition as well as the parents' strategic place in work with language-impaired children. Their suggestions for parents comprise an orienting design for instructing parents in teaching their language-impaired child. Their instructions begin with infants' vocalization and imitation and extend through most of the developmental stages of language acquisition.

One might assume that the authors are instructing us about the natural world of children, parents, and homes, expecting that language interventionists will seek supplemental assistance from parents in implementing their strategies of intervention. More realistically, this chapter suggests that interventionists are the supplemental workers and that parents are the first team in stimulating language. In any event, the chapter presents a plan for combining the efforts of significant adults in language intervention projects. The language interventionist has the option of using "Parent as Intervention Agent: From Birth Onward" as a primary or a supplemental approach to language training.

Wetherby and Striefel, in Chapter 7, "Application of the Miniature Linguistic System or Matrix-Training Procedures," discuss miniature linguistic or *matrix-training* systems. A previous chapter by Wetherby (1978) has suggested that most past and present language research can be conceptualized within a miniature linguistic system framework, originally developed by Esper (1925).

In the author's words, the purpose of their chapter is "to illustrate how a miniature linguistic system analysis of language can be used to guide the training of a generalized receptive or productive language repertoire, and to eventually isolate what appear to be some of the critical features involved in the acquisition of generalized language by language-deficient individuals" (p. 320). A literal analysis of the statement suggests that matrix training may indeed be a strategy that can be implemented to teach language skills. This strategy is not easily characterized under the categories described in previous sections. Matrix training can be considered as a *methodological* strategy or as a condition within *design* or *programmatic* strategies. However, because matrix training has not been developed into a prototypal format, the question of its strategic category may be premature, if not irrelevant.

The issue of miniature linguistic systems or matrix training is introduced here to suggest its future applicability and its current importance for researchers and clinicians who wish to use it in designing their programs. As Wetherby and Striefel have emphasized, the training principles are available. The authors provide only a shorthand statement of matrix training. However, the principles they provide may eventually become standard features in generalization training of receptive and productive language responses. The principles are already a firm part of experimental work on language intervention.

Siegel and Spradlin, in Chapter 8, "Programming for Language and Communication Therapy," provide a critique of language and communication therapy and a perspective on the entire volume. Their discussion interprets and delineates the various programs. They also analyze and update several issues critical to intervention programming, i.e., developmental and remedial approaches, nonvocal communication, useful behavioral diagnosis, imitation and language training, receptive and expressive training, and generalization and transfer training. Chapter 8 provides a fitting academic highlight for this extensive discussion of intervention strategies. However, there is much more to be said. Language intervention is a field with an emerging but essentially unstructured set of training parameters. The current state of the art seems to anticipate the significance of things to come.

The book *Language Intervention Strategies* in effect explains much of the progress that has been made to date by an increasing number of application researchers and clinicians. The strategies alluded to in the introduction of this volume serve to categorize the progress. Thus, the progress, current and anticipated, can be identified with *designing, instructing,* and *programming*. The formats that are represented allow for additional practical applications leading to further progress. The practical adaptations of the past few years have given us the means to adapt programs for virtually all language-impaired children. Along with this new reality is the functional inclusion of parents, paraprofessionals, and other willing adults who have aided in generalizing and extending the effects of intervention work into the child's larger environment. Nevertheless we still have far to go in giving all children the means to communicate. Perhaps it is their right to communicate that society must accept as its ultimate accountability.

REFERENCES

Esper, E. A. 1925. A technique for the experimental investigation of associative interference in artificial linguistic material. Lang. Monogr. 1.

Lloyd, L. L. (ed.). 1976. Communication Assessment and Intervention Strategies. University Park Press, Baltimore.

McLean, J. E., Yoder, D. E., and Schiefelbusch, R. L. 1972. Language Intervention with the Retarded. University Park Press, Baltimore.

Miller, J. F. 1978. Assessing children's language behavior: A developmental process approach. *In* R. L. Schiefelbusch (ed.), Bases of Language Intervention, pp. 269–318. University Park Press, Baltimore.

Schiefelbusch, R. L. (ed.). 1978. Bases of Language Intervention. University Park Press, Baltimore.

Schiefelbusch, R. L., and Lloyd, L. L. (eds.). 1974. Language Perspectives—Acquisition, Retardation, and Intervention. University Park Press, Baltimore.

Wetherby, B. 1978. Miniature languages and the functional analysis of verbal behavior. *In* R. L. Schiefelbusch (ed.), Bases of Language Intervention, pp. 397–448. University Park Press, Baltimore.